D1557294

The Collected Poems
and Journals of
Mary Tighe

MARY TIGHE, THE POET
From a painting by G. Brooke

Portrait of Mary Tighe and her husband, mid 1790s, by G. Brooke. Courtesy of Mr. and Mrs. Charles Hamilton of Hamwood House.

The

Collected Poems
and Journals of
Mary Tighe

Edited by
HARRIET KRAMER LINKIN

THE UNIVERSITY PRESS OF KENTUCKY

Publication of this volume was made possible in part by a grant
from the National Endowment for the Humanities.

Scholarly publisher for the Commonwealth,
serving Bellarmine University, Berea College, Centre College of Kentucky,
Eastern Kentucky University, The Filson Historical Society, Georgetown College,
Kentucky Historical Society, Kentucky State University, Morehead State University,
Murray State University, Northern Kentucky University, Transylvania University,
University of Kentucky, University of Louisville, and Western Kentucky University.

Editorial and Sales Offices: The University Press of Kentucky
663 South Limestone Street, Lexington, Kentucky 40508-4008
www.kentuckypress.com

09 08 07 06 05   5 4 3 2 1

Library of Congress Cataloging-in-Publication Data

Tighe, Mary, 1772-1810.
  The collected poems and journals of Mary Tighe / edited by Harriet Kramer Linkin.
    p. cm.
  Includes bibliographical references and index.
  ISBN 0-8131-2343-7 (Hardcover : alk. paper)
  1. Tighe, Mary, 1772-1810—Diaries. 2. Poets, Irish—18th century—Diaries. 3. Poets,
Irish—19th century—Diaries. I. Linkin, Harriet Kramer, 1956- II. Title.
  PR5671.T2A6 2004
  821'.8—dc22   2004018397

This book is printed on acid-free recycled paper meeting the requirements of the
American National Standard for Permanence in Paper for Printed Library Materials.

Manufactured in the United States of America.

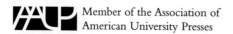 Member of the Association of
American University Presses

For Larry and the memory of our mothers,

Thea Karp Kramer (1910–2001)

and

Lillian Budow Linkin (1920–2000)

CONTENTS

Poems, 1802–1809

JOURNALS

Mary Tighe

Theodosia Blachford

Caroline Hamilton

ACKNOWLEDGMENTS

This project could never have been completed without the help and support of many generous friends, colleagues, scholars, editors, librarians, and institutions. I would like to thank New Mexico State University, which provided significant material support through a scholarly subvention and two research grants. I am deeply grateful to the following archival institutions for permission to quote or cite manuscript materials: the Council of Trustees of the National Library of Ireland, Dublin, for permission to cite from MSS 4742–46, 4800, 4801, 4803, 4804, 4809, 4810, and 10,206; Trinity College Library, Dublin, for permission to cite from MS 1461; the Deputy Keeper of Records, Public Record Office of Northern Ireland, Belfast, for permission to cite from MS D/2685; Chawton House Library, Hampshire, for permission to cite from the Henry and Lucy Moore MS Album: Poems HM 1811; the Royal College of Physicians, London, for permission to cite "Verses Addressed to Henry Vaughan" from the ALS collection; the University of Birmingham, Edgbaston, for permission to cite from MS L Add 1907; the National Library of Wales, Aberystwyth, for permission to cite from MSS 22983B, 22984C, and 22985B; the Huntington Library, San Marino, for permission to cite from shelfmark 328444; and the Beinecke Rare Book and Manuscript Library, Yale University, New Haven, for permission to cite from IN T448 805. Heartfelt thanks for the permission of Mr. and Mrs. Charles Hamilton to reproduce the double portrait of Mary Tighe and her husband at Hamwood House for the frontispiece of this edition and the permission of Llyfrgell Genedlaethol Cymru / The National Library of Wales to reproduce Mary Tighe's watercolor sketch for the final page of *Psyche* from NLW MS 22985B fol 68v. I sincerely appreciate the energy of the librarians at New Mexico State University who were indefatigable in their efforts to locate material as well as the editorial staff at The University Press of Kentucky who were exceptional in their steady commitment to this project. And I am forever and happily indebted to many fine colleagues and friends who provided information, advice, expertise, encouragement, spirit, and cheer:

Steve Behrendt, Ida Boers, Chris Burnham, Gene Cunnar, Stuart Curran, Michael Eberle Sinatra, Lynette Felber, Paula Feldman, Claude Fouillade, Diane Hoeveler, Jennifer Holberg, Elizabeth Kirwan, John Kirwan, Noel Kissane, Greg Kucich, David Latané, Ceridwen Lloyd-Morgan, Laura Mandell, Jim Mays, William McCarthy, Ian Montgomery, Maureen Mulvihill, Stuart O Seanoir, John Pipkin, Alan Richardson, Helen Scott, Nan Sweet, Kathleene West, Susan Wolfson, and Duncan Wu. My deepest thanks go to my husband, Larry Linkin, who has not only lived with the world according to Mary Tighe all this time, but, for far longer, with me; and who has supported, encouraged, and enabled me, in every way, from the moment we first met.

Editorial Note on the Text

The copy texts for Tighe's poems and for the journals are indicated in the notes to each work. In most instances there is only one print or manuscript source available. When more than one print or manuscript copy exists, the notes detail significant variants. Original spelling, punctuation, capitals, and italics are retained for all of the poems, with the following exceptions: modernization of digraph vowels and the long s. Original spelling, punctuation, and italics are retained for the journals, with the following exceptions: modernization of quotation marks, digraph vowels, and the long s; and the consistent use of capital letters to indicate the beginnings of sentences. In addition to providing copy text information and textual variants, editorial notes provide manuscript notes by Tighe or family members; translations of material in French, Italian, or Latin; information on literary or biographical allusions; and glosses for archaic or literary terms.

The following abbreviations are used throughout:

KJV	King James Version
NLI	National Library of Ireland, Dublin
NLW	National Library of Wales, Aberystwyth
PRONI	Public Record Office of Northern Ireland, Belfast
TCD	Trinity College Library, Dublin

Introduction

Mary Blachford Tighe

Mary Blachford Tighe was acclaimed throughout the nineteenth century first and foremost for the intellectual accomplishment and artistry of *Psyche; or, the Legend of Love*, a six-canto allegorical romance of 3,348 lines in Spenserian stanzas that retold the myth of Cupid and Psyche with a subtle feminist slant. Known as the first British woman to compose an epic based on Psyche's experiences, Tighe transformed one of the few myths in Western culture to feature a female as hero, and, with daring and imagination, conflated the story of Psyche's transgressive gazing with the work of visionary women poets. Using portions of the tale Lucius Apuleius relates in *The Golden Ass*, Tighe remythologized the formation of female identity, the nature of romantic love, the expression of female eroticism, competitive relations among women, masculine idealizations of women and beauty, the trajectory of a female quest, female experience of the sublime, and the place of women poets in the Romantic era. Steeped in a rich network of classical and contemporary literature written in Latin, English, French, and Italian, *Psyche* makes daunting reference to works by Homer, Virgil, Horace, Livy, Ovid, Pliny, Plutarch, Dante Alighieri, Francesco Petrarch, Matteo Maria Boiardo, Ludovico Ariosto, Torquato Tasso, Giambattista Marino, Edmund Spenser, Ben Jonson, William Shakespeare, John Milton, Pierre Corneille, Jean de La Fontaine, Moliére, François de Salignac de la Mothe Fénelon, Thomas Otway, Alexander Pope, Oliver Goldsmith, James Thomson, Thomas Gray, William Cowper, Charlotte Smith, Mary Robinson, Joanna Baillie, Ann Radcliffe, Matthew Lewis, Samuel Taylor Coleridge, and William Wordsworth, as if Tighe meant to mark her position in the canons of literary history.

Tighe began composing *Psyche* in 1801, completed the poem in 1802, and published a private edition of *Psyche; or, the Legend of Love* in 1805, a limited printing of fifty copies she gave to relatives, friends, and admirers (including Thomas Moore, Anna Seward, Lady Dacre, Eleanor Butler and

Sarah Ponsonby, William Hayley, William Roscoe, John Wesley, Henry Moore, Joseph Cooper Walker, and William Parnell). These fifty copies were the only ones printed during her lifetime, but they circulated so widely and avidly among enthusiastic readers (who often made their own manuscript copies) that Tighe was celebrated as "the author of *Psyche*" during the remaining five years of her life. The *Quarterly Review* (1811), *British Review* (1811), *British Critic* (1811), and *Eclectic Review* (1813) would later comment on the remarkable circulation history of the 1805 edition, and the extensive "admiration which *the Legend of Love* is known to have excited within the limited sphere of its previous existence."[1] Tighe received many requests for additional copies of *Psyche*, but never pursued a second printing: her fatal struggle with tuberculosis began to impede her physical activities in 1804, and even delayed the printing of the 1805 edition. In 1811 her cousin William Tighe prepared a posthumous edition of *Psyche, with Other Poems* for the general public, comprised of a lightly edited copy of the 1805 *Psyche; or, The Legend of Love* and thirty-nine of the nearly ninety unpublished sonnets and lyrics Tighe composed over the course of her life (her sonnet "To My Mother" was printed with the 1805 *Psyche*). Like *Psyche*, a number of the shorter poems acquired fame through private circulation among admirers who copied manuscript versions into each other's family albums, commonplace books, journals, and diaries. These lyrics showcase the play of a fertile imagination using language and form to make sense of the complexities of love, politics, art, spirituality, family, friendship, memory, and nature with intense feeling, moving imagery, sharp wit, and great technical skill. William Tighe made another seventeen lyrics available in a second posthumous collection, *Mary, a Series of Reflections During Twenty Years* (1811), which was printed privately at a local press in a limited edition of twenty copies and distributed to her intimate friends. Many more lyrics remained in manuscript, as did Tighe's psychologically astute courtship novel, *Selena* (1803), which, like Smith's *Celestina: A Novel* (1791) or Radcliffe's *The Mysteries of Udolpho* (1794), incorporated a number of her lyrics to illuminate the mental states of various characters.

The publication of the 1811 *Psyche* established Tighe's literary reputation for the nineteenth century. Ten prominent periodicals reviewed the 1811 edition with favor, praising it as a work of "extraordinary merits" (*Eclectic Review*) for its intellectual richness, exquisite telling, superb execution, elegant design, superior style, excellent versification, and fine feeling. The *Monthly Review* hailed it as an instant classic "calculated to endure the judgment of posterity, long after the possessors of an ephemeral popularity shall have faded away into a well-merited oblivion," and the *Gentleman's Magazine* predicted it would "long be celebrated by the admirers of genuine poetry." So it was. Catherine Hamilton noted nearly a hundred years later that Tighe's poetry "won the highest praise from competent critics" throughout the century. In 1813 Sir James Mackintosh called *Psyche* "the first female production in our language," having singled out its last three cantos as "the most faultless series of verses ever produced by a woman" the previous year. In 1819 John Wilson named Tighe as one of the three premier national women poets of the age: "Scotland has her Baillie—Ireland her Tighe—England her Hemans" (*Blackwood's Edinburgh Magazine*). In 1820 William Gifford stipulated that "no judicious critic will speak without respect of the tragedies of Miss Baillie, or the Psyche of Mrs. Tighe" or the poems of Mrs. Hemans (*Quarterly Review*). In 1825 Robert Sym placed her with Baillie, Hemans, and Letitia Elizabeth Landon (*Blackwood's Edinburgh Magazine*), and in 1829 Francis Jeffrey lauded her "tenderness, purity, and elegance" in a review of Hemans's *Records of Woman* and *The Forest Sanctuary* (*Edinburgh Review*). While Leigh Hunt praised her Spenserian style in 1847 (*Men, Women, and Books*), George Bethune commended her for her exceptional craft in 1848, and thought Tighe "not equalled in classical elegance by any English female, and not excelled (in that particular) by any male English poet" (*British Female Poets*). David MacBeth ("Delta") Moir considered Tighe superior to Smith for her "powers of imagination" in his 1856 *Sketches*. So too Jane Williams, whose 1861 *Literary Women of England* described *Psyche* as "unquestionably one of the finest poems ever written by a woman; full of imaginative power, passion, and melody" and ranked Tighe as the third greatest British poetess of the century, after Hemans and Baillie. In 1877 Elizabeth Blackburne ranked Tighe third after Hemans and Elizabeth Barrett Browning for *Psyche*'s "sublimity of sentiment, graceful diction, and true poetic strength. . . . It stands alone in the literature of Ireland—pure, polished, sublime—the outpouring of a trammelled soul yearning to be freed" (*Illustrious Irishwomen*). Lady Morgan simply declared Tighe "the first and finest *poetess* of her own or perhaps any country" (1857).[2]

Popular demand for *Psyche* in Britain and the United States led to multiple editions of considerable volume (in 1811, 1812, 1816, 1843, 1844, 1852, and 1853). Longman printed 5,500 copies between 1811 and 1816 (500 in May 1811, 2,000 in August 1811, 2,000 in May 1812, and 1,000 in May 1816), and company ledgers indicate that the first five hundred copies sold out in a month.[3] Furthermore, at least thirty anthologies printed extracts from Tighe's poetry in Britain, the United States, and France through the early twentieth century. In addition to its critical and popular success, Tighe's poetry left its mark on the nineteenth-century literary community of authors. Well established as a major influence on John Keats and Hemans, Tighe's poetry also exerted influence on Lord Byron, Percy Bysshe Shelley, Mary Shelley, Thomas Moore, Lady Morgan, Bernard Barton, Landon, Barrett Browning, Mary Brunton, Charlotte Brontë, Edgar Allan Poe, Emily Dickinson, Christina Rossetti, William Morris, and Charlotte Yonge. She was admired by Coleridge, Hunt, John Hamilton Reynolds, Hayley, Roscoe, Seward, Hannah More, Harriet Bowdler, Jane West, Catherine Fanshawe, Amelia Opie, Maria Abdy, Anna Maria Porter, Lady Dacre, William Howitt, and John Banim, and she received published verse tributes from Moore, Hayley, Roscoe, Dacre, Porter, Barton, Keats, Reynolds, and Hemans, whose *Records of Woman* (1828) concluded with the lyric tribute "The Grave of a Poetess," the only "record" on a contemporary woman.[4]

The strong impression Tighe's poetry made on nineteenth-century readers began to fade in the early twentieth century with the advent of high modernism, when interest in most Romantic-era poets declined. Her work went out of print, and twentieth-century readers came to know of her as a devalued influence on Keats, who invoked the "blessings of Tighe" in his 1815 "To Some Ladies" but rejected them in an 1818 New Year's Eve letter to his brother and sister-in-law: "Mrs. Tighe and Beattie once delighted me—now I see through them and can find nothing in them—or weakness—and yet how many they still delight!" The "many" still delighted by Tighe included the *Quarterly Review*, which had just printed a shattering review of Keats's *Endymion: A Poetic Romance* (1818), no doubt precipitating his remarks. Keats clearly relocated his delight in Tighe shortly after writing this letter: he not only sent his brother George an autograph copy of her 1805 sonnet "Addressed to My Brother" (which was attributed to Keats in the 1883 H. Buxton Forman edition of Keats's *Poetical Works*), but also paid sly homage to Tighe in his "Ode to Psyche," "The Eve of St. Agnes," and "Lamia" (1820). Nevertheless the critics committed to establishing Keats's status after the century turned focus on Keats's 1818 letter and often promoted Keats's reputation by demoting Tighe's. In 1901 Henry Beers acknowledged the poignant beauty in Tighe's verse and imagery but declared her "incapable of such choice and pregnant effects as abound in every stanza of 'St. Agnes.'" In 1909 Arthur Symons observed that Tighe, "one of the most famous of the women poets of her period," was "remembered now because the very early Keats seems to have thought her a poet almost worth imitating." That recognition of Keats's genius hinged on disparaging Tighe's is eminently troubling but eminently traceable in decades of criticism that reduced Tighe to a footnote until feminist and new historical studies in the late 1980s began to refocus attention on Romantic-era women poets.[5]

Among the first to reevaluate Tighe's achievement as a Romantic poet was Donald Reiman, who offered exceptional praise for her voice and verse, and printed not one but two versions of Tighe's *Psyche* for the 1978 Garland Romantic Context series, a facsimile of the 1805 *Psyche; or, the Legend of Love* and a copy of the 1811 *Psyche, with Other Poems* bound with Opie's 1802 *Elegy to the Memory of the Late Duke of Bedford*. After Reiman's editions made Tighe's poetry available to new readers, recognition of Tighe's value as a Romanticist, as a Spenserian, as a woman poet, and as an influence on Keats and Hemans began to appear with steadily increasing frequency in current scholarship.[6] When the Garland series went out of print, Jonathan Wordsworth published a new facsimile edition of the 1811 *Psyche, with Other Poems* for the 1992 Woodstock series, whose introduction not only declared *Psyche* "one of the most accomplished long poems of the Romantic period" but highlighted the "more openly personal, and no less accomplished" lyric poems. Since then selections from Tighe's poetry have appeared in numerous anthologies, including Duncan Wu's landmark 1997 *Romantic Women Poets* (now out of print), which devoted nearly a sixth of the edition to reprint *Psyche* in its entirety.[7] This edition offers the first comprehensive, chronological, annotated collection of Tighe's published and hitherto unpublished poetry—as well as several pertinent unpublished journals by Tighe and family members—to enable a full appreciation of Tighe's achievement as a Romantic-era poet.

BIOGRAPHICAL BACKGROUND

Born in Dublin on October 9, 1772, to an Anglo-Irish family of wealth, privilege, connection, and learning, Mary Blachford was the second child of the Rev. William Blachford and Theodosia Tighe. Her parents married in 1770 and had her older brother, John, in 1771. Blachford, a man of property, attained distinction as librarian of Marsh's Library, St. Patrick's

(1766–1773), but had little direct impact on his daughter: he died seven months into her life, leaving his widow with sole responsibility and excellent economic resources for raising their children. Theodosia Blachford, scion of the prominent Tighe family and early activist for the Methodist movement, firmly believed in liberal education for women, having pursued her own studies with fervor (she published a translation of *The Life of the Baroness de Chantal* in 1787 as well as several religious tracts). Theodosia provided Mary with exceptional opportunity to read widely in English, French, and Italian literature, history, politics, moral philosophy, science, and religion as well as to acquire skill in music and drawing, and, most importantly, encouraged her as a child to compose her own poetry, to translate French and Italian poetry into English, to keep reflective journals, and to record passages from works she admired. A child of distinct intellectual ability, feeling, and imagination, Mary was also blessed with great beauty. When she was fourteen she attracted so much admiration that her mother determined to arrange an early marriage for her to a religious man who would enable her to pursue a life of study. Instead she became romantically entangled with her handsome, hedonistic first cousin Henry Tighe of Rossana (younger brother of William), who fell madly in love with her and drew her away from the contemplative life she led with her mother, into the brilliant social life of the vice-regal court of Dublin, where she became a center of attraction.

Mary Blachford married Henry Tighe on October 5, 1793, though she did not love him: the family connections and his violent passion made refusal difficult. His sister Caroline Hamilton said he was "so violently attached to her that he threatened to go off to America, or to commit some act of violence, if she refused to marry him" (Hamilton journal). Her mother knew that she loved someone else: "I saw my poor child struggling with a foolish & violent passion half insensible to the tenderness of a heart that she was unwilling, indeed seemingly unable to wound by a positive refusal, though she saw her favorite lover, at her feet, in rank & fortune unexceptionable & her equal, at the same time confessing to me her reluctance to any closer connection with H Tighe" (Blachford journal). Her own journal entry on the night before the wedding reads, "My soul draws back with terror & awe at the idea of the event which is to take place tomorrow." They took a house in London, where Henry planned to increase their income of a thousand pounds a year by studying for the bar, but he abandoned his legal studies for a life of idleness. He liked literature better than the law, society better than either, and liked best to display his beautiful, gifted wife before fashionable friends at home or abroad, providing he was in control of that display: Caroline's journal notes that "HT made no acquaintances in the world, where he let his wife go by herself," and a family history by Wilfred Tighe reports on Henry's immense displeasure when he learned that Mary had privately commissioned George Romney to paint her portrait in 1794. Perhaps Henry's anger prompted Mary's remarks to her mother-in-law in May 1795: "Romney has just finished my picture; it is pretty, but perfectly pallid among the high-coloured Lady Hamiltons and Mrs. Tickells; by itself it will look better, I daresay. I wonder how it came to be so pale! I suppose everyone goes rouged to be painted. Bess's picture is more generally approv'd, I think; mine looks as if a pretty woman had wept herself pale and sick" (Ward and Roberts). Neither Mary nor Henry found happiness in the marriage, but Mary confessed the troubling pleasure she found in being the source of so much admiration in 1796: "Very unhappy in my mind—Yet I find it impossible to resist the flattering temptation of being admired, & showing the world that I am so. My conscience this day has been disturbed—I feel uneasy at the vanity, the folly, the dissipation in which I am engaged. Yet without the power to wish myself disengaged from it" (Tighe journal). She took easier pleasure in the Latin lessons she made Henry give her every morning, with a scholarly application that was "sometimes troublesome to him," Caroline writes, "as he had not acquired habits of regularity, but she would not allow him to be absent at the appointed hour for study, her early education having taught her to employ her time diligently, & to her industry in this respect, may be attributed that she was able some years afterwards to undertake the difficult task of composing Psyche" (Hamilton journal).

The Tighes spent most of the 1790s in England, making periodic returns to Ireland for visits to family and friends in Wicklow and Dublin, and for Henry to represent Inistiogue in the Irish Parliament till the Act of Union. Both knew the violence of 1798 firsthand, Henry leading a corps of yeoman troops through the Wicklow Mountains while Mary was besieged at Rossana and in Dublin; and both argued against the Act of Union in 1799, Henry in the Irish Parliament and Mary in her poetry ("There Was a Young Lordling Whose Wits Were All Toss'd Up"). Indeed much of the poetry she wrote during the first eight years of her marriage took place in Ireland, either composed during actual visits or invoked in memory. In 1801 Mary and Henry resettled in Ireland (now making periodic visits to England) and Mary immersed herself in her writing, completing both *Psyche* and *Selena* by the end of 1803. In January 1804 she exhibited signs of the tuberculosis that would debilitate her health over the next six years; she went to England for medical attention in June 1804 and returned to Ireland in September 1805, having completed the printing of *Psyche* that July. Despite her increasing physical difficulties she pursued an active intellectual life, writing a series of strong lyrics (including "Psalm CXXX," "Addressed to My Brother," "Address to the West Wind," "Address to My Harp," "The Shawl's Petition, to Lady Asgill," "Hagar in the Desert," "Imitated from Jeremiah," "Written at West-Aston," "The Lily," and "The Mezereon"), keeping a critical commentary on her prolific reading (NLI MS 4804), maintaining various literary correspondences (notably with the Irish antiquarian Joseph Cooper Walker, preserved in TCD MS 1461), and conversing with the friends who visited (including Thomas Moore, Sydney Owenson, Lady Charlemont, William Parnell, Lady Asgill, Sir Arthur Wellesley, and Lydia White). She died on March 24, 1810, at Woodstock, her cousin William's estate, and was buried in Inistiogue, where an effigy by John Flaxman marks her grave. The task of sorting through her personal papers fell to her mother, who preserved a limited set of Tighe's journal entries (1787–1802) and provided her own feeling commentary on them and Tighe's life (circa 1810). Fifteen years later her cousin Caroline composed a biographical account of Tighe for her family and appended copies of the Tighe and Blachford journals. These three journals, reproduced for the first time in this edition, offer essential material on the circumstances of Tighe's life and the nature and extent of her literary production.[8]

LITERARY PRODUCTION

Tighe's Latin studies provided the scholarly foundation for *Psyche*, which began as a verse translation of the Cupid-Psyche myth from Apuleius's novel *The Golden Ass* but became a rich exploration of the female psyche in its experience of beauty, admiration, love, passion, jealousy, knowledge, ambition, poetry, and much more. In the first two cantos Tighe adapts many of the narrative events that shape the first two-thirds of Apuleius's tale, culminating with the moment of Psyche's transgression, when she looks at Cupid and he leaves. In both tellings, the myth casts Psyche as the youngest of three royal daughters, whose extraordinary beauty prompts men to forsake Venus's shrine to worship her instead. Although Venus orders Cupid to revenge the insult and remove the threat by making

Psyche fall in love with an unworthy being, Cupid falls in love with Psyche himself, and has her carried off to a sumptuous palace for a blissful union contingent on one crucial condition: that Psyche never look at him or ask his name. Happy for a time, Psyche eventually longs for human companionship and visits her jealous sisters, who urge her to find out whether she has, in fact, married a monster. Psyche succumbs to doubt, breaks her vow not to look, and discovers herself married to Cupid, who immediately abandons her. Once Psyche begins her quest to win Cupid back, Tighe sets a new course for her epic, which has nothing to do with the completion of punitive domestic tasks for Venus, such as sorting grain or retrieving wool. Instead the remaining four cantos take Psyche through a dreamlike allegorical landscape, where she faces morally ambiguous situations that reprise aspects of her transgression, testing her responses to what she sees and how she knows. It is her ability to solve these hermeneutic puzzles that effects the restoration of her husband in his true form. In a sharp revision of the myth, Tighe's Psyche faces many of these situations accompanied by an armored knight who turns out to be Cupid in disguise, so that the errant Cupid undergoes an educative journey of his own. Because these hermeneutic puzzles expose the metamorphosing Psyche to a series of emblematic female figures who embody a continuum of cultural roles and psychological profiles that range from complete self-absorption to utter self-abnegation, her acts of interpretation ultimately enact self-identity. By the time Psyche completes her quest and finds Cupid standing beside her, she has effectively redefined her self.

Given Tighe's lived experience as a famous beauty whose marriage is determined by familial conditions rather than personal desire, her selection of the Psyche myth resonates with a potent self-reflexivity. In all six cantos Tighe foregrounds the parallel between Psyche and herself, but with an important difference: she contrasts Psyche as the archetypal romanticized object of desire who transgresses when she looks at Cupid with herself as the narrating woman poet who insists on her capacity to compose visionary poetry when Romantic-era culture teaches her to be the muse. Whereas Psyche is subject to cultural and mythical constraints, Tighe uses her visionary experience to transcend those constraints. Thus just before Psyche commits the act that will place her in the pantheon of females who fall (like Pandora or Eve)—just before Psyche dares to look at her sleeping husband—Tighe interrupts the narrative with a resounding call to her "daring muse!" and "pencil true" to paint the very image

Psyche fears to view in a glorious, sensual, powerful display of authorial control and poetic description:

> Oh, daring muse! wilt thou indeed essay
> To paint the wonders which that lamp could shew?
> And canst thou hope in living words to say
> The dazzling glories of that heavenly view?
> Ah! well I ween, that if with pencil true
> That splendid vision could be well exprest,
> The fearful awe imprudent Psyche knew
> Would seize with rapture every wondering breast,
> When Love's all potent charms divinely stood confest.
>
> All imperceptible to human touch,
> His wings display celestial essence light,
> The clear effulgence of the blaze is such,
> The brilliant plumage shines so heavenly bright
> That mortal eyes turn dazzled from the sight;
> A youth he seems in manhood's freshest years;
> Round his fair neck, as clinging with delight,
> Each golden curl resplendently appears,
> Or shades his darker brow, which grace majestic wears.
>
> Or o'er his guileless front the ringlets bright
> Their rays of sunny lustre seem to throw,
> That front than polished ivory more white!
> His blooming cheeks with deeper blushes glow
> Than roses scattered o'er a bed of snow:
> While on his lips, distilled in balmy dews,
> (Those lips divine that even in silence know
> The heart to touch) persuasion to infuse
> Still hangs a rosy charm that never vainly sues.
>
> The friendly curtain of indulgent sleep
> Disclosed not yet his eyes' resistless sway,
> But from their silky veil there seemed to peep
> Some brilliant glances with a softened ray,
> Which o'er his features exquisitely play,
> And all his polished limbs suffuse with light. (2.190–222)

When Psyche sees what Tighe describes, she becomes "Speechless with awe, in transport strangely lost / Long Psyche stood with fixed adoring eye; / Her limbs immoveable, her senses tost / Between amazement, fear, and ecstasy" (2.235–38), frozen in mute adoration until Cupid wakes up to the moment of betrayal and "ruin's hideous crash bursts o'er the affrighted walls" (2.243). In this very moment that defines Psyche's position in myth and culture as the female who should not have looked, Tighe asserts her own right to look as a visionary woman poet. After this moment, as Psyche begins her quest and seeks to appease Cupid and Venus, Tighe repeatedly suggests that what Psyche needs to do is learn how and when to *negotiate* looking.

Because Tighe constructs a developmental narrative in *Psyche*, one needs to see how each canto builds on episodes in the previous canto to appreciate the value and depth of her work on aesthetics, sexuality, epistemology, and psychology. Readers of *Psyche* will want to look closely at the extended erotic presentation of Cupid and Psyche in canto 1 when he first sees her sleeping on her purple couch and finds himself enchanted by his own gaze; at the intensely sensual description of Cupid's palace of pleasure in canto 1, which culminates with Tighe's coyly abbreviated consummation scene; at the high gothic description of Psyche and Cupid in canto 2 when she gazes at *him* sleeping and tragedy ensues; at the psychologically rich reporting of Psyche's initial sighting of the armored knight who is Cupid in canto 3 when she experiences an unnameable passion she takes care not to name; at the alternate models of female behavior presented to Psyche in canto 3 through her interactions with Varia (the queen of loose delights), Vanity, and Lusinga (flattery); at the emotionally compelling projection and estrangement Psyche must overcome in canto 4 after a sorcerer's mirror images the knight as an unfaithful Cupid in the arms of Varia; at the tempting but limited refuge female community presents in canto 5 as Psyche contemplates a life without Cupid among the women poets who inhabit the realm of Castabella (the queen of chastity); at the philosophically deft portrayal of indifference as independence in canto 6 when Psyche is abducted by the slaves of Glacella (the ice queen); or at the ultimately unsatisfying conclusion of the quest in canto 6 when Psyche finds herself reabsorbed in Cupid's gaze, as "she enraptured lives in his dear eye" (6.528), and Tighe laments returning to her non-visionary life:

> Dreams of Delight farewell! your charms no more
> Shall gild the hours of solitary gloom!

> The page remains—but can the page restore
> The vanished bowers which Fancy taught to bloom?
> Ah, no! her smiles no longer can illume
> The path my Psyche treads no more for me;
> Consigned to dark oblivion's silent tomb
> The visionary scenes no more I see,
> Fast from the fading lines the vivid colours flee! (6.532–40)

"No more," "ah no," "no longer," "no more," "no more": these five reverberating "no's" in the last stanza bring the conjoined narratives of Psyche as Romantic subject and Tighe as woman poet to a devastating finale.

In conjunction with the narrative complexity and romantic self-reflexivity, readers will want to savor the consistent quality of Tighe's language play, which encodes cultural critique through subversive syntax. Although Tighe's preface to the 1805 *Psyche* asked her readers to indulge her love of Spenserian stanzas, which sometimes required her to contort her lines, she claimed, she makes altogether strategic use of the stanza to produce telling inversions that shimmer with secondary meanings. The inversion of the poem's opening lines, for instance, turns a standard bid for clemency into a biting commentary on gender and poetry that invokes the epic opening lines of *The Aeneid*, *Orlando Furioso*, and *The Faerie Queene*:

> Let not the rugged brow the rhymes accuse,
> Which speak of gentle knights and ladies fair,
> Nor scorn the lighter labours of the muse,
> Who yet, for cruel battles would not dare
> The low-strung chords of her weak lyre prepare;
> But loves to court repose in slumbery lay,
> To tell of goodly bowers and gardens rare,
> Of gentle blandishments and amorous play,
> And all the lore of love, in courtly verse essay. (1.1–9)

Equivocal predication blurs the subjects scorned and objects accused: if rugged brows accuse the rhymes and "scorn the lighter labours of the muse," the rhymes accuse the rugged brows and scorn the lighter labours of the muse. Similarly, when Tighe names the cause of Psyche's troubles, that "men her wondrous beauty deified" (1.57), syntactic inversion underscores the reflexivity of male admiration: while men deify Psyche as an object of beauty, admiration of her beauty deifies and objectifies men.

So too the inverted phrasing of Venus's command that Cupid punish Psyche for her beauty, which predicts the reciprocity of romantic enchantment that occurs when Cupid first glimpses Psyche: "'Deep let her heart thy sharpest arrow sting'" (1.120). That linguistic multivalence operates all the way through the poem to open up a wider range of interpretive possibilities for a wider range of readers than the gendered expectations of the time suggest, interpretive possibilities Tighe enjoins her readers to pursue:

> Oh, you for whom I write! whose hearts can melt
> At the soft thrilling voice whose power you prove,
> You know what charm, unutterably felt,
> Attends the unexpected voice of Love:
> Above the lyre, the lute's soft notes above,
> With sweet enchantment to the soul it steals
> And bears it to Elysium's happy grove;
> You best can tell the rapture Psyche feels
> When Love's ambrosial lip the vows of Hymen seals. (1.451–59)

"You best can tell the rapture Psyche feels": infused as it is with intellectual accomplishment and syntactic subtlety, it is the luxurious sensuality and emotional vitality of Tighe's lush style that has made her representation of Psyche's experiences and the imagination of the narrating woman poet so compelling for generations of her readers.

Tighe explores many of the themes she takes up in *Psyche* with greater personal intensity in her lyrics, which reveal an ongoing concern with the psychological dilemma admiration poses at various points in her life: the desire for admiration that conflicts with the pursuit of self-effacing spirituality, the desire for admiration that steals time from interactions with the muse, the desire for a kind of admiration no longer proffered as health or beauty fade. Several of the early poems probe the impact of admiration on the development and coherence of self-identity, reflecting on the delicate tension between yielding the not-yet-formed self to an ideal imaged by external admiration versus the emergence of an authentic selfhood shaped by study, self-examination, and writing. While the speaker of "Verses Written in Solitude, April 1792" berates herself for succumbing to the false charms of flattery, for losing access to her muse because she wants "To fix the attention of admiring eyes, / To move with elegance, and talk with ease; / To be the object of the practised sigh, / To attract the notice, and the ear to please" (17–20), the speaker in "The Vartree" counsels herself to forsake vanity for the safer and more soul-enhancing pleasures of science: "Here, Mary, rest! the dangerous path forsake / Where folly lures thee, and where vice ensnares, / . . . . / Here woo the Muses in the scenes they love; / Let Science near thee take her patient stand" (25–46). It is with fine irony that later poems present the self who finally heeds the call of science, study, and spiritual reflection as secretly longing for admiration, as in "The Shawl's Petition, To Lady Asgill," when Tighe imagines that her shawl would rather grace the shoulders of her beautiful friend than her own worn-out and emaciated form. From the beginning to the end of Tighe's career, tropes and images that figure the emergence of a hidden, repressed, lost, or forgotten self constitute a major component in her lyric poetics, as she contemplates the self transformed by spirituality, admiration, love, friendship, poetry, fame, illness, and death, or in the very process of such transformation: worn sand shifting beneath the crashing waves in "Written at Scarborough"; the twilight modulation of sunset to moonrise in the sonnet "When glowing Phoebus quits the weeping earth"; the work of seasonal transitions in "Written in Autumn" and "Verses Written at the Commencement of Spring"; flowers on the verge of blossoming in "Written at Rossana. November 18, 1799," "On a Night-blowing Cereus," and "The Lily"; the fluctuating moon in "To the Moon" and "The Eclipse. Jan. 24, 1804"; the transfiguring election of Hagar in "Hagar in the Desert"; and always the soul in flight, either to or from the temptations of "Passion's fevered dream!" ("Verses Written in Sickness. December, 1804").

Just as Tighe uses the lyric to examine the formation of the self, she uses the lyric to formulate or structure the self, as if mastery of form can effect self-mastering. Yet so many of the poems that seek to discipline desire through form demonstrate, instead, how desire presents itself in language. In the sonnet "For me would Fancy now her chaplet twine," a speaker asks:

> Shall my distempered heart still idly sigh
> For those gay phantoms, chased by sober truth?
>   Those forms tumultuous which sick visions bring,
>   That lightly flitting on the transient wing
> Disturbed the fevered slumbers of my youth? (8–12)

as if to dismiss "those gay phantoms"; but the recreation of "those forms tumultuous" in the sonnet itself ultimately evokes the desire the speaker admits she can only hope to overcome in the future: "Ah, no! my suffering soul at length restored, / *Shall* taste the calm repose so oft in vain implored" (13–14, my emphasis). In "Written in the Church-yard at Malvern" a speaker contemplates burying desire in form and formality, but her reverie demonstrates how forms induce rather than contain desire, as she imagines and rejects the illusion of closure she might derive *if* she could pay a final tribute at the grave of an unburied (because not yet dead) friend:

> Once more I weep; and wish this grave were thine,
>   Poor, lost, lamented friend! that o'er thy clay
>   For once this last, sad tribute I might pay,
> And, with my tears, to the cold tomb resign
>   Each hope of bliss, each vanity of life,
>   And all the passions agonizing strife. (9–14)

Some poems that set out to bury desire in formal language confess the desire to use language to reexperience passion, to lose rather than gain control, as in the sonnet "As one who late hath lost a friend adored," where the speaker ruefully

> Clings with sick pleasure to the faintest trace
> Resemblance offers in another's face,
> . . . .
> Or in the page, where weeping fancy mourns,
>   I love to dwell upon each tender line,
>   And think the bliss once tasted still is mine;
> While cheated memory to the past returns,
>   And, from the present leads my shivering heart
>   Back to those scenes from which it wept to part (2–14)

or "Address to My Harp," where the speaker intends to recreate the experiences once evoked by the harp she can no longer play through her poetry: "Yet still thy strings, in Fancy's ear, / With soothing melody shall play; / Thy silver sounds I oft shall hear, / To pensive gloom a silent prey" (33–36).

Tighe's lyrics stage complex articulations of the intersection of form and desire: of the efficacy of language and form to contain desire and experience, of the desire to control desire through form, and of the desire to awaken desire through language and form. Sometimes that articulation manifests as a dialectical struggle between the heart and soul torn between desire and control. In the sonnet "Poor, fond deluded heart! wilt thou again" the soul tries to steer the heart away from the "syren song" of "treacherous Pleasure" that makes the heart "throb with wishes vain," but once again the soul's very efforts to describe the "fickle wing / Which Fancy lends thee in her airy flight, / But to seduce thee to some giddy height, / And leave thee there a poor forsaken thing" only tempts the heart to repeat the wrong: "Hope warbles once again, Truth pleads in vain, / And my charmed soul sinks vanquished by her strain" (1–14). Poem after poem depicts the irresistible call of desire despite the hard knowledge purchased by experience, as in the lyric "Pleasure," which warns the heart against the "flattering strains" of "syren Pleasure" but sounds those strains in fantastic, luxurious, sensual images that enchant mariners off the coast of Senegal who are inhaling poison as they gaze at an exotic landscape:

> Thus the charmed mariner on every side
> Of poisoned Senegal's ill-omened tide,
> Eyes the rich carpet of the varied hue
> And plains luxuriant opening to his view:
> Now the steep banks with towering forests crowned,
> Clothed to the margin of the sloping ground;
> Where with full foliage bending o'er the waves,
> Its verdant arms the spreading Mangrove laves;
> And now smooth, level lawns of deeper green
> . . . .
> From cloudless suns perpetual lustre streams,
> And swarms of insects glisten in their beams.
> Near and more near the heedless sailors steer,
> Spread all their canvas, and no warnings hear.
> . . . .
> Even as they gaze their vital powers decay,
> Their wasted health and vigour melt away;
> Till quite extinct the animating fire,
> Pale, ghastly victims, they at last expire. (27–60)

And poems depict the remains or residue of powerful experiences, which alternately prompt the heart's desire or the soul's resolve: the dripping boughs after a tempest passes in "To Time" ("As when the furious tempest is o'erblown, / And when the sky has wept its violence, / The opening heavens will oft let fall a shower, / The poor o'ercharged boughs still drops dispense, / And still the loaded streams in torrents pour"); the plucked flower that might have blossomed in "Written at Rossana. November 18, 1799"; soul hammered to steel by adversity in "To Fortune" ("So the bright steel beneath the hammer's blows / More polished, more refined, and keener grows"); the trembling pennant that looks back to past pleasure in "On Leaving Killarney. August 5, 1800" ("Borne with the struggling bark against the wind, / The trembling pennant fluttering looks behind / With vain reluctance!"); the branch of mezereon that figures Tighe herself as she wonders, in her final poem, how her friends will contemplate her remains.

In addition to poems that meditate on great personal crisis, Tighe's lyrics reflect a wry and sometimes bitter humor about the politics of culture. "The Old Maid's Prayer to Diana" excoriates the politics of beauty and the compulsion to marry well in voicing the comic plea of an "old maid" who begs the virgin goddess Diana for deliverance from the marriage market:

> From the erring attachments of desolate souls,
> From the love of spadille, and of matadore voles
> Or of lap-dogs, and parrots, and monkies, and owls,
>   Be they ne'er so uncommon and clever:
> But chief from the love (with all loveliness flown)
> Which makes the dim eye condescend to look down
> On some ape of a fop, or some owl of a clown,—
>   Diana, thy servant deliver. (25–32)

Poems such as "La Cittadina: On Leaving Rossana," "Acrostics," or "Tho Genius and Fancy Hereafter May Trace" poke fun at the competitive displays required by bluestocking salons even as Tighe displays her ability to participate in them, offering a hilarious portrait of a "typical" Christmas at Rossana in "A Letter from Mrs. Acton to Her Nephew Mr. Evans":

> When with Latin and Greek not a marvel too much,
> With Italian and French and a little high Dutch
> In the midst of such scholars you find yourself placed
> And with questions in Hebrew and Syriac disgrac'd,

> Lest staring around you, you fancy it Babel
> When you hear fifteen languages spoken at table,
> Or venture in English to ask for some beer
> At the poor ignoramus the butler will sneer. (13–20)

Just as these manuscript poems reveal Tighe's unexpected flair for high comedy, the poems from her unpublished novel *Selena* reveal her underappreciated ability to recast her personal voice as the voice of a character or persona. Jonathan Wordsworth notes that "Tighe is a poet of many voices," referring, in part, to her invocations of other poets (Spenser, Milton, Pope, Gray, Cowper, Smith); but the *Selena* poems evidence her skillfulness in creating individual subjectivities for the novel's several writers, male and female poets who inhabit a range of social classes and cultural positions as they explore the psychological ramifications of love lost, such as the aristocratic Lady Trevallyn ("Fled Are the Summer Hours of Joy and Love"), the middle-class Edwin Stanmore ("When the Bitter Source of Sorrow"), or the working-class Methodist Angela Harley ("Oh Seal My Sad and Weary Eyes"). Yet other poems witness with irony the inevitable generational disjunction of parents and children, especially mothers and daughters ("The Hours of Peace"); the differently gendered social displacements of men and women ("To ——c——e": "The youth of broken fortune sent to roam"); and the political-religious conflicts that racked Ireland during Tighe's time, which not only prompted her tragic ballad on "Bryan Byrne, of Glenmalure" but also her fiercely funny exposé of the corrupt parliamentary processes that would lead to the Act of Union, "There Was a Young Lordling Whose Wits Were all Toss'd Up":

> There was a young Lordling whose wits were all toss'd up
>   Seventeen times as high as the Moon,
> What was his object I could not imagine
>   But in his hand he carried a broom—
>
> "Young Lordling, young Lordling, young Lordling says I"
> "Why have you toss'd up your wits so high?"
> "I am going (he cries) with my purse & my broom"
> "To sweep all the members out of this room"—
>
> "Young Lordling, young Lordling, young Lordling I cried
> "Do you think on its ruin the house will decide?

"But his wits were a wool-gathering up in the sky
"And 'union!, a union!,' was all he could cry—

I watch'd in the lobby to look at the fun
For the sweeping already I saw was begun
But the speaker was stubborn & stuck in his chair
Nor the broom nor the purse could do anything there (1–16)

Tighe's more ironic, witty, or politically inflected poems were not published by her cousin William, and thus open up new approaches to Tighe's literary production and the wry sensibility that underscores her vision.

That wry and bittersweet sensibility came to the fore in the autumn of 1804, when Tighe contemplated preparing an edition somewhat like this one before she ultimately determined to print the private copies of *Psyche* that appeared in the summer of 1805. Urged by the members of her literary circle to publish a collection of her poetry for the public, she explained why she decided not to in a Christmas Eve 1804 letter to Joseph Cooper Walker:

I have myself been on the very verge of a most frightful auspice & had almost been persuaded to expose to the mercy of the reviewers, Edinburg *butchers* & all, my poor little Psyche & a volume of smaller poems which I was advis'd to add, as I might, to serve like the straw appendages of a kite, that she might not fall to the ground by her own weight—however after a few nights agitation I found that I have not nerves for it, let my stock of self conceit be as great as it may, so I am very obstinate to the partial solicitations of those who I am sure are chiefly anxious to provide me with what they think would prove amusement—but it is too serious a business for that. (TCD MS 1461)

Readers of this edition will have the opportunity to decide for themselves at long last.

A BRIEF CHRONOLOGY

1772   Mary Blachford is born on October 9 to Theodosia (née Tighe) and William Blachford, second child after John Blachford (born 1771).

1773   Her father dies in May.

1786   She briefly studies as a day scholar at Mr. Este's boarding school on Green's Square in London while her brother attends Eton but returns with her mother to Ireland in May.

1787   She begins to keep a journal of spiritual reflections when she is fourteen.

1788   Her mother proposes an engagement to M. de la Flechere, nephew of John Fletcher, with John Wesley's blessing. Toward the end of the year, she develops a consumptive cough. In December she and her mother visit Rossana, where she renews her friendship with her cousin Henry Tighe (born 1771), who has just returned from school in London.

1789   In August she and her mother travel to London, Tunbridge Wells, and Bath to seek relief for her cough, which lingers till September 1790. Her mother breaks off the proposed engagement to Flechere on account of the cough (and Henry Tighe).

1792   Her brother and Henry Tighe tour Switzerland and France during the summer.

1793   She marries Henry Tighe on October 5. They travel shortly thereafter to England, where they will reside for the most of the 1790s.

1795   She meets Anna Seward in April during a visit to the Ladies of Llangollen, Eleanor Butler and Sarah Ponsonby, in Wales. In May George Romney completes her portrait (begun in April 1794), source of the John Comerford miniature as well as the 1811 Caroline Watson engraving and the 1812 Edward Scriven engraving.

1798   The Tighes spend most of the Rebellion in Ireland and return to

England in late October. They make frequent trips back to Ireland during 1799 and 1800 as the Act of Union is debated, and return for good in 1801.

1801 She begins composing *Psyche; or, the Legend of Love* (completed in 1802).

1803 She completes her five-volume novel, *Selena*, at Rossana.

1804 In January she develops another consumptive cough and travels to England with her husband and mother in June for medical attention. She visits Hannah More and her sisters at Barleywood on a day trip from Bristol.

1805 *Psyche* is published in a limited edition of fifty copies in July. Tighe returns to Ireland with her husband and mother in September, and she spends the next few years residing chiefly in Dublin with periodic stays at Rossana (and other country houses).

1809 She makes a final visit to Woodstock with her mother and husband in May.

1810 Mary Tighe dies on March 24 after a prolonged battle with tuberculosis at Woodstock and is buried on March 27 in Inistiogue.

1811 William Tighe publishes two posthumous editions of Mary Tighe's poetry: *Psyche, with Other Poems* and *Mary, a Series of Reflections During Twenty Years.*

1817 John Blachford dies in July. Theodosia Blachford dies on November 8.

1836 Henry Tighe dies.

POETRY

Poems

1789–1801

August 1789[1]

True happiness is only found
Within fair virtue's sacred bound.[2]

Happy he whose thoughtful mind
    Seeks contentment not on earth,
Nor desires nor seeks to find,
    Riches, honours, joys or mirth.

5   Far retired from care he lives,
    See him calmly, humbly wait,
Peace, beyond what earth e'er gives,
    Is the portion of his state.

Waiting till the appointed hour,
10   That shall speak the solemn word;
Lo, he daily feels the power,
    Of an omnipresent Lord!

Weak repinings at his fate,
    Ne'er disturb his humble breast;
15   Hoping for a better state,
    Satisfied in this to rest.

Lo, his portion is prepared,
    And in this he rests content,
Never hath his spirit dared,
20   Disbelieve the promise sent.

As the glory of his Lord,
    So shall his in heaven be;
He relies upon his word,
    Thus from anxious care set free.

25   Oh that thus my thoughts were stayed
    On that glorious land of rest;
All my cares and sorrows laid
    On my dear Redeemer's breast.

Toiling in this sea of care,
30   Long my weary soul hath been;
Every passion, every fear,
    O'er my heart alternate reign.

Yet I see the happy shore,
    Where my toils for ever cease,
35   Gracious Pilot steer me o'er,
    Bring me to that land of peace.

GOOD FRIDAY, 1790[1]

Here, Oh my soul, fresh comfort take
    From this amazing day!
May gratitude within me wake!
    All worldly thoughts away!

5   For on this day the Godhead died,
    (Amazing thought!) for me!
Pierced were his hands, his feet, his side:
    His soul felt agony.

Oh what return can I then make,
10   For favours so divine?
My gracious Saviour deign to take
    My heart, 'tis all that's mine.

Oh let me suffer, Lord, with thee,
    That I with thee may reign;
15   Oh comfort, bless, and strengthen me,
    While tasting of thy pain.

Oh bring into thy wondrous bliss
    The soul for whom thou'st died,
My only hope and comfort this
20   My Jesus crucified.

To Her Mother. Rossana, 1791[1]

Retired to solitude and soft repose,
　　To thee would I devote this silent hour;
Ere yet in downy sleep these eyes I close,
　　Ten thousand blessings on thine head I'd shower.

5　　Be thine, dear guardian of my helpless youth,
　　Friend of my heart, director of my feet,
Be thine each treasure from the fount of truth;
　　On thee kind heaven distil its comforts sweet.

Not these soft scenes where pleasure reigns with ease,
10　　And grace and beauty mingle all their charms,
Can fully now thine absent daughter please
　　Who longs to rest within a parent's arms.

Bless then, my soul, the Source of every good,
　　For this his dearest and most valued gift,
15　Thy grateful accents tho' in numbers rude
　　And weakly utter'd, thou to heaven mayst lift.

And as when vapours, rising from the earth,
　　Ascend and hover in the clouded skies,
Then in soft rains descending banish dearth,
20　　And bid the flowers in mingled fragrance rise:

So may the gratitude, which swells my heart,
　　And bids my tongue heaven's richest bounties praise,
May it on every act its power impart,
　　Rule every word, and govern all my ways.

From Metastasio, 1791[1]

Vain dreams, and fictions of distress and love,
I idly feigned, but, while I fondly strove
To paint with every grace the tale of woe,
Ah fool! my tears unbid began to flow.

5   O'er the invented griefs I vainly mourn,
    With real sorrow is my bosom torn.
    But has the muse alone the fatal power
    To vex with fancied woes the troubled hour?
    When she resigns her empire o'er my soul,
10   Does reason then this tranquil breast controul?
    Deceived no longer by ingenious art,
    Does wisdom rule each motion of my heart?
    Do no vain loves, no idle passions rage,
    No fond desires my restless thoughts engage?
15   Alas! not only when I write, and sing,
    I soar on fancy's ever varying wing.
    But all my hopes, and all my fears are vain,
    And all my acts but like the tales I feign,
    Vexed by vain cares, by vain delights deceived,
20   In empty dreams I joy, and I am grieved:
    My raving life is one continual cheat,
    And all my wishes but a fond deceit,
    Ah Lord! arouse me from this dream of woes,
    And let me in the arms of truth repose.

SONNET, MARCH 1791[1]

  As the frail bark, long tossed by stormy winds,
  Wearied and scattered a calm haven finds,
  So from a heavy load of cares set free,
  At length, O Lord! my soul returns to thee!
5 Oh sun of light illume my doubtful way,
  And let me from thy paths no longer stray,
  Now hearken kindly to my mournful cries,
  From the dark world now turn to thee mine eyes:
  Oh food of sweetness that can never cloy,
10 Banish my sorrows with thine holy joy!
  Thou gentle stream of soft consoling peace
  O'erflow this heart, and all my tears shall cease,
  Cleanse my repenting soul at mercy's shrine,
  And then, adorn her with thy grace divine.

VERSES WRITTEN IN SOLITUDE, APRIL 1792[1]

Returned at length to solitude, and peace,
　　Once more my heart resumes its loved pursuits;
Once more I seek my lost, poetic ease,
　　And wander searching for Castalia's[2] fruits.

5　　But ah! in vain to me the nine[3] refuse
　　Inspiring succour, and enkindling thought,
Too long alas! I have renounced the muse,
　　Her voice neglected, and her lyre forgot.

Lost in a crowd of folly and of noise,
10　　With vain delight my bosom learned to beat,
Resigned the pleasures I had made my choice,
　　Of calm philosophy and wisdom sweet.

For, in the circles of the vain, and gay,
　　No more her tranquil state my soul enjoyed,
15　　In busy idleness I passed the day,
　　And mirth and dress, and song my hours employed.

To fix the attention of admiring eyes,
　　To move with elegance, and talk with ease;
To be the object of the practised sigh,
20　　To attract the notice, and the ear to please.

The empty flattery which my heart despised,
　　The present frenzy which the dance inspired,
Joys, which my reason never could have prized,
　　And which till tasted I had ne'er desired.

25　　Yet these had charms, which now I blush to own,
　　Powers which I then believed not they possess'd;
The muse to banish from her humble throne,
　　Where she so oft had fired my glowing breast.

But the remembrance of these empty hours
30   Affords no single pleasure to my mind;
My soul regrets her lost collective powers,
    And sighs once more her wonted calm to find;

For folly's influence do I still deplore,
    A vacant gloom she o'er my heart hath spread;
35 The secret charm of solitude is o'er,
    My thoughts are scattered, and the muses fled.

Such was the low ambition of my mind,
    Such were the vain desires I formed,
For such delights my calmer joys resigned,
40   And quenched the fires which had my bosom warmed.

MARCH 1793[1]

———Oh how this spring of youn
Resembles the glory of an April day,
Which now shews all the beauty of the sun,
And by and by a cloud takes all away.

SONNET[1]

As one who late hath lost a friend adored,
　　Clings with sick pleasure to the faintest trace
　　Resemblance offers in another's face,
Or sadly gazing on that form deplored,
5　　Would clasp the silent canvas to his breast:
　　So muse I on the good I have enjoyed,
　　The wretched victim of my hopes destroyed;
On images of peace I fondly rest,
Or in the page, where weeping fancy mourns,
10　　I love to dwell upon each tender line,
　　And think the bliss once tasted still is mine;
While cheated memory to the past returns,
　　And, from the present leads my shivering heart
　　Back to those scenes from which it wept to part.

TO DEATH[1]

O thou most terrible, most dreaded power,
　　In whatsoever form thou meetest the eye!
　　Whether thou biddest thy sudden arrow fly
In the dread silence of the midnight hour;
5　　Or whether, hovering o'er the lingering wretch
　　Thy sad cold javelin hangs suspended long,
　　While round the couch the weeping kindred throng
With hope and fear alternately on stretch;
Oh, say, for me what horrors are prepared?
10　　Am I now doomed to meet thy fatal arm?
　　Or wilt thou first from life steal every charm,
And bear away each good my soul would guard?
That thus, deprived of all it loved, my heart
From life itself contentedly may part.

WRITTEN AT SCARBOROUGH[1]

As musing pensive in my silent home
   I hear far off the sullen ocean's roar,
    Where the rude wave just sweeps the level shore,
Or bursts upon the rocks with whitening foam,
5   I think upon the scenes my life has known;
    On days of sorrow, and some hours of joy;
    Both which alike time could so soon destroy!
And now they seem a busy dream alone;
While on the earth exists no single trace
10   Of all that shook my agitated soul,
    As on the beach new waves for ever roll
And fill their past forgotten brother's place:
    But I, like the worn sand, exposed remain
    To each new storm which frets the angry main.

SONNET[1]

When glowing Phoebus[2] quits the weeping earth,
    What splendid visions rise upon the sight!
    Fancy, with transient charms and colours bright,
To changing forms in Heaven's gay scene gives birth:
5   But soon the melting beauties disappear,
    And fade like those which in life's early bloom
    Hope bade me prize; and the approaching gloom,
These tints of sadness, and these shades of fear,
    Resemble most that melancholy hour
10   Which, with a silent and resistless power,
Shrouded my joy's bright beam in shadowy night:
    Till Memory marks each scene which once shone gay;
As the dark plains, beneath the Moon's soft light,
    Again revealed, reflect a mellowing ray.

Written in Autumn[1]

O Autumn! how I love thy pensive air,
   Thy yellow garb, thy visage sad and dun!
   When from the misty east the labouring Sun
Bursts through thy fogs, that gathering round him, dare
5   Obscure his beams, which, though enfeebled, dart
   On the cold, dewy plains a lustre bright:
   But chief, the sounds of thy reft woods delight;
Their deep, low murmurs to my soul impart
A solemn stillness, while they seem to speak
10   Of Spring, of Summer now for ever past,
   Of drear, approaching Winter, and the blast
Which shall ere long their soothing quiet break:
   Here, when for faded joys my heaving breast
   Throbs with vain pangs; here will I love to rest.

The Vartree[1]

Quivi le piante più che altrove ombrose
E l'erba molle, e il fresco dolce appare.
                          Poliziano[2]

Sweet are thy banks, O Vartree! when at morn
   Their velvet verdure glistens with the dew;
When fragrant gales by softest Zephyrs[3] borne
   Unfold the flowers, and ope their petals new.

5   How bright the lustre of thy silver tide,
   Which winds, reluctant to forsake the vale!
How play the quivering branches on thy side,
   And lucid catch the sun-beam in the gale!

And sweet thy shade at Noon's more fervid hours,
10   When faint we quit the upland gayer lawn
To seek the freshness of thy sheltering bowers,
   Thy chestnut glooms, where day can scarcely dawn.

How soothing in the dark sequestered grove
    To see thy placid waters seem to sleep;
15 Pleased they reflect the *sombre* tints they love,
    As unperceived in silent peace they creep.

The deepest foliage bending o'er thy wave
    Tastes thy pure kisses with embracing arms,
While each charmed Dryad⁴ stoops her limbs to lave
20   Thy smiling Naïad⁵ meets her sister charms.

Beneath the fragrant lime, or spreading beech,
    The bleating flocks in panting crowds repose:
Their voice alone my dark retreat can reach,
    While peace and silence all my soul compose.

25 Here, Mary, rest! the dangerous path forsake
        Where folly lures thee, and where vice ensnares,
    Thine innocence and peace no longer stake,
        Nor barter solid good for brilliant cares.

Shun the vain bustle of the senseless crowd,
30   Where all is hollow that appears like joy;
    Where, the soft claims of feeling disallowed,
        Fallacious hopes the baffled soul annoy.

Hast thou not trod each vain and giddy maze,
    By Flattery led o'er Pleasure's gayest field?
35 Basked in the sunshine of her brightest blaze,
    And proved whate'er she can her votaries yield?

That full completion of each glowing hope,
    Which youth and novelty could scarce bestow,
From the last dregs of Joy's exhausted cup
40   Canst thou expect thy years mature shall know?

Hast thou not tried the vanities of life,
    And all the poor, mean joys of Fashion known?
Blush then to hold with Wisdom longer strife,
    Submit at length a better guide to own.

45   Here woo the Muses in the scenes they love;
      Let Science near thee take her patient stand:
    Each weak regret for gayer hours reprove,
      And yield thy soul to Reason's calm command.

SONNET[1]

Poor, fond deluded heart! wilt thou again
    Listen, enchanted, to the syren song
    Of treacherous Pleasure? Ah, deceived too long,
Cease now at length to throb with wishes vain!
5   Ah, cease her paths bewildering to explore!
    Betrayed so oft! yet recollect the woe
    Which waits on disappointment; taught to know
By sad experience, wilt thou not give o'er
To rest, deluded, on the fickle wing
10   Which Fancy lends thee in her airy flight,
    But to seduce thee to some giddy height,
And leave thee there a poor forsaken thing.
    Hope warbles once again, Truth pleads in vain,
    And my charmed soul sinks vanquished by her strain.

WRITTEN IN THE CHURCH-YARD AT MALVERN[1]

This seems a spot to pensive sorrow dear,
    Gloomy the shade which yields this ancient yew,
    Sacred the seat of Death! soothed while I view
Thy hills, O Malvern, proudly rising near,
5   I bless the peaceful mound, the mouldering cross,
      And every stone whose rudely sculptured form
      Hath braved the rage of many a winter's storm.
Pleased with the melancholy scene, each loss
Once more I weep; and wish this grave were thine,
10   Poor, lost, lamented friend! that o'er thy clay
      For once this last, sad tribute I might pay,
And, with my tears, to the cold tomb resign
    Each hope of bliss, each vanity of life,
    And all the passions agonizing strife.

VERSES WRITTEN AT THE DEVILS BRIDGE, CARDIGANSH[1]

Hic licet occultos proferre impune dolores.
                  Propertius[2]

When pleasure departs, what a blank there remains.
    How dreary each object around us appears!
While the soul, sick of life, from each object refrains,
    And in solitude longs to indulge in vain tears.

5   If the eye of compassion has ceased to look kind,
      If the voice which delighted, no longer is heard;
If sorrows unuttered oppress the sad mind,
    And the labouring breast by no comfort is cheer'd.

When 'tis past, & the moment of pleasure is o'er,
10   When to joys that are gone the sad mourner returns,

While memory faithful still guards in her store,
    The hopes he has lost, & the friend whom he mourns.

Oh! bear him to scenes, where rude Nature appears,
    Let solitude sooth him, & pensive repose,
15 No eye to restrain the sweet freedom of tears,
    No ear to forbid the expression of woes.

Near woods, interrupted by white jutting rocks
    Oh place him beside some river's dark course,
Where the torrents impetuous gush thro' brown oaks,
20   And steep groves reecho their murmurings hoarse.

In a glen deep sequestered, surrounded by woods,
    By mountains o'ertopped, inaccessibly high,
Let him view the swell'd stream's irresistible floods,
    Unappall'd by the tempest which roars thro' the sky.

25 Oh! there let him wander thro' underwoods dark,
    Unmolested by man, by no comforter teiz'd;
No stranger unfeeling his sorrows to mark,
    And unheard be the groans which his bosom have eas'd.—

When Nature deplores her lost beauty & pride,
30   Her drear lamentations more soothing shall sound,
The voice of complaint to his heart is allied,
    And in desolate scenes, is sad sympathy found.

Let Fancy to May's rosy bosom retire,
    And quit the sad season, & shun the sad heart,
35 In the soft vacant breast, let her passion inspire
    And double each pleasure by magical art.—

For treacherous power! while seeming to cheer,
    To sooth his distress, & to soften his woes;
The scenes thou recallest, but rouse the sad tear,
40   And thy warm glowing pictures destroy his repose.

In the regions of sorrow thy lustre is vain,
    It there on no exquisite prospects can shine,
Oh! add not to anguish, nor magnify pain,
    But the wretched to wisdom & reason resign.

45   Thy aid he requests not; he asks not relief,
    From the cruel assistance which thou canst impart,
The image of joy but awakens his grief,
    Of joy, which no longer inhabits his heart.

But thou, cheering Hope! sweet peace breathing guest,
50   Assure him, bright joy on his days soon shall shine,
Dispel this sad gloom, & revisit his breast,
    And whisper, soft pleasure again shall be thine.—

'Tis thou canst pour balm on his anguish alone,
    Though nought can restore, yet thou canst relieve,
55   For his losses compensate, his sorrows atone,
    And teach him with calm resignation to grieve.—

Bryan Byrne, of Glenmalure[1]

Bright shines the morn o'er Carickmure,[2]
    And silvers every mountain stream;
The autumnal woods on Glenmalure[3]
    Look lovely in the slanting beam.

5   And hark! the cry, the cry of joy,
    The hounds spring o'er yon heathy brow!—
"'Tis but the hunter's horn, my boy,
    No death-tongued bugle scares us now."

In vain the widowed mother smiled,
10   And clasped her darling to her breast;
Horror and rage o'er all the child
    A manly beauty strange impressed.

Fierce rolled his eye, of heaven's own hue,
  And the quick blood strong passions told,
15 As fresh the breeze of morning blew
  From his clear brow the locks[4] of gold.

'Tis not alone the horn so shrill;—
  Yon martial plume that waves on high,
Bids every infant nerve to thrill
20   With more than infant agony.

Yet gentle was the soldier's heart,
  Whom 'mid the gallant troop he spied
Who let the gallant troop depart,
  And checked his eager courser's pride.[5]

25 "What fears the child?" he wondering cried,
  With courteous air as near he drew.
"Soldier, away! my father died,
  Murdered by men of blood[6] like you."

Even while the angry cherub speaks,
30   He struggles from the stranger's grasp:
Kissing the tears that bathed her cheeks,
  His little arms his mother clasp.

"And who are these,—this startled pair,[7]
  Who swift down Glenmalure are fled?
35 Behold the mother's maniac air,
  As seized with wild and sudden dread!"

"'Tis Ellen Byrne," an old man cried;
  "Poor Ellen, and her orphan boy!"
Then turned his silvered brow aside,
40   To shun the youth's enquiring eye.

"And is there none to guard the child,
  Save that lone frenzied widow's hand?
These rocky heights, these steep woods wild,
  Sure some more watchful eye demand."

45   "Ah, well he knows each rock, each wood,
          The mountain goat not more secure;
      And he was born to hardships rude,
          The orphan Byrne of Carickmure.

      "That boy had seen his father's blood,
50   Had heard his murdered father's groan;
      And never more in playful mood
          With smiles his infant beauty shone."

      Sad was the pitying stranger's eye:
          "Too well," said he, "I guess the truth;
55   His father, sure, was doomed to die,
          Some poor deluded rebel youth."

      "No rebel he," with eye inflamed,
          And cheek that glowed with transient fire,
      Roused to a sudden warmth, exclaimed
60   The hapless Ellen's aged sire.

      "He did not fall in Tarah's fight,[8]
          No blood of his the Curragh stains,[9]
      Where many a ghost that moans by night
          Of foully broken faith complains.

65   "He triumphed not that fatal day,
          When every loyal cheek looked pale,
      But heard, like us, with sad dismay,
          Of fallen chiefs in Clough's[10] dark vale.

      "For, wedded to our Ellen's love,
70   One house was ours, one hope, one soul:
      Though fierce malignant parties strove,
          No party rage could love control.

      "Though we were sprung from British race,
          And his was Erin's early pride,
75   Yet matched in every loveliest grace,
          No priest could e'er their hearts divide.

"What though no yeoman's arms he bore;
    'Twas party hate that hope forbad:
What though no martial dress he wore,
80   That dress no braver bosom clad.

"And had our gallant Bryan Byrne
    Been welcomed to their loyal band,
Home might I still in joy return
    The proudest father in the land.

85   "For, ah! when Bryan Byrne was slain,
    With him my brave, my beauteous son
His precious life-blood shed in vain;—
    The savage work of death was done!" . . . .

He ceased: for now, by memory stung,
90   His heart's deep wounds all freshly bled,
While with a father's anguish wrung,
    He bowed to earth his aged head.

Yet soothing to his broken heart
    He felt the stranger's sympathy,
95   And age is ready to impart
    Its page of woe to pity's eye.

Yes! it seemed sweet once more to dwell
    On social joys and peaceful days,
And still his darling's virtues tell,
100   And still his Ellen's beauty praise.

"But say," at length exclaimed the youth,
    "Did no one rash, rebellious deed
E'er cloud thy Bryan's loyal truth,
    And justice doom thy boy to bleed?"

105   "No; never rash, rebellious deed
    Was his, nor rash rebellious word;
That day of slaughter saw him bleed,
    Where blushing Justice dropped the sword.

"In Fury's hand it madly raged,
110   As urged by fierce revenge she flew;
With unarmed Innocence she waged
     Such war as Justice never knew."

"'Twas ours (the sorrowing father cried),
     'Twas ours to mourn the crimes of all:
115   Each night some loyal brother died;
     Each morn beheld some victim fall.

"Oh, 'twas a sad and fearful day
     That saw my gallant boys laid low;
The voice of anguish and dismay
120   Proclaimed full many a widow's woe!

"But doubly o'er our fated house
     The accursed hand of murder fell,
And ere our Ellen wept her spouse,
     She had a dreadful tale to tell!

125   "For early on that guilty morn
     The voice of horror reached our ears;
That, from their thoughtless slumber torn,
     Before a helpless sister's tears,

"Beneath their very mother's sight
130   Three youthful brothers butchered lie,
Three loyal yeomen brave in fight,
     Butchered by savage treachery.

"They were my nephews; boys I loved,
     My own brave boys[11] alone more dear;
135   Their rashness oft my heart reproved,
     And marked their daring zeal with fear.

"They were my widowed sister's joy;
     Her hope in age and dark distress;
And Ellen loved each gallant boy
140   Even with a sister's tenderness.

"It was from Ellen's lips I heard
    The tidings sadly, surely true:
To me, ere yet the dawn appeared,
    All pale with fear and grief she flew.

145   "Roused by her call, with her I sought
    The sad abode of misery:
But to the wretched mother brought
    No comfort, but our sympathy.

"On the cold earth,[12] proud Sorrow's throne,
150   In silent majesty of woe,
She sat, and felt herself alone,
    Though loud the increasing tumults grow.

"In throngs the assembled country came,
    And every hand was armed with death:
155   Revenge! revenge! (they all exclaim,)
    Spare no suspected traitor's breath:

"No; let not one escape who owns
    The faith of Rome, of treachery:
This loyal blood for vengeance groans,
160   And signal vengeance let there be!

"What, shall we feel the coward blow,
    And tamely wait a late defence?
No; let us strike the secret foe,
    Even through the breast of innocence!

165   "Poor Ellen trembled as they raved;
    Her pallid cheek forgot its tears;
While from the hand of fury saved,
    Her infant darling scarce appears.

"I saw her earnest searching eye,
170   In that dark moment of alarm,
Ask, in impatient agony,
    A brother's dear, protecting arm.

"Woe! bitter woe, to me and mine!
   Too well his brave, his feeling heart
175   Already could her fears divine,
   And more than bear a brother's part.

"When the first savage blast he knew
   Would bid each deadly bugle roar,
Back to our home of peace he flew:
180   Ah, home of peace and love no more!

"Oh! would to God that I had died
   Beneath my wretched sister's roof!
Thus heaven in mercy had denied
   To my worst fears their utmost proof.

185   "So had these eyes been spared a sight
   That wrings my soul with anguish still,
Nor known how much of life, ere night,
   The blood-hounds of revenge could spill.

"Sinking at once with fear and age,
190   Her father's steps my child upheld;
The mangled victims of their rage
   Each moment shuddering we beheld.

"Down yon steep side of Carickmure,
   Our rugged path we homeward wound;
195   And saw, at least, that home secure,
   'Mid many a smoking ruin round.

"Low in the Glen our cottage lies
   Behind yon dusky copse of oak:
On its white walls we fixed our eyes,
200   But not one word poor Ellen spoke![13]

"We came . . . . the clamour scarce was o'er,
   The fiends scarce left their work of death:—
But never spoke our Bryan more,
   Nor Ellen caught his latest breath.

205 "Still to the corse by horror joined,
  The shrinking infant closely clung,
And fast his little arms intwined,
  As round the bleeding neck he hung.

"Oh, sight of horror, sight of woe!
210 The dead and dying both were there:
One dreadful moment served to show,
  For us was nothing but despair.

"Oh, God! even now methinks I see
  My dying boy, as there he stood,
215 And sought with fond anxiety
  To hide his gushing wounds of blood,[14]

"Ere life yet left his noble breast,
  Gasping, again he tried to speak,
And twice my hand he feebly pressed,
220 And feebly kissed poor Ellen's cheek.

"No word she spoke, no tear she shed,
  Ere at my feet convulsed she fell,
Still lay my children, cold and dead!
  And I yet live, the tale to tell!

225 "She too awoke to wild despair
  With frenzied eye each corse to see,
To rave, to smile with frantic air;
  But never more to smile for me!

"But hold! from yonder grassy slope
230 Our orphan darling calls me hence:
Sweet child, last relic of our hope,
  Of love and injured innocence.[15]

"Soldier, farewel! To thee should power
  Commit the fate of lives obscure,
235 Remember still in fury's hour
  The murdered youths of Glenmalure.

"And chief, if civil broils return,
    Though vengeance urge to waste, destroy;
Ah! pause! . . . . think then on Bryan Byrne,
240   Poor Ellen, and her orphan boy!"

AVAILS IT OUGHT TO NUMBER O'ER[1]

Avails it ought to number o'er
Thy vanished treasures?
These pages then peruse no more
They can't reach thy pleasures.

5   The friend who late so fondly lov'd
Has quitted thee for ever—
And her whom once thine heart approv'd
Thine eyes shall disturb never.

TIME FADES THE LUSTRE OF THE MOON[1]

Time fades the lustre of the moon
The blossoms of the Spring decay,
And melancholy age shall soon,
Chase our joyous youth away.

5   Already we begin to fail
Beneath the weight of fruitless cares
Nor can our tears nor sighs avail
To renovate our dying years

Quit then my soul this tainted earth
10   Yet raise thy prospects higher
Still mindful of thine Heavenly birth
To immortality aspire.

To the Moon[1]

What is it that gives thee, pale Queen of the Night,
    That secret intelligent grace?
Or why do I gaze with such tender delight
    On thy fair, but insensible face?

5   What gentle enchantment possesses thy beam
    Beyond the warm sunshine day?
Thy bosom is cold as the glittering stream,
    Where dances thy tremulous ray.

Canst thou the sad heart of its sorrow beguile,
10   Or grief's fond indulgence suspend?
Yet where is the mourner but welcomes thy smile,
    And loves thee almost as a friend?

The tear that looks bright on thy beam as it flows,
    Unmoved thou dost ever behold;
15   The sorrow that loves in thy light to repose,
    To thee it has never been told:

And yet thou dost sooth me;—and ever I find,
    While watching thy gentle retreat,
A moonlight composure steal over my mind
20   Poetical, pensive, and sweet.

I think of the years that for ever are fled;
    Of follies, by others forgot;
Of joys that have vanish'd; of hopes that are dead
    Of friendships that were, and are not.

25   Those beams that so bright through my casement appear,
    To far distant scenes they extend;
Illumine the dwellings of those that are dear,
    And sleep on the grave of my friend.

Then still I must love thee, mild Queen of the Night!
30   Since feeling and fancy agree,
To make thee a source of unfading delight,
      A friend and a solace to me.

SYMPATHY[1]

Wert thou sad, I would beguile
      Thy sadness, by my tender lay:
Wert thou in a mood to smile,
      With thee, laugh the hours away.

5   Didst thou feel inclined to sleep,
      I would watch, and hover near;
Did misfortune bid thee weep,
      I would give thee tear for tear.

Not a sigh, that heaved thy breast,
10   But I'd echo from my own;—
Did one care disturb thy rest,
      Mine alas! were also flown.

When the hour of death should come,
      I'd receive thy latest sigh;
15   Only ask to share thy tomb,
      Then, contented, with thee die.

CALM DELIGHT[1]

Birds, flowers, soft winds, and waters gently flowing,
      Surround me day and night,
Still sweetly on my heart bestowing
      Content and calm delight.

5   When day's toil wearies, sleep my peace restoring,
      Descends with balmy night;
In bright dreams on my bosom pouring
      Content and calm delight.

SONG[1]

See my love, yon angry deep,
   Hear its wild tumultuous roar,
Think the storm with furious sweep,
   Drives the billows to the shore.

5   On its agitated breast
   Mark yon vessel widely tost,
And the mariner distrest
   'Midst the whelming ruin lost

Such the storms distracting power,
10   Fate prepares for wretched love;
O'er our heads such tempests lower,
   Doom'd distress and fear to prove.

Ah behold! What sudden peace!
   View the calm which reigns at last,
15   How the winds their contest cease!
   Hushed is every ruder blast.

The opening clouds begin to fly,
   The sun shines forth with cheering ray;
The watery mirror of the sky,
20   Is brighten'd in the smiling day.

So, my Love, the heav'ns for us,
   Shall assume a kinder form,
Our distress shall vanish thus,
   Thus, shall fly the cruel storm.

25   Bright the day for us shall shine,
   Gloomy doubt shall disappear,
Peace shall to our pray'rs incline,
   Fled our sorrow, care, and fear.

To ——C——E[1]

The youth of broken fortunes sent to roam
And banish'd early from his smiling home,
With aching heart, indignant, and opprest,
Shame on his cheek, and anguish in his breast,
5   Quits the lov'd scenes he hopes no more to view,
In foreign climes new objects to pursue,
Soon other joys and other sorrows come,
And from his memory fades his distant home;
Yet when revolving time with changeful hand,
10   Once more restores him to his native land,
When stranger like, unwelcom'd and unknown,
He wanders o'er lawns he called his own,
Sees other Lords possess his fair domains
The long lov'd woods and dear paternal plains
15   There as he hails the well-remembered bowers
Each silent witness of his earliest hours,
Regret and tenderness once more return
His eyes their long forgotten sorrows mourn,
Dejected, desolate, he looks around,
20   And treads with reverence on the sacred ground,
Feels all the cheerless gloom he felt before
When first in exile he forsook the shore,
And fondly thinks the scenes he liv'd a boy
Partake his sorrow, as they shared his joy.
25   E'en thus, estrang'd, divided from thy heart,
Reluctant tenderness I bad depart,
For friendship thus denied forgot to care
And hushed the feelings which you scorned to share
But when affection in thy glance I spy
30   Or the sweet smile of kindness meets my eye,
Once more my melting heart with love o'erflows,
Laments its former loss & weeps forgotten woes.

THE HOURS OF PEACE[1]

Stay hours of peace! Awhile delay,
Awhile with grateful Linda[2] stay
And hear her yet contented say
            Stay hours of peace!

5   What though no more the midnight ball
Lures me to answer Folly's call
I shun well pleased th'illumined hall
            For hours of peace.

For you I gladly would forego
10   The splendid circle's idle shew,
Nor sigh, for more than you bestow
            Dear hours of peace

What hath the gay, the busy earth
In all its scenes of noisy mirth
15   More sweet than thee my social hearth
            In hours of peace?

A Mother's partial, tender smile
May time your rapid flight beguile
And woo your stay a little while
20   Oh hours of peace!

The young Anacreon[3] too shall sing
And as he wakes the magic string
Charmed by his notes on hov'ring wing
            Stay hours of peace.

25   No flower hath here the wintry gloom
The Teian[4] rose shall sweetly bloom,
And shed a grateful, soft perfume
            O'er hours of peace

The bough of sportive innocence
30   The look of bright intelligence,

Shall bless the hours of taste and sense
           The hours of peace

No stern reproving glance ye meet
No look but breathes affection sweet
35   Then speed not hence your feathery feet
           Blest hours of peace

What charms those white winged hours can stay?
Alas! while thus I idly pray
E'en now how swift you haste away
40   Dear hours of peace

Like some capricious beauty, coy,
When most persuasion we employ
Most swift you fly the offer'd joy
           Oh hours of peace!—

45   But time shall ne'er your charms devour
For memory still with soothing power
Shall number o'er each happy hour
           The hours of peace.

LA CITTADINA: ON LEAVING ROSSANA 1798[1]

Farewell ye hapless woods,
Which dreary frown o'er the swelled turbid floods,
    Your rude tempestuous roar,
Shall howl discordant in my ears no more—
5   Congenial is your shade
To the sad lover and forsaken maid—
    There spread your sombre gloom
And 'mid the frozen plains your brownest hints assume.
    Hence you unsocial band
10   Retirement and her offspring mute
Study who drives afar with ebon wand,
Joys jocund voice and Pleasure's silver Lute,

Pale science with her patient Lamp
   Silence, assiduous Thought
15 Calm Contemplation by the muses taught
And Application whom no bliss can damp
   With stooping gait, contracted brow,
And eyes whose keen research would no repose allow.

————

   But come ye dear remember'd joys,
20   Hail delightful smoke and noise
   The hurried morn, and daily stroll
   Where the gilded chariots roll;
   While in ev'ry crowded street,
   Pleased the lounging gazers meet;
25   Glittering shops, and splendid sights,
   Gaiety's long festive nights;
   Balls, and Concerts, routs[2] and plays,
   Where the midnight flambeause[3] blaze;
   Joys that gem dark Winter's crown.
30   All the dear delights of town;
   At the call of Mirth and Sport
   Hope invites me to resort;
   Now let plumy[4] footed glee,
   And ever new variety,
35   Lead the sprightly hours along;
   Festive dance, and choral song,
   Hail busy town, and hail with thee,
   Smiling hu'd Society.
   Welcome, Frolic's pleasing train!
40   Now commences Pleasure's reign;
   Quick Imagination pass
   Before my eyes thy magic glass
   Paint the scenes so bright and gay
   The lighted hall at once display;
45   Let me hear the jocund strain
   View the light fantastic train,
   As with many twinkling feet,
   The measur'd cadence oft they beat,
   Wreathed with ever blooming flowers,
50   Forgetting the uncounted hours

When the brisk, unwearied viol,
Calls each active grace to trial;
While the gliding, happy maid,
Conscious views the hommage paid,
55   From the circling crowded rows.
Glances of admiring Beaux;
Round the glowing maid they run
When her pleasing task is done;
Smiles, and adulation bland
60   Eager ask her vacant hand,
Till her soft voice and melting eyes
Declare to whom belong the prize;
Short the toil—the rest how sweet
When delighted partners meet!
65   When no prudent Chaperone's eye
The dangerous whisper can espy!
And the careless, happy band
All around them heedless stand!
Or when the signal bids them share
70   The banquet spread with generous care!
The watchful youth attentive flies
Where his fav'rite maid he spies,
Her yielding hand he then may press,
And ev'ry tender hope confess,
75   And ev'ry swain declare his love,
While soft'ning eyes the tale approve,
Fancy scenes like this bestows,
Images like these she shews
While thro' the crowd and mingling dance
80   Quick I send my eager glance,
And as some well-known friend I spy,
The sudden start, the sparkling eye
Lips brilliant smile, and roseate glow,
Speak with power no words can shew;
85   Let such lively warm delights
Animate remembered nights;
And not infrequent may my ear
Bannister or Siddons hear,[5]
And gratify my curious eyes

90   With all a decent stage supplies,
     And oft with soothing magic power,
     Let music charm the evening hour,
     Warbling soft his melting lays,
     Such emotions skilled to raise,
95   As the feeling breast may move,
     To tenderness and tranquil love,
     Me, eloquence shall oft invite
     Watchful to pass th'unwearied night,
     Then 'midst the senates crowded walls
100 On truth and virtue loud he calls;
     And bids th'unbiassed patriot free
     Nobly stand forth with energy;
     Or leads me to the sacred shrine
     Where Charity and Pity shine,
105 Where pious hopes the soul inspire,
     And kindly breathe a sacred fire,
     While mute enraptured crowds attend
     The widows and the orphan's friend,
     Thus let each feeling fast be bound,
110 By soft persuasions silver sound.
     Till gently stealing o'er my soul
     The smooth melodious currant[6] roll,
     And ev'ry captivated sense
     Owns the power of Eloquence.
115 Oft when calmest hours delight
     The chosen few whom we invite;
     Meeting at the close of day
     In concert decent, sprightly, gay,
     Bless my home, dear cherished center![7]
120 Where no visitors can enter;
     From intrusion sweetly free,
     Banish'd all formality,
     There we taste serenest joys,
     Free from rude and boisterous noise
125 There the heart expands, and there
     Benevolence, and peace appear,
     The anxious brow we there unbend,
     And ev'ry eye reflects a friend.

Reserves cold frosts there melt away
130   Beneath the social genial ray,
While around the blazing pile
The close contracted circle smile.
Or at the board the sparkling bowl
Animates the brilliant soul,
135   And mingling there with wit we see
Sense and mild society,
Charity, benign indulgence,
White rob'd candour, truth's just sentance,[8]
And evermore our feasts to bless
140   A constant guest be cheerfulness;
There oft let Genius guide the tongue,
And taste approve th'unlaboured song;
Let partial judgment smile serene,
Or criticise with gentlest mien;
145   And still refine our merriment
Glistening tender sentiment,
Sweet dove ey'd virgin whom of yore
Fair Venus to Apollo bore,
And gifted by the sacred nine
150   Placed her near Dian's silver shrine,
That her soft voice might pity move
Excuse the crimes of erring Love,
And for her brother's faults atone
With delicacy all her own,
155   Pleased with the infants' gentle charms
The Graces nursed her in their arms;
Smiled at her pains, her timid fear,
Her ready blush, and starting tear,
Inspired her words, and as she grew
160   Taught her each winning art they knew;
Her quick perception, liquid tones
All her father's genius owns,
While her fascinating eyes
Balmy breath and melting sighs,
165   The tender smile, the swelling breast,
Shew the queen of Love confest;
Hand in hand with dimpled mirth

Still may she grace our cheerful hearth;
While Love and Friendship hover round
170   Her pure and consecrated ground,
Oh hours of bliss! Oh night divine!
When shall such feasts again be mine?
Less bright were those which once could charm
The bard within his salvic⁹ farm;
175   And such to me could town afford,
Where peace and pleasure bless my board,
And such delights if thou canst give
Town in thee I still would live.¹⁰

A LETTER FROM MRS. ACTON
TO HER NEPHEW MR. EVANS[1]

I am happy, dear George, to hear you intend
Some time at Rossana this Christmas to spend;
I am pleased in my nephew to see such a spirit
To enterprise boldly I know you inherit
5   Yet before in so arduous a task you engage,
Tho' I know you superior to most of your age,
I think it but friendly to caution you thus
Lest, your memory failing, you come to nonplus.[2]
Whatever you learned at school or at College
10   Brush up for your use at this seat of all knowledge.
For my nephew's appearance I own I must quake
When I think what a moderate figure you'll make;
When with Latin and Greek not a marvel too much,
With Italian and French and a little high Dutch
15   In the midst of such scholars you find yourself placed
And with questions in Hebrew and Syriac[3] disgrac'd,
Lest staring around you, you fancy it Babel
When you hear fifteen languages spoken at table,
Or venture in English to ask for some beer
20   At the poor ignoramus the butler will sneer.
Not a groom but his "aes in presenti"[4] can say
And the son of the cook in pure Latin can pray;
To the housekeeper too should you happen to speak

'Tis fifty to one she will answer in Greek;
25   The Ladies think these are but vulgar attainments
Thrown by to their maids with their old fashion'd raiments
On their toilets no books but Arabic you'll see,
And with native Chinese they present you your tea;
On the carpets are charts of biography spread,
30   And quilts geographical cover the bed;
In alembics by blow pipes with chemic perfection,
The meat is oxided by Harry's direction;
While in sallads they search for the stamens and pistils
The rice pudding cools in rhomboidal chrystals,
35   And the carver takes care tho' the venison he mangles
To part ev'ry portion in proper triangles.
Bread and butter is cut in forms mathematic,
And the tea urn distills with art hydrostatic;
Nay their dances are measured by just trigonometry
40   And they move in the radii as ordered by geometry;
Nor language nor science enough can adorn
For each a poetical genius is born;
While infants they couplets could form in a trice
And lisp in soft numbers of geese and of mice,
45   Not to speak of that wonderful genius from England
Who Priestley[5] and Blair[6] has surpassed by his single hand,
Whose talent for rhyming so copiously flows
His labour is only to speak in plain prose,[7]
When the family, call'd by the bells' silver tine,
50   Assembles to supper, each offers his own,
Whether epic or tragic or comic they choose
Each worships his favorite appropriate muse.
Not a person appears in the family circle
But has verses deserving bays, laurel or myrtle.
55   Not with pencil alone is it Caroline's[8] care
The vices to task, but the persons to spare;
For tho' on her labours the muses all smile
Yet the high polish'd satire's her favorite style
Miss Butticuz[9] modest and timid declares
60   That nothing beyond a poor sonnet she dares;
But it has been whisper'd and I think that the fact is
She prepares for the press a new system of tactics:

Of the georgics an elegant version I hear
From the chymical farmer will shortly appear,[10]
65   There in Mantuan[11] strains his discoveries are sung,
Concentrated essence of gypsum and dung;
Mr. Jones[12] too, I hear, in a poem didactical
Gives hints of politeness both courteous and practical,
Tho' as yet he has only in pastorals dealt,
70   And in smooth strains of sentiment sung what he felt,
Yet this fault I have heard has by critics been found
That in S's too frequent his verses abound;
Camilla[13] indeed, as a foreigner, says
From her lips are expected no vulgar tongued lays,
75   But in the Mandingo, or verses Arabic,
She now and then ventures lines enigrammatic;
Then Mary sings plaintive in notes elegiac,
While her brother I'm told prefers the alcaic.[14]
        To ensure your reception, dear George, I must hope
80   From your pen that some little production may drop;
Some small epic poem or encyclopedia,
(For fifty large jokes, at once they will read ye)
Some treatises critical or philological,
Or at least you may show a new chart Chronological.

ACROSTICS[1]

How many an idly trifling song
Abashed had died upon my tongue,
Rudely hadst thou disdained my muse,
Rudely didst thou to praise refuse.
5   Your judgement oft hath blushed with shame
Tho' partial love could never blame.
Indulgent thus when critics frown,
Good nature smiling yields renown,
Hates the stern task of finding fault
10   Employed l'excuse[2] as kindest taught
Made to engage all hearts, & charm all eyes,
Artless tho' keen, & tho' so witty, wise;
Reason in her assumes the gayest face

Yet still asserts her own distinguished place.
15   Ah lovely maid! the Muse these lines inspires
Not with such genius as thy pencil fires,
No—powers like thine shall every breast inflame
Content thus humbly to admire thy fame
Act like the censes, perfume taught to raise
20   Receive & waft the insence of thy praise.
Or still attendant on thy merit sail
Live in thine honours & partake the gale[3]
If heaven propitious shall attend my prayer
Nor half my vows reject, dispersed in air
25   Eternal smiles thy days shall still attend
Thy charms still blooming, & still loved thy friend
In partial fondness still behold my Love.
Gently condemn, & where thou canst, approve.
Hide my defects, & be no fault of mine
30   Exposed to the keen lash of wit like thine
Sweet is the breath of Rosy Morn.
Unnumbered charms display'd.
Sweeter the blush which can adorn
A bashful modest Maid.
35   No! beauty's own celestial hue
Not half so charmed we see
As when attracted thee we view
Bewitching Modesty.
Of rosy lips & sparkling eyes
40   Unfeeling hearts may tell
These too she has, but still these lies
To please a stronger spell—
Ingenuous worth, discretions seat[4]
Celestial pity's tear
45   A heart prepared for all to feel
Zealous th'opprest to cheer.

THERE WAS A YOUNG LORDLING WHOSE WITS WERE ALL TOSS'D UP[1]

There was a young Lordling[2] whose wits were all toss'd up
    Seventeen times as high as the Moon,
What was his object I could not imagine
    But in his hand he carried a broom—

5   "Young Lordling, young Lordling, young Lordling says I"
    "Why have you toss'd up your wits so high?"
    "I am going (he cries) with my purse & my broom"
    "To sweep all the members out of this room"—

     "Young Lordling, young Lordling, young Lordling I cried
10   "Do you think on its ruin the house will decide?
    "But his wits were a wool-gathering up in the sky
    "And 'union!, a union!,' was all he could cry—

     I watch'd in the lobby to look at the fun
    For the sweeping already I saw was begun
15   But the speaker[3] was stubborn & stuck in his chair
    Nor the broom nor the purse could do anything there

     "Come sweep out, come brush out this troublesome mace[4]
    "The Lordling exclaimed to his servants in place
    "'Tother house[5] is half scoured & the Bishops, good men
20   "Have given us their cassocks to wipe it up clean"—

     But the treasury bench was in strange hubaboo[6]
    And Parnell look'd buff & Fitzgerald look'd blue[7]
    "Who cares says the Lordling (& pushed them away)
    "There is Daly & Corry[8] will serve Castlereagh"—

25   (So Betty with mop & fools head of her own
    From its delicate stand the rich china has thrown
    Nor dreams of its value but runs to her shelf
    And claps in its place some clumsy coarse delf)[9]

See Bury & Monk Mason[10] obeying their Lord
30   With tears in their eyes hobble off at his word
"I want no advice; give your vote, take your pay
"Hold your tongues you old fools & get out of my way"—

Consistency French he could hardly get out
For light as a feather he floated about
35   And when he had got him up close to the door
A puff from behind blew him back on the floor—

The Syllabub[11] youth had prov'd near as light
But gold well applied had just steadied the Knight
And the place of commissions well could dispense
40   With the ballast he wanted of truth & of sense

"To clean out these stables my dear says Sr Boyle[12]
"For a ship like yourself is a mighty great toil
"It's a shame & a sin too to see such a sight!
"In so dirty a work you should take such delight!
(45   "But by jasms[13] my Ld if you wish to succeed
"Bid the nabe[14] little Liffy run thro us with speed—

"Twill save the whole nation a great many pound Sir
"And your English will laugh when they hear how we're drown'ds
"And as we shall be English then we shall laugh too
50   ("The best argument that for the union I know)
"Besides that another advantage is plain
"It will wash out the passage at last thro' Fleet Lane[15]

But Hibernia[16] at last was arous'd by the noise
What a rout there is here with these troublesome boys
55   "Drive out that young fool who destroys my estate
"Ere my house is in ruins break his broom o'er his pate

That business said Caulfeild shall quickly be done
And the spirit of Charlemont[17] spoke thro his son
Your favorite youths shall but lend us a hand
60   And his broom & himself shall be put to a stand—

SONNET[1]

For me would Fancy now her chaplet[2] twine
    Of Hope's bright blossoms, and Joy's fairy flowers,
    As she was wont to do in gayer hours;
Ill would it suit this brow, where many a line
5   Declares the spring-time of my life gone by,
    And summer far advanced; what now remain
    Of waning years, should own staid Wisdom's reign.
Shall my distempered heart still idly sigh
For those gay phantoms, chased by sober truth?
10   Those forms tumultuous which sick visions bring,
    That lightly flitting on the transient wing
Disturbed the fevered slumbers of my youth?
    Ah, no! my suffering soul at length restored,
    Shall taste the calm repose so oft in vain implored.

TO TIME[1]

Yes, gentle Time, thy gradual, healing hand
    Hath stolen from sorrow's grasp the envenomed dart;
    Submitting to thy skill, my passive heart
Feels that no grief can thy soft power withstand;
5   And though my aching breast still heaves the sigh,
    Though oft the tear swells silent in mine eye;
Yet the keen pang, the agony is gone;
    Sorrow and I shall part; and these faint throes
    Are but the remnant of severer woes:
10   As when the furious tempest is o'erblown,
    And when the sky has wept its violence,
The opening heavens will oft let fall a shower,
    The poor o'ercharged boughs still drops dispense,
And still the loaded streams in torrents pour.

Written at Rossana[1]

Dear chestnut bower, I hail thy secret shade,
  Image of tranquil life! escaped yon throng,
  Who weave the dance, and swell the choral song;
And all the summer's day have wanton played:
5   I bless thy kindly gloom in silence laid:
  What though no prospects gay to thee belong;
  Yet here I heed nor showers, nor sunbeams strong,
Which they, whose perfumed tresses roses braid,
Dispersing fear. Their sunny bank more bright,
10   And on their circled green more sweets abound,
Yet the rude blasts, which rend their vestments light,
  O'er these dark boughs with harmless music sound,
  And though no lively pleasures here are found,
Yet shall no sudden storms my calm retreat affright.

Written at Rossana.
November 18, 1799[1]

Oh, my rash hand! what hast thou idly done?
  Torn from its humble bank the last poor flower
  That patient lingered to this wintery hour:
Expanding cheerly to the languid sun
5   It flourished yet, and yet it might have blown, [2]
  Had not thy sudden desolating power
  Destroyed what many a storm and angry shower
Had pitying spared. The pride of summer gone,
  Cherish what yet in faded life can bloom;
10   And if domestic love still sweetly smiles,
If sheltered by thy cot he yet beguiles
  Thy winter's prospect of its dreary gloom,
Oh, from the spoiler's touch thy treasure screen,
To bask beneath Contentment's beam serene!

WRITTEN AT THE EAGLE'S NEST, KILLARNEY. JULY 26, 1800[1]

Here let us rest, while with meridan[2] blaze
   The sun rides glorious 'mid[3] the cloudless sky,
   While o'er the lake no cooling Zephyrs fly,
But on the liquid glass we dazzled gaze,
5   And fainting ask for shade: lo! where his nest
   The bird of Jove[4] has fixed: the lofty brow,
With arbutus and fragrant wild shrubs drest,
   Impendent frowns, nor will approach allow:
Here the soft turf invites; here magic sounds
10   Celestially respondent shall enchant,
While Melody from yon[5] steep wood rebounds
   In thrilling cadence sweet. Sure, life can grant
No brighter hours than this; and memory oft
Shall paint this happiest scene with pencil soft.

WRITTEN AT KILLARNEY. JULY 29, 1800[1]

How soft the pause! the notes melodious cease,
   Which from each feeling could an echo call;
   Rest on your oars; that not a sound may fall
To interrupt the stillness of our peace:
5   The fanning west-wind breathes upon our cheeks
   Yet glowing with the sun's departed beams.
   Through the blue heavens the cloudless moon pours streams
Of pure resplendent light, in silver streaks
Reflected on the still, unruffled lake.
10   The Alpine hills in solemn silence frown,
   While the dark woods night's deepest shades embrown.
And now once more that soothing[2] strain awake!
Oh, ever to my heart, with magic power,
Shall those[3] sweet sounds recal this rapturous hour!

ON LEAVING KILLARNEY. AUGUST 5, 1800[1]

Farewel, sweet scenes! pensive once more I turn
　　Those pointed hills, and wood-fringed lakes to view
　　With fond regret; while in this last adieu
A silent tear those brilliant hours shall mourn
5　For ever past. So from the pleasant shore,
　　Borne with the struggling bark against the wind,
　　The trembling pennant fluttering looks behind
With vain reluctance! 'Mid those woods no more
For me the voice of pleasure shall resound,
10　Nor soft flutes warbling o'er the placid lake
　　Aërial music shall for me awake,
And wrap my charmed soul in peace profound!
Though lost to me, here still may Taste delight
To dwell, nor the rude axe the trembling Dryads fright!

SONNET[1]

Ye dear associates of my gayer hours,
　　Ah! whither are you gone? on what light wing
　　Is Fancy fled? Mute is the dulcet string
Of long-lost Hope? No more her magic powers
5　Scatter o'er my lorn path fallacious flowers,
　　As she was wont with glowing hand to fling
　　Loading with fragrance the soft gales of Spring,
While fondly pointing to fresh blooming bowers,
Now faded, with each dazzling view of bright,
10　Delusive pleasure; never more return,
Ye vain, ideal visions of delight!
　　For in your absence I have learned to mourn;
To bear the torch of Truth with steady sight,
　　And weave the cypress for my future urn.

A Faithful Friend Is the Medicine of Life[1]

Son of Sirach

In the dreams of delight, which with ardour we seek,
    Oft the phantom of sorrow appears;
And the roses of pleasure, which bloom in your cheek,
    Must be steeped in the dew of your tears:

5   'Mid[2] the fountain of bliss, when it sparkles most bright,
    Salt mixtures embitter the spring,
Though its lustre may tremble through bowers of delight,
    In the draught disappointment will sting.

But if Heaven hath one cup of enjoyment bestowed,
10   Unmingled and sweet[3] as its own,
In the streams[4] of affection its bounty hath flowed,
    And there we[5] may taste it alone.

But the pure simple drops Love would seize as his prize
    And defile[6] them with passion's foul tide;
15   While the bowl he prepares as it dazzles our eyes
The poison of anguish can hide.

Let Friendship the stream, as it flows calm and clear,
    Receive unpolluted for me;
Or if tenderness mingle a sigh or a tear,
20   The draught still the sweeter will be.

But let me reject the too-high flavoured bowl
    Affectation or Flattery compose,
From Sincerity's urn thus transparent shall roll
    The cordial[7] of peace and repose.

25   Oh! give me the friend, from whose warm, faithful[8] breast
    The sigh breathes responsive to mine,

Where my cares may obtain the soft pillow of rest,
  And my sorrows may love to recline.

Not the friend who my hours[9] of pleasure will share,
30   But abide not the season of grief;
Who flies from the brow that is darkened by care,
  And the silence that looks for relief.

Not the friend who, suspicious of change or of guile,
  Would shrink from a confidence free;
35 Nor him who with fondness complacent can smile
  On the eye that looks coldly on me.

As the mirror that, just to each blemish or grace,
  To myself will my image reflect,
But to none but myself will that image retrace,
40   Nor[10] picture one absent defect.

To my soul let my friend be a mirror as true,
  Thus my faults from all others conceal;
Nor, absent, those failings or follies renew,
  Which from Heaven and from man he should[11] veil.

THE KISS.—IMITATED FROM VOITURE[1]

When the Sun with am'rous beams
  Greets with kisses soft the Rose;
Pleased the blushing beauty seems,
  And with brighter lustre glows.

5 When his harbinger of joy
  Tells Aurora[2] he is near;
Blushes of celestial dye
  O'er her glowing charms appear.

But a brighter vermeil[3] hue
10   Deepened in my Chloe's[4] face,

Than the modest morn e'er knew,
    Or the Rose's bashful grace.

As I snatched the sudden kiss,
    From my lips my heart hath flown;
15   Ravished by the enchanting bliss,
    And resigned its native throne.

This deserted breast it left,
    Thro' those lips it passed to thine,
Of my "bosom's lord"[5] bereft,
20   Hopeless now I languid pine.—

There a wretched slave enchained,
    Pants the trembling prisoner still;
Still reluctantly retained,
    Captive to thy sovereign will.—

25   See thy sad repentant lover,
    Of himself and thee bereft;
Let him now his peace recover,
    Willing to restore his theft.—

Dearly paid the fatal treasure,
30   Oh! forgive the transient bliss;
Yield me up my bosom's treasure,
    And let me give back the Kiss.—

SONNET[1]

As nearer I approach that fatal day
    Which makes all mortal cares appear so light,
    Time seems on swifter wing to speed his flight,
And Hope's fallacious visions fade away;
5   While to my fond desires, at length, I say,
    Behold, how quickly melted from your sight
    The promised objects you esteemed so bright,

When love was all your song, and life looked gay!
Now let us rest in peace! those hours are past,
10   And with them, all the agitating train
        By which hope led the wandering cheated soul;
Wearied, she seeks repose, and owns at last
        How sighs, and tears, and youth, were spent in vain,
        While languishing she mourned in folly's sad control.

Psyche

1801–1802

Watercolor sketch by Mary Tighe for the final page of the 1803 manuscript copy of *Psyche* prepared for the Ladies of Llangollen. Courtesy of Llyfrgell Genedlaethol Cymru / The National Library of Wales.

PSYCHE; OR, THE LEGEND OF LOVE[1]

Castos docet et pios amores.
Martial[2]

PREFACE

The author, who dismisses to the public the darling object of his solitary cares, must be prepared to consider, with some degree of indifference, the various reception it may then meet. But from those, who write only for the more interested eye of friendship, no such indifference can be expected. I may therefore be forgiven the egotism which makes me anxious to recommend to my readers the tale with which I present them, while I endeavour to excuse in it all other defects but that, which I fear cannot be excused, the deficiency of genius.

In making choice of the beautiful ancient allegory of Love and the Soul, I had some fears lest my subject might be condemned by the frown of severer moralists; however I hope, that if such have the condescension to read through a poem which they may perhaps think too long, they will yet do me the justice to allow, that I have only pictured innocent love, such love as the purest bosom might confess. "*Les jeunes femmes, qui ne veulent point paroitre coquettes, ne doivent jamais parler de l'amour comme d'une chose ou elles puissent avoir part,*" says La Rochefoucault;[3] but, I believe, it is only the false refinement of the most profligate court which could give birth to such a sentiment, and that love will always be found to have had the strongest influence, where the morals have been the purest.

I much regret, that I can have no hope of affording any pleasure to some, whose opinion I highly respect, whom I have heard profess themselves ever disgusted by the veiled form of allegory, and yet

> Are not the choicest fables of the poets,
> Who were the fountains and first springs of wisdom,
> Wrapt in perplexed allegories?[4]

But if I have not been able to resist the seductions of the mysterious fair, who perhaps never appears captivating except in the eyes of her own poet, I have however remembered that my verse cannot be worth much consideration, and have therefore endeavoured to let my meaning be perfectly obvious. The same reason has deterred me from using the obsolete words which are to be found in Spenser and his imitators.[5]

Although I cannot give up the excellence of my subject, I am yet ready to own, that the stanza which I have chosen has many disadvantages, and that it may perhaps be as tiresome to the reader, as it was difficult to the author. The frequent recurrence of the same rhymes is by no means well adapted to the English language, and I know not whether I have a right to offer, as an apology, the restraint which I had imposed upon myself of strictly adhering to the stanza, which my partiality for Spenser first inclined me to adopt.[6]

The loves of Cupid and Psyche have long been a favourite subject for poetical allusion, and are well known as related by Apuleius: to him I am indebted for the outline of my tale in the two first cantos; but, even there, the model is not closely copied, and I have taken nothing from Moliere, La Fontaine, Du Moustier, or Marino. I have seen no imitations of Apuleius except by those authors, nor do I know that the story of Psyche has any other original.[7]

I should willingly acknowledge with gratitude those authors who have perhaps supplied me with many expressions and ideas, but if I have subjected myself to the charge of plagiarism, it has been by adopting the words or images which floated upon my mind, without accurately examining, or being indeed able to distinguish, whether I owed them to my memory or my imagination,

> *Si id est peccatum, peccatum imprudentia est*
> *Poetae, non qui furtum facere studuerit.*
>
> Terentius[8]

And when I confess, that all I have is but the fruit of a much indulged taste for that particular style of reading, let me be excused if I do not investigate and acknowledge more strictly each separate obligation.

Rossana, Jan. 1802

SONNET ADDRESSED TO MY MOTHER

Oh, thou! whose tender smile most partially
  Hath ever bless'd thy child: to thee belong
  The graces which adorn my first wild song,
If aught of grace it knows: nor thou deny
5   Thine ever prompt attention to supply.
  But let me lead thy willing ear along,
  Where virtuous love still bids the strain prolong
His innocent applause; since from thine eye
  The beams of love first charm'd my infant breast,
10 And from thy lip Affection's soothing voice
  That eloquence of tenderness express'd,
Which still my grateful heart confess'd divine:
Oh! ever may its accents sweet rejoice
The soul which loves to own whate'er it has is thine!

Chi pensa quanto un bel desio d'amore
  Un spirto pellegrin tenga sublime;
  Non vorria non averne acceso il core;
Chi gusta quanto dolce il creder sia
  Solo esser caro a chi sola n'e cara,
  Regna in un stato a cui null'altro e pria.

Ariosto, *Eleg.* xii[9]

PSYCHE

ARGUMENT

Proem—Psyche introduced—Her royal origin—Envy of Venus—Her instructions to Cupid—The island of Pleasure—The fountains of Joy and of Sorrow—The appearance of Love—Psyche asleep—Mutually wounded—Psyche reveals her dream to her Mother—The Oracle consulted—Psyche abandoned on the Rock by its decree—Carried by Zephyrs to the island of Pleasure—The Palace of Love—Banquet of Love—Marriage of Cupid and Psyche—Psyche's daily solitude—Her request to her Lover—His reluctant consent.

PSYCHE

Let not the rugged brow the rhymes accuse,
Which speak of gentle knights and ladies fair,
Nor scorn the lighter labours of the muse,
Who yet, for cruel battles would not dare
5   The low-strung chords of her weak lyre prepare;
But loves to court repose in slumbery lay,
To tell of goodly bowers and gardens rare,
Of gentle blandishments and amorous play,
And all the lore of love, in courtly verse essay.

10   And ye, whose gentle hearts in thraldom held
The power of mighty Love already own,
When you the pains and dangers have beheld,
Which erst your lord hath for his Psyche known,
For all your sorrows this may well atone,
15   That he you serve the same hath suffered;
And sure, your fond applause the tale will crown
In which your own distress is pictured,
And all that weary way which you yourselves must tread.

Most sweet would to my soul the hope appear,
20   That sorrow in my verse a charm might find,
To smooth the brow long bent with bitter cheer,
Some short distraction to the joyless mind
Which grief, with heavy chain, hath fast confin'd
To sad remembrance of its happier state;
25   For to myself I ask no boon more kind
Than power another's woes to mitigate,
And that soft soothing art which anguish can abate.

And thou, sweet sprite, whose sway doth far extend,
Smile on the mean historian of thy fame!
30   My heart in each distress and fear befriend,
Nor ever let it feel a fiercer flame

Than innocence may cherish free from blame,
And hope may nurse, and sympathy may own;
For, as thy rights I never would disclaim,
35   But true allegiance offer'd to thy throne,
So may I love but one, by one belov'd alone.

That anxious torture may I never feel,
Which, doubtful, watches o'er a wand'ring heart.
Oh! who that bitter torment can reveal,
40   Or tell the pining anguish of that smart!
In those affections may I ne'er have part,
Which easily transferr'd can learn to rove:
No, dearest Cupid! when I feel thy dart,
For thy sweet Psyche's sake may no false love
45   The tenderness I prize lightly from me remove!

Canto I

Much wearied with her long and dreary way,
And now with toil and sorrow well nigh spent,
Of sad regret and wasting grief the prey,
Fair Psyche through untrodden forests went,
5   To lone shades uttering oft a vain lament.
And oft in hopeless silence sighing deep,
As she her fatal error did repent,
While dear remembrance bade her ever weep,
And her pale cheek in ceaseless showers of sorrow steep.

10   'Mid the thick covert of that woodland shade,
A flowery bank there lay undress'd by art,
But of the mossy turf spontaneous made;
Here the young branches shot their arms athwart,
And wove the bower so thick in every part,
15   That the fierce beams of Phoebus[10] glancing strong
Could never through the leaves their fury dart;
But the sweet creeping shrubs that round it throng,
Their loving fragrance mix, and trail their flowers along.

And close beside a little fountain play'd,
20   Which through the trembling leaves all joyous shone,
And with the cheerful birds sweet music made,
Kissing the surface of each polish'd stone
As it flow'd past: sure as her favorite throne
Tranquillity might well esteem the bower,
25   The fresh and cool retreat have call'd her own,
A pleasant shelter in the sultry hour,
A refuge from the blast, and angry tempest's power.

Woo'd by the soothing silence of the scene
Here Psyche stood, and looking round, lest aught
30   Which threaten'd danger near her might have been,
Awhile to rest her in that quiet spot
She laid her down, and piteously bethought
Herself on the sad changes of her fate,
Which in so short a space so much had wrought,
35   And now had rais'd her to such high estate,
And now had plung'd her low in sorrow desolate.

Oh! how refreshing seem'd the breathing wind
To her faint limbs! and while her snowy hands
From her fair brow her golden hair unbind,
40   And of her zone[11] unloose the silken bands,
More passing bright unveil'd her beauty stands;
For faultless was her form as beauty's queen,
And every winning grace that Love demands,
With mild attemper'd dignity was seen
45   Play o'er each lovely limb, and deck her angel mien.

Though solitary now, dismay'd, forlorn,
Without attendant through the forest rude,
The peerless maid of royal lineage born
By many a royal youth had oft been woo'd;
50   Low at her feet full many a prince had sued,
And homage paid unto her beauty rare;
But all their blandishments her heart withstood;
And well might mortal suitor sure despair,
Since mortal charms were none which might with hers compare.

55 Yet nought of insolence or haughty pride
 Found ever in her gentle breast a place;
 Though men her wondrous beauty deified,
 And rashly deeming such celestial grace
 Could never spring from any earthly race,
60 Lo! all forsaking Cytherea's[12] shrine,
 Her sacred altars now no more embrace,
 But to fair Psyche pay those rites divine,
Which, Goddess! are thy due, and should be only thine.

 But envy of her beauty's growing fame
65 Poison'd her sisters' hearts with secret gall,
 And oft with seeming piety they blame
 The worship which they justly impious call;
 And oft, lest evil should their sire befall,
 Besought him to forbid the erring crowd
70 Which hourly throng'd around the regal hall,
 With incense, gifts, and invocations loud,
To her whose guiltless breast, ne'er felt elation proud.

 For she was timid as the wintry flower,
 That, whiter than the snow it blooms among,
75 Droops its fair head submissive to the power
 Of every angry blast which sweeps along
 Sparing the lovely trembler, while the strong
 Majestic tenants of the leafless wood
 It levels low. But, ah! the pitying song
80 Must tell how, than the tempest's self more rude,
Fierce wrath and cruel hate their suppliant prey pursued.

 Indignant quitting her deserted fanes,
 Now Cytherea sought her favorite isle,
 And there from every eye her secret pains
85 'Mid her thick myrtle[13] bowers conceal'd awhile;
 Practis'd no more the glance, or witching smile,
 But nurs'd the pang she never felt before,
 Of mortified disdain; then to beguile
 The hours which mortal flattery sooth'd no more,
90 She various plans revolv'd her influence to restore.

She call'd her son with unaccustom'd voice;
Not with those thrilling accents of delight
Which bade so oft enchanted Love rejoice,
Soft as the breezes of a summer's night:
95   Now chok'd with rage its change could Love affright;
As all to sullen[14] discontent a prey,
Shunning the cheerful day's enlivening light,
She felt the angry power's malignant sway,
And bade her favourite boy her vengeful will obey.

100   Bath'd in those tears which vanquish human hearts,
"Oh, son belov'd!" (the suppliant goddess cries,)[15]
"If e'er thy too indulgent mother's arts
"Subdued for thee the potent deities
"Who rule my native deep, or haunt the skies;
105   "Or if to me the grateful praise be due,
"That to thy sceptre bow the great and wise,
"Now let thy fierce revenge my foe pursue,
"And let my rival scorn'd her vain presumption rue.

"For what to me avails my former boast
110   "That, fairer than the wife of Jove confest,
"I gain'd the prize thus basely to be lost?[16]
"With me the world's devotion to contest
"Behold a mortal dares; though on my breast
"Still vainly brilliant shines the magic zone.[17]
115   "Yet, yet I reign: by you my wrongs redrest,
"The world with humbled Psyche soon shall own
"That Venus, beauty's queen, shall be ador'd alone.

"Deep let her drink of that dark, bitter spring,
"Which flows so near thy bright and crystal tide;
120   "Deep let her heart thy sharpest arrow sting,
"Its temper'd barb in that black poison dyed.
"Let her, for whom contending princes sigh'd,
"Feel all the fury of thy fiercest flame,
"For some base wretch to foul disgrace allied,
125   "Forgetful of her birth and her fair fame,
"Her honours all defil'd, and sacrific'd to shame."

Then, with sweet pressure of her rosy lip,
A kiss she gave bath'd in ambrosial dew;
The thrilling joy he would for ever sip,
130   And his moist eyes in ecstasy imbrue.[18]
But she whose soul still angry cares pursue,
Snatch'd from the soft caress her glowing charms;
Her vengeful will she then enforc'd anew,
As she in haste dismiss'd him from her arms,
135   The cruel draught to seek of anguish and alarms.

'Mid the blue waves by circling seas embrac'd
A chosen spot of fairest land was seen;
For there with fav'ring hand had Nature plac'd
All that could lovely make the varied scene:
140   Eternal Spring there spread her mantle green;
There high surrounding hills deep-wooded rose
O'er placid lakes; while marble rocks between
The fragrant shrubs their pointed heads disclose,
And balmy breathes each gale which o'er the island blows.

145   Pleasure had call'd the fertile lawns her own,
And thickly strew'd them with her choicest flowers;
Amid the quiet glade her golden throne
Bright shone with lustre through o'erarching bowers:
There her fair train, the ever downy Hours,[19]
150   Sport on light wing with the young Joys entwin'd;
While Hope, delighted, from her full lap showers
Blossoms, whose fragrance can the ravish'd mind
Inebriate with dreams of rapture unconfin'd.

And in the grassy centre of the isle,
155   Where the thick verdure spreads a damper shade,
Amid their native rocks conceal'd awhile,
Then o'er the plains in devious streams display'd,
Two gushing fountains rise; and thence convey'd,
Their waters through the woods and vallies play,
160   Visit each green recess and secret glade,
With still unmingled, still meand'ring way,
Nor widely wand'ring far, can each from other stray.

But of strange contrast are their virtues found,
And oft the lady of that isle has tried
165 In rocky dens and caverns under ground,
The black deformed stream in vain to hide;
Bursting all bounds, her labours it defied;
Yet many a flowery sod its course conceals
Through plains where deep its silent waters glide,
170 Till secret ruin all corroding steals,
And every treacherous arch the hideous gulph reveals.

Forbidding every kindly prosperous growth,
Where'er it ran, a channel bleak it wore;
The gaping banks receded, as though loth
175 To touch the poison which disgrac'd their shore:
There deadly anguish pours unmix'd his store
Of all the ills which sting the human breast,
The hopeless tears which past delights deplore,
Heart-gnawing jealousy which knows no rest,
180 And self-upbraiding shame, by stern remorse opprest.

Oh, how unlike the pure transparent stream,
Which near it bubbles o'er its golden sands!
Th' impeding stones with pleasant music seem
Its progress to detain from other lands;
185 And all its banks, inwreath'd with flowery bands,
Ambrosial fragrance shed in grateful dew:
There young Desire enchanted ever stands,
Breathing delight and fragrance ever new,
And bath'd in constant joys of fond affection true.

190 But not to mortals is it e'er allow'd
To drink unmingled of that current bright;
Scarce can they taste the pleasurable flood,
Defil'd by angry Fortune's envious spite;
Who from the cup of amorous delight
195 Dashes the sparkling draught of brilliant joy,
Till, with dull sorrow's stream despoiled quite,
No more it cheers the soul nor charms the eye,
But 'mid the poison'd bowl distrust and anguish lie.

Here Cupid tempers his unerring darts,
200   And in the fount of bliss delights to play;
Here mingles balmy sighs and pleasing smarts,
And here the honied draught will oft allay[20]
With that black poison's all-polluting sway,
For wretched man. Hither, as Venus will'd,
205   For Psyche's punishment he bent his way:
From either stream his amber vase he fill'd,
For her were meant the drops which grief alone distill'd.

His quiver, sparkling bright with gems and gold,
From his fair plumed shoulder graceful hung,
210   And from its top in brilliant chords enroll'd
Each little vase resplendently was slung:
Still as he flew, around him sportive clung
His frolic train of winged Zephyrs light,[21]
Wafting the fragrance which his tresses flung:
215   While odours dropp'd from every ringlet bright,
And from his blue eyes beam'd ineffable delight.

Wrapt in a cloud unseen by mortal eye,
He sought the chamber of the royal maid;
There, lull'd by careless soft security,
220   Of the impending mischief nought afraid,
Upon her purple couch was Psyche laid,
Her radiant eyes a downy slumber seal'd;
In light transparent veil alone array'd,
Her bosom's opening charms were half reveal'd,
225   And scarce the lucid folds her polish'd limbs conceal'd.

A placid smile plays o'er each roseate lip,
Sweet sever'd lips! why[22] thus your pearls disclose,
That slumbering thus unconscious she may sip
The cruel presage of her future woes?
230   Lightly, as fall the dews upon the rose,
Upon the coral gates of that sweet cell
The fatal drops he pours; nor yet he knows,
Nor, though a God, can he presaging tell
How he himself shall mourn the ills of that sad spell!

235   Nor yet content, he from his quiver drew,
         Sharpen'd with skill divine, a shining dart:
         No need had he for bow, since thus too true
         His hand might wound her all exposed heart;
         Yet her fair side he touch'd with gentlest art,
240   And half relenting on her beauties gaz'd;
         Just then awaking with a sudden start
         Her opening eye in humid lustre blaz'd,
Unseen he still remain'd, enchanted and amaz'd.

         The dart which in his hand now trembling stood,
245   As o'er the couch he bent with ravish'd eye,
         Drew with its daring point celestial blood
         From his smooth neck's unblemish'd ivory:
         Heedless of this, but with a pitying sigh
         The evil done now anxious to repair,
250   He shed in haste the balmy drops of joy
         O'er all the silky ringlets of her hair;
Then stretch'd his plumes divine, and breath'd celestial air.

         Unhappy Psyche! soon the latent wound
         The fading roses of her cheek confess,
255   Her eyes bright beams, in swimming sorrows drown'd,
         Sparkle no more with life and happiness
         Her parents fond exulting heart to bless;
         She shuns adoring crowds, and seeks to hide
         The pining sorrows which her soul oppress,
260   Till to her mother's tears no more denied,
The secret grief she owns, for which she ling'ring sigh'd.

         A dream of mingled terror and delight
         Still heavy hangs upon her troubled soul,
         An angry form still swims before her sight,
265   And still the vengeful thunders seem to roll;
         Still crush'd to earth she feels the stern control
         Of Venus unrelenting, unappeas'd:
         The dream returns, she feels the fancied dole;[23]
         Once more the furies[24] on her heart have seiz'd,
270   But still she views the youth who all her sufferings eas'd.

Of wond'rous beauty did the vision seem,
And in the freshest prime of youthful years;
Such at the close of her distressful dream
A graceful champion to her eyes appears;
275   Her lov'd deliverer from her foes and fears
She seems in grateful transport still to press;
Still his soft voice sounds in her ravish'd ears;
Dissolv'd in fondest tears of tenderness
His form she oft invokes her waking eyes to bless.

280   Nor was it quite a dream, for as she woke,
Ere heavenly mists conceal'd him from her eye,
One sudden transitory view she took
Of Love's most radiant bright divinity;
From the fair image never can she fly,
285   As still consum'd with vain desire she pines;
While her fond parents heave the anxious sigh,
And to avert her fate seek holy shrines
The threaten'd ills to learn by auguries and signs.

And now, the royal sacrifice prepar'd,
290   The milk-white bull they to the altar lead,
Whose youth the galling yoke as yet had spar'd,
Now destin'd by the sacred knife to bleed:
When lo! with sudden spring his horns he freed,
And head-long rush'd amid the frighted throng:
295   While from the smoke-veil'd shrine such sounds proceed
As well might strike with awe the soul most strong;
And thus divinely spoke the heav'n inspired tongue:

"On nuptial couch, in nuptial vest array'd,
"On a tall rock's high summit Psyche place,
300   "Let all depart, and leave the fated maid
"Who never must a mortal Hymen[25] grace,
"A winged monster of no earthly race
"Thence soon shall bear his trembling bride away;
"His power extends o'er all the bounds of space,
305   "And Jove himself has own'd his dreaded sway,
"Whose flaming breath sheds fire, whom earth and heaven obey."

With terror, anguish, and astonishment
The oracle her wretched father hears,
Now from his brow the regal honors rent,
310   And now in frantic sorrow wild appears.
Nor threaten'd plagues, nor punishment he fears,
Refusing long the sentence to obey,
Till Psyche, trembling with submissive tears,
Bids them the sacrifice no more delay,
315   Prepare the funeral couch and leave the destin'd prey.

Pleas'd by th'ambiguous doom the Fates promulge,[26]
The angry Goddess and enamour'd Boy
Alike content their various hopes indulge;
He, still exploring with an anxious eye
320   The future prospect of uncertain joy,
Plans how the tender object of his care
He may protect from threaten'd misery;
Ah sanguine Love! so oft deceiv'd, forbear
With flattering tints to paint illusive hope so fair.

325   But now what lamentations rend the skies!
In amaracine wreaths[27] the virgin choir
With Io Hymen[28] mingle funeral cries:
Lost in the sorrows of the Lydian lyre[29]
The breathing flutes' melodious notes expire;
330   In sad procession pass the mournful throng
Extinguishing with tears the torches' fire,
While the mute victim weeping crowds among,
By unknown fears oppress'd, moves silently along.

But on such scenes of terror and dismay,
335   The mournful Muse delights not long to dwell,
She quits well pleas'd the melancholy lay,
Nor vainly seeks the parents' woes to tell,
But what to wond'ring Psyche then befell
When thus abandon'd, let her rather say,
340   Who shuddering looks to see some monster fell
Approach the desert rock to seize his prey,
With cruel fangs devour, or tear her thence away.

When lo! a gentle breeze began to rise,
Breath'd by obedient Zephyrs round the maid,
345   Fanning her bosom with its softest sighs
Awhile among her fluttering robes it stray'd,
And boldly sportive latent charms display'd:
And then, as Cupid will'd, with tenderest care
From the tall rock, where weeping she was laid,
350   With gliding motion through the yielding air
To Pleasure's blooming isle their lovely charge they bear.

On the green bosom of the turf reclin'd,
They lightly now th'astonish'd virgin lay,
To placid rest they sooth her troubled mind;
355   Around her still with watchful care they stay,
Around her still in quiet whispers play;
Till lulling slumbers bid her eyelids close,
Veiling with silky fringe each brilliant ray,
While soft tranquility divinely flows
360   O'er all her soul serene, in visions of repose.

Refresh'd she rose, and all enchanted gaz'd
On the rare beauties of the pleasant scene.
Conspicuous far a lofty palace blaz'd
Upon a sloping bank of softest green;
365   A fairer edifice was never seen;
The high rang'd columns own no mortal hand,
But seem a temple meet for Beauty's queen.
Like polish'd snow the marble pillars stand
In grace-attemper'd majesty sublimely grand.

370   Gently ascending from a silvery flood,
Above the palace rose the shaded hill,
The lofty eminence was crown'd with wood,
And the rich lawns, adorn'd by nature's skill,
The passing breezes with their odours fill;
375   Here ever blooming groves of orange glow,
And here all flowers which from their leaves distil
Ambrosial dew in sweet succession blow,
And trees of matchless size a fragrant shade bestow.

The sun looks glorious mid a sky serene,
380   And bids bright lustre sparkle o'er the tide;
The clear blue ocean at a distance seen
Bounds the gay landscape on the western side,
While closing round it with majestic pride,
The lofty rocks mid citron groves arise;
385   "Sure some divinity must here reside,"
As tranc'd in some bright vision Psyche cries,
And scarce believes the bliss, or trusts her charmed eyes.

When lo! a voice divinely sweet she hears,
From unseen lips proceeds the heavenly sound;
390   "Psyche approach, dismiss thy timid fears,
"At length his bride thy longing spouse has found,
"And bids for thee immortal joys abound;
"For thee the palace rose at his command,
"For thee his love a bridal banquet crown'd;
395   "He bids attendant nymphs around thee stand
"Prompt every wish to serve, a fond obedient band."

Increasing wonder fill'd her ravish'd soul,
For now the pompous portals open'd wide,
There, pausing oft, with timid foot she stole
400   Through halls high dom'd, enrich'd with sculptur'd pride,
While gay saloons appear'd on either side
In splendid vista opening to her sight;
And all with precious gems so beautified,
And furnish'd with such exquisite delight,
405   That scarce the beams of heaven emit such lustre bright.

The amethyst was there of violet hue,
And there the topaz shed its golden ray,
The chrysoberyl and the sapphire blue
As the clear azure of a sunny day,
410   Or the mild eyes where amorous glances play;
The snow white jasper and the opal's flame,
The blushing ruby and the agate grey,
And there the gem[30] which bears his luckless name
Whose death by Phoebus mourn'd, ensur'd him deathless fame.

415   There the green emerald, there cornelians glow,
    And rich carbuncles pour eternal light,
    With all that India and Peru can shew,
    Or Labrador can give so flaming bright
    To the charm'd mariner's half dazzled sight:
420   The coral paved baths with diamonds blaze:
    And all that can the female heart delight
    Of fair attire, the last recess displays,
  And all that Luxury can ask, her eye surveys.

    Now through the hall melodious music stole,
425   And self-prepar'd the splendid banquet stands,
    Self-pour'd the nectar sparkles in the bowl,
    The lute and viol touch'd by unseen hands
    Aid the soft voices of the choral bands;
    O'er the full board a brighter lustre beams
430   Than Persia's monarch at his feast commands:
    For sweet refreshment all inviting seems
  To taste celestial food, and pure ambrosial streams.

    But when meek eve[31] hung out her dewy star
    And gently veil'd with gradual hand the sky,
435   Lo! the bright folding doors retiring far,
    Display to Psyche's captivated eye
    All that voluptuous ease could ere[32] supply
    To sooth the spirits in serene repose,
    Beneath the velvet's purple canopy
440   Divinely form'd a downy couch arose,
  While alabaster lamps a milky light disclose.

    Once more she hears the hymeneal strain,[33]
    Far other voices now attune the lay,
    The swelling sounds approach, awhile remain,
445   And then retiring faint dissolved away:
    The expiring lamps emit a feebler ray,
    And soon in fragrant death extinguished lie:
    Then virgin terrors Psyche's soul dismay,
    When through the obscuring gloom she nought can spy
450 But softly rustling sounds declare some Being nigh.

Oh, you for whom I write! whose hearts can melt
At the soft thrilling voice whose power you prove,
You know what charm, unutterably felt,
Attends the unexpected voice of Love:
455   Above the lyre, the lute's soft notes above,
With sweet enchantment to the soul it steals
And bears it to Elysium's happy grove;[34]
You best can tell the rapture Psyche feels
When Love's ambrosial lip the vows of Hymen seals.

460   "'Tis he, 'tis my deliverer! deep imprest
"Upon my heart those sounds I well recal,"
The blushing maid exclaimed, and on his breast
A tear of trembling ecstasy let fall.
But, ere the breezes of the morning call
465   Aurora[35] from her purple, humid bed,
Psyche in vain explores the vacant hall,
Her tender lover from her arms is fled
While sleep his downy wings had o'er her eye-lids spread.

Again the band invisible attend,
470   And female voices sooth the mournful bride;
Light hands to braid her hair assistance lend,
By some she sees the glowing bracelet tied,
Others officious hover at her side,
And each bright gem for her acceptance bring,
475   While some, the balmy air diffusing wide,
Fan softer perfumes from each odorous wing
Than the fresh bosom shed of earliest, sweetest spring.

With songs divine her anxious soul they cheer,
And woo her footsteps to delicious bowers,
480   They bid the fruit more exquisite appear
Which at her feet its bright profusion showers:
For her they cull unknown, celestial flowers;
The gilded car[36] they bid her fearless guide,
Which at her wish self-moved with wondrous powers,
485   The rapid bird's velocity defied,
While round the blooming isle it rolled with circuit wide.

Again they spread the feast, they strike the lyre,
But to her frequent questions nought reply,
Her lips in vain her lover's name require,
490   Or wherefore thus concealed he shuns her eye.
But when reluctant twilight veils the sky,
And each pale lamp successively expires;
Again she trembling hears the voice of joy,
Her spouse a tender confidence inspires,
495   But with a fond embrace ere dawn again retires.

To charm the languid hours of solitude
He oft invites her to the Muse's lore,
For none have vainly e'er the Muse pursued,
And those whom she delights, regret no more
500   The social, joyous hours, while rapt they soar
To worlds unknown, and live in fancy's dream:
Oh, Muse divine! thee only I implore,
Shed on my soul thy sweet inspiring beams,
And pleasure's gayest scene insipid folly seems!

505   Silence and solitude the Muses love,
And whom they charm they can alone suffice;
Nor ever tedious hour their votaries prove:
This solace now the lonely Psyche tries,
Or, while her hand the curious[37] needle plies,
510   She learns from lips unseen celestial strains;
Responsive now with their soft voice she vies,
Or bids her plaintive harp express the pains
Which absence sore inflicts where Love all potent reigns.

But melancholy poisons all her joys,
515   And secret sorrows all her hopes depress,
Consuming languor every bliss destroys,
And sad she droops repining, comfortless.
Her tender lover well the cause can guess,
And sees too plain inevitable fate
520   Pursue her to the bowers of happiness.
"Oh Psyche! most beloved, ere yet too late,
"Dread the impending ills and prize thy tranquil state."

In vain his weeping love he thus advised;
She longs to meet a parent's sweet embrace,
525   "Oh were their sorrowing hearts at least apprised
"How Psyche's wondrous lot all fears may chase;
"For whom thy love prepared so fair a place!
"Let but my bliss their fond complaints repress,
"Let me but once behold a mother's face,
530   "Oh spouse adored! and in full happiness
"This love-contented heart its solitude shall bless.

"Oh, by those beauties I must ne'er behold!
"The spicy-scented ringlets of thine hair:
"By that soft neck my loving arms enfold,
535   "Crown with a kind consent thy Psyche's prayer!
"Their dear embrace, their blessing let me share;
"So shall I stain our couch with tears no more.
"But, blest in thee, resign each other care,
"Nor seek again thy secret to explore,
540   "Which yet, denied thy sight, I ever must deplore."

Unable to resist her fond request,
Reluctant Cupid thus at last complied,
And sighing clasped her closer to his breast.
"Go then, my Psyche! go, my lovely bride!
545   "But let me in thy faith at least confide,
"That by no subtle, impious arts betrayed,
"Which ah! too well I know will all be tried,
"Thy simply trusting heart shall e'er be swayed
"The secret veil to rend which fate thy screen hath made.

550   "For danger hovers o'er thy smiling days,
"One only way to shield thee yet I know;
"Unseen I may securely guard thy ways
"And save thee from the threatened storm of woe;
"But forced, if known, my Psyche to forego,
555   "Thou never, never must again be mine!
"What mutual sorrows hence must ceaseless flow!
"Compelled thy dear embraces to resign,
"While thou to anguish doomed for lost delights shalt pine.

"Solace thy mind with hopes of future joy!
560   "In a dear infant thou shalt see my face;
        "Blest mother soon of an immortal boy[38]
        "In him his father's features thou shalt trace!
        "Yet go! for thou art free, the bounds of space
        "Are none for thee: attendant zephyrs[39] stay,
565   "Speak but thy will, and to the wished for place
        "Their lovely mistress swift they shall convey:
    "Yet hither ah! return ere fades the festive day.

        "Light of my soul, far dearer than the day!"
        (Exulting Psyche cries in grateful joy)
570   "Me all the bliss of earth could ill repay
        "For thy most sweet, divine society;
        "To thee again with rapture will I fly,
        "Nor with less pleasure hail the star of eve
        "Than when in tedious solitude I sigh;
575   "My vows of silent confidence believe,
    "Nor think thy Psyche's faith will e'er thy love deceive."

        Her suit obtained, in full contentment blest,
        Her eyes at length in placid slumbers close.
        Sleep, hapless fair! sleep on thy lover's breast!
580   Ah not again to taste such pure repose!
        Till thy sad heart by long experience knows
        How much they err, who to their interest blind,
        Slight the calm peace which from retirement flows;
        And while they think their fleeting joys to bind
585   Banish the tranquil bliss which heaven for man designed!

CANTO II

ARGUMENT

Introduction—Dangers of the World—Psyche conveyed by Zephyrs awakes once more in the paternal mansion—Envy of her Sisters—They plot her ruin—Inspire her with suspicion and terror—Psyche's return to the Palace of Love—Her disobedience—Love asleep—Psyche's amazement—The flight of Love—Sudden banishment of Psyche from the island of Pleasure—Her lamentations—Comforted by Love—Temple of Venus—Task imposed on Psyche conditional to her reconciliation with Venus—Psyche soothed and attended by Innocence—Psyche wandering as described in the opening of the first Canto.

Canto II

Oh happy you! who blest with present bliss
See not with fatal prescience future tears,
Nor the dear moment of enjoyment miss
Through gloomy discontent, or sullen fears
5   Foreboding many a storm for coming years;
Change is the lot of all. Ourselves with scorn
Perhaps shall view what now so fair appears;
And wonder whence the fancied charm was born
Which now with vain despair from our fond grasp is torn!

10   Vain schemer, think not to prolong thy joy!
But cherish while it lasts the heavenly boon;
Expand thy sails! thy little bark shall fly
With the full tide of pleasure! though it soon
May feel the influence of the changeful moon,
15   It yet is thine! then let not doubts obscure
With cloudy vapours veil thy brilliant noon,
Nor let suspicion's tainted breath impure
Poison the favoring gale which speeds thy course secure!

Oh Psyche, happy in thine ignorance!
20   Couldst thou but shun this heart tormenting bane;
Be but content, nor daringly advance
To meet the bitter hour of threatened pain;
Pure spotless dove! seek thy safe nest again;
Let true affection shun the public eye,
25   And quit the busy circle of the vain,
For there the treacherous snares concealed lie;
Oh timely warned escape! to safe retirement fly!

Bright shone the morn! and now its golden ray
Dispelled the slumbers from her radiant eyes,
30   Yet still in dreams her fancy seems to play,
For lo! she sees with rapture and surprise
Full in her view the well-known mansion rise,
And each loved scene of first endearment hails;
The air that first received her infant sighs
35   With wondring ecstasy she now inhales,
While every trembling nerve soft tenderness assails.

See from the dear pavilion, where she lay,
Breathless she flies with scarce assured feet,
Swift through the garden wings her eager way,
40   Her mourning parents ravished eyes to greet
With loveliest apparition strange and sweet:
Their days of anguish all o'erpaid they deem
By one blest hour of ecstasy so great:
Yet doubtingly they gaze, and anxious seem
45   To ask their raptured souls, "Oh, is this all a dream?"

The wondrous tale attentively they hear,
Repeated oft in broken words of joy,
She in their arms embraced, while every ear
Hangs on their Psyche's lips, and earnestly
50   On her is fixed each wonder speaking eye;
Till the sad hour arrives which bids them part,
And twilight darkens o'er the ruddy sky;
Divinely urged they let their child depart,
Pressed with a fond embrace to each adoring heart.

55   Trusting that wedded to a spouse divine
Secure is now their daughter's happiness,
They half contentedly their child resign,
Check the complaint, the rising sigh suppress,
And wipe the silent drops of bitterness.
60   Nor must she her departure more delay,
But bids them now their weeping Psyche bless;
Then back to the pavilion bends her way,
Ere in the fading west quite sinks expiring day.

But while her parents listen with delight
65   Her sisters hearts the Furies[40] agitate:
They look with envy on a lot so bright,
And all the honors of her splendid fate,
Scorning the meanness of their humbler state;
And how they best her ruin may devise
70   With hidden rancour much they meditate,
Yet still they bear themselves in artful guise,
While 'mid the feigned caress, concealed the venom lies.

By malice urged, by ruthless envy stung
With secret haste to seize their prey they flew,
75   Around her neck as in despair they clung;
Her soft complying nature well they knew
And trusted by delaying to undo;
But when they found her resolute to go
Their well laid stratagem they then pursue,
80   And while they bid their treacherous sorrows flow
Thus fright her simple heart with images of woe.

"Oh hapless Psyche! thoughtless of thy doom!
"Yet hear thy sisters who have wept for thee,
"Since first a victim to thy living tomb,
85   "Obedient to the oracle's decree,
"Constrained we left thee to thy destiny.
"Since then no comfort could our woes abate;
"While thou wert lulled in false security,
"We learned the secret horrors of thy fate,
90   "And heard prophetic lips thy future ills relate.

"Yet fearing never to behold thee more
"Our filial care would fain the truth conceal;
"But from the sages cell, this ring we bore,
"With power each latent magic to reveal:
95   "Some hope from hence our anxious bosoms feel
"That we from ruin may our Psyche save,
"Since Heaven propitious to our pious zeal,
"Thee to our frequent prayers in pity gave,
"That warned, thou yet mayest shun thy sad untimely grave.

100   "Oh! how shall we declare the fatal truth?
         "How wound thy tender bosom with alarms?
         "Tell how the graces of thy blooming youth,
         "Thy more than mortal, all-adored charms
         "Have lain enamoured in a sorcerer's arms?
105   "Oh Psyche! seize on this decisive hour,
         "Escape the mischief of impending harms!
         "Return no more to that enchanted bower,
     "Fly the magician's arts, and dread his cruel power!

         "If, yet reluctant to forego thy love,
110   "Thy furtive joys and solitary state,
         "Our fond officious care thy doubts reprove,
         "At least let some precaution guard thy fate,
         "Nor may our warning love be prized too late;
         "This night thyself thou mayst convince thine eyes,
115   "Hide but a lamp, and cautiously await
         "Till in deep slumber thy magician lies,
     "This ring shall then disclose his foul deformities.

         "That monster by the oracle foretold,
         "Whose cursed spells both gods and men must fear,
120   "In his own image thou shalt then behold,
         "And shuddering hate what now is prized so dear;
         "Yet fly not then, though loathsome he appear,
         "But let this dagger to his breast strike deep;
         "Thy coward terrors then thou must not hear,
125   "For if with life he rouses from that sleep
    "Nought then for thee remains, and we must hopeless weep."

         Oh! have you seen, when in the northern sky
         The transient flame of lambent lightning plays,
         In quick succession lucid streamers fly,
130   Now flashing roseate, and now milky rays,[41]
         While struck with awe, the astonished rustics gaze?
         Thus o'er her cheek, the fleeting signals move,
         Now pale with fear, now glowing with the blaze
         Of much indignant, still confiding love,
135   Now horror's lurid hue, with shame's deep blushes strove.

On her cold, passive hand the ring they place,
And hide the dagger in her folding vest;
Pleased the effects of their dire arts to trace
In the mute agony that swells her breast,
140   Already in her future ruin blest:
Conscious that now their poor deluded prey
Should never taste again delight or rest,
But sickening in suspicion's gloom decay,
Or urged by terrors rash their treacherous will obey.

145   While yet irresolute with sad surprise,
Mid doubt and love she stands in strange suspense,
Lo! gliding from her sister's[42] wondering eyes
Returning Zephyrs gently bear her thence;
Lost all her hopes, her joys, her confidence,
150   Back to the earth her mournful eyes she threw,
As if imploring pity and defence;
While bathed in tears her golden tresses flew,
As in the breeze dispersed they caught the precious dew.

Illumined bright now shines the splendid dome,
155   Melodious accents her arrival hail:
But not the torches' blaze can chase the gloom,
And all the soothing powers of music fail;
Trembling she seeks her couch with horror pale,
But first a lamp conceals in secret shade,
160   While unknown terrors all her soul assail.
Thus half their treacherous counsel is obeyed,
For still her gentle soul abhors the murderous blade.

And now, with softest whispers of delight,
Love welcomes Psyche still more fondly dear;
165   Not unobserved, though hid in deepest night,
The silent anguish of her secret fear.
He thinks that tenderness excites the tear
By the late image of her parents' grief,
And half offended seeks in vain to cheer,
170   Yet, while he speaks, her sorrows feel relief,
Too soon more keen to sting from this suspension brief!

Allowed to settle on celestial eyes
Soft sleep exulting now exerts his sway,
From Psyche's anxious pillow gladly flies
175   To veil those orbs, whose pure and lambent ray
The powers of heaven submissively obey.
Trembling and breathless then she softly rose
And seized the lamp, where it obscurely lay,
With hand too rashly daring to disclose
180   The sacred veil which hung mysterious o'er her woes.

Twice, as with agitated step she went,
The lamp expiring shone with doubtful gleam,
As though it warned her from her rash intent.
And twice she paused, and on its trembling beam
185   Gazed with suspended breath, while voices seem
With murmuring sound along the roof to sigh;
As one just waking from a troublous dream,
With palpitating heart and straining eye,
Still fixed with fear remains, still thinks the danger nigh.

190   Oh, daring muse![43] wilt thou indeed essay
To paint the wonders which that lamp could shew?
And canst thou hope in living words to say
The dazzling glories of that heavenly view?
Ah! well I ween, that if with pencil true
195   That splendid vision could be well exprest,
The fearful awe imprudent Psyche knew
Would seize with rapture every wondering breast,
When Love's all potent charms divinely stood confest.

All imperceptible to human touch,
200   His wings display celestial essence light,
The clear effulgence[44] of the blaze is such,
The brilliant plumage shines so heavenly bright
That mortal eyes turn dazzled from the sight;
A youth he seems in manhood's freshest years;
205   Round his fair neck, as clinging with delight,
Each golden curl resplendently appears,
Or shades his darker brow, which grace majestic wears.

      Or o'er his guileless front the ringlets bright
      Their rays of sunny lustre seem to throw,
210   That front than polished ivory more white!
      His blooming cheeks with deeper blushes glow
      Than roses scattered o'er a bed of snow:
      While on his lips, distilled in balmy dews,
       (Those lips divine that even in silence know
215   The heart to touch) persuasion to infuse
    Still hangs a rosy charm that never vainly sues.

      The friendly curtain of indulgent sleep
      Disclosed not yet his eyes' resistless sway,
      But from their silky veil there seemed to peep
220   Some brilliant glances with a softened ray,
      Which o'er his features exquisitely play,
      And all his polished limbs suffuse with light.
      Thus through some narrow space the azure day
      Sudden its cheerful rays diffusing bright,
225   Wide darts its lucid beams, to gild the brow of night.

      His fatal arrows, and celestial bow
      Beside the couch were negligently thrown,
      Nor needs the god his dazzling arms, to show
      His glorious birth, such beauty round him shone
230   As sure could spring from Beauty's self alone;
      The bloom which glowed o'er all of soft desire,
      Could well proclaim him Beauty's cherished son;
      And Beauty's self will oft these charms admire,
    And steal his witching smile, his glance's living fire.

235   Speechless with awe, in transport strangely lost
      Long Psyche stood with fixed adoring eye;
      Her limbs immoveable, her senses tost
      Between amazement, fear, and ecstasy,
      She hangs enamoured o'er the Deity.
240   Till from her trembling hand extinguished falls
      The fatal lamp—He starts—and suddenly
      Tremendous thunders echo through the halls,
    While ruin's hideous crash bursts o'er the affrighted walls.

Dread horror seizes on her sinking heart,
245   A mortal chillness shudders at her breast,
Her soul shrinks fainting from death's icy dart,
The groan scarce uttered dies but half exprest,
And down she sinks in deadly swoon opprest:
But when at length, awaking from her trance,
250   The terrors of her fate stand all confest,
In vain she casts around her timid glance,
The rudely frowning scenes her former joys enhance.

No traces of those joys, alas, remain!
A desert solitude alone appears.
255   No verdant shade relieves the sandy plain,
The wide spread waste no gentle fountain cheers,
One barren face, the dreary prospect wears;
Nought through the vast horizon meets her eye
To calm the dismal tumult of her fears,
260   No trace of human habitation nigh,
A sandy wild beneath, above a threatening sky.

The mists of morn yet chill the gloomy air,
And heavily obscure the clouded skies;
In the mute anguish of a fixed despair
265   Still on the ground immoveable she lies;
At length with lifted hands and streaming eyes,
Her mournful prayers invoke offended Love,
"Oh let me hear thy voice once more (she cries)
"In death at least thy pity let me move,
270   "And death, if but forgiven, a kind relief will prove.

"For what can life to thy lost Psyche give,
"What can it offer but a gloomy void?
"Why thus abandoned should I wish to live?
"To mourn the pleasure which I once enjoyed,
275   "The bliss my own rash folly hath destroyed;
"Of all my soul most prized, or held most dear,
"Nought but the sad remembrance doth abide,
"And late repentance of my impious fear;
"Remorse and vain regret what living soul can bear!

280   "Oh art thou then indeed for ever gone!
       "And art thou heedless of thy Psyche's woe!
       "From these fond arms for ever art thou flown,
       "And unregarded must my sorrows flow!
       "Ah! why too happy did I ever know
285   "The rapturous charms thy tenderness inspires?
       "Ah! why did thy affections stoop so low?
       "Why kindle in a mortal breast such fires,
   "Or with celestial love inflame such rash desires?

       "Abandoned thus for ever by thy love
290   "No greater punishment I now can bear,
       "From fate no farther malice can I prove,
       "Not all the horrors of this desert drear,
       "Nor death itself can now excite a fear,
       "The peopled earth a solitude as vast
295   "To this despairing heart would now appear;
       "Here then, my transient joys for ever past,
   "Let thine expiring bride, thy pardon gain at last!"

       Now prostrate on the bare unfriendly ground,
       She waits her doom in silent agony;
300   When lo! the well known soft celestial sound
       She hears once more with breathless ecstasy,
       "Oh! yet too dearly loved! Lost Psyche! Why
       "With cruel fate wouldst thou unite thy power,
       "And force me thus thine arms adored to fly?
305   "Yet cheer thy drooping soul, some happier hour
   "Thy banished steps may lead back to thy lover's bower.

       "Though angry Venus we no more can shun,
       "Appease that anger and I yet am thine!
       "Lo! where her temple glitters to the sun.
310   "With humble penitence approach her shrine,
       "Perhaps to pity she may yet incline;
       "But should her cruel wrath these hopes deceive,
       "And thou, alas! must never more be mine,
       "Yet shall thy lover ne'er his Psyche leave,
315   "But if the fates[45] allow, unseen thy woes relieve.

"Stronger than I, they now forbid my stay;
"Psyche beloved, adieu!" Scarce can she hear
The last faint words, which gently melt away;
And now more faint the dying sounds appear,
320   Borne to a distance from her longing ear;
Yet still attentively she stands unmoved,
To catch those accents which her soul could cheer,
That soothing voice which had so sweetly proved
That still his tender heart offending Psyche loved!

325   And now the joyous sun had cleared the sky,
The mist dispelled revealed the splendid fane;
A palmy grove majestically high
Screens the fair building from the desert plain;
Of alabaster white and free from stain
330   Mid the tall trees the tapering columns rose;
Thither, with fainting steps, and weary pain,
Obedient to the voice at length she goes,
And at the threshold seeks protection and repose.

Round the soft scene immortal roses bloomed,[46]
335   While lucid myrtles in the breezes play;
No savage beast had ever yet presumed[47]
With foot impure within the grove to stray,
And far from hence flies every bird of prey;
Thus, mid the sandy Garamantian wild,[48]
340   When Macedonia's lord pursued his way,
The sacred temple of great Ammon smiled,
And green encircling shades the long fatigue beguiled:

With awe that fearfully her doom awaits
Still at the portal Psyche timid lies,
345   When lo! advancing from the hallowed gates
Trembling she views with reverential eyes
An aged priest. A myrtle bough supplies
A wand, and roses bind his snowy brows:
"Bear hence thy feet profane (he sternly cries)
350   "Thy longer stay the goddess disallows,
"Fly, nor her fiercer wrath too daringly arouse!"

His pure white robe imploringly she held,
And, bathed in tears, embraced his sacred knees;
Her mournful charms relenting he beheld,
355   And melting pity in his eye she sees;
"Hope not (he cries) the goddess to appease,
"Retire at awful distance from her shrine,
"But seek the refuge of those sheltering trees,
"And now thy soul with humble awe incline
360   "To hear her sacred will and mark the words divine."

"Presumptuous Psyche! whose aspiring soul
"The God of Love has dared to arrogate;
"Rival of Venus! whose supreme control
"Is now asserted by all ruling fate,
365   "No suppliant tears her vengeance shall abate
"Till thou hast raised an altar to her power,
"Where perfect happiness, in lonely state,
"Has fixed her temple in secluded bower,
"By foot impure of man untrodden to this hour!

370   "And on the altar must thou place an urn
"Filled from immortal beauty's sacred spring,
"Which foul deformity to grace can turn,
"And back to fond affection's eyes can bring
"The charms which fleeting fled on transient wing;
375   "Snatched from the rugged steep where first they rise,
"Dark rocks their crystal source o'ershadowing,
"Let their clear water sparkle to the skies
"Where cloudless lustre beams which happiness supplies!

"To Venus thus for ever reconciled,
380   "This one atonement all her wrath disarms,
"From thy loved Cupid then no more exiled
"There shalt thou, free from sorrow and alarms,
"Enjoy for ever his celestial charms.
"But never shalt thou taste a pure repose,
385   "Nor ever meet thy lover's circling arms,
"Till all subdued that shall thy steps oppose,
"Thy perils there shall end, escaped from all thy foes."

With meek submissive woe she heard her doom,
Nor to the holy minister replied;
390   But in the myrtle grove's mysterious gloom
She silently retired her grief to hide.
Hopeless to tread the waste without a guide,
All unrefreshed and faint from toil she lies:
When lo! her present wants are all supplied,
395   Sent by the hand of Love a turtle[49] flies,
And sets delicious food before her wondering eyes.

Cheered by the favoring omen, softer tears
Relieve her bosom from its cruel weight:
She blames the sad despondence of her fears,
400   When still protected by a power so great,
His tenderness her toils will mitigate.
Then with renewed strength at length she goes,
Hoping to find some skilled in secret fate,
Some learned sage who haply might disclose
405   Where lay that blissful bower the end of all her woes.

And as she went, behold with hovering flight!
The dove preceded still her doubtful way;
Its spotless plumage of the purest white,
Which shone resplendent in the blaze of day,
410   Could even in darkest gloom a light display;
Of heavenly birth, when first to mortals given
Named Innocence. But ah! too short its stay;
By ravenous birds it fearfully was driven
Back to reside with Love, a denizen of heaven.

415   Now through the trackless wild, o'er many a mile
The messenger of Cupid led the fair,
And cheered with hope her solitary toil,
Till now a brighter face the prospects wear,
Past are the sandy wastes and deserts bare,
420   And many a verdant hill, and grassy dale,
And trace, that mortal culture might declare,
And many a wild wood dark, and joyous vale
Appeared her soul to sooth, could soothing scenes avail.

But other fears her timid soul distress,
425   Mid strangers unprotected and alone,
The desert wilderness alarmed her less
Than cities, thus unfriended and unknown;
But where the path was all by moss o'ergrown,
There still she chose her solitary way,
430   Where'er her faithful Dove before had flown
Fearful of nought she might securely stray,
For still his care supplied the wants of every day.

And still she entered every sacred grove
And homage paid to each divinity,
435   But chief the altar of almighty Love,
Weeping embraced with fond imploring eye;
To every oracle her hopes apply,
Instructions for her dangerous path to gain:
Exclaiming oft, with a desponding sigh,
440   "Ah! how through all such dangers, toil and pain,
"Shall Psyche's helpless steps their object e'er attain?"

And now remote from every peopled town
One sultry day a cooling bower she found:
There, as I whilom[50] sung, she laid her down,
445   Where rich profusion of gay flowers around
Had decked with artless shew the sloping ground,
There the wild rose and modest violet grow,
There all thy charms, Narcissus![51] still abound:
There wrapt in verdure fragrant lilies blow,
450   Lilies that love the vale, and hide their bells of snow.

Thy flowers, Adonis![52] bright vermilion shew,
Still for his love the yellow crocus[53] pines,
There, while indignant blushes seem to glow,
Beloved by Phoebus his Acanthus[54] shines,
455   Her drooping head still Reseda reclines[55]
With faithful homage to his golden rays,
And, though mid clouds their lustre he resigns,
An image of the constant heart displays,
While silent still she turns her fond pursuing gaze.

460   And every sweet that spring[56] with fairy hands
        Scatters in thy green path, enchanting May!
        And every flowering shrub there clustring stands
        As though they wooed her to a short delay,
        Yielding a charm to sooth her weary way;
465   Soft was the tufted moss, and sweet the breeze,
        With lulling sound the murmuring waters play,
        With lulling sound from all the rustling trees
    The fragrant gale invites to cool refreshing ease.

        There as she sought repose, her sorrowing heart
470   Recalled her absent love with bitter sighs;
        Regret had deeply fixed the poisoned dart,
        Which ever rankling in her bosom lies;
        In vain she seeks to close her weary eyes,
        Those eyes still swim incessantly in tears,
475   Hope in her cheerless bosom fading dies,
        Distracted by a thousand cruel fears,
    While banished from his love for ever she appears.

        Oh! thou best comforter of that sad heart
        Whom fortune's spite assails; come, gentle sleep,[57]
480   The weary mourner sooth! for well the art
        Thou knowest in soft forgetfulness to steep
        The eyes which sorrow taught to watch and weep;
        Let blissful visions now her spirits cheer,
        Or lull her cares to peace in slumbers deep,
485   Till from fatigue refreshed and anxious fear
    Hope like the morning star once more shall re-appear.

CANTO III

ARGUMENT

Praise of Love—Psyche's Champion, with his attendant Constance, described—
The Knight assumes the command of Passion, who appears as a Lion—Psyche
proceeds under the protection of the Knight—Persuaded to repose in the Bower of
loose Delight—Her escape from thence—Led by Innocence to Retirement—Psyche

meets Vanity and Flattery—Betrayed by them into the power of Ambition—
Rescued by her Knight.

Canto III

Oh who art thou who darest of love[58] complain?
He is a gentle spirit and injures none!
His foes are ours; from them the bitter pain,
The keen, deep anguish, the heart-rending groan,
5   Which in his milder reign are never known.
His tears are softer than the April showers,
White-handed Innocence supports his throne,
His sighs are sweet as breath of earliest flowers,
Affection guides his steps, and peace protects his bowers.

10   But scarce admittance he on earth can find,
Opposed by vanity, by fraud ensnared,
Suspicion frights him from the gloomy mind,
And jealousy in vain his smiles has shared,
Whose sullen frown the gentle godhead scared;
15   From passion's rapid blaze in haste he flies,
His wings alone the fiercer flame has spared;
From him ambition turns his scornful eyes,
And avarice, slave to gold, a generous lord denies.

But chief inconstancy[59] his power destroys,
20   To mock his lovely form, an idle train
With magic skill she dressed in transient toys,
By these the selfish votaries she can gain
Whom Love's more simple bands could ne'er detain.
Ah! how shall Psyche through such mortal foes
25   The fated end of all her toils attain?
Sadly she ponders o'er her hopeless woes,
Till on the pillowy turf she sinks to short repose.

But as the careless lamb whom playful chance
Thoughtless of danger has enticed to rove,
30   Amidst her gambols casts a sudden glance
Where lurks her wily foe within the grove,

Anxious to fly, but still afraid to move,
All hopeless of escape—so looks the maid,
Such dread her half-awakened senses prove,
35   When roused from sleep before her eyes dismayed
A knight all armed appears close mid the embowering shade.

Trembling she gazed, until the stranger knight
Tempering with mildest courtesy, the awe
Which majesty inspired, low in her sight
40   Obeisance made; nor would he nearer draw,
Till, half subdued surprise and fear, he saw
Pale terror yielding to the rosy grace,
The pure congealed blood begin to thaw,
And flowing through her crystal veins apace
45 Suffuse with mantling blush her mild celestial face.

Gently approaching then with fairest speech
He proffered service to the lonely dame,
And prayed her that she might not so impeach
The honor of his youth's yet spotless fame,
50   As aught to fear which might his knighthood shame;
But if her unprotected steps to guard,
The glory of her champion he might claim,
He asked no other guerdon[60] or reward,
Than what bright honor's self might to his deeds award.

55   Doubting and musing much within her mind,
With half suspicious, half confiding eye,
Awhile she stood; her thoughts bewildered find
No utterance, unwilling to deny
Such proffered aid, yet bashful to reply
60   With quick assent, since though concealed his face
Beneath his helm, yet might she well espy
And in each fair proportion plainly trace
The symmetry of form, and perfect youthful grace.

Hard were it to describe the nameless charm
65   That o'er each limb, in every action played,
The softness of that voice, which could disarm

The hand of fury of its deadly blade:
In shining armour was the youth arrayed,
And on his shield a bleeding heart he bore,
70   His lofty crest light plumes of azure shade,
There shone a wounded dragon bathed in gore,
And bright with silver beamed the silken scarf he wore.

His milk-white steed with glittering trappings blazed,
Whose reins a beauteous boy attendant held,
75   On the fair squire with wonder Psyche gazed,
For scarce he seemed of age to bear the shield,
Far less a ponderous lance, or sword to wield;
Yet well this little page his lord had served,
His youthful arm had many a foe repelled,
80   His watchful eye from many a snare preserved,
Nor ever from his steps in any danger swerved.

Graced with the gift of a perpetual youth,
No lapse of years had power his form to change;
Constance was named the boy, whose matchless truth
85   Though oft inticed with other lords to range
Nor fraud, nor force could from that knight estrange;
His mantle of celestial blue was made,
And its bright texture wrought with art so strange
That the fresh brilliant gloss could never fade,
90   And lustre yet unknown to Psyche's eyes displayed.

Thus while she gazed, behold with horrid roar
A lion from the neighbouring forest rushed,
A golden chain around his neck he bore,
Which richly glowing with carbuncles[61] blushed,
95   While his fierce eye-balls fiery rage had flushed:
Forth steps the youth before the affrighted fair,
Who in his mighty paw already crushed
Seems in the terrors of her wild despair,
And her mute quivering lips a death-like paleness wear.

100   But scarce the kingly beast the knight beheld,
When crouching low, submissive at his feet,

His wrath extinguished, and his valour quelled,
He seemed with reverence and obeisance sweet
Him as his long acknowledged lord to greet.
105   While, in acceptance of the new command,
Well pleased the youth received the homage meet,
Then seized the splendid chain with steady hand
Full confident to rule, and every foe withstand.

And when at length recovered from her fear,
110   The timid Psyche mounts his docile steed,
Much prayed she tells to his attentive ear
(As on her purposed journey they proceed)
The doubtful course the oracle decreed:
And how observant of her friendly guide,
115   She still pursued its flight, with all the speed
Her fainting strength had hitherto supplied:
What pathless wilds she crossed! What forests darkling wide!

Which having heard, the courteous knight began
With counsel sweet to sooth her wounded heart;
120   Divinely eloquent, persuasion ran
The herald of his words, ere they depart
His lips, which well might confidence impart,
As he revealed how he himself was bound
By solemn vow, that neither force nor art
125   His helmet should unloose, till he had found
The bower of happiness, that long sought fairy ground.

"I too (he said) divided from my love,
"The offended power of Venus deprecate,[62]
"Like thee, through paths untrodden, sadly rove
130   "In search of that fair spot prescribed by fate,
"The blessed term of my afflicted state,
"Where I, the mistress of my soul shall find,
"For whose dear sake no toil to me seems great,
"Nor any dangers to my search assigned
135   "Can from its purpose fright my ardent longing mind.

"Psyche! thy soft and sympathising heart
"Shall share the rapture of thy loyal knight,
"He too, in thy content shall bear a part,
"Blest witness of thy new restored delight;
140   "My vows of true allegiance here I plight,
"Ne'er to forsake thee till thy perils end,
"Thy steps to guard, in thy protection fight,
"By counsel aid, and by my arm defend,
"And prove myself in all, thy champion and thy friend."

145   So on they went, her cheerless heart revived,
By promised succour in her doubtful way,
And much of hope she to herself derived,
From the warm eagerness his lips display
In their pursuit to suffer no delay:
150   "And sure, (she softly sighed) my dearest Lord,
"Thy watchful love still guides me as I stray,
"Not chance alone could such an aid afford,
"Lo! beasts of prey confess the heaven-assisted sword."

Now from his crystal urn, with chilling hand,
155   Vesper[63] had sprinkled all the earth with dew,
A misty veil obscured the neighbouring land,
And shut the fading landscape from their view;
A beaten path they eagerly pursue,
(For now refreshment and repose they need
160   As Psyche weary of long travel grew)
Where by a river's bank it seemed to lead,
Along its sinuous course they heedlessly proceed.

At length the lordly beast that bore the knight
Explored the river's depth with sudden bound,
165   Psyche, who heard the plunge with strange affright,
Her champion reassured with welcome sound,
That he the other bank had safely found;
And, while he spoke, emerging from the shade,
A joyous goodly train appear around,
170   Of many a gallant youth and white robed maid,
Who grateful welcome gave, and courteous greeting paid.

Quick through the trees a thousand torches blazed,
The gloom to banish, and the scene disclose
To Psyche all irresolute, amazed:
175   A bridge with stately arch at distance rose,
Thither at once the gay assembly goes,
Not unattended by the charmed knight,
Inviting Psyche to partake repose,
Pointing where shone their bower illumined bright,
180   Their bower so passing fair, the bower of loose Delight.

At length with timid foot the bridge she past,
And to her guardian knight clung fearfully,
While many a doubting glance around she cast,
If still her watchful dove she might espy;
185   Feebly it seemed on labouring wing to fly,
Till, dazzled by the sudden glare around,
In painful trance it[64] closed its dizzy eye,
And had it not fair Psyche's bosom found,
Its drooping pinion soon had touched the unhallowed ground.

190   Hence there arose within her heart sore dread
Which no alluring pleasure could dispel;
The splendid hall with luscious banquet spread,
The soft-breathed flutes which in sweet concert swell,
With melody of song unspeakable;
195   Nor the light dancing troop in roses drest,
Could chase the terrors which she dared not tell,
While fondly cherished in her anxious breast
She strove in vain to sooth the fluttering bird to rest.

On a soft downy couch the guests are placed,
200   And close behind them stands their watchful page,
But much his strict attendance there disgraced,
And much was scorned his green and tender age,
His calm fixed eye and steady aspect sage:
But him nor rude disdain nor mockery,
205   Nor soothing blandishments could e'er engage,
The wanton mazes of their sports to try,
Or from his lord to turn his firm adhering eye.

White bosomed nymphs around with loosened zones
All on the guests obsequiously tend,
210   Some sing of love with soft expiring tones,
While Psyche's melting eyes the strain commend;
Some o'er their heads the canopy suspend,
Some hold the sparkling bowl, while some with skill
Ambrosial showers and balmy juices blend,
215   Or the gay lamps with liquid odours fill
Whose many coloured fires divinest sweets distil.

And now a softer light they seemed to shed
And sweetest music ushered in their queen.
Her languid steps by winged boys are led,
220   Who in their semblance might have Cupids been;
Close wrapt in veils her following train was seen;
Herself looked lovely in her loose attire,
Her smiling eyes gave lustre to the scene,
And still where'er they turned their wanton fire
225   Each thrilling nerve confessed the rapture they inspire.

The stranger guests she viewed with welcome glad,
And crowned the banquet with reception sweet,
To fill the glowing bowl her nymphs she bad,
And graceful rising from her splendid seat
230   She would herself present the sparkling treat;
When lo! the dove alarmed with sudden start,
Spurned the bright cup and dashed it at her feet,
For well he knew 'twas mixed with treacherous art
To sting his Psyche's breast with agonizing smart.

235   Regardless of her supplicating tears
Each eye with vengeful rage the insult sees,
Her knight's protection now in vain appears;
The offended sovereign anxious to appease,
A thousand hands prepare the dove to seize:
240   Nor was this all, for as the tumult rose,
Sudden more thick than swarm of summer bees,
The secret dens their venomed hoards disclose,
And horror at the sight her vital spirits froze.

Hissing aloud with undulations dire,
245   Their forked tongues unnumbered serpents show,
Their tainted breath emitting poisonous fire
All turn on Psyche as their mortal foe;
But he, whose arm was never weak or slow,
Now rushed before her with resistless spring,
250   On either side the oft-repeated blow
Repulsed the malice of their deadly sting,
While sparks of wrathful fire from their fierce jaws they fling.

"Fly, Psyche! these are slander's hellish brood!
"Contest I know is vain," her champion cried.
255   Her passage now the opposing train withstood,
Struck with disgust their hideous forms she spied,
For lo! each silken veil is thrown aside,
And foul deformity, and filth obscene,
With monstrous shapes appear on every side;
260   But vanished is their fair and treacherous queen,
And with her every charm that decked the enchanted scene.

Meanwhile the dove had soared above their reach,
But hovered still in anxious Psyche's sight,
Precursor of escape, it seemed to teach
265   Whither she safest might direct her flight,
And find a pass-port[65] in her foes' despite;
One rugged path there lay with briars o'ergrown,
Then dark and dismal with the shades of night,
Thither the dove on rapid wing had flown,
270   Conspicuous mid the gloom its silver plumage shone.

Yet she delayed, o'ercome by terror's power,
And scarce her fainting form the knight could shield,
When lo! still active in the trying hour,
Constance rushed fearless through the dreadful field,
275   With breast-plate firm invulnerably steeled,
He heeded not the storms which round him press,
To any perils he disdained to yield,
Endued with prudence as with hardiness,
And ever skilled to bring due succour in distress.

280   Lo! swift returning on his master's steed,
       In his right hand he held the lion's chain,
       The mighty beast his gentleness could lead
       Though little used to bear the curb or rein,
       And mid those groves accustomed to remain,
285   Yet now prepared, with sweet submissive grace,
       He ready stands the knight to bear again,
       While trembling Psyche on the steed they place,
     Which swift as lightning flies far from the dreadful chase.

       Rough was the rude wild way, and many a thorn
290   Tore her loose garments in their rapid flight,
       O'er many a league the panting fair is borne,
       Till now, emerging from the shades of night,
       The grey-eyed morn stole forth her pallid light.
       Then first she paused unable to proceed
295   Exhausted with fatigue, and pain, and fright.
       "Turn, Psyche," cried the youth, "relax thy speed,
     "And see thyself at length from thy pursuers freed."

       Mid the thick forest, was a lonely dell,
       Where foot of man was seldom known to tread,
300   The sloping hills all round, in graceful swell,
       The little green with woods environed:
       Hither the dove their passive course had led.
       Here the thin smoke blue rising mid the trees,
       Where broad and brown the deepest umbrage[66] spread,
305   Spoke the abode of safe retired ease,
     And Psyche gladly there her dove descending sees.

       In lowly cottage, walled with mossy sod,
       Close by a little spring's perpetual rill,
       A hermit dwelt, who many a year had trod
310   With sacred solitude that pine-clad hill,
       And loved with holy images to fill
       His soul enrapt; yet courteous them[67] besought
       A while secluded here to rest; and still
       Replete with kind and hospitable thought,
315   To a sequestered bower the wearied Psyche brought.

Skilled in the virtue of each healing flower,
And the wild fruit's restoring juice to blend,
He spreads the frugal fare of wholesome power,
And heedfully his cares their wants attend,
320   A docile ear to his advice they lend,
And sage instruction from his precepts take,
Which much their future journey may befriend;
Wisdom with soothing eloquence he spake,
Pleased to resolve their doubts, and all their cares partake.

325   In those sweet placid scenes awhile they rest,
Till Psyche finds her fainting strength revive,
And here her dove, as in a quiet nest,
Delighted seems to sportive joy alive,
And hence they surest confidence derive.
330   He plumes his wings, and through his swelling throat
(No more a ruffled, fearful fugitive)
In gentle murmurs pours his dulcet note,
While Psyche listening sits in some still vale remote.

Oh! have you never known the silent charm
335   That undisturbed retirement yields the soul,
Where no intruder might your peace alarm,
And tenderness hath wept without control,
While melting fondness o'er the bosom stole?
Did fancy never, in some lonely grove,
340   Abridge the hours which must in absence roll?
Those pensive pleasures did you never prove,
Oh you have never loved! you know not what is love!

They do not love, who can to these prefer
The tumult of the gay, or folly's roar;
345   The Muse they know not; nor delight in her
Who can the troubled soul to rest restore,
Calm contemplation: Yes, I must deplore
Their joyless state, even more than his who mourns
His love for ever lost; delight no more
350   Unto his widowed heart indeed returns,
Yet, while he weeps, his soul their cold indifference spurns.

But if soft hope illumines fancy's dream,
Assuring him of love and constancy,
How exquisite do then the moments seem,
355   When he may hide himself from every eye
And cherish the dear thought in secrecy,
While sweet remembrance sooths his thrilling heart,
And brings once more past hours of kindness nigh,
Recals the look of love when forced to part,
360   And turns to drops of joy the tears that sadly start.

Forgetful of the dangers of her way,
Imagination oft would Psyche bear
To her long travel's end, and that blest day,
When Love unveiled should to her eyes appear;
365   When she might view his charms exempt from fear,
Taste his pure kisses, feel his balmy sighs,
Rest in the fond embrace of arms so dear,
Gaze with soft rapture on his melting eyes,
And hear his voice divine, the music of the skies!

370   Their destined course impatient to achieve,
The knight is urgent onward to proceed:
Cheered with recruited strength they take their leave
Of their kind host, and pay their grateful meed[68]
Of warmest thanks sincere; onward they speed
375   Their sunless journey long through forests green,
And tangled thickets rank with many a weed,
And when at closing day a hut is seen,
They seek the humble roof, nor scorn its welcome mean.

It happened once that early roused from sleep,
380   (Ere her damp veil the virgin morn had cast
From her pale face, not yet with blushes deep
Lovely suffused, as when approaching fast
His herald star proclaims her spouse at last)
Psyche forsaking soon her homely bed,
385   Alone had fearless the low threshold past,
And, to beguile the hours which lingering fled,
Light o'er the dewy plain walked forth with nimble tread.

Yet though the knight close wrapt in slumber lay,
Her steps, at distance, still the page pursued,
390   Fearful that danger might befal her way,
Or lest, entangled in the mazy wood,
Returning she should miss the pathway rude.
The lark now hails the sun with rapturous song,
The cheerful earth resounds with gratitude,
395   O'er the gay scene, as Psyche tript along,
She felt her spirits rise, her lightened heart grow strong.

And hark, soft music steals upon the ear!
'Tis woman's voice most exquisitely sweet!
Behold two female forms approaching near
400   Arrest with wonder Psyche's timid feet;
On a gay car, by speckled panthers fleet[69]
Is drawn in gallant state a seeming queen,
And at her foot on low but graceful seat,
A gentle nymph of lovely form is seen,
405   In robe of fairest white, with scarf of pleasant green.

In strains of most bewitching harmony,
And still adapted to her sovereign's praise,
She filled the groves with such sweet melody,
That, quite o'ercome with rapture and amaze,
410   Psyche stood listening to the warbled lays;
Yet with a sullen, scarce approving ear
Her mistress sits, but with attentive gaze,
Her eyes she fixes on a mirror clear
Where still by fancy's spell, unrivalled charms appear.

415   And, as she looked with aspect ever new,
She seemed on change and novel grace intent,
Her robe was formed of ever varying hue
And whimsically placed each ornament;
On her attire, with rich luxuriance spent,
420   The treasures of the earth, the sea, the air,
Are vainly heaped her wishes to content;
Yet were her arms and snowy bosom bare
And both in painted pride shone exquisitely fair.

Her braided tresses in profusion drest,
425   Circled with diadem, and nodding plumes,
Sported their artful ringlets o'er her breast,
And to the breezes gave their rich perfumes;
Her cheek with tint of borrowed roses blooms:
Used to receive from all rich offerings,
430   She quaffs with conscious right the fragrant fumes
Which her attendant from a censer flings,
Who graceful feeds the flame with incense while she sings.

Soon as her glance fair Psyche's form had caught
Her soft attendant smiling she addressed:
435   "Behold Lusinga![70] couldst thou ere[71] have thought
"That these wild woods were so in beauty blest?
"Let but that nymph in my attire be drest
"And scarce her loveliness will yield to mine!
"At least invite her in our bower to rest,
440   "Before her eyes let all my splendor shine,
"Perhaps to dwell with us, her heart we may incline."

With softest smile applauding all she heard,
Lusinga bowing left her golden seat,
And Psyche, who at first in doubt, had feared
445   While listening to the lay so silver sweet,
Now passive followed with unconscious feet;
Till Constance, all alarmed, impatient flew,
And soft his whispers of the maid entreat
To fly the Syren's song,[72] for well he knew
450   What lurking dangers hence would to his Lord ensue.

"Oh do not trust her treacherous lips," he cried,
"She is the subtle slave of Vanity,
"Her queen, the child of folly, and of pride,
"To lure thee to her power each art will try,
455   "Nor ever will release thee peaceably."
He spoke, but spoke in vain, for lo! from far,
Of giant port[73] they fast approaching spy
A knight, high mounted on a glittering car,
From whose conspicuous crest flames wide a dazzling star.

460   "Psyche! escape! Ambition is at hand!"
    The page exclaims: while swift as thought he flies;
    She would have followed, but with parley bland,
    Lusinga soon her terrors pacifies.
    "Fair nymph, ascend my car," the sovereign cries,
465   "I will convey thee where thy wishes lead,
    "Haply the safest course I may advise
    "How thou thy journey mayst perform with speed;
  "For ne'er in woods to dwell such beauty was decreed."

    So gently urgent her consent they wooed
470   With much persuasion of the stranger knight;
    That yielding Psyche now no more withstood,
    But pointing out to her observant sight
    The humble cot where she had passed the night,
    She prayed her kind conductress there to turn,
475   And promised to herself what vast delight
    Her wondering knight would feel at her return,
  And with what blushing shame, the timid page would burn.

    But scarcely had she climbed the fatal car
    When swifter than the wind the panthers flew,
480   The traversed plains and woods, receding far,
    Soon shut from trembling Psyche's anxious view
    The spot where she had left her guardian true;
    With desperate efforts, all in vain she tries
    To escape the ills which now too sure she knew
485   Must from her ill-placed confidence arise,
  Betrayed—Ah! self-betrayed, a wretched sacrifice.

    She strove to quit the car with sudden bound,
    Ah vain attempt! she now perceived too late,
    A thousand silken trammels,[74] subtly wound
490   O'er her fair form, detained her as she sate:
    Lost in despair she yields to her sad fate,
    And silent hears but with augmented fright
    The queen describe her brother's splendid state,
    Who now outstripped them by his rapid flight,
495   And prest his foaming steeds to gain the arduous height.

High o'er the spacious plain a mountain rose,
A stately castle on its summit stood:
Huge craggy cliffs behind their strength oppose
To the rough surges of the dashing flood;
500   The rocky shores a boldly rising wood
On either side conceals; bright shine the towers
And seem to smile upon the billows rude.
In front the eye, with comprehensive powers,
Sees wide extended plains enriched with splendid bowers.

505   Hither they bore the sad reluctant fair,
Who mounts with dizzy eye the awful steep;
The blazing structure seems high poised in air,
And its light pillars tremble o'er the deep:
As yet the heavens are calm, the tempests sleep,
510   She knows not half the horrors of her fate:
Nor feels the approaching ruin's whirlwind sweep:
Yet with ill-boding fears she past the gate,
And turned with sickning dread from scenes of gorgeous state.

In vain the haughty master of the hall
515   Invites her to partake his regal throne,
With cold indifference she looks on all
The gilded trophies, and the well-wrought stone
Which in triumphal arches proudly shone:
And, as she casts around her timid eye,
520   Back to her knight her trembling heart is flown,
And many an anxious wish, and many a sigh
Invokes his gallant arm protection to supply.

Sudden the lurid heavens obscurely frown,
And sweeping gusts the coming storm proclaim;
525   Flattery's soft voice the howling tempests drown,
While the roofs catch the greedy lightning's flame.
Loud in their fears, the attendant train exclaim
The light built fabric ne'er can stand the blast,
And all its insecure foundations blame,
530   Tumultuously they rush: the chief aghast
Beholds his throne o'erturned, his train dispersing fast.

Psyche dismayed, yet thoughtful of escape,
In anxious silence to the portal prest;
And freedom would have hailed in any shape
535   Though seen in death's tremendous colours drest:
But ah! she feels the knight's strong grasp arrest
Her trembling steps. "Think not" he cries, "to fly
"With yon false crowd who by my favours blest,
"Can now desert me when with changeful eye
540   "Inclement fortune frowns from yon dark angry sky."

While yet he spoke loud bursts the groaning hall,
With frightful peal the thundering domes resound,
Disjointed columns in wild ruin fall,
While the huge arches tremble to the ground.
545   Yet unappalled amid the crush is found
The daring chief: his hold he firm maintains
Though hideous devastation roars around;
Plunged headlong down his prey he still sustains,
Who in his powerful grasp in death-like swoon remains.

550   Down sinks the palace with its mighty lord,
Hurled from the awful steep with vehemence
Even to the floods below, which angry roared
And gaping wide received the weight immense:
Indignant still, with fearless confidence
555   He rose, high mounting o'er the heaving waves;
Against their rage one arm is his defence,
The other still his lovely burden saves,
Though strong the billows beat, and fierce the tempest raves.

The blazing star yet shone upon his brow,
560   And flamed triumphant o'er the dashing main;[75]
He rides secure the watery waste, and now
The sheltering shore he might in safety gain,
The sheltering shore he shuns with proud disdain,
And breasts the adverse tide. Ah rash resource!
565   Yon vessel, Prince, thou never shalt attain!
For plunging 'mid the deep, with generous force,
See where the lion's lord pursues thy hardy course!

Psyche a well known voice to life restores,
Once more her eyes unclosing view the light,
570   But not the waters, nor receding shores,
One only object can arrest her sight,
High o'er the flood she sees her valiant knight,
And sudden joy, and hopes scarce trusted cheer
Even in that awful moment's dread affright,
575   Her feeble cry indeed he cannot hear,
But sees her out-stretched arms, and seems already near.

In vain the giant knight exerts his strength,
Urged by the impetuous youth the lion prest,
And gaining fast upon his flight, at length,
580   Prepared his daring progress to arrest,
He[76] seized with furious jaw his struggling breast.
Gasping he loosed his hold—and Psyche lost
The o'erwhelming wave with ruin had opprest,
But Constance ever near when needed most,
585   The sinking beauty caught and bore her to the coast.

Stung with the shame of the relinquished prey,
Mad with revenge and hate and conscious pride,
The knight recovers[77] from his short dismay,
And dashed[78] resistless through the foaming tide;
590   The billows yielding to his arm divide,
As rushing on the youth he seeks the shore;
But now a combat strange on either side
Amid the waves begins; each hopes no more
The engulphing deep his foe shall e'er to light restore.

595   Beside the cold inhospitable lands
Where suns long absent dawn with lustre pale,
Thus on his bark the bold Biscayen stands,[79]
And bids his javelin rouse the parent whale:
Fear, pain, and rage at once her breast assail,
600   The agitated ocean foams around,
Lashed by the sounding fury of her tail,
Or as she mounts the surge with frightful bound,
Wide echoing to her cries the bellowing shores resound.

Fierce was the contest, but at length subdued
605   The youth exulting sees his giant foe.
With wonder still the enormous limbs he viewed
Which lifeless now the waves supporting show;
His starred helm, that now was first laid low,
He seized as trophy of the wonderous fight,
610   And bade the sparkling gem on Constance glow,
While Psyche's eyes, soft beaming with delight,
Through tears of grateful praise applaud her gallant knight.

CANTO IV

ARGUMENT

Introduction—Sympathy—Suspicion—Psyche benighted—Credulity represented, according to a Picture by Apelles,[80] as an old Woman the devoted prey of Slander, or the Blatant Beast—Contest between the Knight and Slander—The Knight wounded—Slander flies—Credulity leads Psyche to the Castle of Suspicion— Psyche deluded, laments the desertion of her Knight to the train of Inconstancy— Psyche betrayed by Suspicion into the power of Jealousy—Persuaded by him that her Knight, by whom she was then abandoned, was indeed Love—Psyche delivered by her Knight—Reconciliation.

Canto IV

Full gladsome was my heart ere while to tell
How proud Ambition owned superior Love;
For ah! too oft his sterner power could quell
The mild affections which more gently move,
5   And rather silent fled than with him strove:
For Love content and tranquil saw with dread
The busy scenes Ambition's schemes approve,
And by the hand of Peace obscurely led,
From pride of public life disgusted ever fled.

10   There are who know not the delicious charm
Of sympathising hearts, let such employ
Their active minds; the trumpet's loud alarm

Shall yield them hope of honourable joy,
And courts may lure them with each splendid toy:
15   But ne'er may vanity or thirst of fame
The dearer bliss of loving life destroy!
Oh! blind to man's chief good who Love disclaim,
And barter pure delight for glory's empty name!

Blest Psyche! thou hast 'scaped the tyrant's power!
20   Thy gentle heart shall never know the pain
Which tortures pride in his most prosperous hour:
Yet dangers still unsung for thee remain,
Nor must thou unmolested hope to gain
Immortal beauty's never failing spring,
25   Oh! no—nor yet tranquillity attain:
But though thy heart the pangs of doubt may sting,
Thy faithful knight shall yet thy steps in safety bring.

Warned by late peril now she scarcely dares
Quit for one moment his protecting eye:
30   Sure in his sight, her soul of nought despairs,
And nought looks dreadful when that arm is nigh
On which her hopes with confidence rely;
By his advice their constant course they bend,
He points where hidden danger they should fly,
35   On him securely, as her heaven-sent friend,
She bids her grateful heart contentedly depend.

Oh! who the exquisite delight can tell,
The joy which mutual confidence imparts!
Or who can paint the charm unspeakable
40   Which links in tender bands two faithful hearts?
In vain assailed by fortune's envious darts,
Their mitigated woes are sweetly shared,
And doubled joy reluctantly departs:
Let but the sympathising heart be spared,
45   What sorrow seems not light, what peril is not dared?

Oh! never may suspicion's gloomy sky
Chill the sweet glow of fondly trusting love!

Nor ever may he feel the scowling eye
Of dark distrust his confidence reprove!
50   In pleasing error may I rather rove,
With blind reliance on the hand so dear,
Than let cold prudence from my eyes remove
Those sweet delusions, where nor doubt nor fear
Nor foul disloyalty nor cruel change appear.

55   The noble mind is ever prone to trust,
Yet love with fond anxiety is joined;
And timid tenderness is oft unjust,
The coldness which it dreads, too prompt to find,
And torture the too susceptible mind.
60   Hence rose the gloom which oft o'er Psyche stole
Lest he she loved, unmindful or unkind,
Should careless slight affection's soft control,
Or she long absent lose her influence o'er his soul.

'Twas evening, and the shades which sudden fell
65   Seemed to forebode a dark unlovely night,
The sighing wood-nymphs from their caves foretell
The storm which soon their quiet shall affright:
Nor cheering star, nor moon appears in sight,
Nor taper twinkles through the rustling leaves
70   And sheds afar its hospitable light,
But hark! a dismal sound the ear receives,
And thro' the obscuring gloom the eye strange forms perceives.

It was a helpless female who exclaimed,
Whose blind and aged form an ass sustained:
75   Misshaped and timorous, of light ashamed,
In darksome woods her hard-earned food she gained,
And her voracious appetite maintained,
Though all devouring yet unsatisfied;
Nor aught of hard digestion she disdained,
80   Whate'er was offered greedily she tried,
And meanly served, as slave, whoever food supplied.

A cruel monster now her steps pursued,
Well known of yore and named the Blatant Beast,[81]
And soon he seized his prey with grasp so rude,
85   So fiercely on her feeble body prest,
That had the courteous knight not soon released
Her unresisting limbs from violence,
She must have sunk by his rough jaws opprest;
The spiteful beast, enraged at the defence,
90   Now turned upon the knight with foaming vehemence.

But when his fury felt the couched[82] spear,
On Psyche's unarmed form he bellowing flew;
'Twas there alone the knight his rage could fear,
Swifter than thought his flaming sword he drew,
95   And from his hand the doubtful javelin threw
Lest erring it might wound the trembling fair:
Eager the cruel monster to subdue
He scorned to use his shield's protecting care,
And rashly left his side in part exposed and bare.

100   Sharp were the wounds of his avenging steel,
Which forced the roaring beast to quit the field:
Yet e'er[83] he fled, the knight unused to feel
The power of any foe, or ere[84] to yield
To any arm which sword or spear could wield,
105   Perceived the venom of his tooth impure;
But, with indignant silence, unrevealed
The pain he bore, while through the gloom obscure
The beast in vain pursued urged on his flight secure.

And now the hag, delivered from her fear,
110   Her grateful thanks upon the knight bestowed,
And as they onward went, in Psyche's ear
Her tongue with many a horrid tale o'erflowed,
Which warned her to forsake that venturous road,
And seek protection in the neighbouring grove;
115   Where dwelt a prudent dame, who oft bestowed
Her sage advice, when pilgrims doomed to rove
Benighted there had else with lurking dangers strove.

The knight now softly bade his charge beware
Nor trust Credulity whom well he knew:
120   Yet he himself, harassed with pain and care,
And heedful of the storm which fiercer grew,
Yielded, a path more sheltered to pursue;
Where[85] soon entangled in a gloomy maze
Psyche no longer has her knight in view,
125   Nor sees his page's star-crowned helmet blaze;
Close at her side alone the hag loquacious stays.

Fearful she stops, and calls aloud in vain,
The storm-roused woods roar only in reply,
Anxious her loved protector to regain
130   She trembling listens to Credulity,
Who points where they a glimmering light may spy,
Which through the shade of intervening trees,
And all the misty blackness of the sky,
Casting a weak and dubious ray she sees,
135   And fain[86] by this would seek her terrors to appease.

Yet hoping that, allured by that same light
Which singly seemed through all the gloom to shine,
She there at last might meet her wandering knight,
Thither her footsteps doubtingly incline
140   As best the uncertain path they could divine,
All tangled as it wound through brake[87] and briar:
While to affright her soul at once combine
A thousand shapeless forms of terror dire,
Here shrieks the ill-omened bird, there glares the meteor's fire.

145   In the deep centre of the mazy wood,
With matted ivy and wild vine o'ergrown,
A Gothic castle solitary stood,
With massive walls built firm of murky stone;
Long had Credulity its mistress known,
150   Meagre her form and tawny was her hue,
Unsociably she lived, unloved, alone,
No cheerful prospects gladdened e'er her view,
And her pale hollow eyes oblique their glances threw.

Now had they reached the sad and dreary bower
155   Where dark Disfida[88] held her gloomy state,
The grated casements strong with iron power,
The huge port-cullis creaking o'er the gate,
The surly guards that round the draw-bridge wait,
Chill Psyche's heart, with sad foreboding fears;
160   Nor ever had she felt so desolate
As when at length her guide the porter hears,
And at the well-known call reluctantly appears.

In hall half-lighted with uncertain rays,
Such as expiring tapers transient shed,
165   The gloomy princess sat, no social blaze
The unkindled hearth supplied, no table spread
Cheered the lone guest who weetless[89] wandered,
But melancholy silence reigned around,
While on her arm she leaned her pensive head,
170   And anxious watched, as sullenly she frowned,
Of distant whispers low, to catch the doubtful sound.

Startled to hear an unaccustomed noise,
Sudden she rose, and on the intruders bent
Her prying eye askance; but soon the voice
175   Of her old slave appeased her discontent,
And a half welcome to her guests she lent;
Her frequent questions satisfied at last,
Through all the neighbouring woods her scouts she sent
To seek the knight, while Psyche's tears flowed fast,
180   And all the live-long[90] night in anxious woe she past.

The sullen bell had told the midnight hour,
And sleep had laid the busy world to rest,
All but the watchful lady of that bower,
And wretched Psyche: Her distracted breast
185   The agony of sad suspense opprest,
Now to the casement eagerly she flies,
And now the wished-for voice her fancy blest:
Alas! the screaming night-bird only cries;
Only the drear obscure there meets her straining eyes.

190   Has thy heart sickened with deferred hope?
     Or felt the impatient anguish of suspense?
     Or hast thou tasted of the bitter cup
     Which disappointment's withered hands dispense?
     Thou knowest the poison which o'erflowed from hence
195   O'er Psyche's tedious, miserable hours.
     The unheeded notes of plaintive Innocence
     No longer sooth her soul with wonted[91] powers.
While false Disfida's tales her listening ear devours.

     Of rapid torrents, and deep marshy fens,
200   Of ambushed foes, and unseen pits they tell,
     Of ruffians rushing from their secret dens,
     Of foul magicians and of wizard spell,
     The poisoned lance, and net invisible;
     While Psyche shuddering sees her knight betrayed
205   Into the snares of some enchanter fell,[92]
     Beholds him bleeding in the treacherous shade,
Or hears his dying voice implore in vain for aid.

     At length the cruel messengers return,
     Their trampling steeds sound welcome in her ear;
210   Her rapid feet the ground impatient spurn,
     As eagerly she flies their news to hear.
     Alas! they bring no tidings which may cheer
     Her sorrowing soul opprest, disconsolate!
     "Dismiss" they cry, "each idly timid fear!
215   "No dangers now thy faithless knight await,
"Lured by a wanton fair to bowers of peaceful state.

     "We saw him blithely follow where she led,
     "And urged him to return to thee in vain:
     "Some other knight insultingly he said,
220   "Thy charms might soon for thy protection gain,
     "If still resolved to tread with weary pain
     "The tedious road to that uncertain land,
     "But he should there contentedly remain;
     "No other bliss could now his heart demand
225   "Than that new lady's love, and kindly proffered hand.

A while she stood in silent wonder lost,
And scarce believes the strange abandonment;
No fears like this her heart had ever crost,
Nor could she think his mind so lightly bent
230   Could swerve so quickly from its first intent;
Till sudden bursting forth in angry mood
Disfida gave her indignation vent,
"Ah well I know" she cried, "that wicked brood
"Whose cursed ensnaring arts in vain my cares withstood.

235   "Vile Varia's fickle and inconstant train,
"Perpetual torments of my harassed days;
"Their nightly thefts my fruits, my flowers sustain,
"Their wanton goats o'er all my vineyards graze,
"My corn lies scattered, and my fences blaze,
240   "My friends, my followers, they basely lure,
"I know their mischievous detested ways!
"My castle vainly have I built so sure
"While from their treacherous wiles my life is insecure.

"But I will lead thee to the glittering sands,
245   "Where shines their hollow many-coloured fane:
"There, as the circling group fantastic[93] stands,
"Thy truant knight perhaps thou mayst regain
"From the light arts of that seductive train."
She paused—but Psyche spoke not in reply;
250   Her noble heart, which swelled with deep disdain,
Forbad the utterance of a single sigh,
And shamed the indignant tear which started to her eye.

At length with firm, but gentle dignity
And cold averted eye she thus replies:
255   "No! let him go: nor power nor wish have I
"His conduct to control. Let this suffice
"Before my path a surer guardian flies,
"By whose direction onward I proceed
"Soon as the morn's first light shall clear the skies."
260   She ceased, then languishing her griefs to feed,
Her cold dark chamber sought from observation freed.

'Twas there regret indulged the bitter tear,
She feels herself forsaken and alone;
"Behold" she cries, "fulfilled is every fear,
265   "Oh! wretched Psyche, now indeed undone!
"Thy love's protecting care no more is shown,
"He bids his servant leave thee to thy fate,
"Nor longer will the hopeless wanderer own,
"Some fairer, nobler spouse, some worthier mate,
270   "At length by Venus given shall share his heavenly state.

"Oh! most adored! Oh! most regretted love!
"Oh! joys that never must again be mine,
"And thou lost hope, farewell!—vainly I rove,
"For never shall I reach that land divine,
275   "Nor ever shall thy beams celestial shine
"Again upon my sad unheeded way!
"Oh! let me here with life my woes resign,
"Or in this gloomy den for ever stay,
"And shun the scornful world, nor see detested day."

280   "But no! those scenes are hateful to mine eyes,
"And all who spoke or witnessed my disgrace;
"My soul with horror from this dwelling flies
"And seeks some tranquil, solitary place
"Where grief may finish life's unhappy race!"
285   So past she the long night, and soon as morn
Had first begun to show his cheerful face,
Her couch, which care had strewn with every thorn,
With heavy heart she left, disquieted, forlorn.

Not thus Disfida suffered her to part,
290   But urged her there in safety to remain,
Repeating oft to her foreboding heart
That fairy land she never could attain;
But when she saw dissuasion was in vain,
And Psyche bent her journey to pursue,
295   With angry brow she called a trusty train
And bade them keep the imprudent fair in view,
And guard her dangerous path with strict observance true.

In vain their proffered service she declines,
And dreads the convoy of the scowling band;
300   Their hateful presence with her loss combines,
She feels betrayed to the destroyer's hand;
And trembling wanders o'er the dreary land;
While as she seeks to escape Disfida's power,
Her efforts still the officious guards withstand,
305   Led in vain circles many a tedious hour,
Undistanced still she sees the gloomy turrets lower.

Till wearied with her fruitless way, at length
Upon the ground her fainting limbs she threw,
No wish remained to aid exhausted strength,
310   The mazy path she cared not to pursue,
Since unavailing was the task she knew:
Her murmuring guards to seek for food prepare,
Yet mindful of their charge, still keep in view
The drooping victim of their cruel care,
315   Who sees the day decline in terror and despair.

Hark! a low hollow groan she seems to hear
Repeated oft; wondering she looks around:
It seemed to issue from some cavern near,
Or low hut hidden by the rising ground;
320   For, though it seemed the melancholy sound
Of human voice, no human form was nigh;
Her eye no human habitation found,
But as she listening gazed attentively,
Her shuddering ears received the deep and long drawn sigh.

325   The guard who nearest stood now whispering said,
"If aught of doubt remain within thy mind,
"Or wish to know why thus thou wert betrayed,
"Or what strange cause thy faithless knight inclined
"To leave the charge he with such scorn resigned,
330   "Each curious thought thou now mayst satisfy,
"Since here the entrance of a cave we find,
"Where dwells, deep hid from day's too garish eye,
"A sage whose magic skill can solve each mystery."

He staid not her reply, but urged her on
335 Reluctant to the dark and dreary cave;
No beam of cheerful Heaven had ever shone
In the recesses of that gloomy grave,
Where screaming owls their daily dwelling crave.
One sickly lamp the wretched master shewed;
340 Devouring fiend! Who now the prey shall save
From his fell gripe,⁹⁴ whose hands in blood imbrued,
In his own bosom seek his lacerated food?

On the damp ground he sits in sullen woe,
But wildly rolls around his frenzied eye,
345 And gnaws his withered lips, which still o'erflow
With bitter gall; in foul disorder lie
His black and matted locks; anxiety
Sits on his wrinkled brow and sallow cheek;
The wasted form, the deep-drawn, frequent sigh,
350 Some slow consuming malady bespeak,
But medicinal skill the cause in vain shall seek.

"Behold," the treacherous guard exclaimed, "behold,
"At length Disfida sends thy promised bride!
"Let her, deserted by her knight, be told
355 "What peerless lady lured him from her side;
"Thy cares her future safety must provide."
Smiling maliciously as thus he spoke,
He seemed her helpless anguish to deride,
Then swiftly rushing from the den he broke,
360 Ere from the sudden shock astonished she awoke.

She too had fled, but when the wretch escaped
He closed the cavern's mouth with cruel care,
And now the monster placed his form mis-shaped
To bar the passage of the affrighted fair;
365 Her spirits die, she breathes polluted air,
And vaporous visions swim before her sight:
His magic skill the sorcerer bids her share,
And lo! as in a glass, she sees her knight
In bower remembered well, the bower of loose Delight.

370 But oh! what words her feelings can impart!
  Feelings to hateful envy near allied!
  While on her knight her anxious glances dart,
  His plumed helmet, lo! he lays aside;
  His face with torturing agony she spied,
375 Yet cannot from the sight her eyes remove.
  No mortal knight she sees had aid supplied,
  No mortal knight in her defence had strove;
 'Twas Love! 'twas Love himself, her own adored Love.

  Poured in soft dalliance at a lady's feet,
380 In fondest rapture he appeared to lie,
  While her fair neck with inclination sweet
  Bent o'er his graceful form her melting eye,
  Which his looked up to meet in ecstasy.
  Their words she heard not, words had ne'er exprest,
385 What well her sickening fancy could supply,
  All that their silent eloquence confest,
 As breathed the sigh of fire from each impassioned breast.

  While thus she gazed, her quivering lips turn pale,
  Contending passions rage within her breast,
390 Nor ever had she known such bitter bale,[95]
  Or felt by such fierce agony opprest:
  Oft had her gentle heart been sore distrest,
  But meekness ever has a lenient power
  From anguish half his keenest darts to wrest;
395 Meekness for her had softened sorrow's hour,
 Those furious fiends subdued which boisterous souls devour.

  For there are hearts that, like some sheltered lake,
  Ne'er swell with rage, nor foam with violence;
  Though its sweet placid calm the tempests shake,
400 Yet will it ne'er with furious impotence
  Dash its rude waves against the rocky fence,
  Which nature placed the limits of its reign:
  Thrice blest! who feel the peace which flows from hence,
  Whom meek-eyed gentleness can thus restrain,
405 Whate'er the storms of fate, with her let none complain!

That mild associate Psyche now deserts,
Unlovely passions agitate her soul,
The vile magician all his art exerts,
And triumphs to behold his proud control;
410   Changed to a serpent's hideous form, he stole
O'er her fair breast to suck her vital blood;
His poisonous involutions[96] round her roll;
Already is his forked tongue imbrued,
Warm in the stream of life, her hearts pure purple flood.

415   Thus wretchedly she falls Geloso's[97] prey!
But her, once more, unhoped for aid shall save!
Admitted shines the clear blue light of day
Upon the horrors of that gloomy grave;
Her knight's soft voice resounds through all the cave,
420   The affrighted serpent quits his deadly hold,
Nor dares the vengeance of his arm to brave,
Shrunk to a spider's form, while many a fold
Of self-spun web obscene the sorcerer vile enrolled.

Scarce had the star of his attendant youth
425   Blazed through the cavern, and proclaimed the knight,
When all those spells and visions of untruth,
Bred in dark Erebus,[98] and nursed in night,
Dissolving vanished into vapour light;
While Psyche, quite exhausted by her pains,
430   And hardly trusting her astonished sight,
Now faint and speechless in his arms remains,
Nor memory of the past, nor present sense retains.

Borne from the cavern, and to life restored,
Her opening eyes behold her knight once more,
435   She sees whom lost with anguish she deplored;
Yet a half-feigned resentment still she bore,
Nor sign of joy her face averted wore,
Though joy unuttered panted at her heart;
In sullen silence much she pondered o'er
440   What from her side induced him to depart,
And all she since had seen by aid of magic art.

Was it then all a false deluding dream
That wore the semblance of celestial Love?
On this her wavering thoughts bewildered seem
445   At length to rest; yet onward as they move,
Though much his tender cares her doubts reprove,
And though she longs to hear, and pardon all,
Silence she still preserves: awhile he strove
Her free and cheerful spirits to recall,
450   But found the task was vain; his words unnoticed fall.

Now in his turn offended and surprised,
The knight in silence from her side withdrew;
With pain she marked it, but her pain disguised,
And heedless seemed her journey to pursue,
455   Nor backward deigned to turn one anxious view
As oft she wished; till mindful of his lord,
Constance alarmed affectionately flew,
Eager to see their mutual peace restored,
And blames[99] her cold reserve in many a soft breathed word.

460   "O Psyche! wound not thus thy faithful knight,
"Who fondly sought thee many an anxious hour,
"Though bleeding yet from that inglorious fight,
"Where thou wert rescued from the savage power
"Of that fell beast who would thy charms devour:
465   "Still faint with wounds, he ceased not to pursue
"Thy heedless course: let not displeasure lower
"Thus on thy brow: Think not his heart untrue!
"Think not that e'er from thee he willingly withdrew!"

With self-reproach and sweet returning trust,
470   While yet he spoke, her generous heart replies,
Soft melting pity bids her now be just,
And own the error which deceived her eyes;
Her little pride she longs to sacrifice,
And ask forgiveness of her suffering knight;
475   Her suffering knight, alas! no more she spies,
He has withdrawn offended from her sight,
Nor can that gentle voice now hope to stay his flight.

Struggling no more her sorrows to restrain,
Her streaming eyes look round with anxious fear;
480   Nor are those tender showers now shed in vain,
Her soft lamenting voice has reached his ear,
Where latent he had marked each precious tear;
Sudden as thought behold him at her feet!
Oh! reconciling moment! charm most dear!
485   What feeling heart thy pleasures would repeat,
Or wish thy dearly purchased bliss, however sweet?

The smiles of joy which swell her glowing cheek,
And o'er her parting lips divinely play,
Returning pleasure eloquently speak,
490   Forgetful of the tears which lingering stay,
(Like sparkling dew drops in a sunny day)
Unheeded tenants of rejoicing eyes;
His wounds her tender care can well repay,
There grateful kindness breathes her balmy sighs,
495   Beneath her lenient hand how swiftly suffering flies!

Freed from the mazes of Disfida's groves,
The opening landscape brightens to their view;
Psyche, with strength revived, now onward moves
In cheerful hope, with courage to renew
500   Repeated toils, and perils to pursue:
Thus when some tender plant neglected pines,
Shed o'er its pendant head the kindly dew,
How soon refreshed its vivid lustre shines!
Once more the leaf expands, the drooping tendril twines.

505   Thus cheered, the knight intreats her to impart
The dangers which her way had since befell,
Her timid lips refuse to speak the art
Which clothed him in a form she loved so well;
That she had thought him Love, she blushed to tell!
510   Confused she stopped; a gentle pause ensued;
What chance had brought him to the daemon's cell
She then enquires; what course he had pursued,
And who his steps had led throughout the mazy wood.

Sooth[100] he had much to say, though modest shame
515   His gallant deeds forbade him to declare;
For while through those bewildering woods he came,
Assisted by his page's active care,
He had detected Varia's wily snare,
And forced her wanton retinue to flee.
520   With like disgrace, malignant in despair,
Disfida's slaves their plots defeated see,
Their feeble malice scorned, their destined victims free.

But he had marked the traces of their feet,
And found the path which to the cavern led:
525   Whence now, rejoicing in reunion sweet,
Their way together cheerfully they tread,
Exempt awhile from danger and from dread;
While Psyche's heart, with confidence more bold,
Full oft the hour of rapture pictured,
530   When those celestial charms she should behold,
And feel the arms of Love once more his bride enfold.

CANTO V

ARGUMENT

Introduction—Charm of Poetry—Psyche beholds the Palace of Chastity—Pleads for the admission of her Knight—Obtains it through the intervention of Hymen—Hymen celebrating the triumphs of Chastity—Psyche, enraptured, desires to devote herself solely to the service of Chastity—Entrusted by her to the protection of the Knight—Psyche's Voyage—Tempest—Coast of Spleen—Psyche received and sheltered by Patience.

Canto V

Delightful visions of my lonely hours!
Charm of my life, and solace of my care!
Oh! would the muse but lend proportioned powers,
And give me language, equal to declare
5   The wonders which she bids my fancy share,

When rapt in her to other worlds I fly,
See angel forms unutterably fair,
And hear the inexpressive harmony
That seems to float on air, and warble through the sky.

10   Might I the swiftly glancing scenes recall!
Bright as the roseate clouds of summer's eve;
The dreams which hold my soul in willing thrall,
And half my visionary days deceive,
Communicable shape might then receive,
15   And other hearts be ravished with the strain;
But scarce I seek the airy threads to weave,
When quick confusion mocks the fruitless pain,
And all the fairy forms are vanished from my brain.

Fond dreamer! meditate thine idle song!
20   But let thine idle song remain unknown,
The verse which cheers thy solitude, prolong;
What, though it charm no moments but thine own,
Though thy loved Psyche smile for thee alone,
Still shall it yield thee pleasure, if not fame,
25   And when escaped from tumult thou hast flown
To thy dear silent hearth's enlivening flame,
There shall the tranquil muse her happy votary claim!

My Psyche's wanderings then she loves to trace,
Unrols the glowing canvass to my sight;
30   Her chaste calm eye, her soft attractive grace,
The lightning of her heavenly[101] smile so bright,
All yield me strange and unconceived delight:
Even now entranced her journey I pursue,
And gaze enraptured on her matchless knight;
35   Visions of love, pure, innocent and true!
Oh! may your graceful forms for ever bless my view!

See as they tread the green, soft-levelled plain,
Where never weed, nor noxious plant was found!
Psyche, enchanted, bids her knight explain
40   Who rules that lovely and well cultured ground,

Where fairest flowers and purest springs abound:
"Oh! object of my anxious cares," (he cried,
As with a half-breathed sigh he gazed around)
"A stranger here, full oft I vainly tried
45   "Admittance to obtain, and sooth the sovereign's pride.

"Here Castabella[102] reigns, whose brow severe
"Oft chilled my sanguine spirit by its frown;
"Yet have I served her with adoring fear,
"Though her ungrateful scorn will oft disown
50   "The faithful homage by her servant shown;
"Me she hath banished from her fair domain,
"For crimes my loyal heart had never known;
"While thus excluded vainly I complain,
"And feel another's guilt my injured honour stain.

55   "With false assumption of my arms and name,
"Knight of the Bleeding Heart miscalled too long,
"A vile impostor has disgraced my fame,
"And much usurped by violence and wrong,
"Which to the virgin queen by right belong;
60   "On me her irritated vengeance falls,
"On me, repulsed by force of arms so strong
"That, never suffered to approach her walls,
"Unheard, indignant truth in vain for justice calls.

"Yet she alone our progress can assist,
65   "And thou, Oh Psyche! must her favour gain,
"Nor from thy soft entreaties ere[103] desist
"Till thou free entrance for thy knight obtain;
"Here let his faithful services remain
"Fixed on thy grateful heart! nor thou consent,
70   "Nor let their force thy gentleness constrain
"To leave him, thus disgraced, yet innocent,
"Thine undeserved neglect forsaken to lament."

While yet he speaks, before her ravished eyes
The brilliant towers of Castabella shine;
75   The sun that views them from unclouded skies

Sheds not through heaven a radiance more divine;
The adamantine walls with strength combine
Inimitable lustre ever clear;
Celestial temple! 'tis not lips like mine
80   Thy glories can reveal to mortal ear,
Or paint the unsullied beams which blaze for ever here.

Approaching now the well defended gates,
Which placed at distance guard the sacred fane,
Their lowly suit a stern repulse awaits,
85   The timid voice of Psyche pleads in vain,
Nor entrance there together can they gain:
While yet they stay, unwilling to retreat,
The dove, swift-sailing through the ethereal plain,
Has reached already Castabella's seat,
90   And in her spotless breast has found a welcome sweet.

Caressing oft her well remembered guest,
Serener smiles illumed her softened brow,
The heaven-sent messenger her soul confest,
And mildly listened to his murmurs low,
95   Which seemed in pleading eloquence to flow;
His snowy pinions then he wide displayed,
And gently lured her from her throne to go
Even to the gates, where Psyche blushing stayed
Beside her awe-struck knight half doubtingly afraid.

100   That form majestic might the bravest awe;
Yet Psyche gazed with love unmixed with fear,
And felt those charms her soul attracted draw
As to maternal tenderness most dear;
Congenial souls! they at one glance appear
105   Linked to each other by a mutual tie:
Her courteous voice invites her to draw near.
And lo! obedient to their sovereign's eye,
To Psyche's willing steps the barriers open fly.

But to the lion, and his gallant lord
110   Sudden the affrighted guards the portals close.

Psyche looks back, and mindful of her word,
Mindful of him who saved her from her foes,
Guide of her course, and soother of her woes,
The tear that started to her downcast eye,
115   The deepening blush which eloquently rose,
Silent assistant of the pleading sigh,
To speed the unuttered suit their powers persuasive try.

And now the knight, encouraged to approach,
Asserts his injured fame, and justice claims,
120   Confutes each charge, repels each foul reproach,
And each accusing falsehood boldly shames,
While conscious innocence his tongue inflames;
A firm attachment to her reign he vows,
The base impostor's guilty madness blames,
125   And, while the imputed crimes his spirit rouse,
No intercourse with him his nobler soul allows.

Mean time his faithful page had not been mute,
And he had found a ready warm ally;
For (while his master urged the eager suit,)
130   As through the goodly train he cast his eye,
He chanced exulting mid the group to spy
A joyous youth, his fondly cherished friend;
Hymen, the festive, love-attending boy,
Delighted his assistance hastes to lend,
135   Laughing unbars the gates, and bids the parley end.

Around their queen the timid virgins crowd,
Who half consentingly receives the knight,
And checks her sportive boy, whose welcome loud
Speaks his gay triumph and his proud delight;
140   Yet graceful smiles her happy guests invite
To share the feast with sacred honours blest;
The palace opens to their dazzled sight;
Still as they gazed, the adoring eye confest
That wondering awe which filled each consecrated breast.

145   All was divine, yet still the fairest queen
        Like Dian[104] mid her circling nymphs appear'd,
        Or as Minerva[105] on Parnassus[106] seen,
        When condescendingly with smiles she cheered
        The silent Muses who her presence feared:
150   A starry crown its heavenly radiance threw
        O'er her pale cheek; for there the rose revered
        The purer lilies of her saint-like hue,
    Yet oft the mantling blush its transient visits knew.

        The hand of Fate, which wove of spotless white
155   Her wondrous robe, bade it unchangeable
        Preserve unsullied its first lustre bright,
        Nor ere[107] might be renewed that sacred spell
        If once destroyed; wherefore to guard it well
        Two hand-maids she entrusts with special care,
160   Prudence and Purity, who both excel,
        The first in matron dignity of air,
    The last in blooming youth unalterably fair.

        Favourite of heaven! she at her birth received
        With it the brilliant zone that bound her waist,
165   Which, were the earth of sun and stars bereaved,
        By its own light beneficently cast
        Could cheer the innocent and guide the chaste:
        Nor armour ever had the virgin bore,
        Though oft in warlike scenes her youth she past,
170   For while her breast this dazzling cestus[108] wore,
    The foe who dared to gaze beheld the light no more.

        But when her placid hours in peace are spent,
        Concealed she bids its latent terrors lie,
        Sheathed in a silken scarf, with kind intent
175   Wove by the gentle hand of Modesty;
        And see, the blushing maid with down-cast eye
        Behind her mistress hides her charms retired!
        While foremost of the group, of stature high,
        Firm Courage lifts her brow by Truth inspired,
180   Who holds a crystal lamp in flames celestial fired.

See, fresh as Hebe[109] blooming Temperance stand,
Present the nectared fruits, and crown the bowl!
While bright-eyed Honour leads the choral band,
Whose songs divine can animate the soul,
185   Led willing captive to their high control:
They sing the triumphs of their spotless queen,
And proudly bid immortal fame enrol
Upon her fairest page such as had been
The champions of her cause, the favourites of her reign.

190   From Pallas[110] first begins the lofty song,
And Cynthia[111] brightest goddess of the skies;
To her the virgin deities belong,
And each beholds her with a sister's eyes;
The mystic honours next of Fauna rise;[112]
195   Her solemn rites which purest hands require;
And Vesta,[113] who her virgins taught to prize,
And guard the sacred symbols of the fire
Which earth could ne'er revive if suffered to expire.

Emblem divine of female purity!
200   Whose trust betrayed to like sad fate shall doom;
Pursued by scorn, consigned to infamy,
The hapless victims perish in their bloom
Mid the dark horrors of a living tomb;[114]
Effulgent queen! Thou wilt the pure defend
205   From the dark night of this opprobrious gloom;
Nor even with life thy favouring smiles shall end,
They bid illustrious fame beyond the grave extend.

First of the noble youths whose virtue shone
Conspicuous chief in Castabella's train,
210   They sing the firm unmoved Bellerophon;[115]
And Peleus[116] flying the Magnesian plain,[117]
Pursued by all a wanton's fierce disdain.
You too, Hyppolytus,[118] their songs employ!
Beloved by Phaedra, but beloved in vain;
215   With the chaste honours of the Hebrew boy,[119]
Which time shall ne'er obscure, nor idle scorn destroy.

Nor was unsung whom on Hymettus' brow[120]
The bright Aurora wooed with amorous care;
He, mindful of his sacred nuptial vow,
220   Refused the goddess though celestial fair,
Breathing pure perfumes and ambrosial air:
Of wanton Circe's baffled arts they tell,
And him, too wise her treacherous cup to share,[121]
Who scored the enchantress, and her mystic spell,
225 And all the Syrens' arts could gloriously repel.[122]

The long tried virtue of his faithful spouse
Now sweetly animates the tuneful string,
Unsullied guardian of her virgin vows!
Who twice ten years had wept her wandering king.[123]
230   Acastus' mourning daughter[124] next they sing,
The chaste embrace which clasped her husband's shade:
And thee Dictynna![125] who, with daring spring,
Called from the Cretan rock on Dian's aid:
And still the goddess loves her favourite luckless maid.

235   Pleased to assume herself a name so dear
She bids her altars to Dictynna rise,
Thus called, she ever turns, with willing ear,
To aid each nymph who for her succour cries.
See how the trembling Arethusa[126] flies
240   Through pathless woods, o'er rocks and open plains;
In vain to escape the ravisher she tries,
Fast on her rapid flight Alpheus gains,
And scarce her fainting strength the unequal course sustains.

And now more near his dreaded step she hears,
245   His lengthened shadow flies before her feet,
Now o'er her neck his panting breath appears
To part her locks, which, in disorder sweet,
Ambitious seemed to fan the fervid heat
That flushed her glowing cheek, and heightened charms;
250   Hear how her gasping sighs for aid entreat!
"Dictynna! pitying see my just alarms,
"And snatch thy fainting maid from those polluting arms."

The goddess hears, and in a favouring cloud
Conceals her suppliant from Alpheus' sight;
255   In vain he looks around, and calls aloud,
And wondering seeks the traces of her flight,
Enveloped, still she views him with affright,
An icy coldness creeps o'er all her frame,
And soon, dissolving in a current bright,
260   The silver stream retains her honoured name,
And still unmingled flows, and guards its virgin fame.

'Twas thus Castalia's[127] sacred fountain sprung,
Once a fair nymph by bright Apollo loved;
To Daphne[128] too his amorous strain he sung,
265   But sung in vain: her heart remained unmoved,
No vain delight her modest virtue proved
To be the theme of all his wanton lays;
To shun the god the silvan scene she roved,
Nor prized the flattery of his tuneful praise,
270   Nor one relenting smile his splendid gifts could raise.

Yet were his lips with eloquence endued,
And melting passion warbled o'er his lyre,
And had she yielding listened as he wooed,
The virgin sure had caught the kindling fire,
275   And fallen a victim to impure desire;
For safety cautious flight alone remained,
While tears of trembling innocence require
Her parents aid; and lo! that aid obtained,
How suddenly her charms immortal laurels gained!

280   Dear to the Muses still her honours live:
And they too glory in their virgin name;
To pure delights their tranquil hours they give,
And fear to mingle with a grosser flame
The chaster fires which heaven hath bid them claim;
285   They smiled when Pan,[129] on Ladon's banks deceived,
The fair Syringa clasped, who snatched from shame,
Already had her tuneful form received,
And to the breathing winds in airy music grieved.

Still in that tuneful form[130] to Dian dear
290   She bids it injured innocence befriend;
Commands her train the sentence to revere,
And in her grove, the vocal reeds suspend
Which Virtue may from calumny defend,
Self-breathed, when virgin purity appears,
295   What notes melodious they spontaneous send!
While the rash guilty nymph with horror hears
Deep groans declare her shame to awe-struck wondering ears.

The spotless virgins shall unhurt approach
The stream's rude ordeal,[131] and the sacred fire;
300   See the pure maid,[132] indignant of reproach,
The dreadful test of innocence require,
Amid the holy priests and virgin choir!
See her leap fearless on the blazing shrine!
The lambent flames bright-circling, all aspire
305   Innoxious[133] wreathes around her form to twine,
And crown with lustrous beams the virgin's brow divine.

Nor was the daring Clusia[134] then unsung,
Who plunged illustrious from the lofty tower,
The favouring winds around the virgin clung,
310   And bear her harmless from the tyrant's power;
Nor those, whom Vesta in the trying hour[135]
Protects from slander, and restores to fame;
Nor Clelia, shielded[136] from the arrowy shower;
Nor thou! whose purest hands[137] the Sibyls claim,
315   And bid the modest fane revere Sulpicia's name.

O'er her soft cheek how arch the dimples play,
While pleased the goddess hears Sinope's wiles![138]
How oft she mocked the changeful lord of day,
And many a silvan god who sought her smiles,
320   But chief when Jove her innocence beguiles:
"Grant me a boon," the blushing maid replies,
Urged by his suit: hope o'er his amorous toils
Exulting dawns. "Thine oath is past," she cries;
"Unalterably pure, thy spotless virgin dies!"

325   Rome shall for ages boast Lucretia's[139] name!
          And while its temples moulder into dust
          Still triumph in Virginia's[140] rescued fame,
          And Scipio's[141] victory over baffled lust;
          Even now the strain prophetically just,
330   In unborn servants bids their queen rejoice;
          And in her British beauties firmly trust;
          Thrice happy fair! who still adore her voice,
    The blushing virgin's law, the modest matron's choice!

          Psyche with ravished ear the strain attends,
335   Enraptured hangs upon the heaven–strung lyre;
          Her kindling soul from sensual earth ascends;
          To joys divine her purer thoughts aspire;
          She longs to join the white robed spotless choir,
          And there for ever dwell a hallowed guest:
340   Even Love himself no longer can inspire
          The wishes of the soft enthusiast's breast,
    Who, filled with sacred zeal, would there for ever rest.

          Despising every meaner low pursuit,
          And quite forgetful of her amorous care,
345   All heedless of her knight, who sad and mute
          With wonder hears the strange ungrateful fair,
          A prostrate suppliant, pour the fervent prayer
          To be received in Castabella's train,
          And that in tranquil bliss secluded there,
350   Her happy votary still she might remain,
    Free from each worldly care, and each polluting stain.

          With gracious smile the Queen her favorite heard,
          And fondly raised, and clasped her to her breast;
          A beam of triumph in her eye appeared,
355   While ardent Psyche offered her request,
          Which to the indignant knight her pride confest:
          "Farewell, mistaken Psyche!" he exclaims,
          Rising at length with grief and shame opprest,
          "Since thy false heart a spouse divine disclaims,
360   "I leave thee to the pomp which here thy pride enflames.[142]

"Yet stay, impetuous youth," the Queen replies,
Abashed, irresolute as Psyche stands,
"My favorite's happiness too dear I prize,
"Far other services my soul demands
365   "Than those which here in these sequestered lands
"Her zeal would pay: no, let her bear my fame
"Even to the bowers where Love himself commands:
"There shall my votary reign secure from blame,
"And teach his myrtle groves to echo to my name."

370   "My lovely servant still defend from harms,
"And stem with her yon strong opposing tide:
"Haste, bear her safely to her lover's arms!
"Be it thy care with steady course to guide
"The light-winged bark I will myself provide;
375   "Depart in peace! thou chosen of my heart!
"Leave not thy faithful knight's protecting side.
"Dear to me both, oh may no treacherous art
"Your kindred souls divide, your fair alliance part!

"Here rest to-night! to-morrow shall prepare
380   "The vessel which your destined course shall speed;
"Lo! I consign my Psyche to thy care,
"Oh gallant youth! for so hath Fate decreed,
"And Love himself shall pay the generous meed."
She said, and joined their unreluctant hands.
385   The grateful knight, from fear and sorrow freed,
Receives with hope revived the dear commands,
And Psyche's modest eye no other law demands.

Now Peace with downy step and silent hand
Prepares for each the couch of soft repose:
390   Fairest attendant! she with whispers bland
Bids the obedient eye in slumbers close;
She too the first at early morning goes
With light-foot Cheerfulness the guests to greet.
Who soothed by quiet dreams refreshed arose,
395   Ready the labours of the day to meet,
But first due homage pay at Castabella's feet.

Bright was the prospect which before them shone;
Gay danced the sun-beams o'er the trembling waves;
Who that the faithless ocean had not known,
400   Which now the strand in placid whispers laves,
Could e'er believe the rage with which it raves
When angry Boreas[143] bids the storm arise,
And calls his wild winds from their wintry caves?
Now soft Favonius[144] breathes his gentlest sighs,
405   Auspicious omens wait, serenely smile the skies.

The eager mariners now seize the oar,
The streamers flutter in the favoring gale;
Nor unattended did they leave the shore;
Hymen, whose smiles shall o'er mischance prevail,
410   Sits at the helm, or spreads the swelling sail;
Swift through the parting waves the vessel flies,
And now at distance scarce can Psyche hail
The shore, so fast receding from her eyes,
Or bless the snowy cliffs which o'er the coast arise.

415   Pleased with her voyage and the novel scene,
Hope's vivid ray her cheerful heart expands;
Delighted now she eyes the blue serene,
The purple hills, and distant rising lands,
Or, when the sky the silver queen commands,
420   In pleasing silence listens to the oar
Dashed by the frequent stroke of equal hands,
Or asks her knight if yet the promised shore
May bless her longing eyes when morn shall light restore?

The impatient question oft repeated thus
425   He smiling hears, and still with many a tale,
Or song of heavenly lore unknown to us
Beguiles the live-long night, or flagging sail
When the fresh breeze begins their bark to fail.
Strong ran the tide against the vessel's course,
430   And much they need the kind propitious gale
Steady to bear against its rapid force,
And aid the laboring oars, their tedious last resource.

But lo! the blackening surface of the deep
With sullen murmurs now begins to swell,
435   On ruffled wing the screaming sea fowl sweep
The unlovely surge, and piteous seem to tell
How from the low-hung clouds with fury fell
The demons of the tempest threatening rage;
There, brooding future terrors, yet they dwell,
440   Till with collected force dread war they wage,
And in convulsive gusts the adverse winds engage.

The trembling Psyche, supplicating Heaven,
Lifts to the storm her fate-deploring eye,
Sees o'er her head the livid lightnings driven,
445   Then, turned in horror from the blazing sky,
Clings to her knight in speechless agony:
He all his force exerts the bark to steer,
And bids the mariners each effort try
To escape the rocky coast which threatens near,
450   For Hymen taught the youth that dangerous shore to fear.

Who has not listened to his tuneful lay,
That sings so well the hateful cave of Spleen?
Those lands, submitted to her gloomy sway,
Now open to their view a dreary scene,
455   As the sad subjects of the sullen queen
Hang o'er the cliffs, and blacken all the strand;
And where the entrance of the cave is seen
A peevish, fretful, melancholy band,
Her ever wrangling slaves, in jarring concert stand.

460   Driven by the hurricane they touch the shore,
The frowning guards prepare to seize their prey,
The knight (attentive to the helm no more)
Resumes his arms, and bids his shield display
Its brilliant orb: "Psyche, let no dismay
465   "Possess thy gentle breast," he cheerly cries,
"Behind thy knight in fearless safety stay,
"Smile at the dart which o'er thee vainly flies,
"Secure from each attack their powerless rage despise.

"Soon shall the fury of the winds be past,
470   "Serener skies shall brighten to our view,
"Let us not yield to the imperious blast
"Which now forbids our vessel to pursue
"Its purposed course; soon shall the heavens renew
"Their calm clear smile; and soon our coward foes,
475   "Despairing thus our courage to subdue,
"Shall cease their idle weapons to oppose,
"And unmolested peace restore our lost repose."

Still as he spoke, where'er he turned his shield
The darts drop quivering from each slackened bow,
480   Unnerved each arm, no force remains to wield
The weighty falchion,[145] or the javelin throw;
Each voice half choked expires in murmurs low,
A dizzy mist obscures their wondering sight,
Their eyes no more their wonted fury know,
485   With stupid awe they gaze upon the knight,
Or, as his voice they hear, trembling disperse in flight.

Yet raged the storm with unabated power;
A little creek the laboring vessel gains;
There they resolve to endure the blustering hour,
490   The dashing billows, and the beating rains.
Soon as the bark the sheltering bay attains,
And in the shallows moored securely rides,
Attentive still to soften all her pains,
The watchful knight for Psyche's ease provides;
495   Some fisher's hut perchance the shelving harbour hides.

Deep in the steril bank a grotto stood,
Whose winding caves repel the inclement air,
Worn in the hollowed rock by many a flood
And sounding surge that dashed its white foam there,
500   The refuge now of a defenceless fair,
Who issuing thence, with courteous kind intent
Approached the knight, and kindly bad him share
Whatever good indulgent Heaven had lent
To cheer her hapless years in lonely suffering spent.

505   More sweet than Health's fresh bloom the wan hue seemed
        Which sat upon her pallid cheek; her eye,
        Her placid eye, with dove-like softness beamed;
        Her head unshielded from the pitiless sky,
        Loose to the rude wild blast her tresses fly,
510   Bare were her feet which prest the shelly shore
        With firm unshrinking step; while smilingly
        She eyes the dashing billows as they roar,
And braves the boisterous storms so oft endured before.

        Long had she there in silent sorrow dwelt,
515   And many a year resigned to grief had known;
        Spleen's cruel insolence she oft had felt,
        But never would the haughty tyrant own,
        Nor heed the darts which, from a distance thrown,
        Screened by her cavern she could safely shun;
520   The thorny brakes she trod for food alone,
        Drank the cold stream which near the grotto run,
And bore the winter's frosts and scorching summer's sun.

        In early youth, exchanging mutual vows,
        Courage had wooed and won his lovely bride;
525   Tossed on those stormy seas, her daring spouse
        From her fond arms the cruel waves divide,
        And dashed her fainting on that rock's rough side.
        Still hope she keeps, and still her constant heart
        Expects to hail with each returning tide
530   His dear remembered bark; hence can no art
From those unlovely scenes induce her to depart.

        When the vexed seas their stormy mountains roll,
        She loves the shipwrecked mariner to cheer;
        The trembling wretch escaped from Spleen's control,
535   Deep in her silent cell conceals his fear,
        And panting finds repose and refuge here;
        Benevolently skilled each wound to heal,
        To her the sufferer flies, with willing ear
        She wooes them all their anguish to reveal,
540   And while she speaks, they half forget the woes they feel.

Now to her cave has Patience gently brought
Psyche, yet shuddering at the fearful blast,
Largely she heaped with hospitable thought
The blazing pile, and spread the pure repast;
545   O'er her chilled form her own soft mantle cast,
And soothed her wearied spirits to repose,
Till all the fury of the storm is past,
Till swift receding clouds the heavens disclose,
And o'er subsiding waves pacific sunshine glows.

CANTO VI

ARGUMENT

Introduction—The power of Love to soften adversity—Exhortation to guard Love from the attacks of Ill-temper, which conduct to Indifference and Disgust—Psyche becalmed—Psyche surprised and carried to the Island of Indifference—Pursued and rescued by her Knight—The Voyage concluded—Psyche brought home beholds again the Temple of Love—Is reunited to her Lover, and invited by Venus to receive in Heaven her Apotheosis—Conclusion.

Canto VI

When pleasure sparkles in the cup of youth,
And the gay hours on downy wing advance,
Oh! then 'tis sweet to hear the lip of Truth
Breathe the soft vows of love, sweet to entrance
5   The raptured soul by intermingling glance
Of mutual bliss; sweet amid roseate bowers,
Led by the hand of Love, to weave the dance,
Or unmolested crop life's fairy flowers,
Or bask in Joy's bright sun through calm unclouded hours.

10   Yet they, who light of heart in May-day pride
Meet love with smiles, and gaily amorous song,
(Though he their softest pleasures may provide,
Even then when pleasures in full concert throng)
They cannot know with what enchantment strong

15   He steals upon the tender suffering soul,
         What gently soothing charms to him belong,
         How melting sorrow owns his soft control,
  Subsiding passions hushed in milder waves to roll.

         When vexed by cares and harassed by distress,
20   The storms of fortune chill thy soul with dread,
         Let Love, consoling Love! still sweetly bless,
         And his assuasive balm benignly shed;
         His downy plumage o'er thy pillow spread
         Shall lull thy weeping sorrows to repose,
25   To Love the tender heart hath ever fled,
         As on its mother's breast the infant throws
  Its sobbing face, and there in sleep forgets its woes.

         Oh! fondly cherish then the lovely plant,
         Which lenient Heaven hath given thy pains to ease;
30   Its lustre shall thy summer hours enchant,
         And load with fragrance every prosperous breeze,
         And when rude winter shall thy roses seize,
         When nought through all thy bowers but thorns remain,
         This still with undeciduous charms shall please,
35   Screen from the blast and shelter from the rain,
  And still with verdure cheer the desolated plain.

         Through the hard season Love with plaintive note
         Like the kind red-breast tenderly shall sing,
         Which swells mid dreary snows its tuneful throat,
40   Brushing the cold dews from its shivering wing,
         With cheerful promise of returning spring
         To the mute tenants of the leafless grove.
         Guard thy best treasure from the venomed sting
         Of baneful peevishness; oh! never prove
45 How soon ill-temper's power can banish gentle Love!

         Repentance may the storms of passion chase,
         And Love, who shrunk affrighted from the blast,
         May hush his just complaints in soft embrace,
         And smiling wipe his tearful eye at last:

50   Yet when the wind's rude violence is past
          Look what a wreck the scattered fields display!
          See on the ground the withering blossoms cast!
          And hear sad Philomel[146] with piteous lay
     Deplore the tempest's rage that swept her young away.

55   The tears capricious beauty loves to shed,
          The pouting lip, the sullen silent tongue,
          May wake the impassioned lovers tender dread,
          And touch the spring that clasps his soul so strong;
          But ah beware! the gentle power too long
60   Will not endure the frown of angry strife;
          He shuns contention, and the gloomy throng
          Who blast the joys of calm domestic life,
     And flies when discord shakes her brand with quarrels rife.

          Oh! he will tell you that these quarrels bring
65   The ruin, not renewal of his flame:
          If oft repeated, lo! on rapid wing
          He flies to hide his fair but tender frame;
          From violence, reproach, or peevish blame
          Irrevocably flies. Lament in vain!
70   Indifference comes the abandoned heart to claim,
          Asserts for ever her repulsive reign,
     Close followed by disgust and all her chilling train.

          Indifference, dreaded power! what art shall save
          The good so cherished from thy grasping hand?
75   How shall young Love escape the untimely grave
          Thy treacherous arts prepare? or how withstand
          The insidious foe, who with her leaden band
          Enchains the thoughtless, slumbering deity?
          Ah never more to wake! or e'er expand
80   His golden pinions to the breezy sky,
     Or open to the sun his dim and languid eye.

          Who can describe the hopeless silent pang
          With which the gentle heart first marks her sway?
          Eyes the sure progress of her icy fang

85   Resistless, slowly fastening on her prey;
        Sees Rapture's brilliant colours fade away,
        And all the glow of beaming sympathy;
        Anxious to watch the cold averted ray
        That speaks no more to the fond meeting eye
90   Enchanting tales of love, and tenderness, and joy.

        Too faithful heart! thou never canst retrieve
        Thy withered hopes: conceal the cruel pain!
        O'er thy lost treasure still in silence grieve,
        But never to the unfeeling ear complain;
95   From fruitless struggles dearly bought refrain,
        Submit at once—the bitter task resign,
        Nor watch and fan the expiring flame in vain;
        Patience, consoling maid, may yet be thine,
    Go seek her quiet cell and hear her voice divine!

100   But lo! the joyous sun, the soft-breathed gales
        By zephyrs sent to kiss the placid seas,
        Curl the green wave, and fill the swelling sails,
        The seamen's shouts, which jocund hail the breeze,
        Call the glad knight the favoring hour to seize;
105   Her gentle hostess Psyche oft embraced,
        Who still solicitous her guest to please
        On her fair breast a talisman had placed,
    And with the valued gem her parting blessing graced.

        How gaily now the bark pursues its way
110   Urged by the steady gale! while round the keel
        The bubbling currents in sweet whispers play;
        Their force repulsive now no more they feel;
        No clouds the unsullied face of heaven conceal,
        But the clear azure one pure dome displays,
115   Whether it bids the star of day reveal
        His potent beams, or Cynthia's milder rays
    On deep cerulean skies invite the eye to gaze.

        Almost unconscious they their course pursue,
        So smooth the vessel cuts the watery plain,

120   The wide horizon to their boundless view
       Gives but the sky, and Neptune's ample reign:
       Still the unruffled bosom of the main
       Smiles undiversified by varying wind;
       No toil the idle mariners sustain,
125   While, listless, slumbering o'er his charge reclined,
     The pilot cares no more the unerring helm to mind.

       With light exulting heart glad Psyche sees
       Their rapid progress as they quit the shore:
       Yet weary languor steals by slow degrees
130   Upon her tranquil mind; she joys no more
       The never changing scene to wander o'er
       With still admiring eye; the enchanting song
       Yields not that lively charm it knew before,
       When first enraptured by his tuneful tongue
135 She bad her vocal knight the heavenly strain prolong.

       A damp chill mist now deadens all the air,
       A drowsy dullness seems o'er all to creep,
       No more the heavens their smile of brightness wear,
       The winds are hushed, while the dim glassy deep
140   Oppressed by sluggish vapours seems to sleep;
       See his light scarf the knight o'er Psyche throws,
       Solicitous his lovely charge to keep
       From still encreasing cold; while deep repose
     Benumbs each torpid sense and bids her eye-lids close.

145   Now as with languid stroke they ply the oars,
       While the dense fog obscures their gloomy way;
       Hymen, well used to coast these dangerous shores,
       Roused from the dreaming trance in which he lay,
       Cries to the knight in voice of dread dismay,
150   "Steer hence thy bark, oh! yet in time beware;
       "Here lies Petrea,[147] which with baneful sway
       "Glacella[148] rules, I feel the dank cold air,
     "I hear her chilling voice, methinks it speaks despair!"

Even while he speaks, behold the vessel stands
155   Immoveable! in vain the pilot tries
The helm to turn; fixed in the shallow strands,
No more obedient to his hand, it lies,
The disappointed oar no aid supplies
While sweeping o'er the sand it mocks their force.
160   The anxious knight to Constance now applies,
To his oft tried assistance has recourse,
And bids his active mind design some swift resource.

Debating doubtfully awhile they stood,
At length on their united strength rely,
165   To force the bark on the supporting flood;
They rouse the seamen, who half slumbering lie,
Subdued and loaded by the oppressive sky.
Then wading mid the fog, with care explore
What side the deepest waters may supply,
170   And where the shallows least protect the shore,
While thro' their darksome search the star sheds light before.

Mean time deep slumbers of the vaporous mist
Hang on the heavy eye-lids of the fair;
And Hymen too, unable to resist
175   The drowsy force of the o'erwhelming air,
Laid at her feet at length forgets his care.
When lo! Glacella's treacherous slaves advance,
Deep wrapt in thickest gloom; the sleeping pair[149]
They seize, and bear away in heedless trance,
180   Long ere her guardian knight suspects the bitter chance.

Thus the lorn traveller imprudent sleeps
Where his high glaciers proud Locendra[150] shews;
Thus o'er his limbs resistless torpor creeps,
As yielding to the fatal deep repose
185   He sinks benumbed upon the Alpine snows,
And sleeps no more to wake; no more to view
The blooming scenes his native vales disclose,
Or ever more the craggy path pursue,
Or o'er the lichened steep[151] the chamois chase renew.

190   Lo! to their queen they bear their sleeping prey,
        Deep in her ice-built castle's gloomy state,
        There on a pompous couch they gently lay
        Psyche, as yet unconscious of her fate,
        And when her heavy eyes half opening late
195   Dimly observe the strange and unknown scenes,
        As in a dream she views her changed estate,
        Gazing around with doubtful, troubled mien,
Now on the stupid crowd, now on their dull proud queen.

        With vacant smile, and words but half exprest,
200   In one ungracious, never-varying tone,
        Glacella welcomes her bewildered guest,
        And bids the chief supporter of her throne
        Approach and make their mighty mistress known.
        Proud Selfishness, her dark ill-favoured lord!
205   Her gorgeous seat, which still he shared alone
        He slowly leaves obedient to her word,
And ever as he moved the cringing train adored.

        Nought of his shapeless form to sight appears,
        Impenetrable furs conceal each part;
210   Harsh and unpleasing sounds in Psyche's ears
        That voice which had subdued full many a heart;
        While he, exerting every specious art,
        Persuades her to adore their queen's control;
        Yet would he not Glacella's name impart,
215   But with false title, which she artful stole
From fair Philosophy, deludes the erring soul.

        "Rest happy fair," he cries, "who here hast found
        "From all the storms of life a safe retreat,
        "Sorrow thy breast henceforth no more shall wound,
220   "Nor care invade thee in this quiet seat:
        "The voice of the distressed no more shall meet
        "Thy[152] sympathizing ear; another's woes
        "Shall never interrupt the stillness sweet,
        "Which here shall hush thee to serene repose,
225   "Nor damp the constant joys, these scenes for thee disclose.

"Fatigue no more thy soft and lovely frame
"With vain benevolence and fruitless care;
"No deep heaved sigh shall here thy pity claim,
"Nor hateful want demand thy wealth to share;
230   "For thee shall Independence still prepare
"Pleasures unmingled, and for ever sure;
"His lips our sovereign's peaceful laws declare,
"Centre existence in thyself secure,
"Nor let an alien shade thy sunshine ere[153] obscure."

235   He spoke, and lo! unnumbered doors unfold,
And various scenes of revelry display;
Here Grandeur sunk beneath the massive gold;
Here discontented Beauty pined away,
And vainly conscious asked her promised sway;
240   Here Luxury prepared his sumptuous feast,
While lurking Apathy behind him lay
To poison all the insipid food he drest,
And shake his poppy crown o'er every sated guest.

The hireling minstrels strike their weary lyre,
245   And slumber o'er the oft repeated strain;
No listless youth to active grace they fire,
Here Eloquence herself might plead in vain,
Nor one of all the heartless crowd could gain;
And thou, oh! sweeter than the Muses song,
250   Affection's voice divine! with cold disdain
Even thou art heard, while mid the insulting throng
Thy daunted, shivering form moves timidly along!

Thus o'er the oiled surface softly slides
The unadmitted stream, rapid it flows,
255   And from the impervious plain pellucid glides;
Repulsed with gentle murmurs thus it goes,
Till in the porous earth it finds repose,
Concealed and sheltered in its parents breast;
Oh! man's best treasure in this vale of woes!
260   Still cheer the sad; and comfort the distrest,
Nor ever be thy voice by Selfishness opprest!

Psyche with languid step he leads around,
And bids her all the castle's splendor see;
Here Dissipation's constant sports abound,
265   While her loose hand in seeming bounty free,
Her scentless roses, painted mimickry,
Profusely sheds; here Pride unheeded tells
To nodding crowds his ancient pedigree;
And Folly with reiterated spells
270 To count her spotted cards the yawning group compels.

"See how, attentive to her subjects ease,"
To their reluctant prey exclaims her guide,
"Each fleeting joy of life she bids them seize,
"Anxious for each gay pastime to provide;
275   "See her fast spreading power increasing wide,
"Adored and worshipped in each splendid dome!
"Lo! Beauty glows for ever at her side,
"She bids her cheek the unvarying rose assume;
"And Bacchus[154] sees for her his votive ivy bloom.

280   "Is aught then wanting in this fairy bower?
"Or is there aught which yet thy heart can move?"
That heart, unyielding to their sovereign's power,
In gentle whispers sighing answers, "Love!"
While scornful smiles the fond reply reprove,
285   "Lo!" he exclaims, "thy vanquished Cupid view;
"He oft with powerful arms had vainly strove
"Our sovereign's rocky fortress to subdue,
"Now, subject to her reign, he yields obedience due."

Wondering she gazed around, and where he points,
290   An idiot child in golden chains she spies,
Rich cumbrous gems load all his feeble joints,
A gaudy bandage seels[155] his stupid eyes,
And foul Desire his short-lived torch supplies;
By the capricious hand of Fashion led,
295   Her sudden starts with tottering step he tries
Submissive to attend; him had she bred,
And Selfishness himself the nursling ever fed.

With lustre false his tinsel arms to deck
Ungraceful ornaments around him shone,
300   Gifts of his sportive guide; she round his neck
A glittering cord insultingly had thrown,
Loading its pendant[156] purse with many a stone
And worthless dross, and ever as he went,
His leaden darts, with wanton aim unknown,
305   Now here, now there, in careless chance she sent,
That oft their blunted force in empty air was spent.

Shocked, from the gross imposture Psyche turned
With horror and disgust her fearful eye;
Her fate forlorn in silent anguish mourned,
310   And called her knight with many a hopeless sigh;
But see, the crowds in sudden tumult fly!
The doors, fast closing to exclude some foe,
Proclaim to Psyche's hopes her hero nigh:
Escaping from her guard she flies, when lo!
315   His form the bursting gates in awful beauty shew.

"Fly from these dangerous walls," his page exclaims;
"Swift let us haste our floating bark to gain!
"See thy knight's wondrous dart in terror flames;
"Soon shall these ice-built walls no shape retain!
320   "Nor can their Queen his dreaded sight sustain."
Scarcely she heard while rapidly she fled,
Even as a bird, escaped the wily train[157]
The fowler with destructive art had spread,
Nor panting stays its flight, nor yet forgoes its dread.

325   See how astonished now the crowd supine,
Roused by his potent voice confused arise,
In tottering masses o'er their heads decline
Dissolving walls; they gaze with wild surprise,
And each affrighted from the ruin flies;
330   Pitying he views the vain unfeeling band
Beneath his care, a vile and worthless prize,
Their Queen alone his vengeful arms demand,
But unknown force was her's[158] his terrors to withstand.

A shield she had of more than Gorgon[159] power,
335 And whom she would she could transform to stone,
     Nor ever had it failed her till that hour;
     She proves his form invincible alone,
     And calls its force petrific on her own.
     Amazed he sees the indurated[160] train,
340 The callous tenants of the silent throne,
     And all the marble subjects of their reign,
Inviolably hard, their breathless shape retain.

     The magic shield he thence in triumph bore,
     Resolved, in pity to the human race,
345 Her noxious hands its might should guide no more,
     And bade the seas conceal its Hydra[161] face;
     Oh! kindly meant, though much defeated grace!
     For though the o'erwhelming weight of sounding waves
     Conceal its rugged orb a little space,
350 Snatched by Glacella from the dark deep caves,
Once more the arm of Love with potent spell it braves.

     But Psyche, rescued from their cruel scorn,
     Urges her knight to hasten from the shore;
     The buoyant vessel on the billows borne
355 Rides proudly o'er the mounting surge once more;
     Again they spread the sails, the feathered oar
     Skims with impatient stroke the sparkling tide;
     The blushing Hymen now their smiles restore
     Again to frolic gaily at their side,
360 Tho' still their playful taunts reproach their slumbering guide.

     Psyche looks back with horror on the coast;
     Black, drear, and desolate is all the scene:
     The rocky cliffs still human shape may boast;
     There the sad victims of the cruel Queen,
365 Memorials of her baneful power, are seen;
     No vine crowned hills, no glowing vales appear,
     Nor the white cottage laughs upon the green,
     The black and leafless thorn alone is there,
And the chill mountains lift their summits wild and bare.

370   Her spirits lighten as they leave behind
          The dreary prospect of Glacella's isle;
          She blest with gladdened heart the light-winged wind
          That bears her swiftly from a scene so vile;
          With glistening eye, and hope's prophetic smile,
375   She hears her knight foretel their dangers o'er,
          That sure success shall crown their fated toil,
          And soon arriving at that happy shore,
      Love shall again be found, and leave his bride no more.

          Now, from light slumbers and delicious dreams,
380   The jocund cry of joy aroused the fair;
          The morn that kissed her eyes with golden beams,
          Bade her the universal transport share;
          Divinely breathed the aromatic air,
          And Psyche's heart, half fainting with delight,
385   In the peculiar odour wafted there
          Recalled the breezes which, o'er scenes most bright,
      Their wings of perfume shook, and lingering stayed their flight.

          The lovely shore the mariners descry,
          And many a gladsome cheer the prospect hails;
390   Its graceful hills rise full before the eye,
          While eagerly expanding all their sails
          They woo the freshness of the morning gales;
          The approaching scenes new opening charms display,
          And Psyche's palpitating courage fails,
395   She sees arrived at length the important day,
      Uncertain yet of power the mandate to obey.

          But one dear object every wish confines,
          Her spouse is promised in that bower of rest;
          And shall the sun, that now so cheerful shines,
400   Indeed behold her to his bosom prest,
          And in his heavenly smiles of fondness blest?
          Oh! 'tis too much! exhausted life she fears
          Will struggling leave her agitated breast,
          Ere to her longing eyes his form appears,
405   Or the soft hand of Love shall wipe away her tears.

Oh! how impatience gains upon the soul
When the long promised hour of joy draws near!
How slow the tardy moments seem to roll!
What spectres rise of inconsistent fear!
410   To the fond doubting heart its hopes appear
Too brightly fair, too sweet to realize;
All seem but day-dreams of delight too dear!
Strange hopes and fears in painful contest rise,
While the scarce trusted bliss seems but to cheat the eyes.

415   But safely anchored in the happy port,
Led by her knight the golden sands she prest;
His heart beat high, his panting breath heaved short,
And sighs proclaim his agitated breast
By some important secret thought opprest:
420   "At length," he cries, "behold the fated spring!
"Yon rugged cliff conceals the fountain blest,
    ("Dark rocks its crystal source o'ershadowing,)
"And Constance swift for thee the destined urn shall bring."

He speaks, but scarce she hears, her soul intent
425   Surveys as in a dream each well known scene;
Now from the pointed hills her eye she bent
Inquisitive o'er all the sloping green;
The graceful temple meet for Beauty's queen,
The orange groves that ever blooming glow,
430   The silvery flood, the ambrosial air serene,
The matchless trees that fragrant shade bestow,
All speak to Psyche's soul, all seem their queen to know.

Let the vain rover, who his youth hath past
Misled in idle search of happiness,
435   Declare, by late experience taught at last,
In all his toils he gained but weariness,
Wooed the coy goddess but to find, that less
She ever grants where dearest she is bought;
She loves the sheltering bowers of home to bless,
440   Marks with her peaceful hand the favourite spot,
And smiles to see that Love has home his Psyche brought.

On the dear earth she kneels the turf to press,
With grateful lips and fondly streaming eyes,
"Are these the unknown bowers of Happiness?
445 "Oh! justly called, and gained at last!" she cries,
As eagerly to seize the urn she flies.
But lo! while yet she gazed with wondering eye
Constance ascends the steep to gain the prize,
The eagle's eyry is not built so high
450 As soon she sees his star bright blazing to the sky.

With light and nimble foot the boy descends,
And lifts the urn triumphant in his hand;
Low at the turf-raised altar Psyche bends,
While her fond eyes her promised Love demand;
455 Close at her side her faithful guardians stand,
As thus with timid voice she pays her vows:
"Venus, fulfilled is thine adored command,
Thy voice divine the suppliant's claim allows,
"The smile of favour grant, restore her heavenly spouse.

460 Scarce on the altar had she placed the urn,
When lo! in whispers to her ravished ear
Speaks the soft voice of Love! "Turn, Psyche, turn!
"And see at last, released from every fear,
"Thy spouse, thy faithful knight, thy lover here!"
465 From his celestial brow the helmet fell,
In joy's full glow, unveiled his charms appear,
Beaming delight and love unspeakable,
While in one rapturous glance their mingling souls they tell.

Two tapers thus, with pure converging rays,
470 In momentary flash their beams unite,
Shedding but one inseparable blaze
Of blended radiance and effulgence bright,
Self-lost in mutual intermingling light;
Thus, in her lover's circling arms embraced,
475 The fainting Psyche's soul, by sudden flight,
With his its subtlest essence interlaced;
Oh! bliss too vast for thought! by words how poorly traced!

Fond youth! whom Fate hath summoned to depart,
And quit the object of thy tenderest love,
480   How oft in absence shall thy pensive heart
Count the sad hours which must in exile move,
And still their irksome weariness reprove;
Distance with cruel weight but loads thy chain
With every step which bids thee farther rove,
485   While thy reverted eye, with fruitless pain,
Shall seek the trodden path its treasure to regain.

For thee what rapturous moments are prepared!
For thee shall dawn the long expected day!
And he who ne'er thy tender woes hath shared,
490   Hath never known the transport they shall pay,
To wash the memory of those woes away:
The bitter tears of absence thou must shed,
To know the bliss which tears of joy convey,
When the long hours of sad regret are fled,
495   And in one dear embrace thy pains compensated!

Even from afar beheld, how eagerly
With rapture thou shalt hail the loved abode!
Perhaps already, with impatient eye,
From the dear casement she hath marked thy road,
500   And many a sigh for thy return bestowed:
Even there she meets thy fond enamoured glance;
Thy soul with grateful tenderness o'erflowed,
Which firmly bore the hand of hard mischance,
Faints in the stronger power of joy's o'erwhelming trance.

505   With Psyche thou alone canst sympathise,
Thy heart benevolently shares her joy!
See her unclose her rapture beaming eyes,
And catch that softly pleasurable sigh,
That tells unutterable ecstasy!
510   While hark melodious numbers through the air,
On clouds of fragrance wafted from the sky,
Their ravished souls to pious awe prepare,
And lo! the herald doves the Queen of Love declare.

With fond embrace she clasped her long lost son,
515   And gracefully received his lovely bride,
"Psyche! thou hardly hast my favour won!"
With roseate smile her heavenly parent cried,
"Yet hence thy charms immortal, deified,
"With the young Joys, thy future offspring fair,
520   "Shall bloom for ever at thy lover's side;
"All ruling Jove's high mandate I declare,[162]
"Blest denizen of Heaven! arise its joys to share."

She ceased, and lo! a thousand voices, joined
In sweetest chorus, Love's high triumph sing,
525   There, with the Graces and the Hours entwined,
His fairy train their rosy garlands bring,
Or round their mistress sport on halcyon wing;
While she enraptured lives in his dear eye,
And drinks immortal love from that pure spring
530   Of never-failing full felicity,
Bathed in ambrosial showers of bliss eternally!

Dreams of Delight farewell! your charms no more
Shall gild the hours of solitary gloom!
The page remains—but can the page restore
535   The vanished bowers which Fancy taught to bloom?
Ah no! her smiles no longer can illume
The path my Psyche treads no more for me;
Consigned to dark oblivion's silent tomb
The visionary scenes no more I see,
540   Fast from the fading lines the vivid colours flee!

Poems

1802–1809

LORD OF HEARTS BENIGNLY CALLOUS[1]

Lord of Hearts benignly callous
   Come Insensibility,
Stop the streams which feeling hallows
   Smother each impassioned sigh.

5   Let this bosom idly beating
   Task at length a moment's peace!
Passion's tide at length retreating
   Bid the furious tempest cease.

O'er my path once sweetly smiling
10   Crowned with flowers, unseen his dart,
Love with blushes soft beguiling
   Seized my fascinated heart.

Soon the traitor rudely rending
   From my brow the rosy crown,
15   Pityless of storms impending
   Drove me forth to Fate's dark frown.

Harassed, struggling, faint and weary
   Long kind Hope reluctant clung,
Shudd'ring at my prospects dreary
20   All her brilliant chords unstrung.

Thus the quivering lamp expiring
   Sudden shines with trembling beams
Extinguished now, now life desiring
   Shoots forth momentary gleams.

25   Mute her voice, and dropt her lyre
   Now at last she sinks opprest,
Day's bright beams with her retire
   O'er me clouds and darkness rest.

Joy and Hope and Love and Pleasure!
30   Here I bid you all adieu!
Thee sweet Peace my last best treasure
      All my wishes now pursue.

O'er my senses softly stealing
      Blest Indifference kindly come!
35 From this agony of feeling
      Hide me in thy tranquil gloom.

Banish each bright form delusive,
      From my aching eyes remove,
Fancy's torch with glare obtrusive
40   Visions of seductive Love!—

Tis Thy Command, and Edwin Shall Obey[1]

Tis thy command, and Edwin shall obey
      My voice shall sound submissive to thy will,
Tho' sad my lute and mournful be my lay
      Yet tis enough, thy slave obeys thee still.

5   Poor as I am, my love how dare I own
      No boon to offer, but a faithful heart,
Unblest with fortune's gifts, obscure, unknown
      With nought my portion but this tuneful art.

Yet pardon sentiments as warm and pure
10   As tho' by royal lips they were profest,
My thoughts are noble, tho' my state obscure
      And truth and honour harbour in this breast.

The Muses too have deign'd to touch my tongue
      Early they charmed my simple ravished ear,
15 Each rising sun a tender hopeless song
      To thee I'll raise if thou will gently hear.

No hope presumptuous shall my bosom fire,
   My sole ambition only thee to please,
A look shall pay the efforts of my lyre,
20   A smile the highest boon my soul would seize.

Attendant on thy steps Oh might I guard
   Protect, defend thee with an anxious eye,
No ill should reach thee which this arm could ward
   Thy servant would I live thy champion die.

25   Art thou for some blest youth reserved by fate
   The nuptial song I'll raise, the garland weave
Nor mix my woes nor envy his high state
   But boast myself thy minstrel and thy slave.

WHEN THE BITTER SOURCE OF SORROW[1]

When the bitter source of sorrow
   When the last farewell is sighed,
With no hope to cheer tomorrow
   Joys kind promises denied.

5   Yet we dwell with ling'ring pleasure
   On that distant doubtful day,
Which may yield us back our treasure
   All our sorrows to repay.

Can the tender heart declare
10   Meeting what it fondly loves
Why the bliss cannot compare
   With the pang which parting proves

Happy hour so long expected!
   Joy impatiently desired
15   Disappointed half dejected
   What have I from thee acquired?

Take again the transient pleasure
　　Willingly I yield it up,
But restore my dearest treasure
20　　Give me back delicious Hope.

THE PICTURE. WRITTEN FOR ANGELA[1]

Yes, these are the features already imprest
　　So deep by the pencil of Love on my heart;
Within their reflection they find in this breast,
　　Yet something is wanting—Ah where is the art
5　That to painting so true can that something impart?

Oh where is the sweetness that dwelt[2] on that lip?
　　And where is the smile that enchanted my soul?
From those roses no sweet dew of Love can I sip,[3]
　　Nor meet the soft glance that[4] with magic controul
10　O'er the chords of my heart so bewitchingly stole.

Cold, cold is that eye unimpassioned its beams,
　　They speak not of tenderness Love or delight!
Oh where is the heart-thrilling rapture that streams
　　From the heavenly blue of that circle so bright
15　That sunshine of pleasure which gladdened my sight.

Yet come to my bosom oh image adored!
　　And sure thou shalt feel the soft flame of my heart,
The glow sympathetic once more be restored
　　Once more it shall warm thee, ah cold as thou art,
20　And to charms so beloved its own feelings impart.

Oh come and while others his form may behold
　　And he on another with fondness may smile;
To thee shall my wrongs, shall my sorrows be told,
　　And the kiss I may give thee those[5] sorrows the while
25　Like the memory of joys which are past shall beguile!

FLED ARE THE SUMMER HOURS OF JOY AND LOVE[1]

Fled are the summer hours of joy and love!
   The brilliant season of delight is o'er
Alone mid leafless woods I silent rove
   The voice so dear enchants these bowers no more!
5   Yet sweet the stillness of this calm retreat,
   As toward the sunny bank I pensive stray,
The muse affords her consolations sweet,
   And sooths with memory's charms my lonely way—
Here led by Flora[2] o'er the pathless wild
10   I woo sweet Nature in her private haunts
The rarer flower which long neglected smiled
   My curious eye unspeakably enchants—
Ev'n now the season our mild Autumn yields
   Forbids not yet my timid foot to roam,
15   A languid Sun illumes yet verdant fields
   And many a lingering blossom yet can bloom—
While smiling science shews her Withering's page[3]
   And half unveils her most attractive face,
Reveres the memory of the Swedish sage[4]
20   And bids me nature's charms delighted trace
But if the gloomy clouds or northern blast
   Endear the comforts of our social hearth,
How swift the calm domestic hours are past!
   How far superior to the hours of mirth!—
25   Oft when my heart the call of joy would spurn
   By sad involuntary gloom opprest,
To thee my plaintive harp I languid turn
   Thy silver sounds can sooth my soul to rest—
Or wrapt in loved imagination's dream
30   I hear the voice I see the form so dear,
In visionary charms they present seem
   The well known accents vibrate on mine ear—
I see those eyes of bright celestial blue,
   Those laughing eyes beam love and sympathy,
35   And o'er the mantling cheek the rosy hue
   The blush of kindling hope and tender joy—

I have not lost thee then my soul's best part!
    I still can hear thee talk of love and bliss!
Can pour out all the fulness of my heart,
40   Oh what felicity can vie with this!
How oft will fancy thro' the watchful nights
    Picture thy form my sorrows to beguile,
The glance of soft affection now delights
    Now archly gay I see thy sportive smile
45   I see thee oft with pensive tender eye
    Mark our blue hills thy gay horizon bound
While fond imagination with a sigh
    Measures the space of the far distant ground—
Beyond those hills constrained a while to dwell
50   Full many a lonely hour the thought can cheer
The shades of sorrow oft it can dispel
    And turn to tenderness the saddest tear—
But thou whose image never quits this heart
    Art thou unmindful of thine absent love
55   Ah no! I bid the cruel thought depart
    And each suggestion of distrust reprove—
And yet too oft awaking from my trance,
    My brilliant day-dream of unreal joy,
I think with anguish that thy tender glance
60   Has charmed in vain my captivated eye—
Sad victim of each heart forboding care
    I think with pity on my future lot
Even now some happier eye thy smiles may share
    Thy vows of tenderness to me forgot—
65   On such sad doubts each trembling thought employed
    Oh what a dreary silence there appears!
Life offers nothing but a joyless void
    While my youth wastes in unavailing tears—
Thou canst not see me in those cruel hours
70   Thou knowest not Love but as he smiles and charms
Thy stronger mind feels not dejection's powers
    Nor knows the pang which tenderness alarms—
Yet let thine heart the pains of absence share,
    Oh! be but constant and I yet am blest,
75   Alive to each suspicion kindly spare
    The trembling feelings of this anxious breast!—

SONNET[1]

'Tis past the cruel anguish of suspence
    Shall vex my soul no more—I know him lost
    For ever lost to me—and all that most
On earth I valued, bought with dear expense
5   Of peaceful nights, and days of innocence
    Lies withered in my grasp—Oh idle cost
    Of squandered hours! Oh vows of anguish tost
To the wild winds, that mocked the eloquence
    Of grief indignant, yet constrained to speak!
10   Now all is past, the desolating storm
    No longer may the bowers of bliss deform
    Its furious malice has no more to seek
Each high aspiring hope lies all laid low
Sweep on ye powerless winds, o'er your fall'n trophies blow!—

OH SEAL MY SAD AND WEARY EYES[1]

Oh seal my sad and weary eyes
    Sleep soft suspence of human woe!
The day's long hours may sure suffice
    For sighs to swell and tears to flow!

5   Oh be the night to sorrow dear
    Sacred to cheering calm repose
Nor let the secret wasting tear
    Forbid the watchful lid to close.

Let me resign this load of grief
10   In thy divinely soothing arms,
For thou canst yield some short relief
    Ev'n to the soul Remorse alarms—

How blest are they who lay them down!
    And sleep to wake in life no more!
15   At least if dreams of power unknown
    Haunt not Death's dark, and silent shore.

What hope in life for me remains?
   What prospect cheers the dreary gloom?
Ungrateful heart! forget thy pains
20   Love shall some future night illume!

Banish the agonising thought
   How swift the parting hour must come,
Be future woes no longer sought
   Nor thus anticipate thy doom.

25 I yet may hope some blissful night
   Shall bring me all in life I prise,
And to my captivated sight
   Restore the joy of these fond eyes!—

His tender voice I yet shall hear
30   His eye shall beam delight and love!
The happy hour that brings him near
   Awhile shall every pang remove.

Breathless with trembling joy once more
   This agitated heart shall leap,
35 The hours of long impatience oer
   Shall hail once more his well known step!—

Assured his heart is only mine
   On this dear hope enchanted dwell,
And let its influence benign,
40   Suspicious dreary clouds dispel

Come dear delusions! loved deceit
   This weight of fear awhile remove
With flattering dreams my reason cheat
   Hide every form that threatens Love!—

45 O say in bonds of happiest fate
   Our days united yet shall live!
Oh say that peace and love await
   The fairer hours our hopes shall give!—

Let me forget the cruel truth
50   That peace with innocence is gone
That ceaseless tears shall waste my youth
    All hope, all bliss, forever gone.

PEACE, PEACE, NOR UTTER WHAT I MUST NOT HEAR[1]

Peace, peace, nor utter what I must not hear
    Too much already hast thou been believed
Think not thy words can reach alone mine ear
    In this weak heart too easily received.

5   Why dost thou mock me with a vain complaint?
    Why speak of feelings which thou dost not know?
Too well thy lips can fond affection paint
    But from thine heart those accents never flow!

What dost thou wish what would this language mean
10   What can the idle boast to thee avail?
To wound my peace, to blast my hours serene
    O'er every hope of future bliss prevail.

Is this thy sport? Ah thoughtless and unjust?
    For I have marked thee with a jealous eye,
15   Since reason first forbad my heart to trust,
    And virtue called me from the snare to fly.

Why should I tell the struggles which have torn
    This simply credulous, this trusting heart?
As down the stream of fond affection borne
20   I saw the tranquil shores of peace depart.

As the light flag when borne against the breeze
    Looks back and trembles with reluctance vain,
My vanquished soul reflects on former ease
    Yet powerless sinks submissive to the chain.

25   Oft when my friendly fate had bad us part
            Thy well feign'd sorrow could prevent my cure,
        And absence cherished in my grateful heart
            Friendship it called so innocent and pure.

        Yet when returned I saw this friend advance
30   Expecting joy to sparkle in his eye,
        Chilled I beheld the cold averted glance
            And proudly checked the involuntary sigh

        Then how with scorn my weakness I despised
            The folly which was lur'd by falsehood's tale
35   When other smiles than those I thought were prised
            Could o'er thy false or changeful heart prevail.

        Back then with trembling haste to wisdoms side
            Offended delicacy, bade me flee,
        Accept my peace restored by wounded pride
40   And think no more of tenderness or thee

        Why then with cruel art and idle pain
            Revive the sentiments I still deplore?
        Why seek what thus you slighted to regain
            And swell this breast with anxious sighs once more

45   In vain the foldings of thine heart I seek
            At length by reason, or by truth to trace,
        Conjecture cannot from thy conduct speak
            But baffled yields to sad surprise her place.

        I sought no arts to captivate thy soul
50   To blast the prospects of thy opening youth
        Such selfish vanity could ne'er control
            The heart which loves with innocence and truth—

        Torture no more this agitated breast
            With false seductive hopes of joy and love,
55   Suffer in calm indifference to rest
            The feelings Prudence bids me disapprove—

Yet a short while and this sad timid eye
   No more shall meet thee with reproachful glance
No claims have I to make or thou deny
60   For ease alone this wearied bosom pants

But to Have Hung Enamoured on Those Lips[1]

But to have hung enamoured on those lips
To drink the passion of those beaming eyes!
Yet, yet to feel th'intoxicating power
Which stole into my heart at every word
5   Of that soft voice that vibrates in my ear—
Thus to have loved and loved to extasy
And be beloved again—Oh rapturous bliss!
Destroyed and lost! Yes all on earth conspired
Against the voice of Heaven; against my hopes;
10   And must I never more indulge the dreams
That love to call thee by a name even yet
More fond more sacred more endeared than lover?
Must I resign the image of delight
When in the gentle pressure of thine arms
15   Methinks I hang upon that neck adored
Gaze on thine angel smile or taste thy kiss?
Forced to abandon thee to give thee up!
Forget the hopeless and forever lost! . . . .
Hence! hence ye terrible ideas hence! . . . .

Pleasure[1]

Ah, syren Pleasure! when thy flattering strains
Lured me to seek thee through thy flowery plains,
Taught from thy sparkling cup full joys to sip,
And suck sweet poison from thy velvet lip,
5   Didst thou in opiate charms my virtue steep,
Was Reason silent, and did Conscience sleep?

How could I else enjoy thy faithless dreams,
And fancy day-light in thy meteor gleams;
Think all was happiness, that smiled like joy,
10   And with dear purchase seize each glittering toy?
Till roused at length, deep rankling in my heart,
I felt the latent anguish of thy dart!
Oh, let the young and innocent beware,
Nor think uninjured to approach thy snare!
15   Their surest conquest is, the foe to shun;
By fight infected, and by truce undone.
Secure, at distance let her shores be past,
Whose sight can poison, and whose breath can blast.
Contentment blooms not on her glowing ground,
20   And round her splendid shrine no peace is found.
If once enchanted by her magic charms,
They seek for bliss in Dissipation's arms:
If once they touch the limits of her realm,
Offended Principle resigns the helm,
25   Simplicity forsakes the treacherous shore,
And once discarded, she returns no more.
Thus the charmed mariner on every side
Of poisoned Senegal's ill-omened tide,[2]
Eyes the rich carpet of the varied hue
30   And plains luxuriant opening to his view:
Now the steep banks with towering forests crowned,
Clothed to the margin of the sloping ground;
Where with full foliage bending o'er the waves,
Its verdant arms the spreading Mangrove[3] laves;
35   And now smooth, level lawns of deeper green
Betray the richness of the untrodden scene:
Between the opening groves such prospects glow,
As Art with mimic hand can ne'er bestow,
While lavish Nature wild profusion yields,
40   And spreads, unbid, the rank uncultured fields;
Flings with fantastic hand in every gale
Ten thousand blossoms o'er each velvet vale,
And bids unclassed their fragrant beauties die
Far from the painter's hand or sage's eye.
45   From cloudless suns perpetual lustre streams,

And swarms of insects glisten in their beams.
Near and more near the heedless sailors steer,
Spread all their canvas, and no warnings hear.
See, on the edge of the clear liquid glass
50   The wondering beasts survey them as they pass,
And fearless bounding o'er their native green,
Adorn the landscape, and enrich the scene;
Ah, fatal scene! the deadly vapours rise,
And swift the vegetable poison flies,
55   Putrescence loads the rank infected ground,
Deceitful calms deal subtle death around;
Even as they gaze their vital powers decay,
Their wasted health and vigour melt away;
Till quite extinct the animating fire,
60   Pale, ghastly victims, they at last expire.

SONNET[1]

Can I look back, and view with tranquil eye
   The course of my sad life? what vain desires
   Have kindled in my heart consuming fires!
That heart accustomed each extreme to try
5   Of hope and chilling fear. What torturing dreams
   Have vexed my soul with phantoms of despair,
   Which wearied now regrets its wasted care!
Repentant shame its former anguish deems
Unworthy of that sacred spark of life
10   From heaven received! Exhausted in the strife
   To thee Oh God! my sinking soul would turn,
To thee devote the remnant of my years;
Oh thou! who seest my sorrows, calm my fears,
   Nor let thy wrath against thy creature burn!

1802¹

Thy Summer's day was long, but couldst thou think
   Deluded fool, it would for ever last?
   Thy sun indeed mid shrouding clouds, is fast
Declining, and must soon for ever sink.
5   But from the long foreboded gloom to shrink.
   Thus in the hopeless depths of languor cast,
   Declares thy brighter hours were idly past
In thoughtless folly. Didst thou never think
That all thy fond heart prized must pass away?
10   And all those sparkling joys, even when most bright
Were but as heavy drops which trembling play
   On the breeze-shaken leaf? Couldst thou delight
With calm security thro' all the day?
   Nor seek a shelt'ring bower for sure approaching night?

TRANQUILLITY, 1802¹

Oh once again Tranquillity!
   My darksome path illume,
Or must I never, never see
   Thy smiles disperse this gloom.

5   Lo! from the tempest-black'ning sky,
   White beams the placid moon;
The clouds before her radiance fly,
   Thro' night's obscurest noon.

A transient calm, a moment's peace,
10   A struggling, lucid ray,
Bids the wild winds a while to cease,
   And seems to promise day.

Short hope! again the gathering storms
   With rage redoubled rise,
15 And heavy darkness deep deforms
   The silvery-gleaming skies.

Alas! even thus there shone for me
 A gentle flattering hour,
And soothed, I hailed Tranquillity!
20 Thy soft restoring power.

Ah hailed in vain! again involved
 Fast bound in misery;
By whirling anguish quick revolved
 On care's black wheel I fly.

25 And is there then no place of rest,
 Is hope extinct and dead?
Has mercy closed her pitying breast,
 And peace for ever fled?

Oh yet return, return once more,
30 Adored Tranquillity!
This fevered heart to health restore,
 Or lull to apathy!—

Object of all my vows! for thee
 I left the rose-crowned bands,
35 That sail on pleasure's silver sea,
 Or tread her golden sands.

For thee I sought, mid silent glades,
 Deep quiet's lonely bowers;
And hid in melancholy shades,
40 Consumed the languid hours.

But not for me thy placid smile
 Illumined quiet's cell,
And here no dreams the heart beguile
 With transient, joyous spell.

45 The languid hours brought no relief,
 Tho' far from crowds and courts,
The care I shunned, the bitter grief,
 To me alone resorts.

To ——[1]

How hard, with anguish unrevealed,
 Easy and gay to appear;
And teach the lip, by sorrow sealed,
 An artful smile to wear!

5 The heart consumed by secret pains
  Which must not, dare not speak;
Whose silent tongue to none complains,
 Must sigh,—or swelling break.

  Then cease by stern reproof to load
10 Fresh sorrows on the opprest;
Strew not with thorns his rugged road
 Who fainting pants for rest.

Verses Written at the Commencement of Spring[1]

Oh, breathe once more upon my brow,
 Soft gale of Spring, forgotten never!
For thus thy breath appeared as now
 In days of joy, ah! lost for ever.

5 Put forth thy fresh and tender leaves,
  Soft Eglantine, of fragrance early,
Thee Memory first revived perceives,
 From childhood's dawn still welcomed yearly.

  Burst from thy leafy sheath once more,
10 Bright Hyacinth! thy splendour showing,
The sun thy hues shall now restore
 In all their foreign lustre glowing.

  Oh, plume again thy jetty wing,
  Sweet Blackbird, charm thy listening lover!

15 For thus, even thus, I heard thee sing,
        When hopes could smile that now are over.

    And thou, dear Red-breast, let me hear,
        Exchanged once more thy wintery measure,
    Thy notes proclaim the spring-tide near,
20   As they were wont in hours of pleasure.

    The Lark shall mount the sapphire skies
        And wake the grateful song of gladness;
    One general peal from earth shall rise,
        And man alone shall droop in sadness.

25 'Twas here by peace and friendship blest,
        I paid to Spring my yearly duty,
    When last she decked her fragrant breast
        In all the glowing pride of beauty.

    'Twas here the cordial look of love
30   From every eye benignly flowing,
    Bade the kind hours in union move,
        Each lip the ready smile bestowing.

    But where the blooming Cherub Boy,
        Who hailed with us the pleasant season,
35 Whose smiles recalled each childish joy,
        That sadder years resigned to Reason?

    Those bright, those laughing eyes, where Love
        And Innocence are seen embracing;
    Those fairy hands, that graceful move
40   Their fancy-formed circles tracing.

    Oh, haste as thou wast wont to do;
        We'll mount yon shrubby steep together:
    Thy care the first wood flowers shall shew,
        Thyself all blooming as the weather.

45   Haste, sweetest Babe, beloved of all!
         Our cheerful hours without thee languish:
      Ah! hush! . . . . he hears no more thy call!
         Ah! hush! . . . . nor wake a parent's anguish!

      That lip of roses glows no more;
50   That beaming glance in night is clouded;
      Those bland endearments all are o'er,
         In death's dark pall for ever shrouded.

      No, Angel sweetness! not for ever,
         Though Heaven from us thy charms hath hidden,
55   We joy for thee, though forced to sever;
         O favoured guest, thus early bidden!

      Even o'er thy dying couch, sweet Boy!
         A heavenly Messenger presided;
      He beckoned thee to seats of joy,
60   To fields of endless rapture guided.

      No, not for thee this bitter tear,
         It falls for those yet doomed to sorrow;
      Who feel the load of life severe,
         Who mourn the past, nor hope the morrow.

65   It falls for those who, left behind,
         Must fill their woes allotted measure;
      Who muse in hopes to death consigned
         On visions of departed pleasure.

      For those who through life's dreary night
70   Full many a watchful hour shall number,
      And sigh for long delaying light,
         Or envy those who early slumber.

PLEASURE, 1803[1]

See while the juggler pleasure smiles
    Before our dazzled face,
Enchanted by her various wiles
    We watch each sportive grace,
5   But while the fascinating dame
    Holds fixed our wondering eyes,
She robs us of our peace and fame,
    The gems we most should prize.

THE WORLD, 1803[1]

Oh sacrifice no more thy peace, thy joys
To the ungrateful world! it but insults
Thy wasted anguish, and thy votive cares
When served with faithful, unremitting toil
5   It slights, and once provoked, approves no more;
While virtue, ever graciously is prompt
To pay the smallest offering with a smile.
By present compensation, future peace,
She still rewards each sacrifice; and joys
10   With sweet parental fondness to accept
Repentance, as atonement absolute.

THO GENIUS AND FANCY HEREAFTER MAY TRACE[1]

Tho Genius and Fancy hereafter may trace
    The bright pages, commanded by Thee,
Yet early the friend of thy youth has a place
    And Friendship reserv'd it for me—

5   And here may thine eye with complacence a while
    In tenderness love to repose,
And partially give to the *name* that pleas'd smile
    Which thy judgement on others bestows—

Ev'n thus in thy breast such a place would I claim
10   Tho' others a worthier gain,
Where fix'd in thy Love, tho' thy Judgement may blame
        I securely thro life might remain—

And tho' fonder and closer the ties of delight
        That affection may wind round thine heart,
15   Ev'n there let thy friend still ask as her right
        Some dear yet unoccupied part—

Tho taught in thy garden with lustre to live
        The more brilliant exotick shall glow,
Yet the primrose which Spring shall spontaneously give
20   Still suffer perennial to blow²—

And round the tall shrub whose fragrance divine
        Thou hast purchas'd and shielded with care
The wild woodbine its arms shall with confidence twine
        Tho Nature had planted it there—

THE OLD MAID'S PRAYER TO DIANA¹

Since thou and the stars, my dear goddess, decree,
That Old Maid as I am, an Old Maid I must be,
O hear the petition I offer to thee—
        For to bear it must be my endeavour:
5   From the grief of my friendships all dropping around,²
Till not one whom I loved in my youth can be found—
From the legacy-hunters that near us abound,
        Diana, thy servant deliver.

From the scorn of the young and the flaunts³ of the gay,
10   From all the trite ridicule rattled away
By the pert ones who know nothing wiser⁴ to say,
        Or⁵ a spirit to laugh at them, give her:
From repining at fancied neglected desert,
Or, vain of a civil speech, bridling alert,
15   From finical niceness or slatternly dirt;⁶
        Diana, thy servant deliver.

From over solicitous guarding of pelf,[7]
From humour unchecked—that most obstinate elf—
From every unsocial attention to self,
20   Or ridiculous whim whatsoever:
From the vapourish freaks or methodical airs,
Apt to sprout in a brain[8] that's exempted from cares,
From impertinent meddling in others' affairs,
        Diana, thy servant deliver.

25   From the erring attachments of desolate souls,
From the love of spadille,[9] and of matadore[10] voles,
Or of lap-dogs, and parrots, and monkies, and owls,
        Be they ne'er so uncommon and clever:
But chief from the love (with all loveliness flown)
30   Which makes the dim eye condescend to look down
On some ape of a fop, or some owl of a clown,—
        Diana, thy servant deliver.

From spleen at beholding the young more caressed,
From pettish asperity tartly expressed,
35   From scandal, detraction, and every such pest—
        From all, thy true servant deliver:
Nor let satisfaction depart from her cot[11]—
Let her sing, if at ease, and be patient, if not;
Be pleased when regarded, content when forgot,
40   Till the Fates her slight thread shall dissever.

On a Night-blowing Cereus[1]

These moments stolen from sleeping hours,
Thou fairest, frailest of all flowers,
        To thee I dedicate;
For, ah! before to-morrow's dawn,
5   Thy present beauty will be gone,
        So transient is thy state.

Thoughts, while I gaze, crowd on so fast,
I seize my pen in eager haste,

Lest they should perish too;
10   Instruction to attentive hearts,
Our God by various means imparts—
Him in this plant I view.

Why so much beauty lavish'd here,
Fragrance, that fills the ambient air,
15   But gratitude t'excite?
Well pleased, parental goodness gives
To all that on his bounty lives,
The means of pure delight.

Whilst hanging o'er th'exotic bloom,
20   Approaching fast, I see its doom,
Its life is but a span;
I gaze, I weep, but not for thee,
Thou dost but show *my* destiny,
And that of mortal man.

25   In strength, and beauty, man appears
Fitted to stand the shock of years,
We look, and lo, he's gone;
He sinks untimely to the grave,
Nor friends, nor riches, then can save,
30   Nor birth, nor high renown.

And is it thus with life I cry,
Thus do my short-lived pleasures die,
And yet to life I cling?
And dream I still of bliss below,
35   Where disappointment oft, and woe,
The soul with anguish sting?

Thus have I seen the faithful friend,
O'er some lov'd object fondly bend,
And watch the slow decay,
40   Exert in vain the healing art,
Then with a hopeless broken heart,
Resign to death its prey.

Come, ye fair flowers of human race,
Adorned with each external grace,
45 Come, learn th'unheeded truth;
For you these glories are displayed,
'Tis thus ye blossom, thus ye fade,
  E'en in the bud of youth.

Give me those joys that perish not,
50 Give resignation to my lot—
  The gifts of earth enthrall:
Thy gracious presence, Lord, impart,
Speak peace and pardon to my heart,
  And let the world take all.

55 'Tis wisdom's voice—I hear her say,
To young and old, Seek God, this day:
  To-morrow is not yours,
The sacred pages all declare,
Redeeming mercy, sought by prayer,
60 Eternal bliss insures.

But see, these streaks of orient light,
Remind me of departing night,
  And coming day foretell.
The faded flower no longer blows,
65 Its stamens droop, its petals close—
  Sweet monitress, farewell.

To Cowper & his Mary[1]

Mild spirits ye are gone! together gone
 Where ye shall feel the heavy weight no more
 That presses on humanity! Tis oer
The sympathising pang, the patient groan!
5 The cold dark cloud is past! bright day has shone,
 And Mary never shall again deplore
 Or vainly bid mysterious Heav'n restore
The wounded heart, the "noble mind oerthrown"[2]—

And thou sweet boy whose pure & spotless page
10   So early clos'd. Hea'n hath approving ey'd
The infant critic & the blooming guide
    Of suffering genius & disabled age:
Thou with thy cherub smile rejoic'd to hail
Thy friends at length reliev'd from life's deep shadowy vale.

THE ECLIPSE. JAN. 24, 1804[1]

See the moon in all its glory
    Clear, and full and silvery white;
Dearest Tom[2] would sure be sorry
    Not to see so sweet a sight.

5   See how clear the heavens surround her,
    All of deepest, purest blue;
All serene, no clouds around her,
    Calm, dear boy, and mild as you.

Scarce a little hour is over,
10   Come once more and view the sky,
What a change! what gloomy cover
    Half obscures her from our eye.

Alas! 'tis we alone that sever,
    From her orb that lustre bright,
15   She would shine as clear as ever,
    Only we eclipse her light.

Sweetest boy, believe the lesson;
    Would it were my happy fate,
That my verse might deep impress on
20   Thy pure mind a truth so great.

All our light from heaven we borrow,
    All our peace, and all our joy,
Gloomy care, distress and sorrow,
    We may thus for ever fly.

25 All would shine with cloudless pleasure,
　　　Every object that we viewed,
　Could we place our heart's best treasure
　　　In the purest source of good.

　'Tis our passions, 'tis our vices,
30　　　Interpose 'twixt heaven and man,
　And our folly, that despises
　　　Virtue's joy-bestowing plan.

WRITTEN FOR HER NIECE S.K.[1]

Sweetest! if thy fairy hand
　　Culls for me the latest flowers,
Smiling hear me thus demand
　　Blessings for thy early hours:

5 Be thy promised spring as bright
　　　As its opening charms foretel;
　Graced with Beauty's lovely light,
　　　Modest Virtue's dearer spell.

　Be thy summer's matron bloom
10　　　Blest with blossoms sweet like thee;
　May no tempest's sudden doom
　　　Blast thy hope's fair nursery!

　May thine autumn calm, serene,
　　　Never want some lingering flower,
15　Which affection's hand may glean,
　　　Though the darkling mists may lower!

　Sunshine cheer thy wintry day,
　　　Tranquil conscience, peace, and love;
　And thy wintry nights display
20　　　Streams of glorious light above.

To Fortune. From Metastasio[1]

Unstable Goddess! why, with care severe,
   Still dost thou strew with thorns my rugged path?
Thinkst thou I tremble at thy frowns? or e'er
   Will crouch submissive to avert thy wrath?
5 Preserve thy threats for thine unhappy slaves,
   The shuddering victims of thy treacherous power;
My soul, thou knowest, amid o'erwhelming waves,
   Shall smile superior in the roughest hour.
With me as oft as thou wouldest proudly wage
10   The combat urged by thy malicious ire,
Full well thou knowest, that from thy baffled rage
   My soul has seemed fresh vigour to acquire;
So the bright steel beneath the hammer's blows
More polished, more refined, and keener grows.

To the Memory of Margaret Tighe:

Taken from Us June 7th, 1804.—Ætat 85[1]

Sweet, placid Spirit! blest, supremely blest,
Whose life was tranquil, and whose end was rest;
'Tis not for thee our general tears shall flow,
Our loss is selfish, selfish is our woe:
5 We mourn a common parent, common friend,
Centre, round whom thy children loved to bend:
Where hands divided, met again to move
In one sweet circle of united love:
We mourn the tender, sympathising heart
10 So prompt to aid, and share the sufferer's part;
The liberal hand, the kindly patient ear,
Pity's soft sigh, and ever ready tear;
The graceful form, yet lovely in decay,
The peace inspiring eye's benignant ray;
15 The lip of tenderness that soothed the sad,
And loved to bid the innocent be glad;
The gently, softening, reconciling word,

The ever cheerful, hospitable board:
The unassuming wisdom, pious prayers,
20   The still renewed, prolonged, maternal cares:
All—all are lost!—of thee, blest Saint, bereft,
We mourn, to whom impoverished life is left:
Mourn for ourselves! Secure thy lot must be,
With those who pure in heart their God shall see.

Verses Addressed to Henry Vaughan[1]

Verses written by Mrs. Tighe in the blank leaves of a
Horace è done Henry Vaughan London Oct 9: 1804

Quod me non movet oestimatione
Verum ut Muypoouvov—
                       Catullus[2]

Could e'er the genius sense, or skill
    Of those by Phoebus[3] lov'd avail,
To bid in spite of fate's firm will
    The medicinal art prevail;

5   Then had Healths precious gifts been mine
    On this auspicious natal day,
Nor should I languid thus repine
    While life's sad hours consume away.

For, fav'rite of Apollo's care
10   And richly gifted as thou art,
The God his science bad thee share,
    And Nature gave thee feeling heart.

Nor gave in vain—since tho' too oft
    Sweet Health resists thy potent sway,
15   And her gay smiles, and slumbers soft
    Refuse thy summons to obey—

Yet well thou knowst, with gentler spell,
   To smooth the couch of pain and fear,
The darkest shades with hope dispel,
20   The oppress'd console, the languid cheer.[4]

Nor did the partial God deny,
   The soothing charm of Eloquence,
But bad its powers asswasive[5] try
   To lull the pang-awaken'd sense.

25 And Thee, with mildest manners blest
     Enlightend skill, and polish'd mind
Our confidence secure to rest,
   Propitious Fortune bad us find—

Whate'er thine art could do, is done,
30   With each attentive flattering care,
And pleas'd, I proudly wish to own,
   A more than common interest there.

That grateful on some future day,
   If skill at length have power to save,
35 Delighted Memory may say,
   It was a *friend* these comforts gave!

Who on my natal day bestow'd
   The bard thy faultless taste approv'd,
Whose lyre with sweetest numbers flow'd,
40   By thine own Phoebus most belov'd.

Dear valued gift! full many an hour
   Of weary suffering thou shall cheat!
Thy mildly philosophic power
   Shall charm dark Care from Reason's seat.

45 The fell usurper thence shall flee,
     Contentment all my griefs beguiling,
And Hope thro' heaviest nights shall see
   Tomorrow's Sun still brightly smiling.[6]

Verses Written in Sickness. December, 1804[1]

O thou, whom Folly's votaries slight,
 Domestic Love! assuasive power!
Life's ruby gem, which sheds its light
 Through age and sorrow's darkest hour,

5 Sweeter than Pleasure's syren lay,
  Brighter than Passion's fevered dream!
  Still round my pillow soothing stay,
   Still spread thy kindly lambent beam.

  Alas! for him whose youth has bowed
10 Beneath the oppressive hand of pain;
  Whose claim to pity disallowed
   Bids him the unheeded groan restrain.

  Alas! for him who droops like me,
   Who mourns life's faded vigour flown,
15 But finds no soothing sympathy,
   No tender cares his loss atone.

  For him no wakeful eye of love
   Resists the slumbers health would shed,
  With kind assistance prompt to move,
20 And gently prop the aching head:

  With delicate attention paid
   In hope to minister relief,
  He sees no sacrifices made;
   He sees no Mother's anxious grief!

25 But I, poor sufferer, doomed in vain
   To woo the health which Heaven denied,
  Though nights of horror, days of pain
   The baffled opiate's force deride,

Yet well I know, and grateful feel,
30   How much can lenient kindness do,
From anguish half its darts to steal,
    And faded hope's sick smile renew.

Oh! how consoling is the eye
    Of the dear friend that shares our woes!
35   Oh! what relief those cares supply,
    Which watchful, active love bestows!

And these are mine!—Shall I then dare
    To murmur at so mild a lot?
Nor dwell on comforts still my share
40   With thankful and contented thought?

Though destined to the couch of pain,
    Though torn from pleasures once too dear,
Around that couch shall still remain
    The love that every pain can cheer.

45   And o'er that couch, in fondness bent,
    My languid glance shall grateful meet
The eye of love benevolent,
    The tender smile, the tear most sweet.

And still for me affection's hand
50   Shall o'er that couch her roses shed
And woo from ease her poppied band,
    To twine around this throbbing head.

O pitying Heaven! these comforts spare,
    Though age untimely chill gay hope;
55   May Love still crown the sufferer's prayer,
    And gently smooth life's downward slope!

Psalm CXXX. Imitated, Jan. 1805[1]

From Sorrow's depths to thee I cry,
    O thou! who knowest my inmost fear,
The unuttered prayer, the half-breathed sigh,
    Still let it reach thy pitying ear.

5   Unworthy as I am, from thee
      My soul with hope will mercy claim,
For thou hast made us; thou canst see
    With mercy, crimes which man would blame.

If thou shouldst mark with eye severe,
10   Thy children's faults, ah! who could stand?
Ah! who with boldness could appear,
    Or bless his God's creating hand?

But mercy ever dwells with thee,
    Still to forgiveness thou art prone!
15   That all with fearful hope may see
    Their only refuge is thy throne.

On thee with humble confidence,
    My suffering soul for peace shall wait,
Thy love will comfort speak, and hence
20   Thy word my hopes shall animate.

The languid sufferer doomed to weep
    While painful nights their course delay,
Hopeless of sweet refreshing sleep
    Not more desires the morning ray

25   Than this poor harassed troubled soul
    Hath watched for inly-whispered peace,
Till mercy shall its fears controul,
    And bid its anxious sorrows cease.

And still at mercy's sacred seat
30   Let all thy children, Lord! be found;
For love is there, and at thy feet
    Consoling hopes, and joys abound.

ADDRESSED TO MY BROTHER. 1805[1]

Brother beloved! if health shall smile again
    Upon this wasted form and fevered cheek;
    If e'er returning vigour bids these weak
And languid limbs their gladsome strength regain;
5   Well may thy brow the placid glow retain
    Of sweet content, and thy pleased eye may speak
    Thy conscious self-applause: but should I seek
To utter what this heart can feel, ah! vain
Were the attempt! Yet, kindest friends, as o'er
10   My couch ye bend, and watch with tenderness
The being whom your cares could e'en restore
    From the cold grasp of death; say, can you guess
    The feelings which this lip can ne'er express?
Feelings deep fixed in grateful memory's store!

ADDRESS TO THE WEST WIND, WRITTEN AT PARGATE, 1805[1]

"Breathe, balmy spirit of the West,
    "Why are thy gales so long delayed?
"Why must this lacerated breast
    "Vainly invoke thy lenient aid—

5   "For thee I stayed thro' wintry hours,
    "In patient, long captivity;
"And while stern Eurus[2] ling'ring lours,
    "Still blighted Spring's chill'd touch I flee

"Play round this drooping brow once more,
10   "And gently kiss this fever'd cheek;

"To life, to liberty restore,
    "And hope & health returning speak.—

Thus have I oft with fruitless prayer,
    Wooed the mild Zephyr's tardy wing,
15   Languish'd to taste the fresh pure air,
    The promised healing breath of spring.—

Then wooed in vain; perversely now
    Why send us here unwelcome gales?
Why must no breeze in Heaven but thee,
20   Cling fondly to our fetter'd sails.—

Mild as thou art, thy prisoner still
    I droop; by thee unblest, confined,
To me unfriendly seems thy will,
    Absent or present still unkind.—

25   Go to the couch, where languid pain
    Gasping invokes thy clement power;
Go, sport mid Flora's³ glowing train,
    Or sigh o'er young Love's myrtle bower.—

Soon will I hail thee, welcome, kind,
30   And bid thee on thy pinions bear,
To friends so dear I left behind,
    The kiss of loved affection's tear.—

Close in thy chambers of the West,
    Mid spicy sweets luxurious lie;
35   Or watch near the beloved's breast,
    To steal the perfume of a sigh.—

But hie thee hence! & thou my Foe,
    Whose fatal blasts I dread no more;
For once, propitious Eastwind! blow,
40   And waft us to our Isle's green shore.

IMITATION FROM BOÏELDIEU[1]

"Tu plains mes jours troublés"[2]

No longer weep my days in sorrow past,
Tho' clouds and storms pursue me to the last,
For wisdom's lessons are by sorrow taught
And reason claims the awe-instructed thought.
5   When uncurbed youth all wild with passion's fire
Abandoned every rein to mad desire,
Scarce had I felt the raptured, feverish dream
Ere one rude flash, one strong resistless beam
From faith's bright torch aroused me from the trance
10   And all my pleasures vanished at her glance;
To faithless love I gave my willing soul,
Woo'd his deceits and loved his proud controul,
Nay, when he fled, regretted ev'n my pains
And loath'd the freedom which had burst my claims.
15   Daughters of memory! To your shrine I flew,
And offered all my bleeding heart to you!
To you for fame presumptuously I bowed,
And thought your flattering smiles the claim allowed.
But judgement still repulsed me with a frown,
20   And withered with a look my laurel crown.
    How clouded every view that smiled from far,
How dimmed the lustre of my ruling star!
Ere yet it reached its bright meridian blaze,
Pale, thro' malignant vapours, gleamed its rays
25   No golden threads the fates my days allow,
Spun all with lingering hand and sullen brow
No pleasure strews my path with fairy flowers
Me glory calls not from his glittering towers.
Ah! Why must life resign its joys so soon,
30   And shades untimely blacken o'er its noon!
For bright illusions had its morning chest,[3]
Awhile in flattering dreams my soul was blest,
Too transient error! Vanished ere enjoyed,
Why were thy false delights so soon destroyed?
35   Yet friendship, eloquent the soul to calm,

Shall o'er my sorrows shed her healing balm,
She loves the thorny couch of care to smooth
And share the anguish which she best can sooth.
And sure some pleasure this sad heart had left
40   While of her soft support not quite bereft
This shipwrecked bark its course shall yet maintain,
And, piloted by her, the shores of peace shall gain.
When stern misfortune's lips our hopes reprove,
Bid us despair to please, and cease to love,
45   How sweet e'en then the heart to interest,
And with soft pity touch the generous breast
And when Love's magic charms forever end,
Oh! How consoling is the name of Friend!

ADDRESS TO MY HARP[1]

Oh, my loved Harp! companion dear!
    Sweet soother of my secret grief,
No more thy sounds my soul must cheer,
    No more afford a soft relief.

5   When anxious cares my heart oppressed,
    When doubts distracting tore my soul,
The pains which heaved my swelling breast
    Thy gentle sway could oft control.

Each well remembered, practised strain,
10   The cheerful dance, the tender song,
Recalled with pensive, pleasing pain
    Some image loved and cherished long.

Where joy sat smiling o'er my fate,
    And marked each bright and happy day,
15   When partial friends around me sat,
    And taught my lips the simple lay;

And when by disappointment grieved
    I saw some darling hope o'erthrown,

Thou hast my secret pain relieved;
20   O'er thee I wept, unseen, alone.

Oh! must I leave thee, must we part,
    Dear partner of my happiest days?
I may forget thy much-loved art,
    Unused thy melody to raise,

25   But ne'er can memory cease to love
    Those scenes where I thy charms have felt,
Though I no more thy power may prove,
    Which taught my softened heart to melt.

Forced to forego with thee this spot,
30   Endeared by many a tender tie,
When rosy pleasure blessed my lot,
    And sparkled in my cheated eye.

Yet still thy strings, in Fancy's ear,
    With soothing melody shall play;
35   Thy silver sounds I oft shall hear,
    To pensive gloom a silent prey.

MORNING[1]

————*toties nostros Titania questus*
Præterit, et gelido spargit miserata flagello.
                            Statius[2]

O Morn! I hail thy soft, enchanting breezes,
    Thy soul-felt presence, and reviving light;
Thy glad approach my anxious bosom eases,
    And care and sorrow for a while take flight.

5   Like youth's gay hours, or Spring's delicious season,
    To me once more thy balmy breath appears;
Lost hope returns, assumes the face of reason,
    And half persuades to flight oppressive fears.

While darkened casements vainly light excluded,
10   I wooed propitious sleep with languid sighs,
Care through the gloom his anxious face obtruded,
     And banished slumber from my weary eyes.

The tedious hours I told with watchful anguish,
     And oft, O Morn! accused thy long delay:
15   I hail thee now, no longer vainly languish,
     But quit my couch, and bless refreshing day.

Through the long night impatient, sad, and weary,
     How melancholy life itself appeared!
Lo! cheerful day illumes my prospects dreary,
20   And how diminished are the ills I feared!

Though pleasure shine not in the expected morrow,
     Though nought were promised but return of care,
The light of Heaven could banish half my sorrow,
     And comfort whispers in the fresh, cool air.

25   I hear the grateful voice of joy and pleasure,
     All nature seems my sadness to reprove,
High trills the lark his wild ecstatic measure,
     The groves resound with liberty and love:

Ere his glad voice proclaimed thy dawning early,
30   How oft deceived I rose thy light to hail;
Through the damp grass hoarse accents sounded cheerly,
     As wooed his distant love the wakeful rail.

Oh, you! who murmur at the call of duty,
     And quit your pillow with reluctant sloth,
35   For whom the Morn in vain displays her beauty,
     While tasteless you can greet her smiles so loth;

You cannot know the charm which o'er me stealing,
     Revives my senses as I taste her breath,
Which half repays the agony of feeling
40   A night of horrors, only less than death.

To W. Hayley, Esq.

In Return for a Copy of Cowper's Life, with a Sonnet—
1806[1]

Wake, languid muse! and tell the friendly Bard,
How well the gift, dear signal of regard,
That proudest monument which friendship shews,
While virtue charms us, and while genius glows.
5   The polished verse, the sweetly flattering strain,
Can sooth to soft forgetfulness of pain
The throbbing nerve, whose rest-destroying power
Told the quick pulse thro' many a tedious hour,
For to his ear benevolently kind,
10   I know the voice of gratitude shall find
An ever ready welcome, tho' denied
Wit's brilliant ray, or fancy's graceful pride.
    Ah! to the generous mind, the feeling heart,
What power of song can such delight impart,
15   As the pure, conscious triumph that succeeds
The grateful echo of their own kind deeds?
Not the bright clusters of Parnassian fruit,
Wreathing rich tendrils round Apollo's lute,
Nor his soft pencil's most celestial dye,
20   Pour such enchantment on the glist'ning eye,
As the pale lips which hope reviving speak,
Or the faint smile that brightens sorrow's cheek.
When that faint hope, that renovated smile,
Repay the kindness which could grief beguile,
25   And the full heart, with whispering pride may say,
My soothing cares have chased one pang away.

THE SHAWL'S PETITION, TO LADY ASGILL[1]

Oh, fairer than the fairest forms
Which the bright sun of Persia[2] warms,
Though nymphs of Cashmire[3] lead the dance
With pliant grace, and beamy glance;
5   And forms of beauty ever play
Around the bowers of Moselay;[4]
Fairest! thine ear indulgent lend,
And to thy suppliant Shawl attend!
    If, well content, I left for thee
10   Those bowers beyond the Indian sea,
And native, fragrant fields of rose
Exchanged for Hyperborean[5] snows;
If, from those vales of soft perfume,
Pride of Tibet's far boasted loom,
15   I came, well pleased, thy form to deck,
And, from thy bending polished neck
Around thy graceful shoulders flung,
With many an untaught beauty clung,
Or added to thy brilliant zone[6]
20   A charm that Venus well might own,
Or, fondly twined, in many a fold
To shield those lovely limbs from cold,
Fairest! thine ear indulgent lend,
And to thy suppliant Shawl attend.
25   Oh! by those all attractive charms
Thy slender foot, thine ivory arms;
By the quick glances of thine eyes,
By all that I have seen thee prize;
Oh! doom me not in dark disgrace,
30   An exile from Sophia's[7] face,
To waste my elegance of bloom
In sick and melancholy gloom;
Condemned no more in Beauty's train
To hear the viol's sprightly strain,
35   Or woo the amorous zephyr's play

Beneath the sunbeam's vernal ray;
Banished alike from pleasure's scene,
And lovely nature's charms serene,
Oh, fairest! doom me not to know
40   How hard it is from thee to go!
        But if my humble suit be vain,
If destined to attend on pain,
My joyless days in one dull round,
To one eternal sopha[8] bound,
45   Shut from the breath of heaven most pure,
Must pass in solitude obscure;
At least to cheat these weary hours
Appear with all thy gladdening powers,
Restore thy sweet society,
50   And bless at once thy friend and me.

HAGAR IN THE DESERT[1]

Injured, hopeless, faint, and weary,
    Sad, indignant, and forlorn,
Through the desert wild and dreary,
    Hagar leads the child of scorn.

5   Who can speak a mother's anguish,
           Painted in that tearless eye,
       Which beholds her darling languish,
           Languish unrelieved, and die.

Lo! the empty pitcher fails her,
10   Perishing with thirst he lies,
Death with deep despair assails her,
    Piteous as for aid he cries.

From the dreadful image flying,
    Wild she rushes from the sight;
15   In the agonies of dying
        Can she see her soul's delight?

Now bereft of every hope,
    Cast upon the burning ground,
Poor, abandoned soul! look up,
20   Mercy have thy sorrows found.

Lo! the Angel of the Lord
    Comes thy great distress to cheer;
Listen to the gracious word,
    See divine relief is near.

25   "Care of Heaven! though man forsake thee,
    Wherefore vainly dost thou mourn?
From thy dream of woe awake thee,
    To thy rescued child return.

"Lift thine eyes, behold yon fountain,
30   Sparkling mid those fruitful trees;
Lo! beneath yon sheltering mountain
    Smile for thee green bowers of ease.

"In the hour of sore affliction
    God hath seen and pitied thee;
35   Cheer thee in the sweet conviction,
    Thou henceforth his care shalt be.

"Be no more by doubts distressed,
    Mother of a mighty race!
By contempt no more oppressed,
40   Thou hast found a resting place."—

Thus from peace and comfort driven,
    Thou, poor soul, all desolate,
Hopeless lay, till pitying Heaven
    Found thee, in thy abject state.

45   O'er thy empty pitcher mourning
    Mid the desert of the world;
Thus, with shame and anguish burning,
    From thy cherished pleasures hurled:

See thy great deliverer nigh,
50   Calls thee from thy sorrow vain,
Bids thee on his love rely,
      Bless the salutary pain.

From thine eyes the mists dispelling,
      Lo! the well of life he shews,
55   In his presence ever dwelling,
      Bids thee find thy true repose.

Future prospects rich in blessing
      Open to thy hopes secure;
Sure of endless joys possessing,
60   Of an heavenly kingdom sure.

IMITATED FROM JEREMIAH.
—CHAP. XXXI. V. 15[1]

Hark, the voice of loud lament
      Sounds through Ramah's saddened plain!
There cherished grief, there pining discontent,
      And desolation reign.
5   There, mid her weeping train
See Rachel for her children mourn
      Disconsolate, forlorn!
      The comforter she will not hear,
And from his soothing strains she hopeless turns her ear.
10   Daughter of affliction peace,
      Let, at last, thy sorrows cease,
      Wipe thy sadly streaming eye,
      Look up, behold thy children nigh:
      Lo! thy vows have all been heard,
15   See how vainly thou hast feared!
      See, from the destroyer's land
      Comes the loved, lamented band;
      Free from all their conquered foes
      Glorious shall they seek repose;
20   Surest hope for thee remains,

Smile at all thy former pains;
Joy shall with thy children come,
And all thy gladdened bowers shall bloom

PSYCHE'S ANSWER[1]

Lady, forgive if late the languid lyre,
　　At length responsive to thy sweetest lay,
　　Breathe its low trembling chord with weak essay,
To utter all my grateful thoughts inspire;
5　Forgive, if vacant of poetic fire
　　I seem with frigid heart and dull delay
　　The flattering summons careless to obey;
Woo'd, kindly woo'd, so highly to aspire,
　　And echo the soft name of friend!—for me,
10　Alas! for me, in anguish and in fear,
　　The darkling[2] days have since rolled heavily;
But go, my Psyche! in her partial ear
　　Whisper the sad excuse; and bid her see
In thine, the "sister form" most fair, most dear!

TO LADY CHARLEMONT, IN RETURN FOR HER PRESENTS OF FLOWERS. MARCH, 1808[1]

Yes, though the sullen east-wind storm,
And sunless skies the Spring deform,
The lovely Nina's graceful hand
Can, like a fairy's lily wand,
5　Bid every vernal sweet appear,
And bloom with early fragrance here!
Yes here, even here, they breathe perfume,
Though walls of melancholy gloom,
With northern aspect frowning rude,
10　Each brighter beam of Heaven exclude.
Behold! at Nina's soft command,

The flowers their velvet leaves expand,
And sweet, and blue like her own eye,
(That loves in languid peace to lie,
15   And bending beautiful in shade,
Seems of the amorous light afraid)
Fresh violets here their charms diffuse,
And here, with richly mingling hues,
The gold and purple crocus vie
20   To mock the pomp of majesty.
See how her soul-bewitching smile
Can even selfish love beguile!
While fair Narcissus² bends no more
His snowy beauties to adore,
25   But lifts for once his cups of gold
A fairer image to behold.
Dear Nina! teach a grateful heart
Thine own persuasive, winning art;
So might I best my thanks commend,
30   So please each kind, each cherished friend!
For, as thy hand with smiling flowers
Hath crowned the lingering, wintry hours,
Even thus for me affection's care
Hath sheltered from the nipping air
35   The tender buds of half-chilled hope
That seemed in withering gloom to droop,
And bid them bloom, revived again,
In spite of years, and grief, and pain.
O'er me Affection loves to shed
40   Her comforts full, unmeasured;
To bless my smiling hearth she sends
The dearer smile of dearest friends,
And bids my prison couch assume
No form of pain, no air of gloom;
45   But sweet content and cheerful ease,
All that in solitude can please,
And all that soothing, social love
Can bid its quiet favourites prove,
Wooed by the voice of tenderness,
50   Unite my happy home to bless.

As round that lovely pictured wreath
Where Rubens bid his pencil breathe,[3]
Where touched with all its magic power
Glow the rich colours of each flower,
55   Attendant cherubs sweetly join,
And all their odorous wings entwine;
One cherub guards each blushing flower,
And pure ambrosia seems to shower:
So, Nina, o'er each peaceful day
60   Protecting love and kindness play,
And shed o'er each some balmy pleasure
That grateful memory loves to treasure!

WRITTEN AT WEST-ASTON. JUNE, 1808[1]

Yes, I remember the dear suffering saint,
Whose hand, with fond, commemorative care,
Planted that myrtle on my natal day.
It was a day of joy to him she loved
5   Best upon earth;—and still her gentle heart,
That never felt one passion's eager throb,
Nor aught but quiet joys, and patient woes,
Was prompt to sympathize with all; and most
With that beloved brother.—She had hoped
10   Perchance, that, fondly on his arm reclined
In placid happiness, her feeble step
Might here have wandered through these friendly shades,
This hospitable seat of kindred worth:
And that the plant, thus reared, in future years
15   Might win his smile benignant, when her hand
Should point where, in its bower of loveliness,
Bright spreading to the sun its fragrant leaf,
His Mary's myrtle bloomed.—Ah me! 'tis sad
When sweet affection thus designs in vain,
20   And sees the fragile web it smiling spun
In playful love, crushed by the sudden storm,
And swept to dark oblivion, mid the wreck
Of greater hopes!—Even while she thought of bliss,

Already o'er that darling brother's head
25   The death-commissioned angel noiseless waved
His black and heavy wings: and though she mourned
That stroke, in pious sorrow, many a year,
Yet, even then, the life-consuming shaft
In her chaste breast she uncomplaining bore.
30   Now, both at rest, in blessed peacefulness,
With no impatient hope, regret, or doubt,
Await that full completion of the bliss
Which their more perfect spirits shall receive.
Fair blossomed her young tree, effusing sweet
35   Its aromatic breath; for other eyes
Blushed the soft folded buds, and other hands
Pruned its luxuriant branches: friendship still
Preserved the fond memorial; nay, even yet
Would fain preserve with careful tenderness
40   The blighted relic of what once it loved.
Hard were the wintry hours felt even here
Amid these green protecting walls, and late
The timid Spring, oft chilled and rudely checked,
At last unveiled her tenderest charms, and smiled
45   With radiant blushes on her amorous train:
But no reviving gale, no fruitful dew,
Visits the brown parched leaf, or from the stem,
The withering stem, elicits the young shoots
With hopes of life and beauty; yet thy care
50   Perhaps, dear Sydney, thine assiduous care
May save it still. What can resist the care
Of fond, assiduous love? Oh! it can raise
The shuddering soul, though sunk beneath the black,
Suspended pall of death! Believe this lip,
55   Believe this grateful heart, which best can feel
The life-restoring power of watchful love.

To W.P. Esq. Avondale[1]

We wish for thee, dear friend! for summer eve
Upon thy loveliest landscape never cast
Looks of more lingering sweetness than the last.
    The slanting sun, reluctant to bereave
5   Thy woods of beauty, fondly seemed to leave
Smiles of the softest light, that slowly past
In bright succession o'er each charm thou hast
    Thyself so oft admired. And we might grieve
Thine eye of taste should ever wander hence
10   O'er scenes less lovely than thine own; but here
    Thou wilt return, and feel thy home more dear;
More dear the Muses' gentler influence,
When on the busy world, with wisdom's smile,
And heart uninjured, thou hast gazed awhile.

Written in a Copy of Psyche Which Had Been in the Library of C.J. Fox. April, 1809[1]

Dear consecrated page! methinks in thee
    The patriot's eye hath left eternal light,
    Beaming o'er every line with influence bright
A grace unknown before, nor due to me:
5   And still delighted fancy loves to see
    The flattering smile which prompt indulgence might
    (Even while he[2] read what lowliest Muse could write)
Have hung upon that lip, whose melody
    Truth, sense, and liberty had called their own.
10   For strength of mind and energy of thought,
With all the loveliest weakness of the heart,
    An[3] union beautiful in him had shewn;
And yet[4] where'er the eye of taste found aught
    To praise, he loved the critic's gentlest part.

THE LILY. MAY, 1809[1]

How withered, perished seems the form
    Of yon obscure unsightly root!
Yet from the blight of wintry storm,
    It hides secure the precious fruit.

5   The careless eye can find no grace,
    No beauty in the scaly folds,
Nor see within the dark embrace
    What latent loveliness it holds.

Yet in that bulb, those sapless scales,
10   The lily wraps her silver vest,
'Till vernal suns and vernal gales
    Shall kiss once more her fragrant breast.

Yes, hide beneath the mouldering heap
    The undelighting slighted thing;
15   There in the cold earth buried deep,
    In silence let it wait the spring.

Oh! many a stormy night shall close
    In gloom upon the barren earth,
While still, in undisturbed repose,
20   Uninjured lies the future birth;

And Ignorance, with sceptic eye,
    Hope's patient smile shall wondering view;
Or mock her fond credulity,
    As her soft tears the spot bedew.

25   Sweet smile of hope, delicious tear!
    The sun, the shower indeed shall come;
The promised verdant shoot appear,
    And nature bid her blossoms bloom.

And thou, O virgin Queen of Spring!
30   Shalt, from thy dark and lowly bed,

Bursting thy green sheath's silken string,
   Unveil thy charms, and perfume shed;

Unfold thy robes of purest white,
   Unsullied from their darksome grave,
35   And thy soft petals silvery light
   In the mild breeze unfettered wave.

So Faith shall seek the lowly dust
   Where humble Sorrow loves to lie,
And bid her thus her hopes entrust,
40   And watch with patient, cheerful eye;

And bear the long, cold, wintry night,
   And bear her own degraded doom,
And wait till Heaven's reviving light,
   Eternal Spring! shall burst the gloom.

SONNET WRITTEN AT WOODSTOCK, IN THE COUNTY OF KILKENNY, THE SEAT OF WILLIAM TIGHE. JUNE 30, 1809[1]

Sweet, pious Muse! whose chastely graceful form
   Delighted oft amid these shades to stray,
   To their loved master breathing many a lay
Divinely soothing; oh! be near to charm
5   For me the languid hours of pain, and warm
   This heart depressed with one inspiring ray
   From such bright visions as were wont to play
Around his favoured brow, when, to disarm
The soul subduing powers of mortal ill,
10   Thy soft voice lured him "to his ivyed seat,"
"His classic roses," or "his heathy hill;"
   Or by yon "trickling fount" delayed his feet
Beneath his own dear oaks, when, present still,
   The melodies of Heaven thou didst unseen repeat.

ON RECEIVING A BRANCH OF MEZEREON

Which Flowered at Woodstock. December, 1809[1]

Odours of Spring, my sense ye charm
    With fragrance premature;
And, mid these days of dark alarm,
    Almost to hope allure.
5   Methinks with purpose soft ye come
    To tell of brighter hours,
Of May's blue skies, abundant bloom,
    Her sunny gales and showers.

Alas! for me shall May in vain
10   The powers of life restore;
These eyes that weep and watch in pain
    Shall see her charms no more.
No, no, this anguish cannot last!
    Beloved friends, adieu!
15   The bitterness of death were past,
    Could I resign but you.

But oh! in every mortal pang
    That rends my soul from life,
That soul, which seems on you to hang
20   Through each convulsive strife,
Even now, with agonizing grasp
    Of terror and regret,
To all in life its love would clasp
    Clings close and closer yet.

25   Yet why, immortal, vital spark!
    Thus mortally opprest?
Look up, my soul, through prospects dark,
    And bid thy terrors rest;
Forget, forego thy earthly part,
30   Thine heavenly being trust:—

Ah, vain attempt! my coward heart
  Still shuddering clings to dust.

Oh ye! who sooth the pangs of death
  With love's own patient care,
35 Still, still retain this fleeting breath,
  Still pour the fervent prayer:—
And ye, whose smile must greet my eye
  No more, nor voice my ear,
Who breathe for me the tender sigh,
40 And shed the pitying tear,

Whose kindness (though far far removed)
  My grateful thoughts perceive,
Pride of my life, esteemed, beloved,
  My last sad claim receive!
45 Oh! do not quite your friend forget,
  Forget alone her faults;
And speak of her with fond regret
  Who asks your lingering thoughts.

JOURNALS

Mary Tighe

Extracts from a Journal
of M.B., born 1772[1]

Saturday, 16 February 1787

14 & 4 months old

When I look back & consider my past life (short as it has been) I see in it such an astonishing medley it causes me at times not to know what to think. Some part of my life I have been immersed in sin, & if I may say in the very jaws of the wicked one at others rejoicing in the belief that I was in the favour of God & certainly whether I was in that deceived or not it was the happiest part of my life[.] At other periods I have been in a state which I cannot otherwise describe than by saying that I was asleep. In all these states I am persuaded that I have been drawn graciously to seek my saviour's face, but had I been faithful to these drawings I am sensible that I should not now be in the state I am in—whether I really was in the presence of the blessing which I once professed to enjoy. I am sometimes led to doubt it & at other times to believe. But of this I am certain that I never willingly deceived myself nor God's people. & I know that for many things which I allow myself now, at that time, I should have severely condemned myself. However, I think it is now my desire to set out afresh in the way of the Lord as I have never yet done & may the Lord be my portion.

Sunday 17th [February 1787]

This day I am sensible of having grieved the holy spirit of God by outward sin[.] I went to Bethesda[2]—formerly I could say that my only desire in going to a place of worship was to wait on my God. Alas! am I not greatly fallen!—The Lord have mercy on me.

Monday [1787]

How many days do I live without God in my thoughts! What little things call me off from God! Am I always to live feeling my chain, without the power of breaking it?

Saturday, March 3 [1787]

Alas! am I always to live at this sad dying note. I see more & more my own corruptions & distance from God, but this sight only serves to make me feel more miserable—

Tuesday April 16 [1787?][3]

Yes, my God! I see that thou wilt visit my iniquities with a rod & my sins with scourging.[4] O that it may have the gracious effect for which thou searchest it, may I not burden myself more & more—but submit & own the punishment is just. Dost thou not still call me to seek thy face? & "stoop to ask my love[.]"[5] O may I not turn a deaf ear to the charmer nor be like the deaf adder that stoppeth its ease[6]—

> In the time of my distress
> Thou hast my succour been
> In my utter helplessness
> Restraining me from sin
> Oh how swiftly didst thou love
> To save me in the trying hour!
> Still protect me with thy love,
> And shield me with thy power.[7]

Oh may I then for ever trust that God who is the same for ever & ever.

Monday May 7 [1787]

I have lately experienced God protecting Love in a remarkable manner. May every mercy lead me to seek his face. Indeed I think my heart has lately been drawn afresh to seek the Lord with my whole heart, but how very unfaithful I am to these drawings. Oh Lord help me for I feel that I cannot help myself.

May 21st [1787]

In deep distress—this verse was applied with comfort to my soul.

> "Call upon me in the time of trouble & I will hear thee saith the Lord."[8]

Oh Lord, how many causes have I to praise thee for all that is past & "trust thee for all that's to come"[9]—have mercy upon me & help me to give thee the whole of my faithless unworthy heart—

May 27th [1787]

The all merciful, long-suffering Lord was pleased this evening to visit my soul in a particular manner in private prayer. How graciously is he pleased to encourage me to seek after him

Saturday June 22 [1787?][10]

Of late my soul has been peculiarly exercised & in such a manner as I could speak of to none but to my compassionate high priest & he gave me to feel that he was "touched with the feeling of my infirmities[.]"[11] Oh Lord settle & fix my wandering soul[12]—

> Far, Far from me the world remove,
> And all that keeps me from thy love.

Mr. Wesley is now in town & I think that I feel an expectation of profitting by the opportunities which I am likely to have of meeting him.

Saturday Sep 25th [1787?][13]

Being in great distress & entangled in a snare, out of which I could see no deliverance I found this text sweet to my soul. "If any man lack wisdom let him ask of God, who giveth to all men liberally & upbraideth not"[14] & I was much surprised at hearing Mr. Miles[15] give out for his text that night the very same words. This sermon comforted & profitted me. I found power to cast my care upon God—

Thursday Nov 28 [1787?][16]

This week past these words have been powerfully impressed upon my mind "Nevertheless I have something against thee" because thou hast left thy first love[17]—I heard a sweet sermon upon them—it stirred me up. But I fear my deceitful heart which is ever ready to start aside like a broken bow.[18] I have not profitted as I ought to have done, by the blessed opportunity offered me of seeing the triumphant death of one[19] very dear to me[.]Oh Jesus, if in thy infinite wisdom thou hast appointed for me like sufferings, endue me with like fortitude & resignation. & grant[20] that, like her, having filled up the measure of my sorrows, I may, with her enjoy like Glory for ever & ever. Amen.

Friday July 18 [1788]

Oh My God! How uselessly do I spend my precious time! How unprofitably do I employ it? Day after day & year after year! I go on upbraiding myself, resolving & resolving without the power of fulfilling my resolutions—Oh Lord! exert thy power over my fickle heart, then shall my feet no longer rove? "settled & fixed in thee[.]"[21] Oh let not impressions made by thy spirit be as the early dew & morning cloud which quickly vanish—Truly thou hast been to me strength in the day of my distress—a refuge from the storm, a shadow from the heat.[22]—

1788

Oh Lord! am I always to live as asleep over the pit of destruction! I am as one called by some kind voice to awake & again close my eyes. "Truely the last state of that man is worst than the first."[23] Oh God, ever merciful & gracious snatch me from the threatening ruin. Call me effectually & shake this slumber from my soul & let me cast myself up on thee in the full assurance that thou wilt deliver my lost & dying soul.

Written on the 15th of February the day that she heard Mr. de la Flechier[24] had resolved to return to Switzerland [February 15, 1789]

"Truly God moves in a mysterious way!"[25]
Oh thou who hast been a pillar of fire to thy chosen flock by night,[26] dissipate the surrounding clouds which encompass my trembling feet— shine on my path, make the way plain before me, & give me power to walk therein, whether thou has strewed it with thorns, or adorned it with roses. If a sparrow a worthless sparrow falls not to the ground without my father's notice, how can I doubt his care of me![27] for whom he gave his own son to bleed & die upon the cross—

July 5 1789

It is long since I put pen to this book. How my heart has been since employed I would willingly bury in oblivion. But there is a book kept, a dreadful book! wherein every word & work & thought is registered. Gracious God! give me wisdom to make my calling an election sure[.] Let me work while thou grantest me light. "Lest the night should come wherein no man can work."[28]

Saturday August 21 1790

A year has now elapsed since I have written anything here—It would indeed be impossible to relate how my heart has been since affected, but this to my eternal shame I must own that thou, Oh my God, hast not been in all my thoughts & indeed scarcely in any. Sometimes called off by vanity. & led in the foolish trappings of this world—in the paths of self admiration. Sometimes my heart has been distracted by vain pleasures. False hopes, foolish disappointments, idle pursuits—trifling sorrows, useless alarms & childish vexations—Alas! my thoughts are more intent upon worldly knowledge, worldly fame & worldly pleasures than upon that knowledge which can alone be useful to my immortal soul—but Lord! shall I live ever thus return unto thyself my heart, be no more

Feby 26 [1789?]

Finished the life of Baron Trenck; the man of many sorrows.[29] What a pity, that he has not improved his great afflictions (sent him, no doubt, for that purpose) to his eternal good.

April 11th 1789

Mr. Wesley breakfasted with us in Gardiner's row.[30] I sat next to him—after breakfast he prayed, remembering me in the most tender & ardent manner. When he rose from his knees he took hold of my hand & said "dear Molly, expect that there are blessings in store for you" he turned to my bookcase & said "there are many books here, Molly, not worth your reading" & then observed a good deal on idle books, particularly fine poetry. Said that History & religious books were the best study. Praised French Historians, & condemned Hume[31] & the Abbé Raynal[32] as an enemy to all power human & divine—He spoke about the beggars not in such harsh terms as I have heard even those who are accounted pious persons express themselves. His words were all tenderness & compassion.

Easter Sunday [April 12, 1789]

Mama read some of Romaine on the 107 Psalm.[33] My cough prevented me from going to church—how did I spend my time? Was it in private prayer—alas! alas! my vile heart far other was my employment.

Tunbridge 11th October 1789[34]

Went thro' the high rocks—they are very awful indeed! How wretched must they be who shall be forced to call upon these one day to fall & cover them. Dreadful thought!

Oc25 [1789?]

Finished Julia de Roubigné.[35] I cannot say that I admire the tendency of that book. Her affection to Savillon was certainly wrong & she was guilty in indulging it—Visited Miss Tottenham.[36] Saw her drest for the ball. Did I feel a desire to go? I own I did, but not a longing.

May 1789. Gardiner's row

Lowspirited, perhaps at leaving Rossana[.] If I have not philosophy enough to despise or at least to disregard the gaiety which reigns there, which inclines everyone to eat, & to drink & to rise up to play & to make the pleasures of the present moment their waking passions, I have, at least sense enough to despise myself. Yet I am afraid that it is that the gay scene has seduced my heart that I lament its absence.

1791

How is all happiness, worldly happiness I mean overclouded! Hope sometimes gilds the weary road of life by its sparkling beams, but vain fears & useless cares rob us of even our scanty portions of earthly felicity.—

Lismore[37] 27 August 1791

Looking over Mr. Hume's books I am sorry to say my study was the sorrows of Werther[38] & still sorrier that my taste was so vitiated, that notwithstanding I abhorred the sentiments & moral from my heart yet I could not avoid admiring it. Indeed the language is very pretty & the tenderness that runs thro' it very captivating.

1791 Sep 17 Written in the way to town from Swanlinbar[39]

I confess I feel rather too discontented at the idea of spending a few days at such a place as this. More than such a thing deserves—not without regret I left a place[40] where my vanity was so flattered. Believing low spirits to be partly voluntary, & finding ill humour & discontent to be other disagreeable attendants & being rather disposed to them at present. I resolved to conquer them & partly succeeded.

9th October 1791

This day I am nineteen[.] How shall I express what I feel when I reflect minutely on my past life[.] "What fruit I may indeed well expect had I then in those things of which I am now ashamed."[41] Read over some old letters & papers which gave birth to many reflections. At the end of 1791 these lines—

> Thus was the low ambition of my mind
> Thus were the vain desires I formed,
> For such delights my calmer joys resigned,
> And quenched the fires which had my bosom warmed.[42]

1792 Good Friday April 6

Boswell in his life of Johnson says "at this time every pious thought is kindled in a heart in which there is but a spark of piety"[43]—have I this day found my desires awakened! my love & gratitude influenced or my heart melted by effusions of piety? Heard Shirley[44] preach on "it is finished"[45]—

6 August 1792. Waltrim[46]

Wrote what I could recollect of our visit to Bellevue.[47] I gave way to some such reflections as these. The happiest hours of my life have been alas! imbittered by anxiety & various other pains, sometimes resulting from the source of my pleasures & at others from my pleasures themselves—What have been the fleeting joys expected with such hope & remembered with such tenderness—Can I hope more from what may come than from what has already past?
I have no object upon which to fix hope, nor do I know where to look for pleasure—yet there is a rest for the soul which feels the emptiness of what I still pant for—

Novr 3. [1792]

I do not think Shirley is happy—but who in this world is? I am sure I am not happy[.] Oh shall I never seek happiness where only it is to be found!—

1792 15 December

I think I never received such a shock as on hearing this morning of Mr. Shirley's death. Oh My God—it is thus with us all!—Are we all to be

hurried before thy face with all our corruptions on our heads, unpre-
pared perhaps, to meet thee. My tears flowed fast & my heart broken &
humbled experienced the saddest sensations. God only knows how my
lot in life is to be decided[.] If I repose my confidence in him I know it
will be for the best—This then ought to be all my aim.

23 December Sunday. [1792]

Les engagements du cour[48] falling in my way I could not help reading some
of it, tho' conscious of the unprofitable manner in which I was passing the
Sabbath morning.

30 December [1792]

Oh could I cast my burden on the Lord! Would he not sustain me? Oh
vain illusions of bliss! Imagination, beauty, flattering, tastes I indulged &
prided in to my misery! How far are you from contributing to my peace—

1793. Jany 7

Oh Lord direct me in all my ways & suffer not my feet to slip.[49] Went to
George's church. Heard Mr. Kelly preach a very good sermon indeed.[50]

1793 February 17

Mama read Fenelon[51] & I found great pleasure in hearing it.

21 February [1793]

How, alas! did I rejoice in vanity! Now I am punished in the way in
which I have offended—I exulted in the pride & folly of my heart. & I
fell into the snare as a bird into the net of the fowler.[52] My heart unwill-
ingly owns the anguish which rends it while occupied with these reflec-
tions.

24 February [1793]

Hope, delusive Hope! a broken reed at best but oft a spear—what alas!
have I suffered these last three months! & what have I still to suffer while
my heart still cleaves to earth!—

16 February. [1793]

Went with Lady Jocelyn[53] to the Private Theatre. This was the first play I
ever saw acted[.] It was "Love in a Village[.]"[54] I own the impression it

made upon me was that the stage was an immodest entertainment for women—

Feby 26 [1793]

How merciful is the God with whom we have to do[.] He chastens indeed for our offences, but it is to make us feel his hand, while there may be hope. And this has been the case with poor John![55] Never did I see such a change in temper, judgment & the whole conduct!

1793.

Wrote to HT.[56] Left the matter to his own decision—I trust it shall be ordered as shall be best[.]

October 4th [1793]

My soul draws back with terror & awe at the idea of the event which is to take place tomorrow. Oh My God! Let it not be unattended with thy blessing.

October 6th. [1793]

In the presence of twenty people I yesterday plighted my faith—& gave my hand————————

1794 January 4th

Unhappy in myself, offensive to others, desponding in my heart. I could have wished to have escaped from scenes my soul is weary of. Ay, but to die & go we know not where. Here is the rub[.][57] Solitude at least is preferable.

27 Feby. [1794?]

Finding myself unable to attend to anything I gave myself up to my own imaginations—how very wrong this is. I was soon convinced of it—I hope in future to be preserved from it—

Manchester H.[58] London July 11th [1794?]

There is a corpse laid out in a window opposite the back of our house, which is no very pleasing object to my mind & troubles my imagination—

10 May. [1795?]

At Cecil's chapel[59]—Alas! how do I misemploy my hours & make time pass so, that its existence is marked with evil instead of good to myself & others.

16 June. [1795?]

Sometimes I feel as if I acted wrong in indulging myself even as I do. & at others I think that as long as I do not act sinfully I may be allowed to partake of the pleasures which my present life affords—

Cobham[60] 25 July 1795

Heard of Fortescue's [61] death—

Oh my God I bow in reverence to thy awful & afflicting dispensations— but spare thy worm! Cut me not off in the midst of my sins—spare me a little that I may recover my strength before I go hence & am no more seen[.][62] Oh! thou soul of my departed friend where art thou? Has thou found mercy? Has thou received the onslaught of benefits of thy slighted redeemer.

My God! how cold is the grave—The receptacle of all we love! & all we fear. Very terrible is the sentence which in one cruel word separates us for ever from those we love. Covered by the devouring tomb, soon forgotten by all! & the immortal soul gone to appear before an unknown God!

Sunday 26 July [1795]

At Church. Found my wounded heart relieved by pouring out its sorrows & fears before God—

August 11th [1795?]

Oh Lord give me a feeling for my own awful situation—awaken me, before I go hence, & am no more seen.

Holyhead[63] August 11th [1795?]

"Gone to that bourne from which no traveller returns"![64]—How soon, my Lord, may that also be my fate! I could not look at that great & tremendous ocean, which I was ordained to cross, without some apprehensions on my own part.—Tho' so smooth & flattering with prosperous gales how shortly might the scene be changed & a few hours turn into threatening forms & fatal waves the now placid elements—But even thus is our life! So smiles the morn, & thus uncertain are its smiles. Heavenly father! Thy children are in thy hands! Surely thou dost not, thou canst not will their destruction!—

1 December 1795

My life was embittered to me—some tidings I heard that made me loath the light & long to be concealed in the peaceful silent tomb, which holds all that our ancestors loved & so much of what was once so dear to ourselves. Ere this I have known sorrow & often wiped from my cold brow the dew of anguish. God had indeed given me shame, but alas! if sin is to be severely punished how much more have I to endure! O being of Mercy! Afflict not thus thy creature[.]

1796 March 25th Sunday at Mary's Abbey[65]

I had many serious thoughts this day & indeed, for sometimes past about my way of life or rather state of mind. I begin clearly to discern that I cannot serve God & Mammon. That the latter is my idol can I deny to myself? What remains is alarming. & what is the consequence of not serving God? Yet I still cling to pleasure which I perceive gliding delusively from my grasp, and I seek to persuade the accusing spirit within me that God is surely too just to punish with eternal death, the weakness of a being he has not created strong. But in vain—& I have not power to pray—Oh why was I created?

March 25 [1796 or 1797?]

Very unhappy in my mind—Yet I find it impossible to resist the flattering temptation of being admired, & showing the world that I am so. My conscience this day has been disturbed—I feel uneasy at the vanity, the folly, the dissipation in which I am engaged. Yet without the power to wish myself disengaged from it.

Rossana 5th October, my wedding day. [1797]

Four years! spent, alas! for the greatest part in empty trifles, & vain amusements.

9th My birth day. [October 1797]

This day I am twenty five. What melancholy reflections does this naturally cause! Yet, this day, these serious thoughts found little room

1798 March 28

How long shall my soul be agitated by vain dreams. What is it that capti-
vates my better judgment & thus subjects me to the cruel stings of disap-
pointed hopes—Hopes empty as vanity itself—What is it I desire or what
illusion is it I regret!—Oh! that my hopes were fixed where true joy only
is to be found.[66]

Shepherd of Israel! dost thou sleep & suffer thy wandering sheep to be
devoured by the wolves of the forest. Wilt thou not have compassion on
the flock of thy pasture & go in search of the one unhappy stray lamb.[67]

August 4th 1798

Ah fools! ever ready to dream of pleasure & catch at the empty shade of
what exists no where.

August 27. [1798]

Heard of George Fortescue's being shot by the French, at Ballina[68]—how
untimely has been the fate of these two unfortunate brothers! The com-
panions of my gay & foolish hours.

Dublin 5 June 1799

We are to go to Rossana in a week. Alas! are my pleasures past like the
leaves of this exquisite rose! & is there nothing remaining but the thorn.
Oh too damnable!—

March 5 1800

Oh what a dream is life! When shall I awake?[69]

26th [March 1800?]

was the finest day that eer shone & my heart felt some of that delicious
sensibility which it is the property of Spring alone to bestow[.] But how
deadened all my sensations are?—Within these two years I am scarce the
same being which once hailed with animation the pleasures of life

29 [March 1800?]

Melancholy & unhappy.

15 April [1800?]

Sat up in my own room till near one melancholy & unhappy.

April 23 [1800?]

Spent the night at a gay party without any pleasure. Nor was that all—pain & mortification, self reproach & regret oppressed my heart & made my very existence a burthen—

April 25th [1800?]

Spent a miserable morning. Gloomy thoughts oppressed me & I vainly sought for refuge in philosophy or in my feeble attempts at devotion. How often in the gloom of my soul do I say how blest are they who sleep to wake no more! Oh My God! how often have I desired to be as the insensible dust & asked my Creator why I was called into existence if I have not the power of obeying his supreme will? Oh No. I feel that his Love is beyond my thoughts—

1802

Prayed for restoration of health to my soul.

Her diary ends here.[70]

Theodosia Blachford

OBSERVATIONS ON THE FOREGOING JOURNAL BY HER MOTHER, MRS. BLACHFORD[1]

How often have I thought when gazing at my poor child's dejected countenance, faded beauty, blasted hopes & vain pursuits, how the thoughts that oppressed my heart if well expressed would "Point a moral & adorn a tale"[2]—

I am very inadequate to the expression of them nor have I any female child, nor grandchild, to whom I can hope that they may be useful yet, after inspecting all her journals & papers I feel a desire to leave some account of God's judgments on myself, thro' her, & of that Mercy which endureth for ever—

She was born on the 9th of October 1772 & lost her dear father on the May following, to which circumstance her beautiful lines on the Myrtle at West Acton allude. The promise of beauty, intelligence & vigorous health, which she gave in infancy & childhood added to a very caressing, & flattering manner, naturally endeared her peculiarly to me & inspired me with the brightest hopes respecting her future destiny. Yet as to this world I think my sole earnest & anxious wish was that she might get a loving & beloved companion in a religious & amiable guide. But how inconsistent with this desire was my wish & strenuous endeavors to have her excel in all vain, & elegant accomplishments? Yet for these pursuits I made to myself many excuses such as that I had no right to deprive her of those advantages to which her rank in life entitled her etc. All this, in a certain sense, might be true, but my own heart convinces, & did convince me at the time, of my undue anxiety on this subject. "I laboured for that which was not bread & found the acquisition proved ashes of gravel in my mouth."[3]

So early as seven years old she had a very extraordinary dream of the day of judgment[4] which was followed with very sweet observings & impressions of religion & many outward exercises of real or supposed devotion, particularly abstaining from meat & pleasant food & great attachment to the Methodists, & though I did not entirely approve of either of these expressions of devotion, yet I exulted in the root from whence they proceeded. But Oh! what shame have I here to take to myself! How slightly was my heart affected by this mercy & how improperly was it, at this time, engrossed! Alas, alas! there is no need on my account, to record its wanderings. It is written there as with a pen of iron & with the point of a diamond.[5]

My attachment, at this time, to my sweet child was very weak in comparison to what it was in after years. Indeed I do not think that I loved her then as much as most mothers would have loved such a child, & certainly saw her faults in a strong light, & reproved them with severity, the more on account of her religious profession. She was scarcely fourteen when she awakened my solicitude by being noticed by daring & artful young men every way her inferiors & though her openness with me prevented any very serious apprehensions on the subject, yet it made me prematurely anxious to see her well disposed of. Nor was this the only evil that resulted from those addresses, which, however scorned, gave my poor child a relish for admiration.

I have reason to believe that she listened when fifteen, with more complacency than she owned to me, or even perhaps to herself, to a designing man of a religious profession of whose prior engagements she was ignorant—which I am sure, if I had not discovered he would have slighted—Her reflections on this subject, in her journal, are natural, innocent & just—In the course of this year I embraced with unaccountable warmth the prospect of her marrying Monr de la Flechier (nephew to Mr. Flechier of Madeley), with my eyes open to all the consequences of her being settled a thousand miles from hence. My heart became so set upon this match that I do not think any temporal disappointment, except her not having children, & a similar circumstance, ever gave me so much pain at its not being accomplished.

From this period, till that of her last breath, almost all my anxieties, & my tenderest affections & hourly cares centered in her. Though I felt far more value for her brother some time after, yet I still felt something, with regard to her & her dependant state that was more interesting & produced more anxiety—Towards the conclusion of this year 1788 she was visited with a most extraordinary cough or spasm, every day from two in the afternoon till nine in the evening. At this period she showed such indifference to Mr de la Flechier & as I fancied, a partiality to H Tighe, that I thought it my duty to break off the connection, which I did with her full approbation. We now removed, at the beginning of 1789 to a pleasant habitation in Gardiner's row—she was no longer treated as a child. We lived as perfect friends & notwithstanding this cough, which was termed nerves & my solicitude for her health & happiness & my regret at seeing her evident increasing lukewarmness in religion—I say, notwithstanding this, I suppose this period of my life had as much worldly satisfaction in it as any other since I was a widow.

My children's prospects were bright, they were universally admired in our circle, & whatever secret dissatisfaction I might have in regard to their tempers, I was pleased to see their conduct, upon the whole, exemplary & praiseworthy. Mary's indisposition never preyed very hard upon my mind, nor upon her's—Our Physician's kindness & attention soothed us daily. Her finding in him, an affectionate & attached admirer, tended, perhaps, to confirm, in her mind, a fatal tendency to the love of admiration. Partly to break his encreasing attachment & to try change of air, & to obtain the best advice, I took her to London in August 1789, & afterwards by the advice of the Physician there, first to Tunbridge & then to Bath. In the last of which places her extraordinary complaint took a sudden turn for the better on the 25th of November, & from that day, gradually decreased & almost the same proportion that it had encreased the preceding year till it finally ceased the 8th of September 1790 having lasted from its first seemingly trivial commencement exactly two years.

In speaking of this period I have omitted a circumstance that had very important consequences. At the latter end of December 1788, when we lodged a little way out of town, on account of her cough Mrs Tighe[6] pressed us to go to Woodstock. I who had always a secret dread of any intimacy with the family refused positively, but she, who is ever too much bent on carrying her point, sent her carriage & horses all the way to town for us, using at the same time such arguments as induced me against my better impulses to yield rather than seem so positive and ungrateful as to send back the carriage empty. Here we found H Tighe, after a separation of more than two years grown a *very handsome* & captivating young man in his appearance though only eighteen years of age & here I observed marks of attachment between him & my poor Mary that I determined to break off entirely the proposed, & by me intended match between her & Mr de la Flechier—To this she willingly consented, but not without some kind of tender regret & denied, I believe without insincerity that she had

any more serious regard for Harry than was warranted by their relation-
ship & intimacy from childhood.—We returned to town the 14th of
January 1789 & the day after I wrote to Mr de la Flechier a decided
refusal pleading her want of health. During her stay at Woodstock though
only about three weeks she had, as appears by her journal discontinued a
regular devout application to God to guide & bless her future lot, which
she had for some time faithfully observed.—

Notwithstanding this letter to Mr de la Flechier & his despairing
answer, I still nourished a secret hope that time & events might still bring
about this marriage. For which I was strongly solicitous, nor ever resigned
the hope, till I heard, with no small dejection, of his marriage in Feby
1790 soon after our return from Bath.

From this time, while her cough was rapidly declining, & her beauty
& manners daily improving, her connection with HT filled me with very
uneasy apprehensions. I foresaw much misery & embarrassment, though
not in the shape I met it & yet the advantages were so flattering, & many
of the objections so inexplicable that I felt quite embarrassed how to act.
Nor did I feel at liberty to put a positive negative on what I then believed
to be & in fact really then was, her wish. I knew, indeed, that he was not
religious—& this should have determined me to take a more decided
part. But I thought him moral & was convinced of his being very pecu-
liarly blest with generosity & good nature—an opinion he has never given
me reason to alter. In the mean time I hoped that something would occur
either on her side, or his to lessen an attachment I did not think had taken
very deep root in either. For *never* did I regard this union but with pain
and apprehension, tho' I felt, for him, a tender partiality which the most
bitter consequences have never entirely destroyed.

I could not help going once or twice, in the summer, to Rossana
without an open breach, nor could I prevent the young people from
meeting daily while Mrs Tighe was in town.

Besides my hope of a more desirable connection in the family, & my
fears, on that account of disobliging John, increased my weakness & dread
of giving offence. Sadly God in punishment for my multiplied offences,
& wretched infidelities, left me at this time, to my own poor blinded
judgment & weak attempts to steer my child at this important crisis. She
was, in a good degree, ductile, & very affectionate & confiding in her man-
ner to me. & though her religious impressions had evidently declined yet
still she was sensible to her obligations to me as a mother, & a friend &
would not in any great instance have departed from their dictates.

But devoted to literary studies, to the charms of poetry & fond of the flattery she everywhere received, but particularly of that she continually met with from Harry & his mother I saw with uneasiness the sad & natural consequences of these deviations—Her religious journal ends the 21st of August 1790—with these sad words.

> A year has now elapsed since I wrote anything in this book. It were indeed impossible to relate how my heart has been since affected, but to my shame & condemnation thou O God! has been not in all my thoughts, indeed scarcely in any. Sometimes called off by vanity & led in the foolish trappings of the world in the paths of self admiration—sometimes my heart has been distracted by vain pleasures, false hopes, foolish disappointments, idle pursuits, trifling sorrows, fond desires, useless alarms & childish vexations, etc. etc.

From this, & several other passages of her religious journal, it is evident that during the continuance of her cough she had many deep convictions of sin yet was her life at that time, outwardly innocent & regular, at least in comparison of that she led after her marriage—when immersed in vanity & dissipation she seemed but seldom to awake to any sense of her deviations from a path, that she always acknowledged to be, the only one that led to peace & life eternal.

In the Autumn of 1791 we went with John to Swanlinbar, where her vanity, & alas! mine too were much flattered by the admiration she met with there. At the same time that I observed with grief & disappointment its effects upon her disposition. She remarks herself its ruinous effects in her journal (dated Brittas)[7] 17 Sepr & strove in some degree to arise from the ennui it produced. The following winter & Spring were seasons of great vanity & false exultation. Did I enjoy the triumphs of her beauty & captivating manner? Every voice that reached me sounded her praises— I took, I suppose, too much delight in these applauses tho', at the time, convinced they could tend to no real good, & on that account, felt many a bitter pang.

Her brother was then just of age & not of a turn, *at this time,* to help, but to draw her back from seriousness by the books she found in his study & his ideas *then* of life & manners. I have sometimes thought that she had a prophetic spirit—his first entrance into fashionable vanity, a few days before he was of age was, as has been almost all his errors, remarkably checked. She helped to dress both him & H. Tighe (for a masquerade at

Harristown[8] twenty miles from Dublin) about five oclock on a January evening & on seeing them setting out gaily, she turned from the window, she had opened to look at them, repeating these lines from Gray's Ode:

> Fair laughs the morn, & soft the Zephyr's blow
> While proudly riding o'er the azure realm
> In gallant trim the guilded vessel goes,
> Youth at the prow & pleasure at the helm
> Regardless of the sweeping whirlwind's sway
> That hushed in grim repose, expects his evening prey[9]

They were joined by three other youths as gay as themselves, but returned, in a few hours, with cloaths stained with blood, to tell us that they had been attacked by highwaymen who had wounded one of their companions whom they had left in Mr. Richards'[10] care—poor John's entrance into life has been in respect to punishment, similar to the fate that has ever since attended him. Oh! that now the hand of my God may turn on him for good. Neither he nor my poor Mary have had their portion in this life—My heart sinks at recording the next scene from which I may date the period of all my happiness in her. We went, as usual, at this season to pay a visit at Rossana,[11] the seemingly, mutual attachment was now too evident to be overlooked. John and I thought she gave to it improper encouragement & we both suspected Harry of trifling—on this account I spoke to her more plainly than I should otherwise have done. & afterwards of my own accord, on being accused by Harry, explained. The consequences were most fatal—fatal indeed!—H Tighe declared himself avowedly & she gave a kind of a consent. But Harry's mother. . . .[12]

The summer of 1792 was a season to me of great anxiety on account of this intended marriage & the doubtful engagement subsisting between my poor child & Henry Tighe, who with John spent the greater part of the following summer in Switzerland & France notwithstanding the convulsions which then agitated Europe. John returned in November but HT was kept in London by his mother!!—

From this period all was wretchedness to me such wretchedness as I had no idea of before—I felt with bitterness the fickleness of my poor child & was made, by concealing it, a partaker in her sin, when a candid & more ingenuous confession might have saved years of misery. I saw the right path, but the fear of offending my poor suffering child & the dread of the effects of the displeasure we had already experienced & by my poor Mary's injunctions I closed my lips even to my dearest friend & sister & which, I far more regret to my dear John who was then entering on a blessed path, & was every way qualified to advise—I thought that I had no right to communicate the entrusted secret of another—yet am I not thereby justified—my anxiety, & fear of man, joined to the evident sufferings of my weak child quite overpowered me & these things[,] added to John's illness & its consequences, made the whole of this winter by far the bitterest I had ever past. Yet surely I was very ungrateful to let these afflictions swallow up, in a great measure, my sense of God's mercy in visiting with light & grace the heart of my poor afflicted son.

Anxiety, sorrow & terror, with some gleams of hope, filled up to me the following winter of 1792 & summer of 1793 while I saw my poor child struggling with a foolish & violent passion half insensible to the tenderness of a heart that she was unwilling, indeed seemingly unable to wound by a positive refusal, though she saw[13] her favorite lover, at her feet, in rank & fortune unexceptionable & her equal, at the same time confessing to me her reluctance to any closer connection with H Tighe. Had not his mother behaved to Mary so that it was impossible to confide in her & alienated our affections from her this never could have been. But let me look off from second causes & own, with my mouth in the dust,[14] that the punishment, as to me was just.

The 5th of October 1793—tied the fatal knot which occasioned sixteen years of sad regret & wanderings to two young people apparently eminently qualified to receive & confer happiness—"all who saw envied & in envy loved[.]" But how little can be judged from external appearances[.] I was not long deceived, & from that day I have been convinced that it is not impossible to conceal the deepest anguish.

My poor child was soon settled in London under the guidance of a youth whose tenderness never failed, but whose want of principle, & knowledge of the world encouraged her in every vanity & folly, into which the love of admiration draws our weak sex, & into such snares as none, I believe escape from, unhurt, who dare to frequent the scenes of fashionable resort—For above eight years, she trod this dangerous and fatal path—Let her own journals & poetry declare what happiness she found in it!—That she escaped what the world calls guilt, & its attendant infamy, I am thankful for *now*, but scarcely could be so, during all this time while I saw her standing on the edge of a dreadful precipice, & wasting health, time, & what was still more precious than either, the graces & invitations of God's holy spirit—

In 1802 she forsook the Ballroom & Theatre, but was, perhaps not less misemployed in the pursuits of literature which she had never entirely neglected, nor were her literary companions less dreaded by me, than her fashionable admirers. Her Psyche, & Selena are monuments of her power & taste. They were the productions of the two following years, begun in 1801 & were both, composed, written & copied out fair sometime before the end of 1803.

During all this time she had patiently borne my continual remonstrances which however did not seem to have any effect though her conscience was often smitten her lamentations were melancholy, her convictions keen, but vanity still prevailed as is expressed in her sonnet dated the Spring of 1797 which begins

"Poor fond deluded heart wilt thou again[.]" Indeed almost all her poetry, as well as her cast of countenance declared her internal unhappiness.

On the 27th of January 1804 HT & she came to town after having spent the preceding two months & the greatest part of 1803 at Rossana, except during occasional short periods when they resided in Dominick St—she spent in all more than eight months at Rossana during which time she finished & wrote out fair, her Selena (five volumes) & was seemingly in better health & spirits than she had been for some years. However she brought a cough with her to town to which neither she, nor I paid sufficient attention, though on all other occasions I had been too anxious about her health—unavailing anxiety!—This sad cough never left her till it brought her to her grave six years afterwards—She went in May to Rossana where she grew so much worse that HT determined she should go to Bristol to which place I was easily prevailed upon to accompany them—Our residence there from the end of June till the latter end of August was to me (notwithstanding her illness) a more agreeable period than I usually passed in their society. She was serious, if not pious, & she & Harry seemed more affectionate & united than I had seen them for a long time, which I imputed to their separation from evil society which tended to alienate them from each other daily more & more.

In the latter end of August we went to London & by the advice of Dr Vaughan[15] were preparing for a journey to Lisbon when the arrival of John, his wife & child, & various accidents, first delayed, & then prevented it—Madeira was now preferred. To this she had a decided aversion & I could not heartily join in pressing it—So the whole winter & part of the summer was spent in union with John's family, between Chelsea and Brompton & we did not separate till August.

The year 1805 was a sad one. I saw my poor son in contact with a woman I believed profligate & knew to be profane, imperious & violent.[16] I knew that Harry was treading crooked paths & witnessed the daily decline of my poor suffering child—Dreadful post of observation darker every hour!—In August 1805 we turned our faces to Ireland— spent with the William Tighes & Blachfords some weeks at Birmingham, talking of Madeira & consulting Dr. Bree.[17]

After a very dangerous passage from Parkgate[18] we arrived in Dublin on the 10th of September & flattered ourselves the next two months which Mary spent between Dominick St, Rossana Bellevue & Vevai[19] (where John resided) that she was getting better. About the middle of November she came to Dominick St & staid there the next seven months, till the middle of June 1806, sometimes better & sometimes worse, saw a good deal of company, chiefly literary persons, & had the Blachfords in the house for three weeks—This visit was not very pleasant to either party. Indeed, no one could, I think, ever find Camilla a pleasant guest. & as both Mary & Henry found her a jealous & not goodnatured spy & in many respects oppressive, I was very glad when she left them. But felt much at the chagrin it was natural for John to feel in comparing their manner to his at Brompton. He could not possibly be sensible of the extreme difference of circumstances, tho' I do not mean to compare their dispositions in this respect—however great allowances must be made for straightened circumstances & constant ill health—bad attendance & an uncomfortable home & many particulars better forgotten than remembered—but John's unvarying & attentive kindness to her she ever remembered as she ought—

The summer of 1806 from June till the 19th of October she spent between Rossana & Vevai except one fortnight in August in Dublin, in which time she visited Mrs Brooke[20] in her dying bed. When she came to town in October it was to many doubtful whether she has lost ground or not, but I saw, I thought, an evident decline, yet not more than I expected—it was a few weeks before her return this time to town, that I lost my dear kind & faithful friend, Henry Brooke. My poor Mary was not in town above a month till she was seized with a violent rheumatic fever, attended with symptoms that everyone supposed would soon destroy her exhausted frame, but she revived a little about the end of December or beginning of January & was able, for a few weeks, to come into the drawing room—but her limbs were gone for ever. Early in February she relapsed & for several days no one thought it possible she could survive many more. She had now a blessed call to turn to her redeemer. Her sufferings were dreadful in her stomach & in all her inward parts. No one could say what ail'd her—but my soul was greatly cheered while witnessing her agonies, to see that her heart turned to her saviour with faith & penitence. She continued in extreme suffering & in a sweet spirit of patience & love, till the month of April, when to our great astonishment she again revived. It was at this time she wrote "Hagar in the desert"—

In the beginning of August 1807 she was so much recovered as to be able to leave town to go to Rossana, but finding that it did not agree with her, she returned soon to town by Altadore[21] (then John Blachford's) & stayed in Dominick St till the 20 of September when she went to Mr. Evans's Portraine[22] & was very hospitably entertained there for four weeks & returned to Dublin the next month, seemingly much better, except as to her limbs—

She held up tolerably well this winter & saw a good deal of company, much more than I approved of—indeed I grieved much at this circumstance as I thought it greatly deadened the impressions she had on her soul the preceding year. Tho' I trust their fruit was not lost—at the latter end of May 1808 she went to Rossana but returned to town in July after visiting Altadore for the last time, Avondale, & Westaston[,] where she wrote "The Myrtle.["][23] Early in August I went to Woodstock with her—we stayed at Woodstock till the end of October & we all thought the residence there agreed with her. The next winter was spent nearly as the last, nor did we think she lost any ground till about April when she had a slight fever which encreased her languor & weakness.

In the beginning of May 1809 she wrote the Lily & was able to go to Rosanna the 13th but returned to town the 8th of June & on the 13th of the same month set off for Woodstock spending ten days on the road between Hamwood, Mullycash & Kilfane.[24] On the 24th I joined them at Woodstock. But Oh what did I feel when I leaned forward to kiss her as she held out her hand to draw me to her, I saw evidently the hand of death stamped upon her face, & was from that moment, persuaded that she could never leave Woodstock but in her coffin; yet—we talked, & smiled, & seemed chearful. From this time till the 6th of August she went out almost every day either on a car, or in a carriage, & sometimes on horseback led by the servant, as was the case the last time she was out, before this great & deadly illness, with which she was seized I think, on the 7th of August while Henry was attending the Assizes of Kilkenny. It seemed to be the gout or rheumatism in her stomach, but I believe that not one of her many Physicians ever knew the real cause of her sufferings (her extraordinary sufferings) tho' I suppose it is too certain that the fatal illness she had in December 1800 laid the foundation of them.

We now thought her hour was indeed come but it pleased God to prolong her life for more than seven months. After this attack she lived in great solitude, seeing no one but Harry, her faithful maid Caroline & myself & occasionally Mr Innis[25]—Her brother during this period paid her three visits & by his desire, to her great comfort Mr. Richards came to her at an early period of her illness—her patience, gentleness, & kindness were great—her bodily sufferings were not all she had to contend with, but whatever she could not remedy she suffered silently. & was very grateful for every instance of attention & kindness which indeed she met with from every individual of the family. Her various, & multiplied complaints increased in number & painfulness from this time tho' with many intervals of comparative ease & cheerfulness. Yet all thro' she listened to reading dictated letters & directed the economy of the family. Every morning she called on me to read the Scriptures & generally to read some of the hymns with which she had been well acquainted in her youth. I read several religious books to her chiefly lives, in the course of the winter— she was particularly struck with the experience of Taylor a malefactor[26] & exclaimed "I wish I was that man"!—but when Harry was present, he or I read something of an amusing kind, as she thought that anything not really evil was to be preferred to our sitting staring at her, or perhaps, disputing as we were certainly not of one mind, tho' I bless God, that I ever loved him, nor have any reason to doubt his affectionate regard for me.[27]

About Christmas, or a little before she grew dropsical & wrote to Mr. Richards for his real opinion, which he so answered that with a sad look, & a tear, she threw his letter on the couch, & said "He gives me up[.]" It was, at this period, I think, she wrote the Mezerion, & received the sacrament from Mr Ker[.][28] Soon after this, the water she was oppressed with getting vent thro' her feet, she seemed much relieved & her feet become sore, I had some, tho' but little hope, that her life might be prolonged. She continued thus, about a month, till her feet became decidedly mortified & from that period, I gave her up. Indeed, I had done so with some transient intervals of a faint hope from the moment I saw her on the 24th of June when I met her at Woodstock.

About the middle of February she was anxious to leave her room, to which she had been confined since August & went into the adjoining drawing room two or three times & even suffered us to dine in the same room with her & eat with more pleasure & appetite than was customary to her in health & seemed to take comfort in seeing us with her at meal time—Yet, all this time, I gazed at her, as a dying person—Early in March, at her earnest request, the weather being very mild for the season, she was out three times round the lawn, in a carriage, but she looked so faint & ghastly that it was to me a very sad & mournful spectacle, nor could I consider it, by any means, as a proof of her amendment[.]

The violent pains returning in her limbs she did not go out after the 9th or 10th of March but on Wednesday the 21st, her brother being expected, she went into the drawing room between twelve & one oclock in order to get her room cleaned. & this she did without any previous notice—as the fire was low, the air very sharp & the windows not sufficiently close she evidently got a cold which fell on her poor worn lungs. I was aware of the danger & entreated her to let me put her shawl on her, & stuff the window frames, at her back, which I had always done when I knew she was coming out of her room but with her usual reluctance to any care about herself she would not suffer me. My poor, dear, Love was, I am sure tired by my over solicitude for all her interests, temporal & spiritual & like all other sins, it brought, to me, its own punishment.

Oh! how bitter it proved to me, at this time & indeed during the whole of her illness. God knows.

On this Wednesday, Mar 21st she was delayed in the drawing room, contrary to her inclinations till near five o-clock getting something done to the chair in which she sat, day & night, for many months past she had not attempted to lie down, or go to bed—About one o-clock while she sat on the couch in the drawing room, John arrived—She was extremely pleased & affected & seemed greatly revived at seeing him—But during her detention in the drawing room, it became extremely cold, so that before she returned to her own room she was herself sensible of having caught cold, & of extreme fatigue so that she declined letting us dine with her as she had first intended & as had been our custom during the last fortnight—But we drank tea with her & sat in her room till ten oclock, while John read, I know not what, but I think it was some new work that Mrs Seymour[29] had sent her—In the course of the evening he told her a piece of news which I though afflicted her, but she said nothing—She mentioned to John Mrs Seymour's desire of a motto & bid him look out for one. These are the only circumstances I remember of that evening's conversation. On Thursday morning the 22d she complained much of the increase of her cold & oppression on her chest. I read to her as usual in the morning. The lesson in the New Testament was the 26th of St. Matthew which I felt in a very peculiar manner & applied it, in my mind, to the agonies which I dreaded as coming on her, tho' by no means more apprehensive of the great change, than I had been frequently in the course of the last seven months—About one or two o-clock she was laid for a little resting (tho' sitting) on the couch & called for H Tighe & J Blachford—Caroline & I were already in the room. Leaning on her arm she made an effort of peculiar animation & told us "that the fear of death had for many years oppressed her but she thanked God it was taken away. & that she believed God would be merciful to her for that she felt him the strength of her heart, & that he would be her portion for ever & ever & ever."[30]

This was spoken with such animation of countenance as to surprise & cheer us all—the more for its marked contrariety to her lamentations the preceding week often expressed in these affecting words "Thy rebukes Oh Lord, have broken my heart."[31] Her eyes & countenance were so animated that we feared, at first, some degree of delirium, but every one of the few words she spake during the remaining 38 hours of her earthly existence proved the contrary[.] She was perfectly collected & gave a proof of it about six hours before her death, in understanding an obscure Latin sentence, that John read to her as a fit motto for Mrs Seymour, & the just criticism she made upon it. I am not certain whether it was the evening of the 22d or the next, the one immediately preceding her death that, while we were sitting round her, she looked earnestly at the Moon which shone in full at her window, & without words spoke to the heart of every person present more than I can pretend to explain & she said with a mild & melancholy expression "What is Life!"[32]

After tea she made John read something, but what it was I cannot recollect, I only know that it was some trifling book, merely to break the form of a sad circle.—My heart yearned to read something more suitable, but I feared disputation which was always most disturbing to her.

Early in the evening she had had a blister put on by Mr Innis who, on that account staid all night, at Woodstock, as it was not to be taken off till three in the morning. Till then neither Harry, nor John went to bed, but sat up in their rooms, while I, to my great comfort, obtained leave to lie down, in my cloaths on the bed, behind her chair.—The event of *Friday night* has entirely taken away from me the events of that day. I only know that Innis did not leave the house, that in the morning, she washed her hands & mouth & settled herself as usual & that I read to her afterwards, as they fell out in the course of our reading, the 14th of Job, the 27th of Matthew & out of the small Methodist hymn book the Hymns beginning

"Father in the name I pray"[33]—&
"Oh thou to whose all searching sight"[34]—

She then mended her old shawl & it was never after taken off till I took it some hours after her death from her poor breathless corpse, as we took her out of her chair to lay her on a bed—

John & Henry spent, I think, a great part of the morning in her room—After dinner about six oclock she expressed to Mr Innis as she did frequently to me a wish that he would pray for her, which he thought was with a view that we should outwardly join in prayer & Caroline came up to call me. But just as we reached the door of her room John & Henry came in from the dining room which prevented our attempting it—Oh! how happy are they who at such an awful scene as this have those about them whose hearts & lips are so touched as to be enabled to pour out their souls without being dismayed or embarrassed by the fear of man— She said to me this evening some sentence of which I could understand only three words "*You—sweet prayer.*" Her voice was so weak that I who was more deaf than usual, could not understand her & her respiration so difficult that I was afraid of paining her by desiring her to repeat what she said—(She told me herself, before Thursday, that what Mr Innis said had been greatly blessed to her & that he spoke very sweetly on the way of salvation—she had during all his attendance a great regard for & good opinion of him.) Her oppression increased towards night so that he put a fresh blister on her chest[.] In the course of this evening she gave me so sweet & kind a farewell kiss as I never can forget. It seemed to say what will you do without me? & frequently warmed her poor cold face on mine. Once she put her death cold hands in my bosom from the dreadful feel of which I involuntarily shrunk. Oh! why did I not rather press them to my heart? At ten oclock she insisted upon the gentlemen's leaving the room & as she had taken by Innis's desire half a grain of Opium we wished the room to be kept as quiet as possible. When the men were gone I dreaded her dismissing me, as I had not gone to bed the night before, & she was always very reluctant to my staying at night, but when I supplicated for permission to stay, to my great comfort & surprise she said with the sweetest kindest look "I would rather you staid" the last words she ever addressed to me—About eleven or twelve o-clock Caroline went to bed & I lay down, without taking off my cloaths, on the bed behind her chair. I heard her in the night frequently speak to the nurse in a soft voice but always sensibly, but tho' I was often up, at the fire, looking at my watch, I was afraid of disturbing her, by speaking as she seemed comparatively easy & slumbering & I was fearful of arousing her after taking Opium. How I regret that in those two or three hours (from 12 to 3) I did not speak to her, can only be imagined by those who loved with the same anxiety & fondness that I did. But God does all things well & I feel that I was not worthy of the blessing I so anxiously desired of a parting blessing & embrace[.] While talking to the nurse I heard her speak of John & Little William[35] with kindness & pleasure & all she said was cheerful. At half past two the nurse, as usual, called Caroline Turpin from whose hands my poor Love received the yolk of an egg, as was usual with her, at that hour, saying, at the time to Caroline "what will you do for me"[36]— she took the cup in her own hand & swallowed it entirely, though she generally left a part of it—In the meantime the nurse called Innis, as had been agreed upon, & he no sooner felt her pulse than he desired me to call Harry & John directly—when I returned she did not appear to me worse than I had frequently seen her. She called for "*Ether*" which was the last word I heard from those dear lips I had so often watched the opening. Innis bid Caroline hasten Harry & John but before they could reach the room she was gone for ever, from this scene of pain & sorrow without a groan, or sigh, or even a gasp.

The whole of the time from her swallowing the egg to her last breath, we all think, could not have exceeded ten minutes, in the former part of which ten minutes she had given, with the utmost propriety, directions for the carman who was to go to Kilkenny the following morning. For some minutes I could not believe her really dead—as I had several times seen her so faint as to believe her gone—when it was just a doubt, the first feeling I recollect was thankfulness that she had escaped those last horrors & agonies I had so long dreaded for her. & I felt no doubt then of her being safe lodged in the bosom of infinite Love, so true is the promise that in the hour of anguish "God will provide."[37]

So ended my dream of thirty seven years continuance, filled with bright hopes vain elation, wasting anxieties & cruel anguish. Indeed I do not think that there is any passion my heart is capable of feeling which was not by her exercised to the utmost.

The three days & a half her body remained above the earth it realised that hymn she so much admired, often repeating the first line of it

"Ah lovely appearance of death"[38]

looking far better, fairer & younger than she had done for many months before, so that on Tuesday at one oclock in the afternoon, tho' she had died in the night on Friday (that is on two o-clock on Saturday morning the 24th of March) she looked so well, that I would not suffer her coffin to be closed till Innis painfully, oh how painfully convinced me of the necessity. "But this corruption shall put on incorruption & this mortal shall put on immortality.["][39]

She was buried at Inistiogue on Tuesday afternoon the 27 March 1810 in a new tomb where HT intends to have some memorial of her— I saw the spot before I left Woodstock, a short time after the crowd that attended her funeral was dispersed.

She bears the long cold wintry night
And bears her own degraded doom
And waits till Heaven's reviving light
Eternal Spring shall burst the gloom.[40]

In this account I have omitted her wish expressed to Innis, the evening before her death, that it might take place that night, yet without the smallest impatience, but with great thankfulness for the frame of mind in which she found herself. She said that death was but one dark spot in our external existence.

More than three months before her death in the evening of the 21st of December she was seized with a faintness, apparently the faintness of death. On her recovering a little from it but while I thought her in the gasp of death she called to me for pen & paper & wrote two sides of a half sheet which she desired me to direct to Henry Tighe. I could scarcely believe that she was in her senses. But the contents proved the contrary— I asked her what I was to do with it & she bad me give it, after her death to HT. She had before written the following words. "Dearest Mama, to you I leave the trouble & sorrow of looking over my papers"—& at the same time bequeathed to her brother fifty volumes requesting him to write in them, these words "From my only sister, from her to whom I was most dear from infancy to death."

It is but justice to HT to add how she concluded this note, written, as I have said, the 21st of December before her death; after providing for (her maid) Caroline, she added.

> Generous, dearest love! do not mind anything else I may have left, but I promised kind Caroline that she should never want & you will fulfill my promise—my beloved! My last hours have been comforted by your tenderness, & only embittered by the grief that I have not been to you such as you deserved—Oh! take care of yourself, & do not let a mistaken generosity lead you to hurt yourself for ever in Society. Adieu, but not for ever, we shall meet above—

The concluding sentence proves how deeply she thought upon a subject to which she scarcely ever alluded even to me, I believe not above three times in her life, tho' she knew I was acquainted with it. Nor, I believe, ever to anyone else except to her brother, when she saw him a few weeks before her death—She expressed herself in nearly the same terms as in her last paper, at the conclusion of a will she wrote 9th August 1807.

The paper was written with a trembling hand but legible.

Caroline Hamilton

MARY TIGHE[1]

I have often wished to give some account of the Author of Psyche, but year has passed after year while I have still shrunk from the difficulty of telling only what could interest an impartial reader. However, as no person will probably preserve any memorial of her if I do not, I shall not delay any longer to relate whatever I can now remember worth preserving. Her father Mr Blachford, was a clergyman of the established church. He was a man of unblameable character, but not, I understand remarkable for talents for literature. [2] He married at the age of forty, Theodosia Tighe, daughter of William Tighe of Rossana in the Co of Wicklow, whose wife was Lady Mary Bligh sister to Lord Darnley.[3] Theodosia lost her mother early & in a great measure educated herself. Half a century ago a governess was not considered, as at present, an indispensable member of every gentleman's family[4]—an old nurse generally taught to read & the Parish clerk, to write. & if a young lady possessed any taste for literature, she was permitted to read what she pleased in her father's library which generally consisted of Old Romances, Books of Divinity, & tedious Histories. The advice to a daughter, written by the Marquis of Halifax, which appears to have gone through ten editions, & which I found in the library at Rossana, with Lady Mary Tighes name written in it, shews that little was required of an accomplished woman except to make the most of a drunken husband, to learn how to govern a silly one & to manage the house with economy.[5] The best topics of conversation were derived from a certain degree of worldly wisdom, which gave a habit of reflection without the assistance of much education. Mr. Tighe was a sensible man, his remarks were shrewd, but the gout, to which he was a martyr at no very advanced period of life, had soured his temper, & his daughter past her youth in laborious attendance on him. Finding that he always slept best when somebody read to him, she was obliged to rise, at a very early hour, to take her place at his bed side while the attendant who had read the early part of the night, enjoyed a little repose. They read old histories & travels, among which the most amusing were Mandeville's travels from Aleppo to

Jerusalem & Lord Raleigh's voyage round the world.[6] The histories, I have heard her say, were dry & tedious & as little amusing to the attendant as the Greek writers [were] to Milton's daughters.[7] Theodosia, however, who possessed a very reflective mind acquired a taste to reading superior to most of her contemporaries &, at an advanced period of life, remembered much that she had read by his bed side. Mr. Tighe was a man of considerable property & Rossana, tho' it has now suffered from the hand of time, was once one of the best kept places in Ireland. Its shady walks & magnificent trees, bending over the mountain stream still endear it to a fourth generation.

> Yet live, & long shall flourish, when no more
> Our eyes shall measure their expanding shade,
> These antique chestnuts, & this tapering lime
> Crowning the shelved bank, that well known yew
> Shall still be climbed by many youthful groups
> Of generations yet unborn, as once by us.
>   W. Tighe[8]

In this delightful scene Theodosia passed the early part of her life, in contemplation, & here was early formed her character for piety, for which she was afterwards so much distinguished. A few years after the death of his first wife, Mr. Tighe married again, much to the dissatisfaction of his daughter, who tho' but a child, had been taught to dislike a stepmother.[9] I have heard her tell an anecdote, which shews how early she began to moralise. She was one day much displeased at being contradicted by her stepmother; she quitted the room suddenly, stopped the door after her, & sat down on the stairs to weep. She had read, in the morning, the 5th chapr of Job & the 7th verse. "Man is born to trouble, as the sparks fly upwards"[10] coming into her mind, she repeated it to herself several times & reflecting that she alone could not be exempted from the lot of mankind she was ever afterwards obedient to her mother & it was to her that Mrs Henry Tighe addressed the lines (published among her occasional poems) which begins,

> Sweet Placid spirit, blest, supremely blest!
> Whose life was tranquil, & whose end was rest![11]

Mrs Blachford loved her as much as if she had been her own mother.

She had two children, a son & daughter, both eminent for piety.[12] Theodosia had three brothers. The eldest, William, my father, was universally admired for the uprightness of his character & beloved for his courteous manners, he distinguished himself at Eton, by writing verses, some of which are published in the Musae Etonenses,[13] & he gained the gold medal at Cambridge. He published a letter addressed to his Uncle Lord Darnley on the injury which Ireland sustained from absentees. He died of a fever, in the forty fourth year of his age.[14] His eldest son William was the author of the statistical survey of the Co of Kilkenney & a didactic poem, entitled the Plants besides many other poems, unpublished.[15] Theodosia's second brother Edward, early attached to the Theatre lived much with the actors & wits of his day. He was allowed to excel in the art of reading, which made his society much courted, tho' he could not always restrain the irascibility of his temper & was often ridiculous from his various excentricities. Some laughable anecdotes are told of him in the life of the poet Dermody. He wrote pamphlets & verses in abuse of whiskey, which, together with potatoes, he considered the cause of the misery & degradation of the Irish. He married an heiress, was often in Parliament & had a place under government.[16] His younger brother Richard preferred a more tranquil life & was soon remarkable for his piety. I have heard him relate how he was first led to think upon the subject of religion. When he was young it was not as much the subject of conversation as in our time. His father used to say that the whole of religion was contained in the 8th v 6 of the chapter of the book of Micah "He has shewed thee O Man what is good, & what doth the Lord require of thee, but to do justly, to love mercy. & to walk humbly with thy God"[17] which was then supposed to be an easy task. Richard thought as other people did, till one day, while standing at a door in Wicklow with the clergyman of the parish (Dr. Watts) a beggar asked him for something "for Christ's sake." He said that was an appeal too strong to be resisted & gave him some money. "Why I believe you are become a Methodist Mr. Richard" said the Dr. "A Methodist! I do not know what you mean replied Richard. I never heard of such a thing. Come along with me then, said the clergyman, & I will give you a book which will tell you what a Methodist is." He gave him a small tract, entitled, the character of a christian, written by Mr. Wesley,[18]—it pleased him so much that he copied it & sent the manuscript as a curiosity, to his sister, little imagining, he told me that he could buy as many as he pleased for a penny a piece. The next time he saw her, she told him that if such writings pleased him she would lend him a book which he might like & she took down from her shelf a volume of Mr. Law's works which he read with avidity & from that time, he became a steady disciple of Law's. He published his Life, & several little pamphlets containing extracts from his works, with a few explanatory notes.[19]

It was necessary that I should give some account of Mary's nearest connections to shew that the society in which she lived during the early part of her life, was calculated, in different ways, to inspire her with a taste for reflection & study. In those families where the conversation never rises above the common topics of the day &, where wealth is valued more than knowledge, even genius often lies dormant. Mr Blachford died of a fever three years after his marriage. His death was a severe blow to Theodosia, she had the consolation, however, of witnessing a most remarkable change which took place in his mind, upon his death bed. She saw him pass from a state of the greatest despondency to that of the liveliest hope in the merits of a Redeemer.

Being now mistress of her own actions, Mrs Blachford retired entirely from the world, & as far as was consistent with the education of her son & daughter, followed the example of Law's Miranda.[20] As she had long been in the habit of teaching poor children, she began with some experience, & great ardour, the education of her own. She thought that women could not be so usefully employed as in teaching their children. She disapproved of the higher orders wasting their time in plain work[21] by which she considered that they defrauded the industrious poor. Man, she used to say, was born to labour, but in different ways—The poor, to supply the rich with the necessaries of life & the rich, to gain knowledge for the purpose of disseminating instruction. A sufficient skill in plain work is easily acquired by a sensible woman should her lot in life require the labour of her hands; for such cloaths as would be suitable to her situation are easily made & who would wish her to indulge her vanity by making an appearance far above her means? Many women who have passed their youth round a work table, are obliged to spend more than they can afford in masters, & governesses for their children while they are occupied destroying the neatness & simplicity of their dress in making frills & flounces, their ingenuity enabling them to follow every fashion at a moderate expence.

Mrs Blachford, being too anxious that her children should excel in every mental acquirement, was obliged, after a few years, to give up the instruction of her son. He did not learn as fast as she thought he should & she felt that she could not bear this, with temper, but, before she sent him to school, she had given him the habit of attention & the love of truth & justice for which he was afterwards remarkable. I have heard him say that Law's serious call, which he used to read to her, when a boy, left an impression on his mind, which was never effaced. It taught him the difference between right & wrong, & gave him a tender conscience, which, though it did not contribute to his happiness in this world, brought him, at last, through many vanities & disappointments, to seek for consolation in religion alone.

By his Uncle Edward's advice he was sent at twelve years old, to Eton, where he was made unhappy by his mother's too great anxiety. She allowed him scarcely any pocket money, lest he should spend it foolishly & on this account he was obliged to live separate from his schoolfellows, spending his leisure hours in solitude, reading every book of amusement in the circulating libraries. He never spoke with any pleasure of the time he spent at Eton tho' few boys possessed his talents, or distinguished themselves more than he did in the University of Dublin, where he gained every honour. Mrs Blachford was now left alone with her daughter & here let me observe that Mothers are fortunate who can undertake the education of their daughters, as the generality of young women who are obliged to earn their bread as Governesses, having their own advantage chiefly in view, & possessing but little knowledge, teaching becomes a very irksome task to them. It interferes with their habits of indolence & they endeavour to excuse their own negligence by giving their pupils a character for dullness & obstinacy which they do not deserve & which is not easily forgotten. Even the most conscientious governess does not scruple to ask the advice of visitors & friends of the family when any disagreement takes place between her & her pupils. The more patient mother, on the contrary, finds no difficulty in concealing the little trifling faults which she scarcely perceives & which she knows will cease with childhood. & she feels amply rewarded, for her patience in possessing the whole confidence of her daughter, which gives her the power of forming her taste & opinions & of preserving her from the knowledge of much of the evil of the world. & if a Wise mother, she will value these advantages more than the most correct Parisian accent or even a very good carriage. The tender affection which Mary felt for her mother is expressed in the following lines written at Rossana in 1791, during her first absence from her. [Hamilton transcribes "To Her Mother. Rossana 1791," lines 1–12.]

Mrs Blachford considered that the usual method of educating girls by rigorously appropriating every hour of the day to some task (almost always irksome), dulled the faculties & failed in its object of giving a taste for literature. While children are very young they must be forced to learn certain dry rudiments but a time arrives, when if they have been taught habits of application & if the advantage of possessing knowledge has been impressed upon their minds, they will cheerfully continue their education themselves. It will then afford them great pleasure to read & think alone, without the troublesome interference of a governess, who would imagine them idle when only reading & in whose presence they never could scribble their thoughts on paper, the only means of acquiring the valuable & rare accomplishment of writing correctly & with ease. The first attempts at composition are usually incorrect & contain few new ideas & the cold contemptuous look of a Boarding school grammarian would for ever prevent further education; but the partial mother, who has often experienced herself the difficulty of expressing her thoughts in writing, admires the feeblest attempt at invention & the child's first composition, in this case, is rarely the last.

Many years before any writer on education had dared to call in question the utility of making an unhappy child, learn year after year, columns of spelling from Abbot to Zoology, Mrs Blachford taught spelling by writing. At a very early age Mary's chief employment was copying neatly into blank books, Poems & select passages from good authors which were always well chosen as Mrs Blachford had a warm imagination & great feeling which I have heard her daughter say would have made her a literary character if her education & religious principles had not turned her thoughts another way. Besides transcribing from English authors, Mary translated volumes from French to which I attribute the ease with which she soon learnt to write. She committed much Poetry to memory, repeating what she learnt with great feeling & good taste for her Uncle Edward had taught her to read & considered her as one of the best of his pupils.—He was thought to read so well & had such a love for teaching that many of the young actors of the day solicited his instructions, both in England & Ireland.

Mary had masters to teach her both music & drawing but as these accomplishments were not much valued by her mother she was not encouraged to practice sufficiently to excel in either. She played a little on the Harp, to amuse herself, & the only use she made of her skill in drawing was to ornament with appropriate tail pieces,[22] her occasional little Poems of which she has left many neatly written manuscripts. The books she read were not, I must say, such as a prudent Mother, at present, would give to her daughter, they were mostly works of imagination, in French, English & Italian & to a much indulged taste for these, she attributes in her preface to Psyche whatever talent she possessed as a Poet.[23] In the society of her mother's friends in whose conversation there was always something to excite reflexion & to lead to a knowledge of human nature, her mind was early enlightened to see the vanity of the world, though she afterwards found its pleasure irresistible—I have heard both her & her brother acknowledge the advantage of having been educated among religious people, as it had prevented them from imbibing the vulgar prejudices against Methodism, so universal among those whose minds have not been enlarged by an acquaintance with all descriptions of people. Mary continued, to the last, to love & respect many of her early associates & two or three years before she died, when she had lost the use of her limbs, she was carried to the bed side of one in humble life, who had long been her patient monitor to receive his last blessing.[24] What her opinions were at the age of seventeen may be known from the following lines [Hamilton transcribes "August 1789," lines 1–20, 25–36].

But these good feelings were, alas! soon exchanged for a strong desire to be admired. Her mother could not resist the pleasure she felt in hearing her beauty praised & sent her to some public places, imagining that she could not in any other way, procure acquaintances for her, in her own rank of life & fearing that she might reproach her afterwards if she confined her entirely to the company of poor Methodists. Mary indulged her desire to please, not only in the world where she had some admirers, but in her own family & she was accused of coquetting with her cousin Henry Tighe, who became so violently attached to her that he threatened to go off to America, or to commit some act of violence, if she refused to marry him. He was the second son of Mrs Blachford's beloved brother, considered handsome, & of a most generous, ardent disposition, but not religious, nor even, it was thought, strictly moral.[25] Mary did not love him—but his family, particularly his mother, thought that she had used him ill in gaining his affections & many letters passed between the two mothers—Mary's health suffered from the anxiety of her mind—at length being overcome by the persuasions of his friends & by a generous feeling, which made her think that she had acted wrong in regard him—she married him at the age of one & twenty—he was twenty two & her poor mother bitterly repented to the last hour of her life, having given her consent to this marriage.

They had an income of a thousand a year, but as they did not think that sufficient, it was determined that HT should continue his studies at the Temple[26] & take a small house in London, but HT, though possessed of a great taste for literature, had not the power of applying himself to the dry study of the law. He gave a special pleader[27] a hundred guineas, scribbled two or three times in his office, but learnt nothing, from him, I have heard him say, but to fill a glass of wine for himself at dinner, without attracting notice by asking anyone to drink with him, getting in return for his money only a few good dinners.

Many of the acquaintances which he made at Harrow[28] now idle young lawyers, associated with him to discuss literary subjects & admire his pretty wife. Though her mother had permitted her to go to some assemblies,[29] she had never been at the Theatre & I remember the first time he proposed to take her there. I was with her. He had taken us one evening, out in a carriage, & we knew not where we were going, when we stopped at Drury Lane.[30] She remonstrated, wept, fearing to grieve her poor mother, who had followed her to London & lived in the house with her & who, justly, had a great prejudice against all Theatrical amusements. But Mary had no firmness to resist persuasion & she was so much delighted with Banister & Mrs Siddons,[31] that, from that time, she went frequently to the Play house. Her husband soon abandoned the prospect of rising at the Bar & as he saw no probability of having a family, he sought only for amusement for himself & his wife at water drinking places, in England during some summers & in Dublin during several winters.[32] HT made no acquaintances in the world, where he let his wife go by herself. He spent an idle life, at home, reading for amusement, not profit & associating with those only with whom he felt perfectly at his ease. I often thought him much to be pitied as he saw that his wife did not love him, though he loved her. She felt pity for him too, & was always grateful to him for the instructions which he gave her everyday in Latin, in which she soon made a considerable progress. & she translated, with his help, a variety of authors, not much known & improved her taste by his remarks. She never suffered him to pass a day without reading with her, so ardent was her thirst for improvement. The task was sometimes troublesome to him as he had not acquired habits of regularity, but she would not allow him to be absent at the appointed hour for study, her early education having taught her to employ her time diligently, & to her industry in this respect, may be attributed that she was able some years afterwards to undertake the difficult task of composing Psyche after she had in some measure, lost her health & spirits. A little acrostic addressed to him will show how much she considered herself indebted to him. [Hamilton transcribes the first ten lines of "Acrostics."] Though she spent every evening that she could in society, she always rose early to read for some hours before her companions in dissipation were awake, which her poor mother thought was one means of undermining her health as she never seemed refreshed by sleep.

Her anxious mother always lived in a small lodging near her, continually praying for her & always ready to go to her in an evening if she happened to have no engagement to take her from home. At such times she used to work while her mother or husband read to her if one or two of her nearest relations were not there to join in easy, pleasant conversation, which in her family (more than any other I have since been acquainted with) never flagged. She alludes to her happiness at these times in the following lines, [Hamilton transcribes "La Cittadina: On Leaving Rossana 1798," lines 119–132].

"I cannot agree with you," she says, in a letter to me "that a town life is, at best, a dawdling life. On the contrary there is no where I am so disposed for study, & have enjoyed more leisure. I always stand up for a town retirement, because all the knowledge I have & all the disposition for study to which I owe my chief happiness was acquired in town. I am naturalised to it & what is very singular, I find nothing so conducive to industry as the possibility of being interrupted. I am seldom inclined to sit down to do anything when I know that for six or seven hours, I may remain at it undisturbed. Who is it says that we never employ time with more rigid economy than when we reflect on the many hours which escape contrary to our inclination & who is there that does not derive pleasure from solitude when he perceives the progress he is capable of making while the multitude roll in their carriages thro' the streets & make every wall tremble to its foundation?" She says in another letter,

I drove out in the curricle[33] yesterday, the whole morning & tasted in some degree the exhilarating pleasure belonging to the early spring which you so strongly described & which, I am sure, you feel so warmly at present. I think these delightful sensations belong as much to youth, as to Spring & that every year deadens the keenness with which we hail the reviving charms of nature, so that these like all the other pleasures of life, diminish under the pressure of time. Other causes may however have damped in me the exquisite enjoyment of those temperate breezes, animating beams and fresh verdure which I still feel, at times, "able to chase all sadness but despair."[34] I do not, however agree to your conclusion that having been, in general a resident in town, at this time of year I have never known what were the pleasures of Spring, for I am quite convinced that the country is seen & felt never to such advantage as within a few miles of a great city, having thus all the additional, & striking, charms of novelty & contrast—I languish for the fresh air a thousand times, but cannot deny that I would not give up the society which a town affords one without the severest pain

Yet, though carried away by the love of admiration she felt deeply convinced of the senseless & fruitless vanity of what is generally, but falsely called, a life of pleasure. As appears from the following lines [Hamilton transcribes excerpts from "Pleasure": lines 1–6, 13–18, an additional couplet,[35] and 19–26]. One of the great evils of dissipation is that it blunts the most amiable feelings of human nature—The death of a relation or friend is often but slightly felt, while the mind is occupied with prospects of future amusement. The cessation from balls & parties, which decency requires is often perceived to be irksome & the mind longs to throw off the melancholy which might, otherwise soften the heart & dispose it for receiving religious impressions. Mary's feelings were, however, always alive & after the death of one of her gay companions she wrote to me as follows.

To C.T.
In the gloom of an afflicted hour, when my heart is unable to bestow chearfulness & ease sufficient to mingle in the conversation of common society, why should I intrude myself & my sorrows on my beloved & happy C. Yet I naturally feel comfort in unbosoming myself to her kind and partial ear—I have lost my brother, my too affectionate brother! & God knows when we shall meet again—yet why should I lament his departure—he is indeed separated from me by the Ocean & soon will kingdoms & mountains intervene between us.[36] But there is hope—we may yet enjoy bright hours of happiness together, he may return at no long period of time, better, happier, & as kind to me as I have seen him depart. But Ah! for the dead there is no return! & who knows, he may in some dreadful hour, attended by no agonising sister, be cut off by a sudden & fearful stroke. 'Twas even thus, my poor friend, the unhappy

Fortescue has been sent to appear before an all merciful, but alas, I
fear, too little thought of Creator.[37] You have certainly heard of this
event, you have been like me struck with horror at the account—
No warning given! & Gracious God! to die insensible! without an
hour of sickness in which his terrified soul might fly to the only
refuge of man—I confess the idea haunts me without ceasing. Who
next shall be summoned away? Yet may we not hope that he who
willeth not the death of any sinner has not suffered his unthinking
soul to depart without some moments in which infinite mercy may
have been shewn! O my dear C may not my soul be thus required
& how unfit is it to appear before its judge! What my poor friend
was, I know not—but alas! I know myself & feel that I am
unworthy of being spared, but Merciful Heaven! avert from me this
judgement. From sudden death deliver me! dreadful is the sound of
a companion's death! Ashamed for him, ashamed for myself I have
suffered a shock more violent than I can express. I have begun to
dread the cruel Tyrant, I think upon every friend & consider them
as his devoted prey. The good things which I enjoy, the dear
relations I so much love seem stealing from me—I tremble at my
love for them—while I write a thunderstorm terrifies my
imagination (you know my foolish terrors). You will not be
surprised that I feel inclined "to talk of epitaphs & elegies, of graves
& sepulchres. Lets chuse executors & make our wills[.]"[38] Indeed I
cannot banish from my mind the melancholy end of him, whom I
do not now scruple to call my friend, how remarkable is it that the
very last morning I saw him he should express much terror &
reluctance at going to Ireland & that he should, indeed, only land
on Saturday & be no more on Monday. From what I can gather, I
fear very much that he owes his death to some medicine taken by
mistake—Surely in the midst of Life we are in death! My poor
John![39] One thing peculiarly torments me at this moment. I will
mention it to you with my usual freedom. You know how pious he
is, not in word, but in deed & in truth—& yet *I* so much below
him in this greatest favour of Heaven, dread his present situation.
Thousands of young men, I have known return from Italy—not *one*
alas! but has been corrupted in principle & profligate in manners.
Oh who can say my heart is established. I can never be moved. In
the world the travelled gentleman the man of polished manners &
accomplished mind may please & the charms of his society may

captivate mortals like himself; but alas! what are these when death approaches! Let the friends of him declare who possessed those advantages in no common degree & is now departed—

Yet it cannot be denied that the society of such men of the world, & the ardour with which she seemed to court admiration, drew upon her the censure of many but how innocent her husband considered her may be seen from these few lines which he addressed to her.

> Gay Fashions' daughters' little care
>   Though slander false attack their fame
> They scarcely hate the vicious snare,
>   Why should they dread ideal shame?
>
> Are they the object of some tale,
>   Of others frailties they can tell,
> Be they, or seem they to be frail
>   If others seem the same, tis well.
>
> Yet my sweet Mary shrinks with fear
>   Oft from detractions idlest word,
> Though all who may the scandal hear
>   Must own, must feel the tale absurd
>
>   HT.

Youth & beauty, however, are but of short duration & Mary often felt her spirits depressed from the fancied neglect of friends & the imaginary slights of a world which she had loved too well. It was her idea that learning and talents in women, never excited love &, while young, she was willing to pass for having neither. I remember hearing it remarked that Mrs Tighe was very pretty but had not much sense. Indeed, she often chose for her companions those who were very far below the rest of the world in talents if they loved her. She never tried to shine in conversation & was often considered too silent in company. She was always in the habit of writing a journal, which was a practise recommended by her mother but tho' it gave a fluency to her style, it only gave her survivors the painful trouble of burning it as it contained only the trifling adventures of a gay life, interesting at the time to the writer, but to nobody else—She wrote indeed during her latter years, a kind of more interesting diary & it would be well if many would follow her example.[40] She noted down every book she read & her observations upon them, & it appears that she read a variety of books during the course of the year. It may not be uninteresting to the reader to know her opinion of Milton.

> I have great reason to be dissatisfied with my want of taste if Milton does indeed deserve all the admiration which has been lavished upon him; a great part of what I read in this Poem (which I nevertheless acknowledge to be a wonderful effect of genius) can give me no pleasure, but rather a sentiment of disgust. The speeches he gives to the Heavenly Beings appear to me generally tedious & almost blasphemous. & there are a thousand circumstances which are to me mean & unpoetical as well as unworthy of his subject; to name one. What can be more absurd than his transformation of the Devils into serpents & his converting their applauses into a hiss!—

Though so fond of society there was no period of her life when she did not enjoy retirement & occasional Solitude—while being at Rossana she wrote to me, "in my present situation nothing could be more apropos than your observations on your own life, you exactly describe the calm in which every day passes with me & I sympathise easily with the sentiments which make you feel not only contented, but happy, where, however, your pleasures are not very lively. Alas! the time is perhaps not far distant from each of us, when a victim to sorrows oppressed by cares or tormented by disquietude we shall look back with fond regret upon our present moments & reproach the insensibility & want of gratitude with which we are now possibly sometimes inclined to accuse them of insipidity. & yet I am not ungrateful, even now I feel & acknowledge the pleasures which arise from 'instructive ease, fireside enjoyments, home born happiness & all the comforts which the silent roof of undisturbed retirement—& the hours of long uninterrupted evening know'"[41]—
Another time she wrote:

> In the mean time I try, as I have said, to enjoy my own society & am grateful for peace & tranquility for though I cannot agree with you in thinking this to be "The summit of earthly happiness" yet I think a reasonable person ought always to make out a happiness for himself if he can reflect that he does not suffer actual pain. "Il n'est pas toujours besoin de la jouissance des plaisirs, si on fait un bon

usage de la privation des douleurs, on rend sa condition apres heureuse."[42] I think it is St. Evremont[43] says this & I am sure it is true, though his authority in other sentences may be questionable. I botanise a great deal & when I come home loaded with exquisite beauties & wonders, I say to myself with a degree of triumph & self satisfaction "the world scorns these & calls them by the indiscriminate name of weeds[.]" I am fond of quotation or rather of expressing my own sentiments in better words than my own. Let me say then of Botany that "il y a dans cette occupation un charme que l'on ne sent que dans le plein calme des passions, mais qui suffit seul alors pour rendre la vie heureuse & douce"[44] & indeed I am almost unwilling when I engage in this study, to lay it aside for any other.

As her health declined her love of occupation encreased & it was then she formed the plan of writing a long poem which she used to continue at intervals. In the same way & about the same time, she wrote a novel, Selena, reading out to us the beginning & leaving us to guess how she meant to conclude it. Unlike Miss Edgeworth, who, I remember, told me that she generally finished the entire rough sketch of her story before she filled it up.[45] When Psyche was concluded her husband admired it so much that he persuaded her to let him print fifty copies of it to be distributed among her friends & as a few of them were given to some of the most distinguished characters of the day (C Fox, Mr. Hayley, &c&c) her reputation for talents rose at once[.][46] She received many most complimentary letters & from that moment her society was eagerly sought for by all within reach of her who had any pretentions to literature or talents.

Mr Hayley sent her the following lines with a copy of Cowper's life, 1806. [Hamilton transcribes Hayley's sonnet "Records of Genius! traced by friendship's hand!" lines 1–14.][47] Roscoe, Moore & others wrote verses to her in the same flattering strain & her poor mother, who watched her with unceasing anxiety, saw her now as much exposed to the injurious smiles of the world as in the days of her youth & beauty.[48] Her love of literature & of literary society & the society of those who paid homage to her talents, seemed to make her cling with great tenacity to life—her fears of death had been always very great for she knew well that she would be relieved from them only by such a faith as she daily witnessed in her mother—her friends alarmed by a long continued cough which

became very troublesome in the year 1804 persuaded her to go to Bristol—
she wrote to me from thence:

> We have been in our new lodgings about a fortnight it is in the
> very first situation in Clifton & possesses the finest points of view
> & what is esteemed the best air in the world, but alas! it brings no
> healing on its wings to me. I am not better, nor I fear shall I ever
> again know perfect health, but I hate complaints, remedies & would
> say, Physicians, had I not been restrained by the remembrance of Sol:
> Richards, & the conviction that Dr. Crawford (who however does
> me no good & condemns me to the torture of perpetual blisters) is
> a most amiable man.[49]

Again she wrote describing the view from her window

> —Behind me St. Vincent's Rocks,[50] which (as a Botanist) is a name
> which should be familiar to your ear & from the testimony of
> Withering[51] you will perceive that it is a scene the most favourable
> for such researches. But what I most highly value, the wood with
> which it is covered abounds with Nightingales who keep watch,
> with me, every night, & sooth the painful hours of fatiguing
> exercise from my incessant cough & difficulty of breathing. I hear
> the little plaintive melodists as plain as if they were on my window
> stool, but should hardly have distinguished them from a thrush had
> I not been told to expect a similarity in their first notes. I thought
> of you when I walked to the spot where Withering bid me expect
> the Bee Orchis,[52] but alas! one half withered specimen alone
> remained of all the brilliant garland offered to the Spring—

In another letter she says.

> On Tuesday last, in consequence of an obliging message from
> Hannah More, we paid her a visit of about two hours & a half, at
> her very beautiful cottage situated among the Mendip hills about
> twelve miles from this.[53] The cottage itself, the garden & its ornamental
> buildings vie in elegance & taste with Llangollen.[54] & tho' the
> surrounding scenery cannot boast of the romantic & wild sublimity
> of the Welsh Fairy place, yet few spots in this kingdom can afford
> views of equal beauty (in the rich cultivated style) with Barleywood,

where Hannah More & her two sisters reside. She received us with much affability & to me in particular, gave the kindest looks I ever had from a pair of lively, searching, black eyes, yet in her manners there was an air of protection (as the French call it) & a consciousness of superiority (which though it never offends me) I am quite sensible is not, in itself, such as is best calculated to gain general love. From the village that surrounds her cottage, among many spires, stands conspicuous, the tower of Wrington, the birth place of Locke.

From Bristol she removed to Brompton in the neighbourhood of London from whence she wrote in December 1804.

I have had severe weather & felt it severely, in spite of our six Thermometers, roaring fires & constant warmth which has been so effectually kept up in my rooms, that during this whole hard winter, I have never had my hands cold, nor known anything of the frost except its influence on my chest which is inconceivable. Vaughan shakes his head & says with a disappointed air, "Ah! she must breathe our air though we do warm it"[55]—My nights have been, in general much better this last month, but that is decidedly the effect of medicine, & I am obliged to change the opiates continually as each loses its effect. The first nights of a medicine are to me indeed blessed Sabbaths & my spirits are better than they have been at times when my strength & health had not "failed me."

She wrote in the following January 1805. [Hamilton transcribes "Psalm CXXX. Imitated, Jan. 1805" lines 1–4, 9–12, 21–28.] She returned to Ireland in the course of the summer of 1805 & lived during the following four years, sometimes at Rossana but chiefly in Dominick St where every exertion was made by numerous friends, to alleviate her sufferings. During these years she wrote, Hagar in the desert, The Myrtle, & The Lily which are printed with Psyche & which all discover a mind dissatisfied with itself & endeavoring, though feebly, to look for happiness beyond this world. "The dear suffering saint," mentioned in the Myrtle, was her aunt & namesake, Mary Blachford. I find an account of her death in a letter from Mrs Blachford to my mother, & as Mary often spoke of her during her sufferings, wishing that she might exercise like patience, I shall transcribe it.

May 1788

Ever since I last wrote to you I have spent all my leisure moments at poor Molly Blachford's bed side, who expired this day, between one & two o-clock. For the last twelve months she has borne the most complicated pain & sufferings with the utmost patience & a perfect acquiescence in the divine will, as fully believing it was all the effect of his infinite wisdom & love, & the only possible way for her salvation. Her patience, resignation & love have seemed daily to have encreased from the beginning. She has kept her bed for the last seventeen days & lived, during that time, without any visible sustenance (on account of her weakness of swallow encreasing) except a few drops of whey every day & even that could not be got down during the last six days, so that she was literally starved to death. But "Man lives not by bread alone."[56] As her sufferings encreased, so did her faith & hope. She declared she never knew such transport, nor knew before how to call God her father. May we die the death of the righteous & may our last end be like her's full of faith, hope & love.

T Blachford.

But we must now turn to another scene. While Mary lived in Dominick Street she was visited (as she says herself in one of her letters) by "troops of Friends" all vieing with each other which should contribute most to her amusement. She was latterly not only confined to the house but to her couch, yet the early part of each day was still spent in Study & she had often little evening parties where Moore sang his sweetest songs to a few (perhaps not more than eight or ten) of those who were then most esteemed in Dublin, for rank or talents. Moore visited her constantly & often submitted his works, to her criticism, while they were yet in manuscript. He shewed her one little poem & by her countenance, which was capable of the greatest expression, he saw that she highly disapproved of it—he threw it into the fire—but some months afterwards it appeared in print. Lady Morgan, then Miss Owenson, was often invited to tea to entertain the company, tho' Mary neither liked nor esteemed her, but she tried to bring together those who could talk to amuse her, while she often remained silent, at her work, the little she ever said, at such times, was pointed & interesting.[57] She never attempted to lead the conversation in mixed company, but in a tete à tete no person could be more agreeable, she had such a knowledge of the human heart, such quickness of feeling & listened with so much interest to everything that was said to her. & there were many, at that time who experienced the truth of this—& whose sweet flattery often made her forget her sufferings & her fears of death. Her poor mother felt this & bitterly lamented it. She never let a day pass without visiting her, at a very early hour, to sit by her bed side & read the Bible to her, particularly the Psalms, which I heard Mary recommend to a person in great affliction as what always comforted her most when suffering from sickness or sorrow. Her mother knew them almost all, by heart, & had probably made her very well acquainted with them when she was a child, for she knew well of what consequence it is that parents should let the first impressions on the minds of children be in favour of Religion as our earliest impressions always follow us to the grave. I knew a very eminent Christian whose mind, on her death bed, occasionally wandered, & once, a silly old Ballad roaming in her head, she said with great feeling, "Oh! why will parents suffer their children to learn songs in the nursery!" Mary's sufferings seemed to encrease daily & neither the smiles of Lady Charlemont, the kind looks of William Parnell, nor the visits of Lady Asgill & Sir Arthur Wellesley, Duke of Wellington, nor the coarser flattery of Lydia White,[58] could stop the progress of her disease—in a note to me she said that many of her days were "lost to her from her incapability of doing anything but sit with her head leaning on the pillowed arm of her couch in a state between sleeping & waking" & during every night her sufferings from difficulty of breathing were very great & sometimes "her head" she said "never for one moment reposed upon her pillow" yet on what she called her "well days" her friends left her very few minutes alone after two oclock. She had for some time lost the use of her limbs, but still her active mind found amusement in literature & she read almost every new publication & the arrival of every new review seemed to give her great pleasure. She read, I remember, about this time, a little tract, one of the first published, giving an account of a man at Bath, who was sentenced to be executed but whose fears of death were entirely removed before he left his prison by faith in Christ.[59] "Oh," she said, "how willingly would I exchange places with him"!—

The physicians thought that change of air might be of use to her & in July 1808 she was removed to Rossana & as an instance of the tenderness of her disposition I shall transcribe a part of one of her letters from thence, to me—

I was much annoyed at finding myself evidently & seriously the worse for my journey & change of air so that the days I passed at Bushy[60] & on my first arrival here were days of great suffering—but I have now, at least recovered my ground & enjoy inexpressibly the extreme transition from the black walls at Dominick St & Walter's[61] odious prospect to our magnificent chestnuts & all the full bloom of fragrance & beauty in the gardens—we have no mignionette in bloom but I saw dearest Caroline's kind remembrance of me in some that has just made its appearance & cannot tell you how pleasing it was to my heart when I was told you had sowed these pots for me. I intend to save some of the seed & will never be, I hope, a year without reviving this dear & sweet proof of your love—

In the summer of 1809 she went to Woodstock & there her poor mother had the satisfaction of seeing her removed from the flattering society which she considered so injurious to her. During the Autumn her bodily infirmities daily encreased. She had few visitors. This country was not scattered, as it now is, with pious ministers & intellectual & refined as she was she was glad to find in the Village of Inistiogue, a scotch Sergeant (whom she believed to be a Christian), to pray with her. While her mother read to her she used to employ her poor emaciated hands making cloaths for cripples like herself as she used to call them for whom she felt a great pity & it was for this reason that the money produced after her death, by the publication of Psyche was intended to be appropriated to the support of two lame girls in the House of Refuge.[62] Her mother wrote to me on the second of July 1809.

Poor Mary suffers many variations of painful & dangerous complaints but on the whole, she is, I think considerably better than she was ten days ago, for which we should be thankful, but I cannot keep up my spirits when I look at her in her present sad state, though neither she nor I are unmindful that we have many alleviations in our present affliction—

The vigour of her mind continued unimpaired to the last in December she wrote the Meserion which tho' already published I must insert here. [Hamilton transcribes "On Receiving a Branch of Mezereon Which Flowered at Woodstock. December, 1809," lines 1–48.] She sent these lines to her brother who returned the following answer.

2d February 1810.

My dearest Mary,

If I had the power of giving you half as much pleasure by my letter,
as the six words in your handwriting at the head of your sweet
melancholy verses have given me, what gratification I should have
in writing to you, but tho' I cannot hope this, I must not be
ungrateful in delaying to thank you both for your verses & their
address. I have accepted them as an omen of brighter hours & tho'
you fear to permit yourself to do so yet surely I am not too
confident when I promise myself that the restoration of even a
small degree of bodily power & the unimpaired state of your mind,
so satisfactorily shewn in your very beautiful verses, is a symptom
of the return, however slow, it may be[,] of health & if this much be
the product of winter may you not, as well as I, trust that our
Spring may be a spring to you. Heaven grant that when you read
this you may feel that my confidence is not ill founded & that your
symptoms of strengthening life & lessening pain may be encreased.
I have little to tell you of myself, or my employments that would
interest or amuse you. I am every day busy in doing what I think at
the time necessary & what I find, when it is done unprofitable.
"Semper in augenda festinat et obruitur re"[63] I will not use the
penultimate inauspicious word but contrarily my haste is not
successful—do not believe I can ever forget you or that I cease to
pour the fervent, would it were an availing prayer for you. Adieu.

JB.

Her mother read the bible to her every morning & the day before she
died the chapter which came in its course was the 14th of Job.—"1 Man
that is born of a woman is of few days & is full of trouble—2 He cometh
forth like a flower & is cut down—he fleeth also as a shadow & continueth
not" & when she read & "doest thou open thine eyes upon such an one &
bringest me into judgement with thee"[64] she gave a most expressive look—
towards evening such a coldness came over her that even her brother &
her attendant shrank from her touch—it seemed already the coldness of
death—she was carried for change of air, from the drawing room, of
which she had made a bedchamber, into the saloon, & laid upon the
couch—it was dusk, the window shutters had not been closed & the full

moon appeared with unusual brightness—she cast her languid eyes upon it & uttered, What is life?[65]—it is possible to conceive what her thoughts were at that moment—all life's vanities & follies passed in review before her. Friendships from which she had derived so little profit—pleasures which had always been embittered by reflection—& Fame which now indeed seemed but an empty bubble—everything had sunk to its real value & she felt that she was quickly passing alone into the presence of her God—

Her mother read to her that evening

Jesus, lover of my soul
   Let me to thy bosom fly,
While the distant thunders roll
   While the tempest still is nigh.

Hide me, oh my saviour hide,
   Till the storm of life is past,
Safe into the haven guide,
   Oh receive my soul at last.[66]

She frequently during the last days of her life uttered this mournful lamentation "Thy rebukes, O Lord, have broken my heart"[67] but shortly before her death she turned to her brother & husband, who were both by her bed side & reminded them of the horror she had always felt at the thoughts of death, but with a most animated countenance she said that her terrors were now entirely removed & that she felt that God was the strength of her heart & would be her "portion for ever & ever."[68] After this she spoke but little. Her mother said that she seemed full of peace & kindness & a chearful desire to depart, observing that death was but one dark spot in our existence, tho' before this period she always expressed her wish to continue in a state of the extremest sufferings rather than to be released by death. She retained the perfect use of her faculties to her very last breath, which was without a struggle or a pang so as to appear as if she had fallen asleep.

APPENDIX

Tributes to Mary Tighe

Thomas Moore

TO MRS. HENRY TIGHE, ON READING HER "PSYCHE"[1]

Tell me the witching tale again,
    For never has my heart or ear
Hung on so sweet, so pure a strain,
    So pure to feel, so sweet to hear.

5   Say, Love, in all thy prime of fame,
    When the high heaven itself was thine;
When piety confess'd the flame,
    And even thy errors were divine;

Did ever Muse's hand, so fair,
10   A glory round thy temples spread?
Did ever lip's ambrosial air
    Such fragrance o'er thy altars shed?

One maid there was, who round her lyre
    The mystic myrtle wildly wreath'd;—
15   But all *her* sighs were sighs of fire,
    The myrtle wither'd as she breath'd.

Oh! you, that love's celestial dream,
    In all its purity, would know,
Let not the senses' ardent beam
20   Too strongly through the vision glow.

Love safest lies, conceal'd in night,
    The night where heaven has bid him lie;
Oh! shed not there unhallow'd light,
    Or, Psyche knows, the boy will fly.[2]

25   Sweet Psyche, many a charmed hour,
    Through many a wild and magic waste,
To the fair fount and blissful bower[3]
    Have I, in dreams, thy light foot trac'd!

Where'er thy joys are number'd now,
30   Beneath whatever shades of rest,
The Genius of the starry brow[4]
    Hath bound thee to thy Cupid's breast;

Whether above the horizon dim,
    Along whose verge our spirits stray,—
35   Half sunk beneath the shadowy rim,
    Half brighten'd by the upper ray,[5]—

Thou dwellest in a world, all light,
    Or, lingering here, dost love to be,
To other souls, the guardian bright
40   That Love was, through this gloom, to thee;

Still be the song to Psyche dear,
    The song, whose gentle voice was given
To be, on earth, to mortal ear,
    An echo of her own, in heaven.

Thomas Moore

I Saw Thy Form in Youthful Prime[1]

I saw thy form in youthful prime,
    Nor thought that pale decay
Would steal before the steps of Time,
    And waste its bloom away, Mary!

5   Yet still thy features wore that light,
        Which fleets not with the breath;
     And life ne'er look'd more truly bright
        Than in thy smile of death, Mary!

     As streams that run o'er golden mines,
10   Yet humbly, calmly glide,
     Nor seem to know the wealth that shines
        Within their gentle tide, Mary!
     So veil'd beneath the simplest guise,
        Thy radiant genius shone,
15   And that, which charm'd all other eyes,
        Seem'd worthless in thy own, Mary!

     If souls could always dwell above,
        Thou ne'er hadst left that sphere;
     Or could we keep the souls we love,
20   We ne'er had lost thee here, Mary!
     Though many a gifted mind we meet,
        Though fairest forms we see,
     To live with them is far less sweet,
        Than to remember thee, Mary![2]

     William Stanley Roscoe

SONNET TO MRS. HENRY TIGHE, ON *HER POEM OF "PSYCHE, OR, THE LEGEND OF LOVE"*[1]

     I saw in heaven, before the throne of Jove,
     A vision bright, and midst her odorous bowers
     Fair Psyche sate culling eternal flowers,
     While o'er her stood entranc'd immortal Love!
5   And ever as the blooming wreath she wove,
     Shed from his beaming eyes ecstatic showers;
     And on the amaranthine buds he pours
     His breath, that all the leaves with rapture move.

Fair Psyche smil'd, and rais'd her blissful eyes.
10   "This crown for her whose chaste and hallow'd song
Hath so rejoic'd us midst our native skies,
And echoes still these sapphire vaults along,
For her who sung our wanderings on the earth,
And hail'd with hymns of joy our heavenly birth."

Anna Maria Porter

Lines written after reading the "Corinne" of Madame de Stael, and the "Psyche" of the late Mrs. Henry Tighe, of Rosanna[1]

Magic omnipotent! resistless power
Of Genius, seraph-lipp'd! how doth thy force
Seize the most fixed soul, and bear it on
Thro' every change of passion, pain, or joy!—
5   How mighty is thy sway! how wide its range!
How varied, e'en in uniform design!—
Lo! now thro' different lips, thy voice inspired,
Speaks to my heart; transports, depresses, fills!—
In rapt amazement lost, the same fond theme
10   Wondering I hear, and mark how different each!—
Methinks from deep shades, swells th' Eolian lyre;
While from some twilight grove, soft Philomel
Warbles her rival song.—Hark to the strains!—
That magic instrument which Heaven's own breath
15   Wakes to mysterious music, that sweet harp,
Low to the breeze in dying languor sighs!
Now louder roused, rings like the trumpet's blast
To Glory calling!—next, with temp'rate swell,
Gentle, and soft, and calm, in lulling tone,
20   Spreads rest and tender bliss o'er all things round,
Tuning the mind to dreams of holy peace.—
Now, whispering voices like the heavenly choir,
Scarce breathed, scarce heard, suspend my thrilling heart:

Then moanings, as of melancholy shades,
25   Chill Rapture's pulse.—Anon, from yon dark pass,
Rusheth the wind, and borne on wailing wing,
With piercing blast of sound, sweeps all the strings
In Phrensy's sudden shriek, or demon's yell:
Now resting on one deep and dismal note,
30   Continuous, strange, and wild, it loads the ear
With loud lament of hopeless, fixed despair.—
The strain is o'er!—mute now, the mystic breath!—
Sadness and stillness reign; alone disturbed
By the heart's beatings;—ceased!—in silence fix'd!—
35   ★   ★   ★   ★   ★
Ah, sounds divine! whence flow ye? from yon copse,
Steal on the depth of night, melodious sighs
From Love's own bosom heaved: the warbled lay,
First softly wooing, then lamenting sad,
40   Now trembling with delight, with hope, half bliss,
With dear persuasion of partaken joy,
Soars and descends by turns: all nature melts
To softer charm, beneath its influence pure;
With tenderer light, looks down the pensive moon;
45   With gentler murmur glide the silver streams;
More balmy breathe the flowers; and stiller stand
The listening trees; the human breast o'erflows
With holy rapture; virtue, love, and joy
All swell together, till in tears dissolved,
50   The sweet emotions find their happy way.—
Nightingale of Rosanna! thou art gone!
Snatched 'mid thy tuneful life, to sing above!—
Earth's guilty echoes, dared not answer thee;
(Echoes, so oft devote to Passion's voice,
55   Tuneful indeed, but lawless, and profane.)
Wondering we saw the stream o'erflowing Love,
Yet pure from mortal dross; as tho' it well'd
Strait from the fount of Heaven!—ah, sure it did!
And to that sacred source hath back returned.—
60   How happy they, who 'mid thy native shades
Roved near thee ever, and with tranced ear
Or heard thy liquid notes thro' joyous day,

Mixed, (still pre-eminent,) with Nature's band
Of varied minstrels; or with deeper draught,
65   Drank their rich nectar 'mid the lonely scenes
Of night and silence! happy they! whilst we
(Thro' deep embowering woods, at distance far,)
But heard thee once, tho' never to forget!—
And thou, O harp of strange and wondrous mould!
70   Thou lyre Aeolian! may the air that wakes
Again thy chords, come fraught with peace or joy!
May never blast of madd'ning anguish shake
Those chords; nor the life-with'ring sighs of grief,
Nor blighted hopes, in sad vibration dwell
75   Upon thy mournful strings! when next they speak,
May all blest Araby's innumerous sweets
Hang on the breeze that sweeps them into sound!
May breath of angels aid the blissful gale,
And while thou warblest love, awake the soul
80   To thought of Love's best world, the world of Heaven!

Bernard Barton

STANZAS ON PERUSING PSYCHE,

A Poem, By The Late Mrs. Tighe[1]

"Fond dreamer! meditate thine idle song,
  But let thine idle song remain unknown:"
O guard its beauties from the vulgar throng,
  Unveil its charms to friendship's eye alone.
5   To thee shall friendship's partial praise atone
  For all the incense of the world beside;
Unthinking mirth may slight thy pensive tone,
  Folly may scorn, or ignorance deride:—
The lay so idly sung, let prudence teach to hide.

10   Sweet Minstrel! couldst thou think a song like thine,
  With grace replete, with harmony inspir'd,
Thy timid modesty could e'er confine

Within those limits which thy fears desir'd?
　　Ah no! by all approv'd, by all admir'd,
15　Its charms shall captivate each listening ear;
　　Thy "Psyche," by the hand of taste attir'd,
　　　To virtue, grace, and delicacy dear,
　　Shall consecrate thy name for many a future year.

　　Oh! had indulgent heaven but spar'd thy Lyre,
20　　　Which first it strung and tun'd to melody,
　　How many an heart had felt encreasing fire,
　　　Dwelling enraptur'd on its minstrelsy:
　　How many an ear had drank its harmony,
　　　And listen'd to its strains with sweet delight;
25　But He, whose righteous will is sovereignty,
　　　Hath bid thy sun of glory set in night,
　　And, though we mourn thy loss, we own his sentence right.

　　Yet, plaintive Songstress! on thy gentle lay
　　　Fancy with pensive tenderness shall dwell;
30　Memory shall snatch from Time thy transient day,
　　　And soft regret each feeling breast shall swell.
　　But, why regret? Let faith, exulting, tell
　　　That she, whose tuneful voice had sung before,
　　In allegoric strain, love's witching spell,
35　　　Now sings HIS love whom wondering worlds adore,
　　And still shall chaunt his Praise when time shall be no more.

Felicia Hemans

THE GRAVE OF A POETESS[1]

"Ne me plaignez pas—si vous saviez
Combien de peines ce tombeau m'a épargnées!"[2]

I stood beside thy lowly grave;—
　　Spring-odours breath'd around,
And music, in the river-wave,
　　Pass'd with a lulling sound.

5   All happy things that love the sun
           In the bright air glanc'd by,
       And a glad murmur seem'd to run
           Thro' the soft azure sky.

       Fresh leaves were on the ivy-bough
10   That fring'd the ruins near;
       Young voices were abroad—but thou
           Their sweetness couldst not hear.

       And mournful grew my heart for thee,
           Thou in whose woman's mind
15   The ray that brightens earth and sea,
           The light of song, was shrined.

       Mournful, that thou wert slumbering low,
           With a dread curtain drawn
       Between thee and the golden glow
20   Of this world's vernal dawn.

       Parted from all the song and bloom
           Thou wouldst have loved so well,
       To thee the sunshine round thy tomb
           Was but a broken spell.

25   The bird, the insect on the wing,
           In their bright reckless play,
       Might feel the flush and life of spring,—
           And thou wert pass'd away!

       But then, ev'n then, a nobler thought
30   O'er my vain sadness came;
       Th' immortal spirit woke, and wrought
           Within my thrilling frame.

       Surely on lovelier things, I said,
           Thou must have look'd ere now,
35   Than all that round our pathway shed
           Odours and hues below.

The shadows of the tomb are here,
    Yet beautiful is earth!
What seest thou then where no dim fear,
40   No haunting dream hath birth?

Here a vain love to passing flowers
    Thou gav'st—but where thou art,
The sway is not with changeful hours,
    There love and death must part.

45   Thou has left sorrow in thy song,
      A voice not loud, but deep!
The glorious bowers of earth among,
    How often didst thou weep!

Where couldst thou fix on mortal ground
50   Thy tender thoughts and high?—
Now peace the woman's heart hath found,
    And joy the poet's eye.

Felicia Hemans

LINES WRITTEN FOR THE ALBUM AT ROSANNA[1]

Oh! lightly tread through these deep chestnut-bowers
    Where a sweet spirit once in beauty moved!
And touch with reverent hand these leaves and flowers,
    Fair things, which well a gentle heart hath loved!
5   A gentle heart, of love and grief the abode,
    Whence the bright streams of song in tear-drops flow'd.

And bid its memory sanctify the scene!
    And let the ideal presence of the dead
Float round, and touch the woods with softer green,
10   And o'er the streams a charm, like moonlight, shed;
Through the soul's depths in holy silence felt—
    A spell to raise, to chasten, and to melt!

Felicia Hemans

WRITTEN AFTER VISITING A TOMB, NEAR WOODSTOCK, IN THE COUNTY OF KILKENNY[1]

Yes! hide beneath the mouldering heap,
The undelighting, slighted thing;
There in the cold earth, buried deep,
In silence let it wait the Spring.
> Mrs. Tighe's *Poem on the Lily.*

I stood where the lip of song lay low,
Where the dust had gathered on Beauty's brow;
Where stillness hung on the heart of Love,
And a marble weeper kept watch above.

5   I stood in the silence of lonely thought,
Of deep affections that inly wrought,
Troubled, and dreamy, and dim with fear—
They knew themselves exiled spirits here!

Then didst *thou* pass me in radiance by,
10   Child of the sunbeam, bright butterfly!
Thou that dost bear, on thy fairy wings,
No burden of mortal sufferings.

Thou wert flitting past that solemn tomb,
Over a bright world of joy and bloom;
15   And strangely I felt, as I saw thee shine,
The all that sever'd *thy* life and *mine.*

Mine, with its inborn mysterious things
Of love and grief, its unfathom'd springs,
And quick thoughts wandering o'er earth and sky,
20   With voices to question eternity!

Thine, in its reckless and joyous way,
Like an embodied breeze at play!
Child of the sunlight!—thou wing'd and free!
One moment, *one* moment, I envied thee!

25   Thou art not lonely, though born to roam,
Thou hast no longings that pine for home;
Thou seek'st not the haunts of the bee and bird,
To fly from the sickness of hope deferr'd:

In thy brief being no strife of mind,
30   No boundless passion, is deeply shrined;
While I, as I gazed on thy swift flight by,
One hour of my soul seem'd infinity!

And she, that voiceless below me slept,
Flow'd not her song from a heart that wept?
35   —O Love and Song! though of Heaven your powers,
Dark is your fate in this world of ours.

Yet, ere I turn'd from that silent place,
Or ceased from watching thy sunny race,
Thou, even thou, on those glancing wings,
40   Didst waft me with visions of brighter things!

Thou that dost image the freed soul's birth,
And its flight away o'er the mists of earth,
Oh! fitly thy path is through flowers that rise
Round the dark chamber where Genius lies!

Felicia Hemans

ON RECORDS OF IMMATURE GENIUS[1]

Written after reading *Memorials of the late Mrs. Tighe.*

Oh! judge in thoughtful tenderness of those,
Who, richly dower'd for life, are called to die,
Ere the soul's flame, through storms, hath won repose
In truth's divinest ether, still and high!
5   Let their mind's riches claim a trustful sigh!
Deem them but sad sweet fragments of a strain,
First notes of some yet struggling harmony,
By the strong rush, the crowding joy and pain
Of many inspirations met, and held
10   From its true sphere:—Oh! soon it might have swell'd
Majestically forth!—Nor doubt, that He,
Whose touch mysterious may on earth dissolve
Those links of music, elsewhere will evolve
Their grand consummate hymn, from passion-gusts made free!

NOTES

INTRODUCTION

1. *Quarterly Review* (1811). See the bibliography for a listing of all known reviews of *Psyche*.

2. Tighe figured prominently in much nineteenth century discussion of literature that took up the work of women poets, only some of which is cited above, and she was praised for her lyric poetry as well as *Psyche*: David Main classed her sonnets "with the very best that had been written by women up to her time" in his 1880 *Treasury of English Sonnets*, an encomium repeated by Elizabeth Sharp in her 1887 *Women's Voices*.

3. See the Longman archives in the Reading University Library. I am grateful to Mike Bott for this information.

4. See the appendix of this edition for a sampling of the verse tributes Tighe received from Moore, Roscoe, Porter, Barton, and Hemans. Tributes from Hayley and Dacre are printed in the notes to "To W. Hayley, Esq. in Return for a Copy of Cowper's Life, with a Sonnet—1806" and "Psyche's Answer" (to Dacre's tribute).

5. One interesting exception is Earle Vonard Weller, who sought to demonstrate the significance of Tighe's impact on Keats in *Keats and Mary Tighe* (1928).

6. Marlon Ross, Greg Kucich, Anne Williams, James Chandler, and Andrea Henderson have reexplored the connections between Tighe and Keats; Norma Clarke, Isobel Armstrong, and Susan Wolfson have considered Tighe's impact on Hemans; Susan Stanford Friedman, Mary Loeffelholz, John Anderson, Jonathan Wordsworth, Stephen Behrendt, John Pipkin, James Dunn, Jim Mays, Martin Priestman, Diego Saglia, Laura Mandell, Stuart Curran, and Paula Feldman have examined Tighe's work in the context of other women or contemporary writers; and the editor has published several essays on Tighe's value as a Romantic-era poet.

7. See the bibliography for a comprehensive listing of recent anthologies that include selections from Tighe's *Psyche* and other poems.

8. For additional material on Tighe's life and family, see Mrs. Richard Smith, *The Life of the Rev. Henry Moore* (1844); C.H. Crookshank, *Memorable Women of Irish Methodism* (1882); Eva Mary Bell, *The Hamwood Papers* (1930); Patrick Henchy, *The Works of Mary Tighe* (1957); Elizabeth Mavor, *The Ladies of Llangollen* (1971); Muriel McCarthy, *Marsh's Library* (1980); Mary Lightbown, "Memorial to a Poetess" (1993); Conor O'Brien, "The Byrnes of Ballymanus" (1994); Patricia Butler, "Printing at Rossanagh" (1995); John Kirwan, "William Tighe" (1998); and Ruan O'Donnell, *The Rebellion in Wicklow, 1798* (1998).

August 1789

1. Written in the summer of 1789 and published in 1811 as the first poem in William Tighe's *Mary, a Series of Reflections During Twenty Years* (NLI LO 373, pp. 5–6), prefaced by his comment "Many of these Reflections were written in very early youth, and may be inaccurate; but are not the less valuable to those for whom *alone* this Selection is intended" (3). Tighe's journal entry for July 5, 1789 reflects her effort to focus on spirituality: "It is long since I put pen to this book. How my heart has been since employed I would willingly bury in oblivion. But there is a book kept, a dreadful book! wherein every word & work & thought is registered. Gracious God! give me wisdom to make my calling an election sure. Let me work while thou grantest me light. Lest the night should come wherein no man can work." Caroline Tighe Hamilton (1777–1861), Tighe's sister-in-law, prints this poem in her journal as evidence of Tighe's firm religious conviction at seventeen, omitting lines 21–24.

2. Tighe's epigraph is a variation on an air sung by Irene in Georg Friedrich Händel's oratorio *Theodora*, composed in 1750 with a libretto by Thomas Morell, about a Christian martyr (Theodora) who preserves her chastity: "Bane of virtue, nurse of passions, / Soother of vile inclinations, / Such is, prosperity, thy name. / *True happiness is only found, / Where grace and truth and love abound,* / And pure religion feeds the flame" (act 1, my emphasis).

Good Friday, 1790

1. Written in the spring of 1790 and published in 1811 in *Mary* (7). Tighe's journal entry for August 21, 1790, expresses frustration with her inability to stay focused on spirituality: "A year has now elapsed since I have written anything here—It would indeed be impossible to relate how my heart has been since affected, but this to my eternal shame I must own that thou, Oh my God, hast not been in all my thoughts & indeed scarcely in any. Sometimes called off by vanity. & led in the foolish trappings of this world—in the paths of self admiration. Sometimes my heart has been distracted by vain pleasures. False hopes, foolish disappointments, idle pursuits—trifling sorrows, useless alarms & childish vexations—Alas! my thoughts are more intent upon worldly knowledge, worldly fame & worldly pleasures than upon that knowledge which can alone be useful to my immortal soul—but Lord! shall I live ever thus return unto thyself my heart."

To Her Mother. Rossana, 1791

1. Written in 1791 and published in 1811 in *Mary* (8). According to Caroline Hamilton, Tighe wrote the poem at Rossana during her first absence from her mother (Hamilton journal). In a letter from Rossana dated May 5, 1791, Sarah Tighe tells William Tighe (then in Berlin) that Mary Blachford is a great beauty with great charm who has been out in public and much admired (PRONI MS D/2685/1/34).

From Metastasio, 1791

1. Written in 1791 and published in 1811 in *Mary* (9). Mrs. Richard Smith prints a transcription of an autograph copy Tighe gave to Rev. Henry Moore in *The Life of the Rev. Henry Moore* (1844), titled "Poem or Prefatory Sonnet, by

Signor Abate Metastasio. Translated by Miss Blachford" (218). Pietro Metastasio (1698–1782) was Italy's major Enlightenment poet; Tighe's poem is inspired by his Sonet 1 (1733):

> Sogni e favole io fingo; e pure in carte
> Mentre favole e sogni orno e disegno,
> In lor, folle ch'io son, prendo tal parte,
> Che del mal che inventai piango e mi sdegno.
>   Ma forse, allor che non m'inganna l'arte,
> Più saggio io sono? È l'agitato ingegno
> Forse allor più tranquillo? O forse parte
> Da più salda cagion l'amor lo sdegno?
>   Ah che non sol quelle ch'io canto o scrivo
> Favole son: ma quanto temo o spero,
> Tutto è menzogna, e delirando io vivo!
>   Sogno della mia vita è il corso intero.
> Deh tu, Signor, quando a destarmi arrivo,
> Fa ch'io trovi riposo in sen del Vero! (2:938, lines 1–14)

SONNET, MARCH 1791

1. Written in March 1791 and published in 1811 in *Mary* (10). The first of Tighe's numerous sonnets, composed of seven couplets.

VERSES WRITTEN IN SOLITUDE, APRIL 1792

1. Completed in April 1792 and published in 1811 in *Mary* (11–12). Elizabeth Owens Blackburne prints this poem in *Illustrious Irishwomen* to illustrate Tighe's state of mind in "1792, at the close of a gay Dublin season," as she "mingled in the society which she so despises herself for having been enthralled with, chaperoned by her aunt, Mrs. Tighe" (2:54–55). Tighe quotes an earlier version of the final quatrain in her journal entry for October 9, 1791: "This day I am nineteen. How shall I express what I feel when I reflect minutely on my past life. . . . Read over some old letters & papers which gave birth to many reflections. At the end of 1791 these lines—'Thus was the low ambition of my mind / Thus were the vain desires I formed, / For such delights my calmer joys resigned, / And quenched the fires which had my bosom warmed.'"

2. Castalia] a spring on Mount Parnassus, sacred to Apollo and the Muses, and regarded as a source of inspiration.

3. the nine] The Muses, daughters of Zeus and Mnemosyne (Memory), originally known collectively as the nine and later identified with specific fields: Clio for history, Urania for astronomy, Melpomene for tragedy, Thalia for comedy, Terpsichore for dance, Calliope for epic poetry, Erato for love poetry, Polyhymnia for sacred poetry, and Euterpe for lyric poetry.

MARCH 1793

1. Written in March 1793 and published in 1811 in *Mary* (12).

SONNET ("AS ONE WHO LATE HATH LOST A FRIEND ADORED")

1. Written in London, June 1794 (*Mary* 13) and published in 1811 in *Psyche, with Other Poems* (226).

TO DEATH

1. Written in Cheltenham, August 1795 (*Mary* 13) and published in 1811 in *Psyche, with Other Poems* (235). On July 25, 1795, Tighe learned that a friend had died, and her journal entries reflect how deeply the death disturbed her. On July 25, 1795, at Cobham she writes "My God! how cold is the grave—The receptacle of all we love! & all we fear. Very terrible is the sentence which in one cruel word separates us for ever from those we love. Covered by the devouring tomb, soon forgotten by all! & the immortal soul gone to appear before an unknown God!" On August 11, 1795, at Holyhead she contemplates her voyage to Dublin: "'Gone to that bourne from which no traveller returns'!—How soon, my Lord, may that also be my fate! I could not look at that great & tremendous ocean, which I was ordained to cross, without some apprehensions on my own part.—Tho' so smooth & flattering with prosperous gales how shortly might the scene be changed & a few hours turn into threatening forms & fatal waves the now placid elements— But even thus is our life! So smiles the morn, & thus uncertain are its smiles."

WRITTEN AT SCARBOROUGH

1. Written in Scarborough, August 1796 (*Mary* 13) and published in 1811 in *Psyche, with Other Poems* as "Written at Scarborough. August, 1799" (220). The Tighes lived in Scarborough, England, during the summer of 1796; in a letter dated July 24, 1796, Tighe describes her impression of the sea view to Sarah Tighe: "as I never before liv'd directly within full view of the sea I find it a never failing amusement—Indeed I could not have believ'd that there was such an infinite variety in an object which at a distance appears with such a tiresome sameness—I have from my window the view of the open sea & a beautiful harbour—without the disadvantage of a view which the tide entirely carries away—I hate that circumstance & would rather have no sea at all, than have it only for a few hours with a bare strand the remaining part of the day" (PRONI MS D/2685/2/44).

SONNET ("WHEN GLOWING PHOEBUS QUITS THE WEEPING EARTH")

1. Written in the late 1790s and published in 1811 in *Psyche, with Other Poems* (221).

2. Phoebus] the sun.

WRITTEN IN AUTUMN

1. Written in the late 1790s and published in 1811 in *Psyche, with Other Poems* (222).

THE VARTREE

1. Written in Rossana, July 1797 (*Mary* 13) and published in 1811 in *Psyche, with Other Poems* (244–47). The Vartry River flows through Rossana.

2. "Here more than elsewhere the plants are shady, the grass is soft, and it appears fresh and sweet." Angelo Poliziano (1454–1494) was the name assumed

by Angelo Ambrogini, the Italian humanist and great textual scholar known in English as Politian. Although Tighe uses these lines twice—as epigram to "The Vartree" and in an August 2, 1802 letter to Joseph Cooper Walker (TCD MS 1461/5)—they do not occur in any printed copy of Poliziano's Italian poetry. However lines communicating the same thought appear in Poliziano's *Stanze cominciate per la giostra del magnifico Giuliano di Piero de' Medici* (1475–1478), "Stanzas Begun for the Tournament of the Magnificent Giuliano de' Medici," which describes Julio's efforts to win the love of Simonetta:

> Sovente in questo loco mi diporto,
> qui vegno a soggiornar tutta soletta;
> questo è de' mia pensieri un dolce porto,
> qui l'erba e' fior, qui il fresco aier m'alletta;
> quinci il tornare a mia magione è accorto,
> qui lieta mi dimoro Simonetta,
> all'ombre, a qualche chiara e fresca linfa,
> e spesso in compagnia d'alcuna ninfa. (book 1, stanza 52)

"I often walk in this place, I come here to sojourn alone; this is a sweet haven for my thoughts; here the grass and flowers, here the fresh air attract me; the return from here to my house is short; here, I, Simonetta, rest happily in the shade beside some cool and limpid stream, often in the company of some other nymph" (translated by David Quint, 27).

3. Zephyr] soft gentle breeze.
4. Dryad] tree nymph.
5. Naïad] water nymph.

SONNET ("POOR, FOND DELUDED HEART! WILT THOU AGAIN")

1. Written in March 1797 (NLI MS 4810) or March 1798 (*Mary* 13) and published in 1811 in *Psyche, with Other Poems* (223). Theodosia Blachford cites the sonnet to show how "vanity still prevailed as is expressed in her sonnet dated the Spring of 1797. . . . Indeed almost all her poetry, as well as her cast of countenance declared her internal unhappiness" (Blachford journal).

WRITTEN IN THE CHURCH-YARD AT MALVERN

1. Written in the late 1790s and published in 1811 in *Psyche, with Other Poems* (224). The Tighes probably took the waters at Malvern during a summer visit in the mid- to late-1790s; Caroline Hamilton describes how Henry Tighe "sought only for amusement for himself & his wife at water drinking places, in England during some summers & in Dublin during several winters" (Hamilton journal). Malvern was famous for its springs, its rolling hills, and the Malvern Priory, a church that survived from a fifteenth-century Benedictine monastery.

VERSES WRITTEN AT THE DEVILS BRIDGE, CARDIGANSH

1. Written in the late 1790s and copied by Henry Moore in May 1811 from Tighe's manuscript into the Henry and Lucy Moore MS Album: Poems HM 1811, Chawton House Library (63–66). A devil's bridge usually refers to bridges

in difficult places, such as the Devil's Bridge in Cardiganshire, South Wales, twelve miles east of Aberystwyth, over the river Mynach.

2. "In this place one may reveal hidden anguish without punishment." Tighe takes her epigraph from Propertius's *Sexti Properti Carmina:* "hic licet occultos proferre impune dolores" (1:18, line 3).

BRYAN BYRNE, OF GLENMALURE

1. Written in the autumn of 1798 and published in 1811 in *Psyche, with Other Poems* (281–96). An autograph copy in PRONI MS D/2685/11 contains several interesting variants. William Tighe notes that "The story of Bryan Byrne is founded upon facts which were related to the author in the autumn of 1798: though the circumstances may not have happened in the exact manner which is recorded in the poem, yet it gives but too faithful a picture of the sentiments and conduct of those days. It is certain that at that period several unarmed persons, report says above twenty, were put to death by the troops near Wicklow, to retaliate the murder of many loyalists, and particularly of the three brothers mentioned in this ballad" (*Psyche, with Other Poems* 314). Tighe's ballad conflates at least two highly publicized incidents: first, the execution of the heroic rebel Billy Byrne of Ballymanus, whose life and death would be celebrated in the famous "Ballad of Billy Byrne"; and second, the death of three yeoman, Thomas, Joseph, and James Bryan, who were killed at the Tighes's Ballynockan estate by rebel insurgents during a raid on September 26, 1798.

2. Carickmore] the "great mountain" in Irish, or the Carrick mountain in Wicklow.

3. Glenmalure in county Wicklow saw some of the fiercest battles between the Irish rebels and the British in 1798 and served as a hiding place for the rebel leader Michael Dwyer.

4. locks] "curls" in PRONI MS D/2685/11.

5. PRONI MS D/2685/11 includes an additional stanza between lines 24–25 as follows: "For he had caught the glance of fire / And seen the mother's saddened smile, / And mingled feelings strong inspire / The wish on each to dwell awhile."

6. men of blood] "soldiers" in PRONI MS D/2685/11.

7. PRONI MS D/2685/11 expands lines 33–36 to eight lines with several variants:

And "who are those?" the youth exclaimed
    With pity touched, with wonder, filled;
Ere yet his cooler reason blamed
    The early hatred deep instilled.

But pointing to the startled pair
    While swift down Glenmalure they fled,
He marked the Mother's maniac air,
    As seized with wild and sudden dread.

8. Government forces defeated rebel insurgents on May 26, 1798, in Tarah, county Meath.

9. The Curragh is a grassy plain in county Kildare, where more than three hundred rebel prisoners were executed on May 29, 1798.

10. Clough's] "Clough, the place at which Colonel Walpole was killed, and his detachment defeated by the rebels" (William Tighe's note to *Psyche, with Other Poems* 314). Colonel Walpole was killed on June 4, 1798, in the village of Clough, county Wexford.

11. boys] "boy" in PRONI MS D/2685/11.

12. earth] "ground" in PRONI MS D/2685/11.

13. Lines 201–12 are omitted in PRONI MS D/2685/11.

14. PRONI MS D/2685/11 includes an additional stanza between lines 216–17, as follows: "Dear Ellen faintly he exclaimed, / I could not save our Bryan's life, / Thy brother's love will not be blamed / Unequal, cruel, was the knife."

15. PRONI MS D/2685/11 includes an additional stanza between lines 232–33, as follows: "Behind that birch tree see him stand, / Waving its light boughs gracefully: / While threatning with his baby hand, / He chides me that I talk with thee."

Avails it Ought to Number O'er

1. Written during the late 1790s and copied by Caroline Hamilton into NLI MS 4809.

Time Fades the Lustre of the Moon

1. Written during the late 1790s and copied by Caroline Hamilton into NLI MS 4809.

To the Moon

1. Written in the late 1790s and published in 1823 in Elizabeth Scott's *Specimens of British Poetry* (133–34) under the inaccurate title "To the Moon. From Mrs. Tighe's 'Psyche'" (the poem is not from *Psyche*). Scott also reprints the last twenty lines of "The Mezereon" under the title "On Hope" (264–65).

Sympathy

1. Written in the late 1790s and published in 1858 in Samuel Lover's *The Lyrics of Ireland* (57).

Calm Delight

1. Written in the late 1790s and published in 1890 in Charles A. Read's *Cabinet of Irish Literature: Selections from the Works of the Chief Poets, Orators, and Prose Writers of Ireland* (2:119).

Song ("See my love, yon angry deep")

1. Written in the late 1790s and copied by Caroline Hamilton into NLI MS 4800.

To ——c——e ("The youth of broken fortunes sent to roam")

1. Written in the late 1790s and copied by Caroline Hamilton into NLI MS 4800.

The Hours of Peace

1. Written in the late 1790s and copied by Caroline Hamilton into NLI MS 4800.

2. "Linda" may refer to Tighe herself; Sarah Ponsonby wrote an imitation of *Psyche* 3.19–27 in response to the manuscript copy she and Lady Eleanor Butler

received, which urges "Sweet Linda! meditate thy charming song, / Nor let the charming song remain unknown / The verse which cheers thy solitude prolong / To witch the world with beauties all its own, / Let not thy Psyche smile for thee alone" (IN T448 805, Beinecke Rare Book Room and Manuscript Library, Yale University).

3. Anacreon (ca. 570–480 BC) was famous for writing love poems and drinking songs. Tighe is probably referring to Thomas Moore, who achieved early success with his *Odes of Anacreon* (1800); she calls Moore "Anacreon" in letters to Joseph Cooper Walker (TCD MS 1461).

4. Teian] Anacreon, famous for his ode on the rose and the healing balm of its scent.

LA CITTADINA: ON LEAVING ROSSANA 1798

1. Written in 1798 and copied by Caroline Hamilton into NLI MS 4801 with the title "La Chitadena" crossed out and corrected to "La Cittadina" (or town dweller). Throughout, Tighe plays against the metrical form and content of Milton's "L'Allegro" (ca. 1631).

2. routs] large formal evening parties or social gatherings.

3. flambeause] flaming torches.

4. plumy] adorned with plumes or feathers, such as dancing shoes.

5. John Bannister (1760–1836) and Sarah Siddons (1755–1831), two celebrated actors who performed at the Drury Lane Theatre, a playhouse the Tighes frequently visited in the 1790s, according to Caroline Hamilton, whose journal notes that Mary Tighe was "much delighted with Banister & Mrs. Siddons."

6. currant] probably a transcription error for current.

7. Caroline Hamilton quotes lines 119–32 to evidence the pleasure Mary Tighe experienced during occasional evenings at home during the 1790s (journal).

8. sentance] probably a transcription error for sentence.

9. salvic] healing; probably a reference to Virgil, whose *Georgics* celebrated the farmer's life as an ideal of peace and contentment.

10. Tighe echoes the concluding couplets of "L'Allegro"—"These delights if thou canst give, / Mirth, with thee I mean to live" (lines 151–52)—and Christopher Marlowe's "The Passionate Shepherd to His Love" (1599): "If these delights thy mind may move, / Then live with me, and be my love" (lines 23–24).

A LETTER FROM MRS. ACTON TO HER NEPHEW MR. EVANS

1. Written ca. 1798–1800 and available in autograph copy L. Add 1907 at the Birmingham University Library. The "Mrs. Acton" of the poem refers to Sidney Acton (née Davis), married to Thomas Acton of West Aston in 1780, and addressed as "Sydney" in the poem Tighe wrote at the Acton estate, "Written at West-Aston. June 1808." Mrs. Acton's nephew was George Evans of Portrane, county Dublin; Theodosia Blachford notes that on September 20, 1807, Tighe went to "Mr. Evans's Portraine & was very hospitably entertained there for four weeks" (journal).

2. nonplus] state of utter perplexity.

3. Syriac] a form of Aramaic used by various Eastern churches.

4. aes in presenti] ready money. Tighe might be alluding to the *Eton Latin Grammar,* which contained a phrase from Oliver Goldsmith, "Aes in presenti perfectum format" ("Ready-money makes a man perfect").

5. Joseph Priestley (1733–1804), founding Unitarian who wrote on grammar, education, government, psychology, and more.

6. Hugh Blair (1718–1800), Scottish divine and professor of rhetoric.

7. Tighe probably refers to her uncle Edward Tighe, the dramatist and critic.

8. Tighe's cousin Caroline Hamilton née Tighe was a gifted painter and witty poet.

9. Susan Butticuz later Davis was the daughter of a Swiss clergyman who taught Latin at Harrow and persuaded Sarah Tighe to foster his daughter with her own children.

10. Tighe probably refers to her cousin William Tighe of Woodstock, who might have been working on early drafts of his poem *The Plants* (1808–1811).

11. Mantuan] Mantua was the birthplace of Virgil, who celebrated rural life in his *Georgics*.

12. Mr. Jones is a frequent visitor to Rossana and other family venues (and probably a cousin of George Tighe's on his mother's side, the Jones of Westmeath); Caroline Hamilton refers to him as a ladies' man in her December 11, 1797, manuscript poem "To Captn Huet": "Or poor Mr Jones Sir, whose principle trade is / To talk to and flatter the pretty young Ladies; / The moment you see him you'll easily know / That nature designed him to shine as a Beau, / And since then a very great pity 'twould be / To leave him to hang on a liberty tree" (NLI MS 4801).

13. Mary Tighe's sister-in-law Camilla Blachford was raised in Germany; she married John Blachford in 1796 in Dresden.

14. alcaic] quantitative verse form.

ACROSTICS

1. Written in the 1790s and copied by Caroline Hamilton into NLI MS 4803. Hamilton also prints the first ten lines in her journal to illustrate Tighe's appreciation of her husband "Harry Tighe." The first letters of each line, read vertically, spell out the names of "Harry Tighe," "Maryann Caroline Tighe" (Caroline Hamilton), and "Susanna Butticuz."

2. l'excuse] the excuse.

3. Or still attendant on thy merit sail / Live in thine honours & partake the gale] The manuscript includes a single quotation mark before "Live" to indicate the reference to lines from Pope's *Essay on Man*, Epistle IV: "Oh! while along the stream of time thy name / Expanded flies, and gathers all its fame, / Say, shall my little bark attendant sail, / Pursue the triumph, and partake the gale?" (lines 383–86).

4. seat] probably a transcription error for seal.

THERE WAS A YOUNG LORDLING WHOSE WITS WERE ALL TOSS'D UP

1. Written in 1799 and available in autograph copy NLI MS 10,206, which notes that the poem was written "To the tune of 'There was an old woman toss'd up in a blanket,'" the Mother Goose rhyme:

There was an old woman tossed up in a blanket
Seventeen times as high as the moon.
But where she was going, no mortal could tell it,
For under her arm, she carried a broom.

"Old woman, old woman, old woman," quoth I,
"Whither, ah whither, ah whither so high?"
"To sweep the cobwebs from the sky."
"May I come with you?"
        "Aye, by and by."

In a letter to Sarah Tighe dated December 7, 1798 (PRONI MS D/2685/2/58), Mary Tighe professes herself to be too ignorant to take a stand on the proposed Act of Union (which Sarah Tighe favored), but the specific references Tighe makes to parliamentary activities throughout this poem indicate otherwise. In 1798 William Pitt, the British prime minister, proposed an act of union that would merge the British and Irish Parliaments: Ireland would be represented in the House of Lords by four bishops and twenty-eight representative peers, and in the House of Commons by one hundred members (MPs). The proposed act was strenuously debated in the Irish Parliament for much of 1799 and rejected by a majority of five during the first vote, but accepted by a clear majority in both houses during the second vote, after numerous members received lucrative offers from the British government via Lord Castlereagh, Robert Stewart (1769–1822), Chief Secretary of Ireland.

2. Lordling] young or unimportant lord; petty or insignificant lord.

3. John Foster (1740–1808) was Speaker of the Irish House of Commons 1785–1800, and was stripped of his office for uncompromising opposition to the Act of Union.

4. mace] staff of office; symbol of the Speaker's authority in the House of Commons.

5. The House of Lords voted for the Union before the House of Commons.

6. hubaboo] hubbub, tumult, uproar (a word of Irish origin).

7. Buff and blue were the colors of Charles James Fox (1749–1806), leader of the liberal Whig opposition to William Pitt (1759–1806) and energetic campaigner for Irish independence.

8. Sir John Parnell (1744–1801), Chancellor of the Exchequer, and James Fitzgerald (1742–1835), Prime Serjeant, were dismissed from their positions in 1798 and replaced by Isaac Corry (1755–1813) and St. George Daly (ca. 1751–1829), both of whom voted for the union.

9. delf] earthenware.

10. Charles William Bury (1764–1835), Lord Tullamoore in 1797, Viscount Charleville in 1800, and Earl of Charleville in 1806, supported the Union and sought to influence the vote of the member from Carlow, William Burton (who sold the borough to Bury in 1795); John Monk Mason (1726–1809) voted for the Union in 1799.

11. Syllabub] sillabub, a drink or dish of sweetened milk or cream mixed with wine or cider.

12. Sir Roche Boyle (1743–1807) served in the British army in the war in America and served in the Irish Parliament from 1766–1800, where he fought hard for the Union.

13. jasms] nineteenth-century slang for spirit or energy.

14. nabe] eighteenth-century slang term with a range of meanings, including

the head, the head of a stick, a hat, a coxcomb or fop, or an important person; as a verb, to cheat or steal.

15. Fleet Lane, near the House of Lords, could have been flooded by the River Liffy.

16. Hibernia] Ireland.

17. James Caulfeild, fourth Viscount and first Earl of Charlemont (1728–1799), worked for Irish independence with Henry Grattan (1746–1820) and Henry Flood (ca. 1732–1791) in the 1780s. His son Francis William Caulfeild was a principal leader of the opposition to the union.

Sonnet ("For me would Fancy now her chaplet twine")

1. Written in 1799 and published in 1811 in *Psyche, with Other Poems* (225).

2. chaplet] a wreath or garland for the head.

To Time

1. Written in the late 1790s and published in 1811 in *Psyche, with Other Poems* (227).

Written at Rossana ("Dear chestnut bower, I hail thy secret shade")

1. Written in the late 1790s at Rossana (probably the summer of 1799) and published in 1811 in *Psyche, with Other Poems* (231).

Written at Rossana. November 18, 1799

1. Written at Rossana, November 18, 1799 (*Mary* 13), and published in 1811 in *Psyche, with Other Poems* (230). Tighe's journal entry for June 5, 1799, records "We are to go to Rossana in a week. Alas! are my pleasures past like the leaves of this exquisite rose! & is there nothing remaining but the thorn. Oh too damnable!"

2. blown] flowered.

Written at the Eagle's Nest, Killarney. July 26, 1800

1. Written at Killarney, July 26, 1800, and published in 1811 in *Psyche, with Other Poems* (232). A manuscript copy appears in *Selena* under the title "Sonnet Written at the Eagles Nest" (NLI MS 4746) as a poem that the character Sidney Dallamore writes for his beloved Selena Miltern.

2. meridan] "meridian" in NLI MS 4746.

3. 'mid] "o'er" in NLI MS 4746.

4. The eagle was Jove's bird.

5. yon] "those" in NLI MS 4746.

Written at Killarney. July 29, 1800

1. Written at Killarney, July 29, 1800, and published in 1811 in *Psyche, with Other Poems* (233). A manuscript copy appears in *Selena* under the title "Sonnet Returning at Night" (NLI MS 4746) as a second poem that Sidney Dallamore writes for his beloved Selena Miltern.

2. soothing] "melting" in NLI MS 4746.

3. those] "these" in NLI MS 4746.

On Leaving Killarney. August 5, 1800

1. Written at Killarney, August 5, 1800, and published in 1811 in *Psyche, with*

Other Poems (234). Unlike the first two Killarney sonnets, Tighe does not print "On Leaving Killarney" in *Selena* (NLI MS 4746) but has her narrator refer to it as too precious for Selena Miltern to share: "Two of these [sonnets] are here presented to the reader because they attempt some description of scenes indeed that surpass all language, scenes which are surely ever dear to memory and cannot therefore fail to please in some degree those who have once enjoyed them—But the third was instantly concealed by Selena from every eye but hers, which swam in delighted tenderness as they beamed upon him [Sidney Dallamore] a grateful confession of sympathy in the love and rapture which they had so sweetly expressed" (*Selena* 5:564).

SONNET ("YE DEAR ASSOCIATES OF MY GAYER HOURS")

1. Written in 1800 (*Mary* 13) and published in 1811 in *Psyche, with Other Poems* (228).

A FAITHFUL FRIEND IS THE MEDICINE OF LIFE

1. Written ca. 1800 and published in 1811 in *Psyche, with Other Poems* (248–50). An autograph copy appears as the first poem in Camilla Blachford's album, *Album Camilla 1800* (NLW MS 22983B ff.2–3). Tighe's title comes from "The Wisdom of Jesus, Son of Sirach" or "Ecclesiasticus," in the Apocrypha: "A faithful friend is the medicine of life; and they that fear the Lord shall find him" (6.16).

2. "Medio de fonte leporum / Surgit amari aliquid quod in ipsis floribus angat. Lucr: lib 4" (Tighe's note to NLW MS 22983B). In *De Rerum Natura* Lucretius (Titus Lucretius Carus) (ca. 94–55 BC) observes that "From the midst of the fountain of delights rises something bitter that chokes them all amongst the flowers" (4:1133).

3. sweet] "pure" in NLW MS 22983B.
4. streams] "stream" in NLW MS 22983B.
5. we] "Man" in NLW MS 22983B.
6. defile] "pollute" in NLW MS 22983B.
7. The cordial] "The pure cordial" in NLW MS 22983B.
8. faithful] "feeling" in NLW MS 22983B.
9. hours] "moments" in NLW MS 22983B.
10. Nor] "Or" in NLW MS 22983B.
11. should] "would" in NLW MS 22983B.

THE KISS.—IMITATED FROM VOITURE

1. Written ca. 1800 and copied by Henry Moore in May 1811 from Tighe's manuscript into the Henry and Lucy Moore MS Album: Poems HM 1811, Chawton House Library (57–59). Vincent Voiture (1597–1648) wrote numerous amatory lyrics; Tighe's poem is based on his "Stances" (published in 1650):

Ce soir que vous ayant seulette rencontrée,
Pour guerir mon esprit et le remettre en paix:
J'eus de vous, sans effort, belle et divine Astrée,
La premiere faveur que j'en reçeus jamais.

Que d'attraits, que d'appas vous rendoient adorable!
Que de traits, que de feux me vinrent enflamer!
Je ne verray jamais rien qui soit tant aimable,
Ni vous rien desormais qui puisse tant aimer.

Les charmes que l'Amour en vos beautez recelle,
Estoient plus que jamais puissans et dangereux;
O Dieux! qu'en ce moment mes yeux vous virent belle,
Et que vos yeux aussi me virent amoureux!

La rose ne luit point d'une grace pareille,
Lors que pleine d'amour elle rit au Soleil,
Et l'Orient n'a pas, quand l'Aube se réveille,
La face si brillante, et le teint si vermeil.

Cet objet qui pouvoit esmouvoir une souche,
Jettant par tant d'appas le feu dans mon esprit,
Me fit prendre un baiser sur vostre belle bouche,
Mais las! ce fut plustost le baiser qui me prit.

Car il brusle en mes os, et va de veine en veine,
Portant le feu vengeur qui me va consumant,
Jamais rien ne m'a fait endurer tant de peine,
Ni causé dans mon coeur tant de contentement.

Mon ame sur ma lévre estoit lors toute entiere,
Pour savourer le miel qui sur la vostre estoit;
Mais en me retirant, elle resta derriere,
Tant de ce doux plaisir l'amorce l'arrestoit.

S'esgarant de ma bouche, elle entra dans la vostre,
Yvre de ce Nectar qui charmoit ma raison,
Et sans doute, elle prit une porte pour l'autre,
Et ne luy souvint plus quelle estoit sa maison.

Mes pleurs n'ont pû depuis fléchir cette infidelle,
A quitter un séjour qu'elle trouva si doux:
Et je suis en langueur sans repos, et sans elle,
Et sans moy-mesme aussi lors que je suis sans vous.

Elle ne peut laisser ce lieu tant desirable,
Ce beau Temple où l'Amour est de tous adoré,
Pour entrer derechef en l'Enfer misérable,
Où le Ciel a voulu qu'elle ait tant enduré.

Mais vous, de ses desirs unique et belle Reine,
Où cette ame se plaist comme en son Paradis,

Faites qu'elle retourne, et que je la reprenne
Sur ces mesmes oeillets, où lors je la perdis.

Je confesse ma faute, au lieu de la défendre,
Et triste et repentant d'avoir trop entrepris,
Le baiser que je pris, je suis prest de le rendre,
Et me rendez aussi ce que vous m'avez pris.

Mais non, puis-que ce Dieu dont l'amorce m'enflame,
Veut bien que vous l'ayez, ne me la rendez point;
Mais souffrez que mon corps se rejoigne à mon ame,
Et ne separez pas ce que Nature a joint. (lines 1–52)

Thomas Moore's "To Mrs. ——, On Her Beautiful Translation of Voiture's Kiss" (1801) compliment's Tighe's lyric:

How heavenly was the poet's doom,
    To breathe his spirit through a kiss:
And lose within so sweet a tomb
    The trembling messenger of bliss!

And, sure his soul returned to feel
    That it *again* could ravished be;
For in the kiss that thou didst steal,
    His life and soul have fled to thee. (lines 1–8)

2. Aurora] Roman goddess of the morning.
3. vermeil] vermillion red.
4. Chloe] In place of Voiture's "Astree" (Greek for star) Tighe uses "Chloe," a name that appears in many pastoral poems and means "green shoot" in Greek (an epithet of Demeter).
5. bosom's lord] Tighe refers to *Romeo and Juliet* 5.1, where Romeo declares "If I may trust the flattering truth of sleep, / My dreams presage some joyful news at hand: / *My bosom's lord* sits lightly in his throne; / And all this day an unaccustom'd spirit / Lifts me above the ground with cheerful thoughts. / I dreamt my lady came and found me dead—/ Strange dream, that gives a dead man leave to think!—/ And breathed such life with kisses in my lips, / That I revived, and was an emperor. / Ah me! how sweet is love itself possess'd, / When but love's shadows are so rich in joy!" (1–11, my emphasis).

SONNET ("AS NEARER I APPROACH THAT FATAL DAY")
1. Written in November 1801 (*Mary* 13) and published in 1811 in *Psyche, with Other Poems* (229).

PSYCHE; OR, THE LEGEND OF LOVE
1. Written in 1801–1802 at Rossana and published in 1805 in *Psyche; or, the Legend of Love* (London: James Carpenter). William Tighe published a corrected

copy of *Psyche; or, the Legend of Love* in the 1811 *Psyche, with Other Poems,* but the corrections are not attributed to Tighe. The copy text for this edition follows the 1805 edition, and notes significant differences between the 1805 and 1811 editions checked against the 1803 manuscript copy Tighe prepared for Lady Eleanor Butler and Sarah Ponsonby, the Ladies of Llangollen (NLW MS 22985B).

2. "Teaches pure and affectionate love" (*Epigrams* 10.35.8). Martial (Marcus Valerius Martialis) (ca. AD 40–104) was famous for his witty, satiric, and often coarse epigrams. Epigram 10.35.8–9 advises husbands and wives to read Sulpicia to please one another: "Sed castos docet et probos amores / Lusus, delicias facetiasque" ("she describes pure and honest love, toyings, endearments, and raillery," Loeb translation). Tighe changes Martial's "probos" (true) to "pios." She includes the next line's "Lusus, delicias" (sports, delights) in her 1803 manuscript copy for the Ladies of Llangollen (NLW MS 22985B, f.1).

3. "Young women who do not wish to appear flirtatious should never speak of love as something in which they might be involved" (*Maximes* 418). La Rochefoucauld, François de Marsillac, duc de (1613–1680), courtier, soldier, and moralist, was the author of *Réflexions ou sentences et maximes morales* (1665), usually known as *Maximes,* brief polished reflections on virtue, vice, vanity, etc. Tighe elides a significant portion of the maxim: "Les jeunes femmes qui ne veulent point paraître coquettes, et les hommes d'un âge avancé qui ne veulent pas être ridicules, ne doivent jamais parler de l'amour comme d'une chose où ils puissent avoir part" ("men of an advanced age who do not wish to be ridiculed").

4. Ben Jonson, *The Alchemist* (1612). Subtle asks "Are not the choicest fables of the poets, / That were the fountains and first springs of wisdom, / Wrapt in perplexed allegories?" (2.3.205–7). Tighe changes Jonson's "That" to "Who," emphasizing poets over fables.

5. Eighteenth-century enthusiasm for the poetry of Edmund Spenser prompted a number of poets to try something in his style, e.g., James Thomson's *The Castle of Indolence* (1748), James Beattie's *The Minstrel* (1771), William Blake's "An Imitation of Spenser" (1783), or Samuel Taylor Coleridge's "Lines in Imitation of Spenser" (1795).

6. In a letter to Joseph Cooper Walker, Tighe expresses her great love for Spenser: "from early prejudice I always [illegible] read the fairy queen not as a critick but a lover—I think it is one of the first books I remember reading with delight" (September 8, [1807], Rossana, TCD MS 1461/6 f.159–60). Tighe uses the Spenserian stanza Spenser invented for *The Faerie Queene,* which consists of eight five-foot iambic lines followed by a ninth iambic line of six feet, rhyming ababbcbcc.

7. Lucius Apuleius, *The Golden Ass* (ca. 155); Molière (Jean-Baptiste Poquelin), *Psyché* (1671); Jean de la Fontaine, *Les Amours de Psyché et Cupidon* (1669); Charles Albert Demoustier, *Lettres à Émilie, sur la Mythologie* (1792–1798); Giambattista Marino, *Adone* (1623). Tighe's postscript to the 1803 manuscript offers an earlier version of the 1805 preface, which does not name Marino and stresses that she has seen no English versions of Apuleius's "Cupid and Psyche": "For the outline of my tale in the two first Cantos I am in great part indebted to Apuleius, who has been differently imitated by La Fontaine in a well told prose story, by Moliere

in a *comedic* & Moustier in his Mithologic—I have not seen any English imitation of Apuleius" (NLW MS 22985B, f.70).

8. "If that is a sin, it is the unintentional sin of the poet, who did not mean to steal something" (Prologue to *Eunuchus*, lines 27–28). Terence (Publius Terentius Afer) (ca. 190 or 180–159 BC) was a Roman comic poet who adapted *Eunuchus* from the Greek dramatic poet Menander (ca. 342–292 BC).

9. "He who thinks that a beautiful lover can lift a sad spirit, will want to set her heart on fire; he who knows how sweet it is to know that he is loved only by her, is the sole ruler in this state" (*Elegia* 12, Duncan Wu translation). Ludovico Ariosto (1474–1533) wrote lyrics, satires, and comedies in addition to his great romantic epic *Orlando Furioso* (1532). Tighe cites lines 1–3 and 7–9 of *Elegia* 12, and does not indicate her omission of lines 4–6 of the 46-line elegy: "Se pensa poi che quel tanto n'opprime, / Che l'util proprio e 'l vero ben s'oblia, / Piange in van del suo error le cagion prime." She also changes two words in the first line (not "un" but "il" and not "desio" but "disio").

10. Phoebus] Apollo, the sun.

11. zone] belt.

12. Cytherea] Venus, called Cytherea because of her birth in the sea near Cythera.

13. myrtle] the myrtle was used as an emblem of love and held sacred to Venus.

14. sullen] "sudden" in 1811 edition; "sullen" in 1803 MS copy.

15. cries] "cried" in 1811 edition; "cries" in 1803 MS copy.

16. Venus refers to the judgment of Paris, who awarded her the golden apple marked "for the fairest" over Hera and Athena.

17. the magic zone] the magic girdle Vulcan made for Venus, which compelled anyone she wished to desire her.

18. imbrue] drench, stain.

19. the ever downy Hours] the three goddesses of the seasons (spring, summer, winter) who often attended Venus, as did the three Graces.

20. allay] reduce in intensity.

21. winged Zephyrs light] Cupid is often portrayed with a small group of winged infants (amoretti or amorini); a zephyr is a gentle breeze.

22. why] "while" in 1811 edition; alternate line "And just her ivory teeth its charms disclose" in 1803 MS.

23. dole] grief or sorrow, lamentation.

24. the furies] not capitalized (as in 2.65), so probably not a reference to the Furies.

25. Hymen] Hymen or Hymenaeus was the god of marriage and the marriage feast or song.

26. promulge] proclaim.

27. amaracine wreaths] wreaths made from amaranths, legendary undying flowers.

28. Io Hymen] nuptial chant.

29. Lydian lyre] ancient kingdom in West Asia Minor famed for its music; in music the Lydian mode represents the natural diatonic scale F-F (with an augmented fourth).

30. gem] the hyacinth (or jacinth), a purplish-blue gem named after Hyacinthus, a boy Apollo loved and accidentally killed, from whose blood sprang the hyacinth flower.

31. eve] "Eve" in 1811 edition; "Eve" in 1803 MS.

32. ere] "e'er" in 1811 edition; e're in 1803 MS.

33. hymeneal strain] marriage song.

34. Elysium's happy grove] the abode of the blessed after death.

35. Aurora] goddess of the dawn.

36. car] chariot.

37. curious] intricate, subtle.

38. As in Apuleius, Cupid anticipates a son but Psyche bears a daughter, Pleasure.

39. zephyrs] "Zephyrs" in 1811 edition; "Zephyrs" in 1803 MS.

40. the Furies] the Furiae or Dirae, female divinities who execute the curses pronounced upon criminals, torture the guilty with stings of conscience, and inflict famines and pestilence.

41. Tighe describes the aurora borealis (or northern lights).

42. sister's] "sisters" in 1811 edition; "sisters" in 1803 MS.

43. muse] "Muse" in 1811 edition; "Muse" in 1803 MS.

44. effulgence] radiance.

45. the fates] the three goddesses of destiny.

46. bloomed] "bloom" in 1811 edition; "bloom'd" in 1803 MS. Roses were sacred to Venus.

47. presumed] "presume" in 1811 edition; "presum'd" in 1803 MS.

48. mid the sandy Garamantian wild] "The temple of Jupiter Ammon situated in the midst of the deserts of Libya & particularly describ'd by Quintus Curtius" (Tighe's note to 1803 MS, f.23). Quintus Curtius Rufus, a Roman historian who flourished in the first century, wrote a ten-book history of Alexander the Great, *Historiae Alexandri Magni* (ca. 40), which tells of Alexander's famous expedition across the Egyptian desert to the oracle at the temple of Jupiter Ammon, where he was saluted as Jupiter Ammon's son (4.7).

49. turtle] a turtledove; the dove was sacred to Venus.

50. whilom] formerly.

51. Narcissus] a beautiful youth who rejected the nymph Echo and fell in love with his own reflection in a pool; he pined away and was changed into the flower that bears his name.

52. Adonis] the beautiful youth loved by Venus who was killed by a boar; the anemone sprang from his blood.

53. crocus] "Crocus" in 1811 edition; "Crocus" in 1803 MS. Crocus was a youth who pined for the nymph Smilax; both were transformed into flowers bearing their names (in an alternate version Crocus is accidentally killed by Mercury and transformed into a flower).

54. Acanthus] Acantha was transformed into the acanthus tree when she rejected Apollo.

55. Her drooping head still Reseda reclines] "Reseda Luteola—If worth alteration, the following line may be substituted, to avoid the unfortunate false quantity: *Reseda still her drooping head reclines*" (Tighe's note to 1805 edition, 209). Commonly called a mignonette, the reseda is a pale green plant thought to have curative powers.

56. spring] "Spring" in 1811 edition; "Spring" in 1803 MS.

57. sleep] "Sleep" in 1811 edition; "Sleep" in 1803 MS.

58. love] "Love" in 1811 edition; "Love" in 1803 MS.

59. inconstancy] "Inconstancy" in 1811 edition; "Inconstancy" in 1803 MS.

60. guerdon] recompense.

61. carbuncles] bright red gems, usually garnets cut in a convex, rounded form without facets.

62. deprecate] pray for deliverance from.

63. Vesper] the evening star, Venus.

64. it] "is" in 1811 edition; "Entranc'd it seem'd to close" in 1803 edition.

65. pass-port] "passport" in 1811 edition; "passport" in 1803 MS.

66. umbrage] shade.

67. them] "then" in 1811 edition; "them" in 1803 MS.

68. meed] reward or recompense.

69. speckled panthers] the maenads or bacchants, women who worshipped Bacchus (god of wine and drunken happiness), were often shown wearing panther skins.

70. Lusinga] flattery.

71. ere] "e'er" in 1811 edition; "e're" in 1803 MS.

72. Syren's song] the seductive song of a beautiful, beguiling, dangerous woman; the Sirens were winged sea nymphs whose songs lured unwary mariners to their destruction.

73. port] carriage or bearing.

74. trammels] impediments or restraints, such as nets or fetters.

75. main] ocean.

76. He] "And" in 1811 edition; "He" in 1803 MS.

77. recovers] "recovered" in 1811 edition; "recovers" in 1803 MS.

78. dashed] "dashes" in 1811 edition; "dash'd" in 1803 MS.

79. Thus on his bark the bold Biscayen stands] "The whale fishery, on the coast of Greenland, was first carried on by the sailors of the Bay of Biscay. See Goldsmith's *Animated Nature*, Vol. VI" (Tighe's note to 1805 edition, 209). Oliver Goldsmith, *An History of the Earth, and Animated Nature*, 8 vols. (1774).

80. Apelles (fl. 330–320 BC) was a famous Greek painter. None of his pictures survive, but descriptions of at least thirty did. Tighe refers to "The Calumny," which Sandro Botticelli (ca. 1445–1510) tried to recreate based on a description by Lucian of Samosata (AD ca. 125–200); Botticelli's "The Birth of Venus" is also based on a lost Apelles painting, described by Pliny the Elder (AD 23–79).

81. Blatant Beast] begotten of Envy and Detraction, the monster who personifies slander or calumny in Spenser's *The Faerie Queene* (books 5, 6), based on the Glatysaunt Beast in Sir Thomas Malory's *Le Morte D'Arthur* (1470).

82. couched] lowered to a horizontal position for attack.

83. e'er] "ere" in 1811 edition; "e're" in 1803 MS.

84. ere] "e'er" in 1811 edition; "e're" in 1803 MS.

85. Where] "Now" in 1811 edition; "Where" in 1803 MS.

86. fain] pleased or willing under the circumstances.

87. brake] thicket.

88. Disfida] Suspicion. Instead of *sospetto* or *dubbio*, more common terms for

suspicion in Italian, Tighe employs what *The Monthly Review* (1811) considers a "barbarous compound."

89. weetless] unknowing, unaware.

90. live-long] entire.

91. wonted] habitual, usual.

92. fell] evil or deadly.

93. fantastic] exotic; remote from reality.

94. gripe] tight grasp.

95. bale] physical torment or mental suffering.

96. involutions] entanglements, i.e., serpent coils.

97. Geloso's] Jealousy.

98. Erebus] darkness under the earth, where death dwells.

99. blames] "blamed" in 1811 edition; "blames" in 1803 MS.

100. Sooth] truth, reality, or fact.

101. The lightning of her heavenly] *"E'l lampeggiar del'angelico riso*—Petrarca" (Tighe's note to 1803 MS, f.48). Petrarch (Francesco Petrarca) (1304–1374), *Rime* 292 (line 6), one of the many sonnets which express longing for his beloved Laura. Felicia Hemans also adapts this line for stanza 91 of *The Forest Sanctuary* (1825), written in modified Spenserian stanzas: "With eyes whose lightning laughter hath beguil'd" (line 813).

102. Castabella] Chastity (literally beautiful chastity).

103. ere] "e'er" in 1811 edition; "e're" in 1803 MS.

104. Dian] Diana, virgin goddess of the moon, hunting, and fertility, a protector of women whose attendant virgin nymphs surrounded her to prevent Actaeon from glimpsing her naked form when he hunted near her favorite bathing spot; Actaeon was transformed into a stag and killed by his companions.

105. Minerva] virgin goddess of wisdom and the arts.

106. Parnassus] mountain sacred to the nine Muses, who were usually identified as companions of Phoebus Apollo rather than Minerva.

107. ere] "e'er" in 1811 edition; "e're" in 1803 MS.

108. cestus] girdle or belt.

109. Hebe] Greek goddess of youth and spring, called Juventas (youth) by the Romans.

110. Pallas] the Greek goddess Pallas Athena known to the Romans as Minerva.

111. Cynthia] another name for the virgin goddess of the moon, Diana, based on her Greek counterpart Artemis (born on Mount Cynthus in Delos).

112. The mystic honours next of Fauna] "Fauna, called also the Bona Dea, during her life was celebrated for the exemplary purity of her manners, and after death was worshipped only by women" (Tighe's note to 1805 edition, 209–10). Fauna or Bona Dea (good goddess) presided over virginity and fertility; she was worshipped exclusively by women who never uttered the words "wine" or "myrtle" at their meetings because Faunus (Bona Dea's father) once made Fauna drunk and beat her with a myrtle stick.

113. Vesta] goddess of the hearth, whose sacred fires were maintained by the vestal virgins.

114. Mid the dark horrors of a living tomb] "For an account of the living

embodiment of the guilty Vestals *vide* Dionys: Halicar:" (Tighe's note to 1803 MS, f.51). Dionysius of Halicarnassus (30–7 BC) compiled a twenty-volume history of Rome which includes a description of the pit prepared for vestals found guilty of breaking their vows, who were buried alive.

115. Bellerophon] Bellerophon rejected the advances of Anteia, the wife of Proteus, who sought revenge by telling Proteus that Bellerophon had wronged her.

116. Peleus] Peleus rejected the advances of Astydameia, Acastus's wife, who told her husband that Peleus attempted to seduce her; Acastus took Peleus on a hunting trip and abandoned him.

117. Bellerophon; / And Peleus flying the Magnesian plain] "Ut Praetum mulier perfida credulum / falsis impulerit criminibus, nimis / Casto Bellerophonti / Maturare necem, refert, / Narrat pene datum Pelea Tartaro, / Magnessam Hyppolyten dum fugit abstinens. Hor. *Ode* vii. lib. iii" (Tighe's note to 1805 edition, 210). Tighe quotes lines 13–18 from Horace's (Quintus Horatius Flaccus) *Ode* 3.7 (23 BC), which addresses the constancy of the parted lovers Asterie and Gyges, and how the married Chloe seeks to tempt her houseguest Gyges by telling him "how a perfidious woman by false charges drove credulous Proetus to bring swift death on over-chaste Bellerophon. She tells of Peleus, all but doomed to Tartarus for righteous shunning of Magnessian Hippolyte" (Loeb translation). Tighe spells Horace's "Proetum" as "Praetum" and "Bellerophontae" as "Bellerophonti."

118. Hyppolytus] "Hippolytus" in 1811 edition; "Hypolytus" in 1803 MS. Hippolytus rejected the advances of his stepmother Phaedra, second wife of Theseus, who left a suicide note for Theseus claiming that Hippolytus tried to seduce her.

119. the Hebrew boy] "Joseph" (Tighe's note to 1805 edition, 210). In Genesis 39 Joseph rejects the advances of his master Potiphar's wife, who accuses him of trying to seduce her.

120. whom on Hymettus' brow] "Cephalus" (Tighe's note to 1805 edition, 210). In the notes to the 1803 MS Tighe writes "*Vide* Ovid Metam: lib vii" (f.53). Book 7 of the *Metamorphoses* tells the story of Cephalus and Procris: Cephalus had been happily married to Procris for two months when he was abducted by Aurora, goddess of the dawn, to Mount Hymettus, where he resisted her advances.

121. him, too wise her treacherous cup to share] "Ulysses" (Tighe's note to 1805 edition, 211). Ulysses escaped the enchantments of Circe by using a magic herb Hermes gave him (moly), which prevented her from turning him into a swine as she did other members of his crew.

122. Ulysses repelled the sirens's arts—their seductive singing, which lured mariners to their deaths—by ordering his men to stuff their ears with wax and to tie him to the mast.

123. Ulysses's faithful wife, Penelope, resisted the advances of suitors for twenty years while she waited for her husband's return from the Trojan wars and his sea voyages by insisting that she could not marry until she completed a shroud for Ulysses's father, Laertes, which she wove by day and unravelled each night.

124. Acastus' mourning daughter] "Laodamia" (Tighe's note to 1805 edition, 211). In the notes to the 1803 MS Tighe writes "*Vide* Ovid: Epi: 13" (f.53). In

Heroides Ovid tells of Laodamia, Acastus's daughter, and her husband, Protesilaus, who sought a brave death as the first Greek to leap ashore at Troy (ordained by the oracle to die). The gods honored him by having Hermes return him for one last visit to Laodamia, who refused to part from him a second time and so killed herself.

125. And thee Dictynna!] "A virgin of Crete, who threw herself from a rock into the sea, when pursued by Minos. The Cretans, not contented with giving her name to the rock which she had thus consecrated, were accustomed to worship Diana by the name of her unfortunate votary" (Tighe's note to 1805 edition, 211). Dictynna, also known as Britomartis, survived her leap by falling into some nets and was made into a goddess by Diana.

126. Arethusa] Arethusa, a nymph pursued by the river-god Alpheus, was transformed into the fountain that bears her name by Diana.

127. Castalia's] Castalia, a nymph pursued by Apollo, jumped into the spring at Delphi to escape him and was transformed into the fountain that bears her name on Mount Parnassus, sacred to Apollo and the Muses.

128. Daphne] Daphne, daughter of the river-god Peneus, was pursued by Apollo and changed into a laurel tree by Peneus when she asked him to help her escape; the laurel is Apollo's tree.

129. Pan] Pan pursued the Arcadian nymph Syrinx, who escaped him at the Ladon River where her sister nymphs transformed her into a tuft of reeds; Pan cut the reeds into various sizes and made his panpipe, the syrinx.

130. Still in that tuneful form] "In a grove, sacred to Diana, was suspended a syrinx (the pipe into which the nymph Syringa had been metamorphosed) which was said to possess the miraculous power of thus justifying the calumniated" (Tighe's note to 1805 edition, 211). Tighe's note to the 1803 MS adds "*Vide* Achil: Tat:" (f.54). Achilles Tatius, a Greek rhetorician who flourished in the second century AD, was most famous for his erotic romance *Leucippe and Cleitophon,* the story of love triumphant over numerous obstacles, which influenced the development of the novel.

131. The stream's rude ordeal] "The trial of the Stygian fountain, by which the innocent were acquitted, and the guilty disgraced; the waters rising in a wonderful manner, so as to cover the laurel wreath of the unchaste female, who dared the examination" (Tighe's note to 1805 edition, 212). Tighe's note to the 1803 MS edition adds "*Vide* Ach: Tat:" (f.54). See previous note for Achilles Tatius.

132. See the pure maid] "Chariclea *vide* Heliodor:" (Tighe's note to 1803 MS, f.54). Heliodorus of Emesa flourished in the third century AD and was the author of the romance *Aethiopica,* about parted lovers, Chariclea and Theagenes, who maintain chastity as they travel through strange lands seeking each other. *Aethiopica* influenced Achilles Tatius's *Leucippe and Cleitophon* as well as the development of the novel.

133. Innoxious] harmless, innocuous.

134. the daring Clusia] "Who, to avoid the violence of Torquatus, cast herself from a tower, and was preserved by the winds, which, swelling her garments, supported her as she gently descended to the earth" (Tighe's note to 1805 edition, 212). The *Parallela Minora* in Plutarch's *Moralia* tells the story of Clusia and Torquatus: "When the Romans were warring against the Etruscans, they elected Valerius Torquatus general. When he beheld the king's daughter, whose name was Clusia,

he asked the Etruscan for his daughter; but when he failed to obtain her, he attempted to sack the city. Clusia threw herself down from the battlements; but by the foresight of Venus her garment billowed out, and she came safely to the ground" (Loeb translation).

135. those, whom Vesta in the trying hour] "Claudia, a vestal, who having been accused of violating her vow, attested her innocence by drawing up the Tiber a ship, bearing a statue of the goddess, which many thousand men had not been able to remove. Aemilia, who was suspected of unchastity from having inadvertently suffered the sacred flame to expire, by entrusting it to the care of a novice, but, imploring Vesta to justify her innocence, she tore her linen garment, and threw it upon the extinguished ashes of the cold altar; when, in the sight of priests and virgins, a sudden and pure fire was thus enkindled. Tucia, who being falsely accused, carried water from the Tiber to the forum, in a sieve, her accuser miraculously disappearing at the same time" (Tighe's note to 1805 edition, 212–13). Tighe does not name her sources for these famous examples, but the story of Claudia can be found in St. Jerome's *Against Jovinianus* (book 1), the story of Aemilia in Propertius's *Elegies* (book 4), and the story of Tuccia in Pliny the Elder's *Natural History* (and elsewhere).

136. Nor Clelia, shielded] "*Vide* Liv. lib. 2" (Tighe's note to 1803 MS, f.52). In book 2 of *The History of Rome* Livy (Titus Livius) (59 BC–?AD 17) celebrates the heroism of Cloelia, one of twenty Roman hostages given to the Etruscans, who swam across the Tiber at the head of a group of girls, avoiding a rain of enemy spears and safely leading them all home.

137. thou, whose purest hands] "Sulpicia, a Roman lady of remarkable chastity; chosen by the Sibyls to dedicate a temple to Venus Verticordia, in order to obtain greater purity for her contemporary country-women" (Tighe's note to 1805 edition, 213). The elegiac poet Sulpicia was a contemporary of Tibullus and the only woman writer in the corpus of classical Latin literature. Tighe's preface cites the Martial epigram that refers to her.

138. Sinope's wiles] "The nymph Sinope, being persecuted by the addresses of Jupiter, at length stipulated for his promise to grant her whatever she might ask, and having obtained this promise, claimed the gift of perpetual chastity. 'Sinope / Nympha prius, blandosque Jovis quae luserat ignes / Coelicolis inmota procis.'— Val. Flac. lib. v. ver. 110" (Tighe's note to 1805 edition, 213–14). In the notes to the 1803 MS Tighe writes "*Vide* Apol: Rhod: & after him Val: Flac:" (f. 52). Tighe quotes lines 109–11 from book 5 of Valerius Flaccus's *Argonautica* (late first century AD) for her description of "Sinope, once a nymph and one who mocked Jove's ardent wooing, unmoved by heavenly suitors" (Loeb translation), and notes an earlier version of the story in book 2 of Apollonius Rhodius's *Argonautica* (third century BC), which tells how Sinope used the same ruse to safeguard her virginity from Phoebus Apollo and the river-god Halys as well as Zeus.

139. Lucretia's] Lucretia was the famously beautiful and virtuous wife of Collatinus who rejected the advances of Sextus Tarquinius and was then raped by him. She killed herself after she told her husband and father (the poet Lucretius) to avenge her; the outrage brought about the end of the Roman monarchy and beginning of republican government.

140. Virginia's] Virginia was the daughter of the Roman centurion Lucius Virginius, who stabbed her to death to save her from becoming the sexual slave of Appius Claudius, one of the ten ruling legislators of Rome. Virginius showed the bloody knife to his fellow soldiers, who seized and imprisoned Appius Claudius.

141. Scipio's] In book 21 of *The History of Rome* Livy contrasts the Roman virtues of Publius Cornelius Scipio, who demonstrates clemency and restraint toward surrendered Atanagrum, with the Carthaginian vices of Hannibal, who treats the surrendered Victumulae with cruelty.

142. enflames.] Both the 1811 edition and the 1803 MS conclude the knight's dialogue with a closing quotation mark.

143. Boreas] the north wind.

144. Favonius] the west wind.

145. falchion] sword.

146. Philomel] the nightingale.

147. Petrea] hard, rocklike, stony land; from the Latin "petra" (rock) or Italian "petraia" (quarry, heap of stones).

148. Glacella] Tighe's queen of indifference, from the Latin "glacio" (freeze) or Italian "glassare" (ice, glaze).

149. pair] "fair" in 1811 edition; "fair" in 1803 MS.

150. proud Locendra] "The immense glaciers, which crown the summit of the mountain of Locendra, supply a lake, and, issuing from this source, the river Reuss flows through the valley of St. Gothard" (Tighe's note to 1805 edition, 214). "Locendro" in 1811 edition; "Locendra" in 1803 MS.

151. lichened steep] "The lichen, which is the exclusive winter food of the reindeer in Lapland, contributes also very considerably to the subsistence of the Alpine chamois" (Tighe's note to 1805 edition, 214).

152. Thy] "The" in 1811 edition; "Thy" in 1803 MS.

153. ere] "e'er" in 1811 edition; "e're" in 1803 MS.

154. Bacchus] god of wine and drunken happiness, often depicted with a crown of ivy leaves.

155. seels] blindfolds; in falconry to sew shut the eyes of a falcon during parts of its training.

156. pendant] "pendent" in 1811 edition; alternate line "Where hangs a purse weigh'd down with many a stone" in 1803 MS. The 1811 correction captures the sense of the manuscript line: pendent as hanging.

157. train] net spread by the fowler.

158. her's] "hers" in 1811 edition; "hers" in 1803 MS.

159. Gorgon] the gorgons were three sisters with wings and snaky hair who turned anyone that looked at them into stone.

160. indurated] calloused, hardened.

161. Hydra] a water or marsh serpent with nine heads, each of which, if cut off, grew back as two.

162. Jupiter mandated that Psyche become immortal.

LORD OF HEARTS BENIGNLY CALLOUS

1. Written ca. 1802 and inscribed in *Selena* vol. 1 (NLI MS 4742) as verses

secretly composed by the character Lady Trevallyn (the former Emily Montrose) for a melody sung by the title character Selena Miltern, which makes her think of the man she had hoped but failed to marry, her unfaithful cousin Lord Henry Ortney.

TIS THY COMMAND, AND EDWIN SHALL OBEY

1. Written ca. 1802 and inscribed in *Selena* vol. 1 (NLI MS 4742) as verses written by the character Edwin Stanmore for Selena Miltern, with whom he has fallen in love. The narrator notes that Edwin has been composing poetry for some time, but his first glimpse of Selena provides direction for his amatory imagination: "She was at once his Laura, his Cinthia, his Delia, his Sacchiarissa and his Amoret" (1.402).

WHEN THE BITTER SOURCE OF SORROW

1. Written ca. 1802 and inscribed in *Selena* vol. 2 (NLI MS 4743) as verses written by Edwin Stanmore for Selena Miltern after he learns she is considered as married to Lord Dallamore.

THE PICTURE. WRITTEN FOR ANGELA

1. Written ca. 1802 and inscribed in *Selena* vol. 3 (NLI MS 4744) as verses composed by the character Angela Harley on a portrait of Lord Henry Ortney, the man she secretly loves; Angela's poem is recited by heart to Selena Miltern by Lady Trevallyn, who inadvertently finds the poem in Angela's portfolio of drawings (and who has also loved and lost Henry); published in 1811 in *Psyche, with Other Poems* (269–70).

2. dwelt] "dwells" in *Psyche, with Other Poems*.

3. From those roses no sweet dew of Love can I sip,] "No sweet dew of Love from these roses I sip" in *Psyche, with Other Poems*.

4. that] "which" in *Psyche, with Other Poems*.

5. those] "these" in *Psyche, with Other Poems*.

FLED ARE THE SUMMER HOURS OF JOY AND LOVE

1. Written ca. 1802 and inscribed in *Selena* vol. 3 (NLI MS 4744) as verses by Lady Trevallyn, written the summer before she married, which Selena finds folded in a volume of Withering's botany (see note below) that once belonged to Lord Henry Ortney.

2. Flora] Roman goddess of flowers.

3. Probably William Withering's *A Botanical Arrangement of All the Vegetables Growing in Great Britain with Descriptions of the Genera and Species According to the Celebrated Linnaeus, with an Easy Introduction to the Study of Botany. Shewing the Method of Investigating Plants, and Directions How to Dry and Preserve Specimens* (London, 1776). Tighe refers to Withering in a letter to Caroline Hamilton (Hamilton journal).

4. Tighe refers to the Swedish botanist Carolus Linnaeus (1707–1778).

SONNET ("'TIS PAST THE CRUEL ANGUISH OF SUSPENCE")

1. Written ca. 1802 and inscribed in *Selena* vol. 4 (NLI MS 4745) as one of two poems written by Angela Harley after the end of her affair with Lord Henry

Ortney, found among her papers by Selena Miltern after her death. The sonnet concludes with a rare alexandrine or iambic hexameter line.

OH SEAL MY SAD AND WEARY EYES

1. Written ca. 1802 and inscribed in *Selena* vol. 4 (NLI MS 4745) as the second of two poems written by Angela Harley after the end of her affair with Lord Henry Ortney, found among her papers by Selena Miltern after her death.

PEACE, PEACE, NOR UTTER WHAT I MUST NOT HEAR

1. Written ca. 1802 and inscribed in *Selena* vol. 4 (NLI MS 4745) as verses written by Lady Trevallyn approximately two years before her marriage in response to a passionate song Lord Henry Ortney translates for her (not printed in the novel), which Selena Miltern commits to memory before destroying them in accordance with Lady Trevallyn's request.

BUT TO HAVE HUNG ENAMOURED ON THOSE LIPS

1. Written ca. 1802 and inscribed in *Selena* vol. 5 (NLI MS 4746) as the narrator's translation of sixteen lines from Vincenzo Monti's "A Sua Eccellenza Il Signor Principe Don Sigismondo Ghigi," which the character Sydney Dallamore quotes in a letter to Selena Miltern, his beloved, as he waits for his older brother Lord Dallamore to release Selena from her coerced promise to marry him:

Ma in que' vergini labbri, in que' begli occhi
Aver quest'occhi inebriati, e dolce
Sentirmi ancor nell'anima rapita
Scorrere il suono delle tue parole;
Amar te sola, e riamato amante
Non essere felice, e veder quindi
Contra me, contra te, contra le voci
Di natura e del ciel sorger crudeli
Gli uomini, i pregiudizi e la fortuna:
Perder la speme di donarti un giorno
Nome piú sacro che d'amante, e caro
Peso vederti dal mio collo pendere,
E d'un bacio pregarmi, e d'un sorriso
Con angelico vezzo: abbandonarti . . .
Obliarti, e per sempre . . . Ah lungi, lungi
Feroce idea (lines 150–65)

PLEASURE

1. Written in 1802 (*Mary* 13) and published in 1811 in *Psyche, with Other Poems* (262–65). The 28 lines of "Pleasure" that William Tighe reprints in *Mary* includes an additional couplet: "Let them not listen to her fatal song / Nor trust her pictures, nor believe her tongue" (lines 18–19). Caroline Hamilton includes that couplet in the 22 lines of "Pleasure" she prints in her journal on Tighe, which includes lines 1–6, omits lines 7–12, skips to lines 13–18, prints the couplet above, and concludes with lines 19–26.

2. Europe exported slaves, ivory, and gold from Senegal throughout the

seventeenth and eighteenth centuries. Tighe's discussion of the flora and fauna of Senegal may be based on the writings of the French botanist Michel Adanson (1727–1806), whose "Histoire Naturelle du Sénégal" (1757) appeared in English as "A Voyage to Senegal, the Isle of Goree and the River Gambia" (1759).

3. Mangrove] tree or shrub that grows in muddy, chiefly tropical coastal swamps that are inundated at high tide; mangroves typically have numerous tangled roots aboveground and form dense thickets.

SONNET ("CAN I LOOK BACK, AND VIEW WITH TRANQUIL EYE")
1. Written ca. 1802 and published in 1811 in *Mary* (15).

1802 ("THY SUMMER'S DAY WAS LONG, BUT COULDST THOU THINK")
1. Written in 1802 and published in 1811 in *Mary* (16).

TRANQUILLITY, 1802
1. Written in 1802 and published in 1811 in *Mary* (17–18).

TO ——("HOW HARD, WITH ANGUISH UNREVEALED")
1. Written ca. 1802–1803 and published in 1811 in *Mary* (19).

VERSES WRITTEN AT THE COMMENCEMENT OF SPRING
1. Written in 1802–1803 and published in 1811 in *Psyche, with Other Poems* (251–55). In *Psyche, with Other Poems* William Tighe dates the poem to 1802 and notes that it was "Written at Waltrim, the seat of the Reverend M. Sandys, who had lately lost a beloved child" (314). In *Mary* William Tighe prints eleven stanzas (lines 25–36, 41–72) as an "Extract from Verses written at Mr. S——'s, who had lately lost a beloved Child—1803" (20–21), followed by an "Answer, by Mrs. S——":

O May the same celestial spirit
   That called my boy to endless bliss,
Give thee, sweet Mary, to inherit
   A blessing as divine as his.

May he restore thy long-lost treasure,
   Awake thy torpid soul to joy,
Open new scenes of heavenly pleasure,
   And with new songs thy tongue employ.

May our Redeemer's loving-kindness
   Light up a lamp shall ever blaze,
Shall scatter all remains of blindness,
   And warm thy heart to love and praise.

So shall we when this life is ended
   With Jesu's saints together rise,
Shall see our Lord with hosts attended,
   And meet my cherub in the skies. (22)

Mrs. Sandys was the former Barbara Tighe, Theodosia Blachford's younger sister, who married the Reverend Michael Sandys of Powerscourt in 1776. In a letter to Joseph Cooper Walker postmarked September 21, 1802, Mary Tighe comments on the sad loss of the youngest of the seven children at Waltrim (TCD MS 1461/5).

PLEASURE, 1803

1. Written in 1803 and published in 1811 in *Mary* (23).

THE WORLD, 1803

1. Written in 1803 and published in 1811 in *Mary* (23).

THO GENIUS AND FANCY HEREAFTER MAY TRACE

1. Written in April 1803 for Caroline Hamilton's Album: 1803–1859 (NLW MS 22984C).

2. to blow] to blossom.

THE OLD MAID'S PRAYER TO DIANA

1. Written before 1805 and published in 1827 in *The Amulet, or, Christian and Literary Remembrancer* (107–8). Caroline Hamilton's Album: 1803–1859 (NLW MS 22984C) contains an elegant print copy inscribed in 1805; the poem was reprinted in Elizabeth Mavor's *The Ladies of Llangollen* (1971) in a slightly altered stanzaic format without lines 25–32 and inaccurately attributed to Lady Eleanor Butler as a "Hymn to Diana" (179) from the Parker MS (229). "Old maid" refers to a woman unlikely to marry; "Diana" was the goddess of chastity and virginity.

2. grief . . . dropping] "griefs . . . drooping" in the Parker MS; "grief . . . dropping" in the Hamilton Album (NLW MS 22984C).

3. flaunts] "flouts" in Parker MS and Hamilton Album (NLW MS 22984C).

4. wiser] "better" in Parker MS; "wiser" in the Hamilton Album (NLW MS 22984C).

5. Or] "Oh" in Parker MS; "Or" in the Hamilton Album (NLW MS 22984C).

6. niceness or slatternly] "rudeness or flattering" in Parker MS; "niceness or slatternly" in the Hamilton Album (NLW MS 22984C).

7. pelf] money, especially when gained in a dishonest or dishonorable way.

8. brain] "mind" in Parker MS; "brain" in the Hamilton Album (NLW MS 22984C).

9. spadille] the ace of spades in the card games ombre and quadrille.

10. matadore] any of the highest trumps in ombre, skat, and other card games; also a domino game in which halves are matched so as to make a total of seven.

11. cot] cottage; "lot" in Parker MS; "Cot" in the Hamilton Album (NLW MS 22984C).

ON A NIGHT-BLOWING CEREUS

1. Written ca. 1803–1805 and published in 1827 in *The Amulet, or, Christian and Literary Remembrancer* (374–76). The night-blooming cereus (or cereus grandiflorus) is a neotropical cactus which produces one white, vanilla-scented flower during midsummer nights that blooms over a six-hour period and then withers and dies. Also known as vanilla cactus or queen of the night, it has been used to make a heart tonic to relieve problems related to nerves and debility.

To Cowper & His Mary

1. Written in August 1803 and available in autograph copy in a letter to Joseph Cooper Walker postmarked August 13, 1803 (TCD MS 1461/5). Tighe wrote this sonnet on the poet William Cowper (1731–1800) and his companion Mary Unwin (d. 1796) after reading William Hayley's *The Life, and Posthumous Writings, of William Cowper* (1803), and being struck by Hayley's description of the visit Cowper and Unwin made to him at Eartham, where Hayley's eleven-year-old son and a friend would take the stroke-disabled Mrs. Unwin round the garden twice a day in a chair.

2. "noble mind oerthrown"] Tighe cites Ophelia's description of Hamlet when she believes him to be mad, in *Hamlet* 3.1.150.

The Eclipse. Jan. 24, 1804

1. Written in January 1804 and published in *Mary* (24–25). Tighe spent most of January 1804 in Dublin and would have seen a partial lunar eclipse there.

2. A reference to Tighe's cousin Thomas, second son of her uncle Rev. Thomas Tighe.

Written for Her Niece S.K.

1. Written ca. 1804 and published in 1811 in *Psyche, with Other Poems* (266–67). Tighe's niece Sarah Kelly was the daughter of her cousin Elizabeth Kelly (née Tighe).

To Fortune. From Metastasio

1. Written ca. 1804 and published in 1811 in *Psyche, with Other Poems* (268). Tighe bases her sonnet on Pietro Metastasio's Sonet 22:

> Che speri, instabil dea, di sasse e spine
> Ingombrando a' miei passi ogni sentiero?
> Ch'io tremi forse a un guardo tuo severo?
> Ch'io sudi forse a imprigionarti il crine?
> Serba queste minacce alle meschine
> Alme soggette al tuo fallace impero;
> Ch'io saprei, se cadesse il mondo intero,
> Intrepido aspettar le sue ruine.
> Non son nuove per me queste contese:
> Pugnammo, il sai, gran tempo; e più valente
> Con agitarmi il tuo furor mi rese:
> Ché dalla ruota e dal martel cadente,
> Mentre soffre l'acciar colpi ed offese,
> E più fino diventa e più lucente. (2:949, lines 1–14)

To the Memory of Margaret Tighe

1. Written in June 1804 and published in 1811 in *Psyche, with Other Poems* (256–57). Tighe commemorates her grandmother, Margaret Tighe (née Theaker), Theodosia Blachford's stepmother.

VERSES ADDRESSED TO HENRY VAUGHAN

1. Written in London, October 1804 and available in autograph at the Royal College of Physicians Library, London (ALS collection). Tighe addressed these verses to her doctor, Henry Vaughan, later Sir Henry Halford (from 1809 onwards), who treated her for consumption in 1804. Appointment books indicate that Tighe was scheduled to see him on Friday, October 26, 1804 (MS 2596, Royal College of Physicians, London), but she evidently saw him on her birthday as well. I am grateful to Geoffrey Davenport for this information.

2. "Which does not concern me for what it is worth, but because it is a keepsake" (*Carmina* 12.12–13, Loeb translation). Tighe takes her epigraph from Caius Valerius Catullus, whose *Carmina* 12 berates Marrucine Asini for trying to steal table linens valued for their association with the absent friends who sent them.

3. Phoebus] Apollo was the god of healing.

4. "In eo autem facultate qua consolamur afflictos et edo duci mage perluritos a timore, qua languidos incitamus, et aegimus depressos, omniam Medicorum facite princeps fuit; et si qui medicamentis non cessissent dolores, permulcebat eos, et consopiebat hortationibus et alloquio." ". . . . stetit urna paulum / sicca, dum grato Danai puellas / Carmine mulces" (Tighe's note to manuscript). In the first portion of the note Tighe presents a Latin translation and extension of lines 17–20, followed by a quote from Horace's *Carminum* 3.11.22–24, which invokes and describes Mercury's persuasive charms: "for a little while the jar stood dry, as with thy winning notes thou Danaus' daughters didst beguile" (Loeb translation). Danaus's fifty daughters were compelled to marry their cousins but ordered to stab them to death on their wedding night with knives provided by their father; all but one did so (as the ode details). As punishment they spent eternity trying to fill leaky jars with water.

5. asswasive] assuasive.

6. "Vide Horace Ode X Lib. II et passim: '. . . Informes hyemes reducit / Jupiter; idem / Summovet. Non, si male nunc, et olim / Sic erit" (Tighe's note to manuscript). Tighe quotes lines 15–18 from Horace's *Carminum* 2.10: "Though Jupiter brings back the unlovely winters, he, also, takes them away. If we fare ill to-day, 'twill not be ever so" (Loeb translation).

VERSES WRITTEN IN SICKNESS. DECEMBER, 1804

1. Written in London, December 1804 and published in 1811 in *Psyche, with Other Poems* (258–61).

PSALM CXXX. IMITATED, JAN. 1805

1. Written in London, January 1805 and published in 1811 in *Mary* (26–27). Psalm 130 reads as follows:

Out of the depths have I cried unto thee, O LORD.
Lord, hear my voice: let thine ears be attentive to the voice of my supplications.
If thou, LORD, shouldest mark iniquities, O Lord, who shall stand?
But there is forgiveness with thee, that thou mayest be feared.

I wait for the LORD, my soul doth wait, and in his word do I hope.
My soul waiteth for the Lord more than they that watch for the morning: I
   say, more than they that watch for the morning.
Let Israel hope in the LORD: for with the LORD there is mercy, and with
   him is plenteous redemption.
And he shall redeem Israel from all his iniquities. (KJV, lines 1–8)

Addressed to My Brother. 1805

1. Written in London, 1805 and published in 1811 in *Psyche, with Other Poems*
(237). According to Theodosia Blachford's journal, Tighe spent much of the winter
and summer of 1805 with her brother and sister-in-law, John and Camilla
Blachford, in Chelsea and Brompton Grove.

Address to the West Wind, Written at Pargate, 1805

1. Written in 1805 and copied by Henry Moore in May 1811 from Tighe's
manuscript into the Henry and Lucy Moore MS Album: Poems HM 1811,
Chawton House Library (60–62). Pargate is a quay on the banks of the river Dee
in the northwest of England near Chester; vessels to Dublin generally sailed from
Holyhead, Liverpool, or Parkgate. Theodosia Blachford refers to the dangerous
crossing Tighe made in September 1805 (journal).
   2. Eurus] Eurus is the Greek god of the east wind (child of Eos and Astraeus)
who brings warmth and rain from the east.
   3. Flora] the Roman goddess of flowers.

Imitation from Boïeldieu

1. Written ca. 1801–1805 and copied by Caroline Hamilton into NLI MS
4800. The French composer François-Adrien Boïeldieu (1775–1834) based his
1801 romance "*Tu plains mes jours troublés*" on the following poem by Charles-
Pierre Colardeau (1732–1776), "*A Mon Ami, Stances*":

Tu plains mes jours troublés par tant d'orages,
Mes jours affreux, d'ombres environnes!
Va, les douleurs m'ont mis au rang des Sages;
Et la raison suit les Infortunés.

A tous les goûts d'une folle jeunesse
J'abandonnai l'effor de mes desirs:
A peine, hélas! j'en ai senti l'yvresse,
Qu'un prompt réveil a détruit mes plaisirs.

Brûlant d'amour & des feux du bel âge,
J'idolâtrai de trompeuses Beautés.
J'aimois les fers d'un si doux esclavage;
En les brisant, je les ai regrettés.

J'offris alors aux Filles de Mémoire
Un fugitif de sa chaîne échappé;

Mais je ne pus arracher à la Gloire
Qu'un vain laurier, que la foudre a frappé.

Enfin, j'ai vû de mes jeunes années
L'Astre pâlir, au Midi de son cours:
Depuis long-tems, la main des destinées
Tourne, à regret, le fuseau de mes jours.

Gloire, Plaisir, cet éclat de la vie,
Bientôt pour moi tout est évanoui;
Ce songe heureux, dont l'erreur m'est ravie,
Fut trop rapide; & j'en ai peu joui.

Mais l'Amitié sçait, par son éloquence,
Calmer des maux, qu'elle aime à partager;
Et, chaque jour, ma pénible existence
Devient, près d'elle, un fardeau plus léger.

Jusqu'au tombeau si son appui me reste,
Il est encor des plaisirs pour mon coeur;
Et ce débris d'un naufrage funeste
Pourra, lui seul, me conduire au bonheur.

Quand l'infortune ôte le droit de plaire,
Intéresser est le bien plus doux;
Et l'Amitié nous est encor plus chère,
Lorsque l'Amour s'envole loin de nous. (lines 1–36)

I am grateful to Claude Fouillade for his translation of this poem.
    2. *Tu plains mes jours troublés*] You pity my troubled days.
    3. chest] probably a transcription error for chased.

ADDRESS TO MY HARP
    1. Written ca. 1805 and published in 1811 in *Psyche, with Other Poems* (238–40).

MORNING
    1. Written ca. 1805 and published in 1811 in *Psyche, with Other Poems* (241–43).
    2. "So oft hath Tithonia passed by my groans, and pitying sprinkled me with her cool whip" (*Silvae* 5:4, lines 9–10, Loeb translation). Tighe takes her epigraph from Publius Papinius Statius (AD ca. 45–96), whose verses "To Sleep" invoke Tithonia (Aurora, the dawn goddess, named here after her lover Tithonus) rather than Titania (Diana, the moon goddess).

TO W. HAYLEY, ESQ. IN RETURN FOR A COPY OF COWPER'S LIFE, WITH A SONNET—1806
    1. Written in 1806 and published in 1811 in *Mary* (28). Tighe sent these verses to William Hayley to thank him for the inscribed copy of *The Life and Posthumous*

Writings of William Cowper he sent in 1806, which had been accompanied by a
sonnet addressed to her:

> Records of Genius! traced by friendship's hand!
> Go, & to Psyche's sympathetic eyes
> Fondly display in nature's simple guise
> A Poet's life! whose merit may command
> Perpetual plaudits from his native land,
> And fame, from every polished chime that lies
> Beneath the favour of indulgent skies,
> Wherever minds aspire & hearts expand
> To Psyche say, in truth's endearing tone
> Behold thy favorite bard, whose life & lays
> (If ever man might arrogate such praise)
> May match in purity & grace thy own.
> How would he (if on earth) exult to raise
> And seat thee high on his Parnassian throne. (NLI MS 4810)

The Shawl's Petition, to Lady Asgill

1. Written ca. 1806–1809 and published in 1811 in *Psyche, with Other Poems*
(271–73). Lady Sophia Asgill (née Ogle) and Sir Charles Asgill married in 1788,
seven years after his famous experience as an imprisoned British captain in the
American Revolutionary War. Lord Asgill was active in suppressing the Irish
Rebellion of 1798 and placed in command of the garrison of Dublin in 1800.
Lady Asgill was active in Dublin society and one of the "troops of Friends" who
visited Tighe after she was confined to her couch at the Dominick Street house
in Dublin (Hamilton journal).

2. Persia] now Iran.

3. Cashmire] Kashmir, a region on the border of India and Pakistan; Kashmir
goats provide the fine soft wool used to make cashmere products such as shawls.

4. Moselay] Mosellay, a site at Shiraz in Southern Persia, often mentioned by
the poet Hafiz (1325–1389), whose Persian "Gazel" was translated by Sir William
Jones (1746–1794) as "A Persian Song of Hafiz" (1799):

> Sweet maid, if thou would'st charm my sight,
> And bid these arms thy neck infold;
> That rosy cheek, that lily hand,
> Would give thy poet more delight
> Than all Bocara's vaunted gold,
> Than all the gems of Samarcand.
> Boy, let yon liquid ruby flow,
> And bid thy pensive heart be glad,
> Whate'er the frowning zealots say:
> Tell them, their Eden cannot show
> A stream so clear as Rocnabad,
> A bower so sweet as Mosellay. (1–12)

5. Hyperborean] arctic; frigid.

6. zone] belt. The next line invokes the magic zone or girdle of Venus, which compelled anyone she wished to desire her.

7. Sophia's] Lady Asgill.

8. sopha] the sofa or couch Tighe inhabited, whose spelling invokes "Sophia."

HAGAR IN THE DESERT

1. Written in April 1807 (*Mary* 28) and published in 1811 in *Psyche, with Other Poems* (299–302). In Genesis 21 Hagar and Ishmael are cast out into the wilderness of Beersheba with bread and a bottle of water. After the water is spent, Hagar places Ishmael under a shrub, "and sat her down over against him a good way off, as it were a bow shot: for she said, Let me not see the death of the child. And she sat over against him, and lift up her voice, and wept. And God heard the voice of the lad; and the angel of God called to Hagar out of heaven, and said unto her, What aileth thee, Hagar? fear not; for God hath heard the voice of the lad where he is. Arise, lift up the lad, and hold him in thine hand; for I will make him a great nation. And God opened her eyes, and she saw a well of water; and she went, and filled the bottle with water, and gave the lad drink" (21.16–19, KJV).

IMITATED FROM JEREMIAH.—CHAP. XXXI. v. 15

1. Written ca. 1807 and published in 1811 in *Psyche, with Other Poems* (297–98). Jeremiah 31 prophesies the restoration of the divided states of Israel as a homecoming of Rachel's children: "Thus saith the LORD; A voice was heard in Ramah, lamentation, and bitter weeping; Rahel weeping for her children refused to be comforted for her children, because they were not. Thus saith the LORD; Refrain thy voice from weeping, and thine eyes from tears: for thy work shall be rewarded, saith the LORD; and they shall come again from the land of the enemy. And there is hope in thine end, saith the LORD, that thy children shall come again to their own border" (31.15–17, KJV).

PSYCHE'S ANSWER

1. Written in May 1807 and published in 1821 in Lady Dacre's *Dramas, Translations and Occasional Poems*. Tighe's sonnet offers a belated response to the April 1806 sonnet she received from Barbarina Brand, Lady Dacre (née Ogle) on *Psyche; or, the Legend of Love*, "To Psyche, on Reading Her Poem":

Who hears the lark's wild rapturous carol shrill,
    Nor feels with kindred joy his bosom glow?
    Who, the lone owl's loud dismal shriek of woe,
Nor starts as with a sense of coming ill?
The mingled bleatings that at evening fill
    The dewy air with tender sounds, that flow
    From mother's love, all answering hearts avow,
Such sympathy does nature's voice instil!
    What wonder, then, if the enchanting lay
In which the soul of love and virtue blend
    Their force resistless, and thy heart pourtray,

While all the Nine their fascination lend,
  That the rapt fancy the strong spell obey,
Greeting thee, unknown Psyche! as a friend? (2:237)

2. darkling] growing darkness.

TO LADY CHARLEMONT, IN RETURN FOR HER PRESENTS OF FLOWERS. MARCH, 1808

1. Written in March 1808 and published in 1811 in *Psyche, with Other Poems* (274–77). Anne Bermingham, Countess Charlemont married Francis William Caulfeild, second Earl of Charlemont, on February 9, 1802, and lived with him at Marion House in Dublin, famous for its architectural construction and beautiful gardens. Lady Charlemont was one of the "troops of Friends" who visited Tighe after she was confined to her couch at the Dominick Street house in Dublin (Hamilton journal).

2. Narcissus] a beautiful youth who rejected the nymph Echo and fell in love with his own reflection in a pool; he pined away and was changed into the flower that bears his name.

3. Tighe is probably referring to the "Madonna in Floral Wreath" by Jan Brueghel the Elder and Peter Paul Rubens (ca. 1620).

WRITTEN AT WEST-ASTON. JUNE, 1808

1. Written in June 1808 and published in 1811 in *Psyche, with Other Poems* (278–80). Often referred to as "The Myrtle" by family members, William Tighe notes that "The myrtle was planted by the author's aunt Mary, at West-Aston, the seat of Thomas Acton, esq. in the county of Wicklow. The 'beloved brother' was the author's father, the Reverend William Blachford, who died after a very short illness in the meridian of life, a few months after the birth of his daughter. The myrtle was destroyed by frost in the winter of 1807, notwithstanding the care of Mrs. Acton, who is addressed in this poem by her christian name of Sydney" (*Psyche, with Other Poems* 313–14). As Theodosia Blachford remarks, Tighe made a last series of visits to friends and family during the spring of 1808: "At the latter end of May 1808 she went to Rossana but returned to town in July after vising Altadore for the last time, Avondale, & Westaston, where she wrote 'The Myrtle'" (journal). The "Mrs. Acton" of the poem refers to Sidney Acton (née Davis), married to Thomas Acton of West Aston in 1780, and invoked in Tighe's "A Letter From Mrs. Acton to Her Nephew Mr. Evans." Tighe's aunt and namesake Mary Blachford died in May 1788 after a protracted bout with cancer; she was the younger of William Blachford's two sisters and lived with her sister and brother-in-law, the Radcliffes.

TO W.P. ESQ. AVONDALE

1. Written in Avondale, June 1808 and published in 1811 in *Psyche, with Other Poems* (236). Tighe wrote this sonnet for William Parnell (1780–1821) during her last visit to his estate at Avondale (see previous note for Theodosia Blachford's remarks on Tighe's last tour). William Parnell was a younger son of Sir John Parnell and the grandfather of Charles Stewart Parnell; he took the name Parnell-Hayes when he inherited Avondale in recognition of his father's inheriting the

estate from William Hayes. E.V. Weller reproduces a holograph of Tighe's manuscript copy in *Keats and Mary Tighe,* which shows a variation in the first line: "We *wished* for thee, dear friend! for Summer Eve" (236a, my emphasis).

WRITTEN IN A COPY OF PSYCHE WHICH HAD BEEN IN THE LIBRARY OF C.J. FOX. APRIL, 1809

1. Written in Dublin, April 1809 and published in 1811 in *Psyche, with Other Poems* (219). Tighe inscribed this sonnet in the 1805 copy of *Psyche; or, the Legend of Love* she gave to her friend William Parnell (Huntington Library 328444); Parnell presented his copy to the famous Whig politician Charles James Fox (1749–1806), whose widow returned the copy to Tighe after Fox's death, at Tighe's request.

2. he] "it" in Huntington Library 328444.
3. An] "A" in Huntington Library 328444.
4. yet] "still" in Huntington Library 328444.

THE LILY. MAY, 1809

1. Written in Dublin, May 1809 and published in 1811 in *Psyche, with Other Poems* (303–5).

SONNET WRITTEN AT WOODSTOCK, IN THE COUNTY OF KILKENNY, THE SEAT OF WILLIAM TIGHE. JUNE 30, 1809

1. Written in Woodstock, June 1809 and published in 1811 in *Psyche, with Other Poems* (306). Tighe wrote this sonnet for her cousin William Tighe at the very beginning of her final visit to his estate at Woodstock, where she died in March 1810.

ON RECEIVING A BRANCH OF MEZEREON WHICH FLOWERED AT WOODSTOCK. DECEMBER, 1809

1. Written in Woodstock, December 1809 and published in 1811 in *Psyche, with Other Poems* (307–10). William Tighe concludes his edition with the poem family members referred to as "The Mezereon" and notes "The concluding poem of this collection was the last ever composed by the author, who expired at the place where it was written, after six years of protracted malady, on the 24th of March, 1810, in the thirty-seventh year of her age. Her fears of death were perfectly removed before she quitted this scene of trial and suffering; and her spirit departed to a better state of existence, confiding with heavenly joy in the acceptance of love of her redeemer" (311).

EXTRACTS FROM A JOURNAL OF M.B., BORN 1772

1. The surviving journal entries composed by Mary Blachford Tighe between 1787 and 1802, copied by her cousin Caroline Hamilton (née Tighe) into NLI MS 4810 from the originals preserved by Tighe's mother, Theodosia Blachford. Some of the entries are out of order as copied into NLI MS 4810 and some of the dates Hamilton copied may be inaccurate (indicated in the notes).

2. Tighe refers to the Bethesda Chapel in Dublin. Edward Smyth was appointed minister there in 1786 and John Wesley preached his first sermon at Bethesda in April 1787.

3. April 16 fell on a Monday in 1787, and would not fall on a Tuesday until 1793.

4. See Psalm 89.32: "Then will I visit their transgression with the rod, and their iniquity with stripes" (KJV).

5. Tighe quotes from the third stanza of the Methodist hymn "When shall thy love constrain": "It calls me still to seek thy face, / And stoops to ask my love" (11–12).

6. See Psalm 58.4–5: "Their poison is like the poison of a serpent: they are like the deaf adder that stoppeth her ear; which will not hearken to the voice of charmers, charming never so wisely" (KJV).

7. Tighe quotes the third stanza of the Methodist hymn "To the haven of thy breast": "In the time of my distress / Thou hast my succour been, / In my utter helplessness / Restraining me from sin; / O how swiftly didst thou move / To save me in the trying hour! / Still protect me with thy love, / And shield me with thy power" (17–24).

8. See Psalm 50.15: "And call upon me in the day of trouble: I will deliver thee, and thou shalt glorify me" (KJV).

9. Tighe refers to the last two lines of Joseph Hart's 1759 hymn "This, this is the God we adore": "We'll praise him for all that is past, / And trust him for all that's to come" (7–8).

10. June 22 fell on a Friday in 1787 and a Sunday in 1788. The journal entry suggests 1787 as the likelier date, as Tighe anticipates seeing Wesley, who was in Dublin during June 1787.

11. See Hebrews 4.15: "For we have not an high priest which cannot be touched with the feeling of our infirmities; but was in all points tempted like as we are, yet without sin" (KJV).

12. Tighe misquotes from the tenth stanza of the Methodist hymn "When shall thy love constrain": "Settle and fix my wavering soul" (39).

13. September 25 fell on a Tuesday in 1787; it did not fall on a Saturday until 1790.

14. See James 1.5: "If any of you lack wisdom, let him ask of God, that giveth to all men liberally, and upbraideth not; and it shall be given him" (KJV).

15. Probably a reference to William Myles (1756–1828), an Irish Methodist converted by John Wesley in 1773. He itinerated at his own expense from 1777 to 1782 and was the first Irish preacher to be received into full connection. A letter from Theodosia Blachford to Sarah Tighe postmarked April 26, 1788, suggests that Myles sustained a romantic interest in the young Mary Blachford, and was encouraged in his suit by Mrs. Edward Smyth (PRONI MS D/2685/2/15).

16. November 28 fell on a Wednesday in 1787; it did not fall on a Thursday until 1793.

17. See Revelations 2.4: "Nevertheless, I have something against thee, because thou hast left thy first love" (KJV).

18. See Psalm 78.58 as printed in the *Book of Common Prayer*: "They turned their backs, and fell away like their forefathers; starting aside like a broken bow."

19. "Her aunt Miss M.B." (Caroline Hamilton's note to the manuscript). Tighe's aunt and namesake, Mary Blachford, died in May 1788.

20. "answered I trust, 24th March 1810. TB." (Caroline Hamilton's note to the manuscript, a copy of Theodosia Blachford's annotation, which refers to the date of Tighe's death).

21. See stanza 4 of the Methodist hymn "My God! I know, I feel thee mine": "Jesus, thine all-victorious love / Shed in my heart abroad; / Then shall my feet no longer rove, / Rooted and fixed in God" (13–16).

22. See Isaiah 25.4: "For thou hast been a strength to the poor, a strength to the needy in his distress, a refuge from the storm, a shadow from the heat, when the blast of the terrible ones is as a storm against the wall" (KJV).

23. See Matthew 12.43–45: "When the unclean spirit is gone out of a man, he walketh through dry places, seeking rest, and findeth none. Then he saith, I will return into my house from whence I came out; and when he is come, he findeth it empty, swept, and garnished. Then goeth he, and taketh with himself seven other spirits more wicked than himself, and they enter in and dwell there: and the last state of that man is worse than the first. Even so shall it be also unto this wicked generation" (KJV).

24. Mr. de la Flechier (or Flechere) was the nephew of the Rev. John Fletcher; Tighe's mother explains in her journal that she tried to secure him as a husband for Mary, but broke the engagement in January 1789 after she saw a developing attachment between Mary and Henry Tighe.

25. The first line of William Cowper's famous hymn, "Light Shining Out of Darkness": "God moves in a mysterious way / His wonders to perform; / He plants his footsteps in the sea / And rides upon the storm" (1–4).

26. See Exodus 13.21: "And the LORD went before them by day in a pillar of a cloud, to lead them the way; and by night in a pillar of fire, to give them light; to go by day and night" (KJV).

27. See Matthew 10.29–31: "Are not two sparrows sold for a farthing? and one of them shall not fall on the ground without your Father. But the very hairs of your head are all numbered. Fear ye not therefore, ye are of more value than many sparrows" (KJV).

28. See John 9.4: "I must work the works of him that sent me, while it is day: the night cometh, when no man can work" (KJV).

29. *The life of Baron Frederick Trenck: containing his adventures, his cruel and excessive sufferings, during ten years imprisonment, at the fortress of Magdeburgh, by command of the late King of Prussia* appeared in German in 1786–1787, in French in 1788, and in an English translation by Thomas Holcroft in 1788. Baron Trenck was guillotined on July 26, 1794. Wesley mentions reading this work in his journal entry for Thursday, May 7, 1789 (4:467).

30. Theodosia Blachford writes that she and Mary moved to a house on Gardiner's row in Dublin in early 1789 (journal); Wesley made his last visit to Ireland in 1789, and preached at Bethesda Chapel on April 10 (see Wesley's *Journals* 4:464).

31. David Hume (1711–1776), the Scottish philosopher whose position on evidence and miracles prompted Wesley to comment against "David Hume's insolent book" (*Works* 3:354).

32. Guillaume Thomas François Raynal (1713–1796) was a fierce controversialist

who wrote against the Inquisition and European colonization, among other things; Wesley attacked Raynal in his Sermon 63 as an "enemy to monarchy and revelation."

33. William Romaine (1714–1795) was a leading Calvinist preacher and Hebrew scholar whose sermons and lectures at St. Dunstan-in-the-West drew large crowds; "A Practical Comment on the Hundred and Seventh Psalm" (1755) went through at least four editions.

34. Tighe and her mother left Dublin for London in August 1789, visited spas in Tunbridge and Bath to improve Tighe's health, and returned to Dublin in February 1790.

35. Henry Mackenzie, *Julia de Roubigné* (1777).

36. Probably Anne Caroline Tottenham (1776–1852), who married John David LaTouche on March 16, 1799.

37. Lismore, county Cavan.

38. Goethe's *The Sorrows of Young Werther* (1774) created a sensation as an epistolary novel which told the tale of a young artist who committed suicide after falling in love with a young woman engaged to another man.

39. During the late eighteenth and early nineteenth centuries Swanlinbar (in county Cavan) was one of Ireland's foremost spas.

40. "Swanlinbar" (Caroline Hamilton's note to the manuscript).

41. See Romans 6.21: "What fruit had ye then in those things whereof ye are now ashamed? for the end of those things is death" (KJV). Augustine similarly invokes Romans in chapter 2 of *The Confessions of Saint Augustine:* "What fruit had I then (wretched man!) in those things, of the remembrance whereof I am now ashamed?"

42. An earlier version of what would become the final quatrain of "Verses Written in Solitude, April 1792."

43. In *The Life of Johnson* for AD 1772 Boswell writes "At this time it appears from his 'Prayers and Meditations,' that he had been more than commonly diligent in religious duties, particularly in reading the holy scriptures. It was Passion Week, that solemn season which the Christian world has appropriated to the commemoration of the mysteries of our redemption, and during which, whatever embers of religion are in our breasts, will be kindled into pious warmth" (1:437).

44. Walter Shirley, the son of the great Rev. Walter Shirley, was ordained in 1792 and preached at Bethesda.

45. See John 19.30: "When Jesus therefore had received the vinegar, he said, It is finished: and he bowed his head, and gave up the ghost" (KJV).

46. Waltrim was the home of the Sandys, Tighe's relatives (Barbara Sandys was Theodosia Blachford's younger half-sister).

47. Bellevue House in county Wicklow was the great family estate of the La Touches, built in 1754 by the Dublin banker David La Touche.

48. Engagements of the court.

49. Numerous psalms invoke this trope; see, for instance, Psalm 66.9 ("Which holdeth our soul in life, and suffereth not our feet to be moved") or Psalm 121.3 ("He will not suffer thy foot to be moved: he that keepeth thee will not slumber").

50. Thomas Kelly was ordained in 1792 (with Walter Shirley) and married Tighe's cousin Elizabeth Tighe in 1795. She may have heard him preach at St.

George's Chapel, in Lower Temple Street, Dublin, referred to as Little George's Church after the 1802 construction of St. George's Church in Hardwicke Street, Dublin.

51. Fénelon, François de Salignac de la Mothe (1651–1715) was a French theologian and educator whose didactic romance *Télémaque* (1699) was very popular in the eighteenth century.

52. See Psalm 91.3 ("Surely he shall deliver thee from the snare of the fowler, and from the noisome pestilence") or Psalm 124.7 ("Our soul is escaped as a bird out of the snare of the fowlers: the snare is broken, and we are escaped").

53. Lady Jocelyn, Frances Theodosia née Bligh (d. 1802), one of Tighe's cousins.

54. Isaac Bickerstaffe (1735–1812), *Love in a Village, a Comic Opera* (1763).

55. John Blachford, Tighe's older brother, who had just returned from Europe.

56. Henry Tighe, who had proposed marriage.

57. An allusion to Hamlet's famous soliloquy: "To die, to sleep; / To sleep: perchance to dream: ay, there's the rub; / For in that sleep of death what dreams may come" (3.1.63–65).

58. Tighe was probably living at the house her mother-in-law and aunt Sarah Tighe rented in Manchester Square, London.

59. Tighe may be referring to the Cecil Chapel built in the 1620s for Sir Edward Cecil; alternately, she may be referring to the eminent Rev. Richard Cecil (1748–1810), who preached at Bedford Row Chapel, London.

60. Cobham Hall in Kent, England, was one of the seats of the Earls of Darnley.

61. Thomas James Fortescue (1760–1795) of Ravensdale Park was buried in Clermont Park.

62. See Psalm 39.13: "O spare me, that I may recover strength, before I go hence, and be no more" (KJV).

63. Tighe usually made the voyage between Ireland and England from Holyhead, Wales.

64. From Hamlet's soliloquy (see note above): "The undiscover'd country from whose bourn / No traveller returns" (3.1.78–79).

65. Mary's Abbey in Dublin was the site of numerous meeting-houses in the late eighteenth century.

66. See the collect for the fourth Sunday after Easter in the 1662 *Book of Common Prayer*: "Almighty God, who alone canst order the unruly wills and affections of sinful men; Grant unto thy people, that they may love the thing which thou commandest, and desire that which thou dost promise; that so, among the sundry and manifold changes of the world, our hearts may surely there be fixed, where true joys are to be found."

67. See Matthew 18.12: "How think ye? if a man have an hundred sheep, and one of them be gone astray, doth he not leave the ninety and nine, and goeth into the mountains, and seeketh that which is gone astray?" (KJV).

68. Rev. George Fortescue (1769–1798) was shot by the French on August 23 in an effort to prevent them from entering Ballina, county Mayo after they landed in Kilcummin Bay.

69. See Proverbs 23.35, whose discourse on the dangers of appetite concludes as follows: "They have stricken me, shalt thou say, and I was not sick; they have

beaten me, and I felt it not: when shall I awake? I will seek it yet again" (KJV).

70. The manuscript does not indicate whether the final entry is written by Theodosia Blachford or Caroline Hamilton.

OBSERVATIONS ON THE FOREGOING JOURNAL BY HER MOTHER, MRS BLACHFORD

1. Commentary on Tighe's surviving journal entries and life composed by Theodosia Blachford ca. 1810, copied by Caroline Hamilton into NLI MS 4810.

2. A quotation from Samuel Johnson's *Vanity of Human Wishes* (1749): "He left the name at which the world grew pale, / To point a moral, or adorn a tale" (line 221).

3. See Isaiah 55.2: "Wherefore do ye spend money for that which is not bread? and your labour for that which satisfieth not? hearken diligently unto me, and eat ye that which is good, and let your soul delight itself in fatness" (KJV); Lamentations 3.16: "He hath also broken my teeth with gravel stones, he hath covered me with ashes" (KJV); and Proverbs 20.17: "Bread of deceit is sweet to a man; but afterwards his mouth shall be filled with gravel" (KJV).

4. William Tighe prints a version of Tighe's "Remarkable Dream. 31st Jan 1780, at seven years and three months old" in *Mary*, as transcribed and edited by Theodosia Blachford. A vision of the second coming and day of judgment that describes Jesus leading the good into heaven, and the devil dragging the evil down to hell, the dream ends with a vision of family reconciliation: "I thought I saw my father in a white robe coming to me, and my mamma and brother without robes, arm in arm, who told me we should be happy; which so delighted that it awoke me, and I was sorry to find it only a dream" (36).

5. See Jeremiah 17.1: "The sin of Judah is written with a pen of iron, and with the point of a diamond" (KJV).

6. Mary Tighe's aunt and future mother-in-law Sarah Tighe (née Fownes).

7. Brittas House in county Meath was one of several homes built by the Bligh family.

8. John La Touche's estate was at Harristown.

9. See Thomas Gray, "The Bard: A Pindaric Ode" (1757), lines 71–76. Blachford or Tighe misquotes line 74, which reads "Youth *on* the prow, and Pleasure at the helm" (my emphasis).

10. Solomon Richards (1758–1819), an eminent surgeon who served as president of the Royal College of Surgeons in Dublin. Elsewhere Caroline Hamilton notes that he was a longtime friend of the Tighe family and rented an apartment from her mother, Sarah Tighe, early in his medical career (see NLI MS 4811).

11. "May 1792" (Caroline Hamilton's note to the manuscript).

12. "Was it unnatural that a mother should wish to retard a marriage between her son, scarcely 21, & his cousin whom she thought too fond of admiration? she never approved of the match nor did she think that she had even encouraged it" (Caroline Hamilton's note).

13. "T Singleton, afterwards married to Lord T's daughter & settled in England, a respectable, pleasing person" (Caroline Hamilton's note).

14. See Lamentations 3.29: "He putteth his mouth in the dust" (KJV).

15. Dr. Henry Vaughan (later Sir Henry Halford), who treated her for consumption in London in 1804 and received Tighe's "Verses Addressed to Henry Vaughan."

16. John Blachford's first wife, Camilla.

17. Dr. Robert Bree, a specialist in respiratory disorders (and Fellow of the Royal Society) who would later tell Keats he suffered from anxiety several months before Keats died.

18. Parkgate served as an alternate port to Holyhead for travellers to and from Dublin.

19. Vevay, an area within Bray, county Wicklow.

20. Mrs. Brooke was the wife of Henry Brooke the painter (1738–1806).

21. Altidore Castle, in Kilpeddar, county Wicklow.

22. Portrane House, the seat of George Evans in Portrane, county Dublin.

23. Avondale was the seat of William Parnell; Westaston was the seat of Thomas Acton.

24. Hamwood House, Dunboyne, county Meath was the seat of Charles and Catherine Hamilton; Harristown House, Mullacash, country Kildare was one of the La Touche family houses; and Kilfane House, Thomastown, county Kilkenny was the demesne of Sir John and Lady Powers (and famous for its lush romantic landscape).

25. Tighe's physician at Woodstock.

26. *A Narrow Escape from the Punishment of Death, or The Case of John Taylor and John Burton: Who Were Left for Execution at Huntingdon* (London: Evans and Sons, 1807).

27. "HT her husband" (Caroline Hamilton's note).

28. Theodosia Blachford is probably referring to Rev. James Adams Ker (1760–1825), rector in Listerlin parish, county Kilkenny.

29. Mrs. Seymour was probably Jane Seymour née Thompson (1764–1847), the wife of Thomas Seymour (1762–1821) of Ballymore Castle, county Galway, Ireland. In a letter to Joseph Cooper Walker dated January 21, 1809, Tighe mentions that Mrs. Seymour brought her one of the first copies of Sydney Owenson's *Ida* (TCD MS 1461/7).

30. See Psalm 73.26: "My flesh and my heart faileth: but God is the strength of my heart, and my portion for ever" (KJV).

31. Tighe may have been thinking of Psalm 39, especially verse 11: "When thou with rebukes dost correct man for iniquity, thou makest his beauty to consume away like a moth: surely every man is vanity. Selah" (KJV).

32. In *Mary* William Tighe suggests this sentence alludes to Bishop Gambold's "The Mystery of Life" and prints a copy of the poem: "The following Poem is added, because it was a favourite one with the Author of the foregoing reflections, and probably alluded to in one of the last sentences she ever spoke:—*What is Life?*" (30).

33. Hymn 336 in the 1889 *Methodist Hymnal*: "Father, in the name I pray / Of thy incarnate Love, / Humbly ask, that as my day / My suffering strength may prove; / When my sorrows most increase, / Let thy strongest joys be given; / Jesu, come with my distress, / And agony is heaven!" (1–8).

34. Hymn 339 in the 1889 *Methodist Hymnal*: "O Thou to whose all-searching

sight / The darkness shineth as the light, / Search, prove my heart; it pants for thee; / O burst these bonds, and set it free!" (1–4).

35. John Blachford's son William.

36. The Domenico Feti painting "Ecce Homo" portrayed the crucified Christ with the legend, "This have I done for you—Now what will you do for me?"

37. See Genesis 22.8 for the origin of this phrase: "And Abraham said, My son, God will provide himself a lamb for a burnt offering: so they went both of them together" (KJV).

38. This Protestant hymn is attributed to George Whitefield: "Ah, lovely appearance of death, / What sight upon earth is so fair? / Not all the gay pageants that breathe / Can with a dead body compare. / In solemn delight I survey / A corpse when the spirit is fled / In love with the beautiful clay, / And longing to lie in its stead. / Its languishing pain is at rest, / Its aching and aching are o'er; / The quiet immovable breast / Is pained by affliction no more. / The heart it no longer receives / Of trouble and torturing pain; / It ceases to flutter and beat, / It never shall flutter again" (1–16).

39. See 1 Corinthians 15.53: "For this corruptible must put on incorruption, and this mortal must put on immortality" (KJV).

40. Blachford cites the last stanza of Tighe's "The Lily. May 1809": "And bear the long, cold, wintry night, / And bear her own degraded doom, / And wait till Heaven's reviving light, / Eternal Spring! shall burst the gloom" (lines 41–44).

MARY TIGHE

1. Written by Caroline Hamilton ca. 1825 and available in autograph in NLI MS 4810.

2. William Blachford (1730–1773) was Prebendary of Tasgarrat and served as Librarian of Marsh's Library in Dublin (1766–1773); he married Theodosia Tighe in 1770.

3. Theodosia Blachford (1744–1817) was the daughter of William Tighe (1710–1766) and Lady Mary Bligh (1716–1748), who married in 1736 and had three sons in addition to Theodosia: William Tighe (1738–1782), Edward Tighe (1740–1800), and Richard Tighe (1744–1828).

4. "I question if there is any mention of one idle spectator" (Caroline Hamilton's note).

5. Halifax, George Saville, marquess of (1633–1695), whose essay *A Lady's Gift, or Advice to a Daughter* (1688) was written for his own daughter and went through numerous editions.

6. Mandeville, Sir John, ostensible author of a famous book of *Travels* which first appeared in France in 1356–1357; Ralegh, Sir Walter (1554–1618), whose collected works included "The Discovery of the Large, Rich, and Beautiful Empire of Guiana, with a Relation of the Great and Golden City of Manoa (which the Spaniards Call El Dorado)" (1596).

7. In 1652 John Milton became totally blind and thereafter had his daughters read to him.

8. These lines are by Caroline Hamilton's brother William Tighe, who wrote numerous occasional lyrics as well as his didactic poem *The Plants* (1808–1811).

9. William Tighe (1710–1766) married Margaret Theaker (1719–1804) in 1750.

10. Job 5.7: "Yet man is born unto trouble, as the sparks fly upward" (KJV).

11. "To the Memory of Margaret Tighe: Taken from Us June 7th, 1804.—Etat 85" (1–2).

12. William Tighe (1710–1766) and Margaret Theaker (1719–1804) had a son, Rev. Thomas Tighe (1751–1821) and a daughter, Barbara Tighe (1752–1820) who married Rev. Michael Sandys in 1776.

13. *Musae Etonenses* published verse by students at Eton College, including Thomas Gray.

14. William Tighe (1738–1782), eldest son of William Tighe (1710–1766), married Sarah Fownes (1743–1822) of Woodstock in 1765 and published *A Letter to the Earl of Darnley, on the State of the Poor in Ireland* in 1781.

15. William Tighe (1766–1816) of Woodstock published *Statistical Observations Relative to the County of Kilkenny* in 1802, his didactic poem *The Plants* in 1811, and collections of Mary Tighe's poetry in 1811 (*Psyche, with Other Poems* and *Mary, A Series of Reflections during Twenty Years*).

16. Edward Tighe (1740–1800) was well known during his day as a theater critic; he served as an MP for various boroughs (1763–1797), supported philanthropic causes (especially the education of the poor), and authored several short publications. In addition to being mentioned in James Grant Raymond's *The Life of Dermody* (1806), he is mentioned in memoirs by Anna Seward, Hannah More, Lady Morgan, and Samuel Johnson.

17. Micah 6.8: "He hath shewed thee, O man, what is good; and what doth the LORD require of thee, but to do justly, and to love mercy, and to walk humbly with thy God?" (KJV).

18. John Wesley, *The Character of a Methodist* (1742).

19. In addition to *A Short Account of the Life and Writings of the Late Rev. William Law* (1813), Richard Tighe was known for his *Psalms and Hymns* (1789) and other religious tracts and sermons.

20. In the eighth chapter of *A Serious Call to a Devout and Holy Life* (1729) William Law describes "How the wise and pious use of an estate naturally carries us to great perfection in all the virtues of the Christian life, represented in the character of Miranda."

21. plain work] plain sewing.

22. tail pieces] a small decorative design at the end of a chapter or at the bottom of a page.

23. "extract which may be brought in here. 'Mr Wesley breakfasted with us. he turned to my book case & said "there are many books here Mary not worth your reading & then he made many observations on idle books particularly fine Poetry & said that History & religious books were the best studies for me—he praised French Histories & condemned Hume & the Abbé Raynal as enemies to all Power human & divine'" (Caroline Hamilton's note, which incorporates material from Mary Tighe's journal entry for April 11, 1789).

24. Probably her visit to the Brookes in 1806, mentioned in Thedosia Blachford's journal.

25. Henry Tighe (1768–1836) was the second son of William Tighe (1738–1782) and Sarah Fownes (1743–1822), and older brother of Caroline Hamilton.

26. The group of buildings in London occupied by the Inns of the Court.

27. One who would enter pleas before the court.

28. Harrow] boarding school in London.

29. assemblies] large-scale evening gatherings.

30. Drury Lane Theatre, where Tighe would see John Bannister and Sarah Siddons perform.

31. John Bannister (1760–1836) and Sarah Siddons (1755–1831), two celebrated actors who performed at the Drury Lane Theatre in London.

32. Henry Tighe did become a barrister in 1796 but apparently did not practice.

33. curricle] A two-wheeled chaise drawn by two horses abreast.

34. An allusion to Milton's *Paradise Lost* book 4, when Satan first sees Eden: "purer aire / Meets his approach, and to the heart inspires / Vernal delight and joy, able to drive / All sadness but despair" (lines 153–56). Tighe may also be alluding to the conclusion of Charlotte Smith's sonnet "VIII. To Spring" (1784): "Thy sounds of harmony, thy balmy air, / Have power to cure all sadness—but despair" (13–14).

35. See note to "Pleasure": "Let them not listen to her fatal song. / Nor trust her pictures, nor believe her tongue."

36. John Blachford spent several years traveling in Europe in the 1790s and early 1800s.

37. Thomas James Fortescue (1760–1795), whose death Tighe refers to in her journal entry for July 25, 1795.

38. Tighe refers to Shakespeare's *King Richard the Second* 3.2, where King Richard declares "No matter where—of comfort no man speak: / Let's talk of graves, of worms, and epitaphs, / Make dust our paper, and with rainy eyes / Write sorrow on the bosom of the earth. / Let's choose executors and talk of wills:" (144–48).

39. "her brother" (Caroline Hamilton's note).

40. Tighe's collection of book reviews from 1806–1809 are recorded in NLI MS 4804, which does not contain the discussion of Milton's *Paradise Lost* that follows.

41. An allusion to William Cowper's "The Winter Evening" from book 4 of *The Task* (1785): "I crown thee king of intimate delights, / Fire-side enjoyments, home-born happiness, / And all the comforts that the lowly roof / Of undisturb'd retirement, and the hours / Of long uninterrupted ev'ning, know" (lines 139–43).

42. "It is not alway necessary to take pleasure in pleasure; if one makes good use of the privation of sadness, one can return to a state of happiness afterwards."

43. Saint-Evrémond, Charles de Saint-Denis (1613–1703), the French critic and essayist.

44. "There is a charm in this occupation which one doesn't feel during the full embrace of the passions, but which is enough, by itself, to make life happy and sweet."

45. Maria Edgeworth (1768–1849), the celebrated Anglo-Irish novelist.

46. Charles James Fox (1749–1806), leader of the liberal Whig opposition to

William Pitt (1759–1806) and energetic campaigner for Irish independence; William Hayley (1745–1820), author of *The Triumphs of Temper* (1781), etc.

47. See the note to "To W. Hayley, Esq. in Return for a Copy of Cowper's Life, with a Sonnet—1806" for the complete sonnet.

48. As noted in the introduction, Tighe received tributes from William Roscoe ("Sonnet to Mrs. Henry Tighe, on Her Poem of 'Psyche, or the Legend of Love'"), Thomas Moore ("To Mrs. Henry Tighe, on Reading Her Psyche"), Lady Dacre ("To Psyche, on Reading Her Poem"), John Edwards ("To Mrs Henry Tighe with the Tragedy of Panthea upon Reading Her Poem of Psyche"), Hugh Boyd ("To Mrs. H. Tighe on Her Poem of Psyche"), Joseph Atkinson ("To Mrs. H. Tighe"), William Ball ("To Mrs. H. Tighe") and many others.

49. Solomon Richards (1758–1819); see the note to Theodosia Blachford's journal.

50. The reddish hue of the rocks at St. Vincent's Rocks, Clifton, Bristol, offered a spectacular view to eighteenth-century travelers.

51. William Withering (1741–1799) was a botanist, chemist, geologist, and physician who practiced in Birmingham, England, and discovered digitalis (from foxglove).

52. The bee orchis is a European orchid whose flowers resemble bees in shape and color.

53. In a letter to Joseph Cooper Walker dated July 20, 1804, Tighe mentions that she has been invited to visit Hannah More: "I do not know whether you are an admirer of Hannah More—parties run very high between her defenders & her opposers here—tho' I do not intend to become one of her worshippers yet I think her a very useful character & intend profitting by an offer'd invitation to pay her a visit" (TCD MS 1461/7).

54. Llangollen was the famous and much-visited home of Lady Eleanor Butler and Sarah Ponsonby (Sarah Tighe's cousin).

55. As indicated in the note to Theodosia Blachford's journal, Dr. Henry Vaughan (later Sir Henry Halford) treated her for consumption in London in 1804.

56. See Matthew 4.4: "But he answered and said, It is written, Man shall not live by bread alone, but by every word that proceedeth out of the mouth of God" (KJV).

57. In *Lady Morgan's Autobiography, Diaries, and Correspondence* (London, 1862) W. Hepworth Dixon reprints an undated letter Tighe sent to Sydney Owenson: "My Dear Miss Owenson, I have very often thought of you, and the pleasure you kindly promised me since I had last the pleasure of seeing you; but the weather has been so unfavourable for walking, that I could hardly wish you to come so far unless you dined in the neighbourhood, and could steal an hour for me, as you did before; if it should happen that you could dine with us *at five*, on Thursday, it would make us very happy; but I am so uncertain about Mr. T—, that at present I cannot name any other day. You know you promised to try and prevail on your sister to accompany you; but indeed, I am ashamed to ask, to a sick room, two so much fitter for a ball room. If this does not find you at home, do not trouble yourself to send an answer till my messenger can call again Tuesday. I am, very truly, M. Tighe" (1:322–23).

58. See note to "To Lady Charlemont, in Return for Her Presents of Flowers. March, 1808" for Lady Charlemont; "To W.P. Esq. Avondale" for William Parnell; "The Shawl's Petition, to Lady Asgill" for Lady Asgill; Sir Arthur Wellesley (1769–1852) became the first Duke of Wellington after he won the 1809 Battle of Talavera in the Peninsular Wars against Napoleon; Lydia Rogers White (d. 1827) founded a famous salon on Park Street in London.

59. Another reference to *A Narrow Escape from the Punishment of Death, or The Case of John Taylor and John Burton: Who Were Left for Execution at Huntingdon* (London: Evans and Sons, 1807); see the Blachford journal account.

60. In July 1808 Tighe visited the Howards at Bushy Park on her way to Dominick Street, Dublin from Rossana, as she notes in a letter to Joseph Cooper Walker (TCD MS 1461/6). Tighe's cousin Catherine Bligh married Hugh Howard in 1792.

61. "The coach-maker" (Caroline Hamilton's note).

62. Theodosia Blachford founded the House of Refuge for unemployed and homeless young women on Baggot Street in Dublin in 1802.

63. "Horace Ep. libr. 1,16" (Caroline Hamilton's note). John Blachford quotes line 68 from Horace's *Epistles* 1.16: "ever busied and lost in making money" (Loeb translation).

64. Job 14.1–3: "Man that is born of a woman is of few days and full of trouble. He cometh forth like a flower, and is cut down: he fleeth also as a shadow, and continueth not. And doth thou open thine eyes upon such an one, and bringest me into judgment with thee?" (KJV).

65. See the note to Theodosia Blachford's account, which indicates that William Tighe thought this sentence alluded to Bishop Gambold's poem "The Mystery of Life."

66. The first eight lines of the famous hymn by Charles Wesley (1740), "Jesus, Lover of My Soul," whose third line elsewhere reads as "While the nearer waters roll."

67. See the note to Theodosia Blachford's account, which suggests Tighe may have been thinking of Psalm 39.11.

68. See Psalm 73.26: "My flesh and my heart faileth: but God is the strength of my heart, and my portion for ever" (KJV).

To Mrs. Henry Tighe, On Reading Her "Psyche"

1. Published in Moore's *Juvenile Poems* (1803).

2. "See the story in Apuleius" (Moore's note).

3. "Allusions to Mrs. Tighe's Poem" (Moore's note).

4. "Constancy" (Moore's note).

5. "By this image the Platonists expressed the middle state of the soul between sensible and intellectual existence" (Moore's note).

I Saw Thy Form in Youthful Prime

1. Published in the fourth part of Moore's *Irish Melodies* (1811).

2. "I have made a feeble effort to imitate that exquisite inscription of Shenstone's, 'Heu! quanto minus est cum reliquis versari quam tui meminisse!'" (Moore's note). Moore refers to the epitaph William Shenstone inscribed on an ornamental

urn for his cousin Mary Dolman, who died of smallpox when she was twenty-one, "Ah, how much less all living loves to me, / Than that one rapture of remembering thee."

SONNET TO MRS. HENRY TIGHE, ON HER POEM OF "PSYCHE, OR THE LEGEND OF LOVE"

1. Written ca. 1806 and published in Roscoe's collected *Poems* (1834).

LINES WRITTEN AFTER READING THE "CORINNE" OF MADAME DE STAEL, AND THE "PSYCHE" OF THE LATE MRS. HENRY TIGHE, OF ROSANNA

1. Published in Porter's *Ballad Romances, and Other Poems* (1811)

STANZAS ON PERUSING PSYCHE, A POEM, BY THE LATE MRS. TIGHE

1. Published in Barton's *Metrical Effusions or Verses on Various Occasions* (1812).

THE GRAVE OF A POETESS

1. "'Extrinsic interest has lately attached to the fine scenery of Woodstock, near Kilkenny, on account of its having been the last residence of the author of *Psyche*. Her grave is one of many in the churchyard of the village. The river runs smoothly by. The ruins of an ancient abbey, that have been partially converted into a church, reverently throw their mantle of tender shadow over it.'—*Tales by the O'Hara Family*" (Hemans's note). First published in the *New Monthly Magazine* (1827) and then in *Records of Woman* in 1828. Hemans cites John Banim's *The Fetches* (1825), the second volume and tale of the *Tales, by the O'Hara Family*.

2. "Do not pity me—if you knew how many pains this tomb has spared me!" Hemans cites Madame de Stael's *Corinne* (1807).

LINES WRITTEN FOR THE ALBUM AT ROSANNA

1. "A beautiful place in the county of Wicklow, formerly the abode of the authoress of 'Psyche'" (Hemans's note). Written ca. 1829; published in Hemans's *Poetical Remains* (1836).

WRITTEN AFTER VISITING A TOMB, NEAR WOODSTOCK, IN THE COUNTY OF KILKENNY

1. Written in 1831; published in Hemans's *National Lyrics and Songs for Music* (1834).

ON RECORDS OF IMMATURE GENIUS

1. Written in 1834; published in Hemans's *Poetical Remains* (1836).

BIBLIOGRAPHY

MANUSCRIPTS

Blachford, Theodosia. "Observations on the Foregoing Journal by Her Mother Mrs. Blachford." MS 4810. National Library of Ireland, Dublin.

Hamilton, Caroline. "Caroline Hamilton's Album: 1803–1859." MS 22984C. National Library of Wales, Aberystwyth.

———. Albums. MSS 4800, 4801, 4803, 4809. National Library of Ireland, Dublin.

———. "Mary Tighe." MS 4810. National Library of Ireland, Dublin.

Ponsonby, Sarah. "Sweet Linda!" IN T448 805. Beinecke Rare Book Room and Manuscript Library, Yale University, New Haven.

Tighe family papers. MSS D/2685/1–15. Public Record Office of Northern Ireland, Belfast.

Tighe, Mary. "A Faithful Friend Is the Medicine of Life." Album Camilla 1800. MS 22983B. National Library of Wales, Aberystwyth.

———. "A Letter from Mrs. Acton to Her Nephew Mr. Evans." MS L. Add. 1907. Birmingham University Library, Birmingham, UK.

———. "Extracts from a Journal of M.B. born 1772." Copyist Caroline Hamilton. MS 4810. National Library of Ireland, Dublin.

———. Letters to Joseph Cooper Walker. MSS 1461/5–7. Trinity College Library, Dublin.

———. *Psyche; or, the Legend of Love.* MS 22985B. National Library of Wales, Aberystwyth.

———. Reviews. MS 4804. National Library of Ireland, Dublin.

———. *Selena.* MSS 4742–46. National Library of Ireland, Dublin.

———. "There Was a Young Lordling Whose Wits Were All Toss'd Up." MS 10,206. National Library of Ireland, Dublin.

———. "Verses Addressed to Henry Vaughan." MS ALS Collection. Royal College of Physicians, London.

———. "Written in a Copy of Psyche Which Had Been in the Library of C.J. Fox. April, 1809." 328444. Huntington Library, San Marino, Calif..

TIGHE'S PUBLICATION HISTORY

Psyche; or, the Legend of Love. London: [James Carpenter], 1805.
Psyche, with Other Poems. London: Longman, 1811.

Mary, a Series of Reflections during Twenty Years. [Dublin]: Roundwood, 1811.
Psyche, with Other Poems, 3rd ed. London: Longman, 1811.
Psyche, with Other Poems, 4th ed. London: Longman, 1812.
Psyche, with Other Poems. Philadelphia: Humphreys, 1812.
Psyche, with Other Poems, 5th ed. London: Longman, 1816.
Psyche, with Other Poems. London: Longman, 1843.
Psyche, or, the Legend of Love. London: H.G. Clarke, 1844.
Psyche, or the legend of love: and miscellaneous poems. Halifax: Miner and Sowerby, 1852.
The Works of Apuleius: A New Translation Comprising The Metamorphosis, or Golden Ass, The God of Socrates, The Florida and His Defence, or a Discourse on Magic To Which Are Added a Metrical Version of Cupid and Psyche and Mrs. Tighe's Psyche (a Poem in Six Cantos). Ed. Henry George Bohn. London: Bohn, 1853.
Keats and Mary Tighe: The Poems of Mary Tighe with Parallel Passages from the Work of John Keats. Ed. Earle Vonard Weller. New York: Modern Language Association Press, 1928; reprint, New York: Kraus, 1966.
Psyche; or, the Legend of Love by Mary Tighe (1805). Rpt. ed. Donald H. Reiman. Romantic Context Series No. 114. New York: Garland, 1978.
Elegy to the Memory of the Late Duke of Bedford Written on the Evening of His Interment by Amelia Opie (1802). Psyche, with Other Poems by Mary Tighe (1811). Rpt. ed. by Donald H. Reiman, Romantic Context Series No. 94. New York: Garland, 1978.
Psyche, with other poems 1811. By Mary Tighe. Rpt. ed. Jonathan Wordsworth. Revolution and Romanticism 1789–1834 series. Oxford and New York: Woodstock, 1992.

ANTHOLOGIES AND COLLECTIONS

Lofft, Capel, ed. *Laura: or An Anthology of Sonnets and Elegiac Quatuorzains: English, Italian, Spanish, Portuguese, French, and German; Original and translated; Great part never before published.* 5 vols. London: Crosby, 1814. "Written in a Copy of Psyche Which Had Been in the Library of C.J. Fox."
Harmonica; or, Elegant Extracts of English, Scotch and Irish Melodies from the Most Approved, Popular and Modern Authors. Vol. 2. Cork: J. Bolster, 1818.
Scott, Elizabeth, ed. *Specimens of British Poetry: Chiefly Selected from Authors of High Celebrity, and Interspersed with Original Writings.* Edinburgh: James Ballantyne, 1823. "To the Moon" and lines from "The Mezereon" retitled "On Hope."
Dyce, Alexander, ed. *Specimens of British Poetesses.* London: Rodd, 1825. From *Psyche*, "The Lily."
Knight, Ann, ed. *Poetic Gleanings from Modern Writers: with Some Original Pieces, by a Governess.* London: Harvey and Darton, 1827. "Hagar in the Desert," "Written for Her Neice S. K." retitled "To a Little Girl Gathering Flowers."
The Amulet, or, Christian and Literary Remembrancer. London: Westley and Davis, 1827. "The Old Maid's Prayer to Diana," "On a Night-Blowing Cereus."

The Amulet, or, Christian and Literary Remembrancer. London: Westley and Davis, 1828. "Written at Rossana," "Sonnet: As one, who late hath lost a friend adored."

Montgomery, James, ed. *The Christian Poet: or, Selections in Verse on Sacred Subjects, with an Introductory Essay.* 3rd edition. Glasgow: William Collins, 1828. "On Receiving a Branch of Mezereon."

Mythological Fables. Translated by Dryden, Pope, Congreve, Addison, and Others. Prepared Expressly for the Use of Youth. In One Volume. New York: Dean, 1837. From *Psyche.*

Hall, Samuel Carter, ed. *The Book of Gems: The Modern Poets and Artists of Great Britain.* Vol. 3. London: Bohn, 1838. From *Psyche,* "Hagar in the Desert," "On Receiving a Branch of Mezereon."

Taylor, Emily, ed. *Sabbath Recreations: or, Christian Poetry of a Religious Kind; Taken from the Works of Modern Poets, with Original Pieces Never Before Published.* London: Houlston and Company, 1839. "The Lily."

Rowton, Frederic, ed. *The Female Poets of Great Britain.* London: Longman, 1848. From *Psyche,* "The Lily."

Bethune, George, ed. *The British Female Poets.* Philadelphia: Lindsay and Blakiston, 1848. From *Psyche,* "Sonnet: As one who late hath lost a friend adored," "To Time," "Hagar in the Desert," "On Receiving a Branch of Mezereon."

Morrell, Arthur, ed. *Selections from the British Classics: Burns Crabbe, Leyden, Jones, Moss, Lady Barnard, Oldys, Mrs. Tighe, and Wordsworth.* Morrell's Standard Miniature Library. Vol. 2. New York: Arthur Morrell, 1852. "The Lily."

Chamber, Robert, ed. *Cyclopedia of English Literature.* 2 vols. Boston: Gould and Lincoln, 1853. From *Psyche,* "The Lily."

Cleveland, Charles, ed. *English Literature of the Nineteenth Century.* Philadelphia and Boston: Biddle, 1854. From *Psyche,* "The Lily," "On Receiving a Branch of Mezereon."

Hale, Sarah, ed. *Woman's Record.* New York: Harper, 1855. From *Psyche.*

Willmott, Rev. Robert Aris, ed. *The Poets of the Nineteenth Century.* New York: Harper, 1857. From *Psyche.*

Lover, Samuel, ed. *The Lyrics of Ireland.* London: Houlston and Wright, 1858. "Sympathy."

Pierpont, John, ed. *Lays for the Sabbath: a Collection of Religious Poetry.* Boston: Walker, Wise and Company, 1860. "The Lily."

Wilmott, Rev. Robert Aris, ed. *English Sacred Poetry of the Sixteenth, Seventeenth, Eighteenth and Nineteenth Centuries.* London: George Routledge, 1861. "The Lily."

Chatelain, Jean Baptiste François Ernest, Chevalier de, ed. *Beautés de la Poësie Anglaise.* 2 vols. London: Rolandi, 1862.

Bryant, William Cullen, ed. *The Family Library of Poetry and Song.* New York: Ford, 1870. From *Psyche.*

Main, David M., ed. *A Treasury of English Sonnets Edited from the Original Sources with Notes and Illustrations.* 2 vols. Manchester: Alexander Ireland, 1880. "To Time," "Written at Killarney. July 29, 1800."

Inglis, Robert, ed. *Gleanings from the English Poets, Chaucer to Tennyson.* Edinburgh and London: Gall and Inglis, 1883. From *Psyche.*

Forman, H. Buxton, ed. *The Poetical Works and Other Writings of John Keats.* 4 vols. London, Reeves & Turner, 1883. "Sonnet Addressed to My Brother" [attributed to Keats].

Crowell, Thomas, ed. *Red-Letter Poems by English Men and Women.* New York: Crowell, 1885. From *Psyche,* "The Lily."

Sharp, Elizabeth, ed. *Women's Voices: An Anthology of the Most Characteristic Poems by English, Scotch and Irish Women.* London and New York: White and Allen, 1887. "Written at Killarney. July 29, 1800," "The Lily."

Read, Charles A., ed. *The Cabinet of Irish Literature: Selections from the Works of the Chief Poets, Orators, and Prose Writers of Ireland.* Vol. 2. London: Blackie & Son, 1890. From *Psyche,* "Sympathy," "The Lily," "Calm Delight."

Coates, Henry Troth, ed. *The Fireside Encyclopedia of Poetry.* Philadelphia: Coates, 1901. "Written at Killarney, July 29, 1800."

Ingpen, Roger, ed. *One Thousand Poems for Children: A Choice of the Best Verse Old and New.* Philadelphia: Jacobs, 1903. Rev. and enlarged edition; Philadelphia: Macrae, Smith, 1923. "Written for Her Niece S. K." retitled "To a Little Girl Gathering Flowers."

Graves, Alfred Perceval, ed. *The Book of Irish Poetry.* New York: Stokes, 1915. "To Time."

Kelly, Angeline A., ed. *Pillars of the House: An Anthology of Verse by Irishwomen from 1690 to Present.* 1987; Dublin: Wolfhound Press, 1997. Lines from "Pleasure" retitled "Dissipation," "Written at Killarney. July 29, 1800."

Moffat, Mary Jane, ed. *In the Midst of Winter: Selections from the Literature of Mourning.* New York: Vintage, 1992. "To Time."

McGann, Jerome, ed. *The New Oxford Book of Romantic Period Verse.* New York: Oxford University Press, 1993. From *Psyche.*

Weekes, Ann Owens, ed. *Unveiling Treasures: The Attic Guide to Published Writings of Irish Women Literary Writers: Drama, Fiction, Poetry.* Dublin: Attic Press, 1993. "Sonnet Addressed to My Mother."

Wu, Duncan, ed. *Romanticism: An Anthology.* Oxford: Blackwell, 1994. From *Psyche.*

Ashfield, Andrew, ed. *Romantic Women Poets 1770–1838: An Anthology.* Manchester and New York: Manchester University Press, 1995. "Written at Scarborough," "Sonnet: For me would Fancy now her chaplet twine," "Sonnet: Ye dear associates of my gayer hours," from *Psyche.*

Perkins, David, ed. *English Romantic Writers.* 2nd ed. Fort Worth, Tex.: Harcourt Brace, 1995. From *Psyche.*

Armstrong, Isobel, Joseph Bristow, and Cath Sharrock, eds. *Nineteenth-Century*

Women Poets: An Oxford Anthology. Oxford: Clarendon Press, 1996. From *Psyche,* "The Lily."

Ferguson, Margaret, Mary Jo Salter, and Jon Stallworthy, eds. *The Norton Anthology of Poetry.* 4th edition. New York: Norton, 1996. "Sonnet Addressed to My Mother," from *Psyche.*

Feldman, Paula R. ed. *British Women Poets of the Romantic Era: An Anthology.* Baltimore: Johns Hopkins University Press, 1997. From *Psyche,* "On Receiving a Branch of Mezereon," "Written at Scarborough. August, 1799," "Sonnet: As one who late hath lost a friend adored," "Address to My Harp," "Sonnet, March 1791," "Sonnet: 'Tis past the cruel anguish of suspence."

Jump, Harriet Devine, ed. *Women's Writing of the Romantic Period, 1789–1836: An Anthology.* Edinburgh: Edinburgh University Press, 1997. From *Psyche,* "Written at Scarborough. August, 1799."

Wu, Duncan, ed. *Romantic Women Poets: An Anthology.* Oxford: Blackwell, 1997. *Psyche; or the Legend of Love,* "On Receiving a Branch of Mezereon."

Carpenter, Andrew, ed. *Verse in English from Eighteenth-Century Ireland.* Cork: Cork University Press, 1998. "Written at Rossana, November 18, 1799," "Written at Killarney. July 29, 1800."

Feldman, Paula R. and Daniel Robinson, eds. *A Century of Sonnets: The Romantic-Era Revival 1750–1850.* New York and Oxford: Oxford University Press, 1999. "Written at Scarborough. August, 1799," "Sonnet: As one who late hath lost a friend adored," "Sonnet: When glowing Phoebus quits the weeping earth," "Written in Autumn," "Sonnet: Poor, fond deluded heart!" "Written at Rossana. November 18, 1799," "Written at the Eagle's Nest, Killarney. July 26, 1800," "Written at Killarney. July 29, 1800," "To Death," "Sonnet: Can I look back, and view with tranquil eye," "1802."

Motherhood: A Gift of Love. Philadelphia: Running Press, 1999. From *Psyche.*

DeShazer, Mary K., ed. *The Longman Anthology of Women's Literature.* New York: Longman, 2001. "Sonnet Addressed To My Mother."

Fuller, John, ed. *The Oxford Book of Sonnets.* New York: Oxford, 2001. "Written in Autumn," "Written at the Eagle's Nest, Killarney. July 26, 1800."

Robertson, Fiona, ed. *Women's Writing 1778–1838: An Anthology.* Oxford: Oxford University Press, 2001. From *Psyche.*

Bourke, Angela, Siobhán Kilfeather, Maria Luddy, Margaret Mac Curtin, Gerardine Meaney, Máirín Ní Dhonnchadha, Mary O'Dowd, and Clair Wills, eds. *The Field Day Anthology of Irish Writing, Vols. IV and V: Irish Women's Writings and Traditions.* Ireland: Cork University Press; New York: New York University Press, 2002. From Mary Tighe's "Journal (1787–1802)," "Pleasure."

Wordsworth, Jonathan, and Jessica Wordsworth, eds. *The New Penguin Book of Romantic Poetry.* New York: Penguin, 2003. From *Psyche,* "Address to My Harp," "To Death," "Written at Scarborough."

Works Cited and Recommended Reading

Anderson, John. *Beyond Calliope: Epics by Women Poets of the Romantic Period.* Ph.D. Thesis, Boston College, 1993.

———. "Mary Tighe, *Psyche.*" *A Companion to Romanticism.* Ed. Duncan Wu. Oxford: Blackwell, 1998. 199–203.

———. "Tighe, Mary Blachford." *Encyclopedia of Romanticism: Culture in Britain, 1780s–1830s,* Ed. Laura Dabundo. New York: Garland, 1992. 576.

Ariosto, Lodovico. *Elegie, Sonetti E Canzoni.* Ed. Ardengo Soffici. Lanciano: Carabba, 1911.

Armstrong, Isobel. *Victorian Poetry: Poetry, Poetics and Politics.* London: Routledge, 1993.

Barton, Bernard. *Metrical Effusions or Verses on Various Occasions.* Woodbridge: Loder, 1812.

Beers, Henry A. *A History of English Romanticism in the Nineteenth Century.* New York: Henry Holt, 1901.

Behrendt, Stephen. "Mary Shelley, *Frankenstein,* and the Woman Writer's Fate." *Romantic Women Writers: Voices and Countervoices.* Ed. Paula Feldman and Theresa Kelley. Hanover and London: University Press of New England, 1995. 69–87.

Bell, Eva Mary. *The Hamwood Papers of the Ladies of Llangollen and Caroline Hamilton.* London: Macmillan, 1930.

Bethune, George W. *The British Female Poets: with Biographical and Critical Notices.* Philadelphia: Lindsay and Blakiston, 1848.

Blackburne, Elizabeth Owens. *Illustrious Irishwomen. Being Memoirs of Some of the Most Noted Irishwomen from the Earliest Ages to the Present Century.* 2 vols. London: Tinsley, 1877.

Butler, Patricia. "Printing at Rossanagh." *Ashford and District Historical Journal* 4 (July 1995): 8–14.

Chandler, James. *England in 1819: The Politics of Literary Culture and the Case of Romantic Historicism.* Chicago: University of Chicago Press, 1998.

Clarke, Norma. *Ambitious Heights: Writing, Friendship, Love—The Jewsbury Sisters, Felicia Hemans, and Jane Welsh Carlyle.* New York: Routledge, 1990.

Colardeau, Charles Pierre. *Oeuvres de Colardeau.* 2 vols. Paris: Ballard and LeJay, 1779.

Craik, George. *A Compendious History of English Literature, and of the English Language, from the Norman Conquest.* 2 vols. New York: Scribner's, 1885.

Croker, John Wilson. "Keats, Endymion: A Poetic Romance." *The Quarterly Review* 19:37 (April 1818): 204–8.

Crookshank, C. H. *History of Methodism in Ireland.* 3 vols. Belfast: R. S. Allen and London: T. Woolmer, 1885–88.

———. "Theodosia Blachford." *Memorable Women of Irish Methodism of the Last Century.* London: Wesley-Methodist Book-Room, 1882. 140–50.

Curran, Stuart. "Mothers and Daughters: Poetic Generation(s) in the Eighteenth and Nineteenth Centuries." *Forging Connections: Women's Poetry from the Renaissance to Romanticism.* Ed. Anne K. Mellor, Felicity Nussbaum, and Jonathan F.S. Post. San Marino, Calif.: Huntington Library, 2002. 147–62.

Dacre, Lady Barbarina Brand. *Dramas, Translations and Occasional Poems,* 2 vols. London: John Murray, 1821.

Dix, E.R. McClintock. "The First Edition of Mrs. Tighe's 'Psyche.'" *The Irish Book Lover* 3 (1912): 141–43.

Dixon, W. Hepworth. *Lady Morgan's Autobiography, Diaries, and Correspondence.* 2 vols. London: Allen, 1862.

Dunn, James. "Charlotte Dacre and the Feminization of Violence." *Nineteenth-Century Literature* 53:3 (December 1998): 307–27.

Feldman, Paula. "Women Poets and Anonymity in the Romantic Era." *New Literary History* 33:2 (Spring 2002): 279–89.

Feldman, Paula, and Theresa Kelley. "Introduction." *Romantic Women Writers: Voices and Countervoices.* Hanover and London: University Press of New England, 1995. 1–10.

Fitzpatrick, H.M. "The Ashford Poetess." *Ashford and District Historical Journal* 1 (July 1991): 16–18.

Fitzpatrick, William John. *Lady Morgan; Her Career, Literary and Personal, with a Glimpse of Her Friends, and a Word to Her Calumniators.* London: Skeet, 1860.

Friedman, Susan Stanford. "Gender and Genre Anxiety: Elizabeth Barrett Browning and H.D. as Epic Poets." *Tulsa Studies in Women's Literature* 5:2 (1986): 203–28.

Gifford, William. "Mrs. Hemans's *Poems.*" *The Quarterly Review* 24 (Oct. 1820): 130–39.

Gilbert, Sandra, and Susan Gubar. *The Norton Anthology of Literature by Women.* 1985; New York: Norton, 1996.

Glendinning, Victoria. "Mary, Mary Quite Contrary." *The Irish Times.* March 7, 1974.

Hamilton, Catherine Jane. *Notable Irishwomen.* Dublin: Sealy, Bryers and Walker, 1904.

Hemans, Felicia. *The Poetical Works of Felicia Dorothea Hemans.* London: Oxford University Press, 1914.

Henchy, Patrick. *The Works of Mary Tighe: Published and Unpublished.* The Bibliographic Society of Ireland 6:6. Dublin: At the Sign of the Three Candles, 1957.

Henderson, Andrea. "Keats, Tighe, and the Chastity of Allegory." *European Romantic Review* 10:3 (Summer 1999): 279–306.

Howitt, William. "Mrs. Tighe, the Author of Psyche." *Homes and Haunts of the British Poets.* 2 volumes. 1846; London: Routledge, 1894. 2:281–91.

Hunt, Leigh. *Men, Women, and Books.* New York: Harper, 1847.

Jeffrey, Francis. "Review of *Records of Woman* (2nd ed.) and *The Forest Sanctuary* (2nd ed.), by Hemans." *Edinburgh Review* 50 (October 1829): 32–47.

Keats, John. *The Poetical Works and Other Writings of John Keats, Now First Brought Together, Including Poems and Numerous Letters Not Before Published.* Ed. H. Buxton Forman. 4 vols. London: Reeves and Turner, 1883.

———. *The Letters of John Keats.* Ed. Hyder Edward Rollins. 2 vols. Cambridge: Harvard University Press, 1958.

Kirwan, John. "William Tighe (1766–1816)." *William Tighe's Statistical Observations Relative to the County of Kilkenny.* Kilkenny: Grangesilvia Publications, 1998. viii–xliii.

Kucich, Gregory. "Gender Crossings: Keats and Tighe." *The Keats-Shelley Journal* 44 (1995): 29–39.

———. "Gendering the Canons of Romanticism: Past and Present." *The Wordsworth Circle* 27:2 (1996): 95–102.

———. *Keats, Shelley, and Romantic Spenserianism.* University Park: Pennsylvania State University Press, 1991.

Lightbown, Mary. "Memorial to a Poetess: John Flaxman's Monument to Mary Tighe." *Old Kilkenny Review* 4:5 (1993): 1195–1207.

Linkin, Harriet Kramer. "More than *Psyche:* the Sonnets of Mary Tighe." *European Romantic Review* 13:4 (December 2002): 365–78.

———. "Recuperating Romanticism in Mary Tighe's *Psyche.*" *Romanticism and Women Poets: Opening the Doors of Reception.* Ed. Harriet Kramer Linkin and Stephen C. Behrendt. Lexington: University Press of Kentucky, 1999. 144–62.

———. "Romantic Aesthetics in Mary Tighe and Letitia Landon: How Women Poets Recuperate the Gaze." *European Romantic Review* 7:2 (1997): 159–88.

———. "Romanticism and Mary Tighe's *Psyche:* Peering at the Hem of Her Blue Stockings." *Studies in Romanticism* 35 (1996): 55–72.

———. "Skirting around the Sex in Mary Tighe's *Psyche.*" *Studies in English Literature* 42:4 (Autumn 2002): 731–52.

———. "Teaching the Poetry of Mary Tighe: *Psyche,* Beauty, and the Romantic Object." *Approaches to Teaching British Women Poets of the Romantic Period.* Ed. Stephen C. Behrendt and Harriet Kramer Linkin. New York: Modern Language Association Press, 1997. 106–9.

Loeffelholz, Mary. "'In Place of Strength': Elizabeth Barrett Browning's Psyche Translations." *Studies in Browning and His Circle* 19 (1991): 66–75.

Mackintosh, Sir James. *Memoirs of the Life of the Right Honourable Sir James Mackintosh.* 2 vols. London: Moxon, 1835

Main, David. *A Treasury of English Sonnets.* Manchester: Alexander Ireland, 1880.

Mandell, Laura. "Misogyny and the Canon: The Character of Women in Anthologies of Poetry." *Misogynous Economies: The Business of Literature in Eighteenth-Century Britain.* Lexington: University Press of Kentucky, 1999. 107–28.

Mavor, Elizabeth. *The Ladies of Llangollen: A Study in Romantic Friendship*. London: Michael Joseph, 1971.

Mays, Jim. "The *Lyrical Ballads* in Wicklow." *The Coleridge Bulletin* 11 (Spring 1998). Available online at http://www.friendsofcoleridge.com/Mays.htm.

McCarthy, Muriel. *All Graduates and Gentlemen: Marsh's Library*. Dublin: O'Brien Press, 1980.

Metastasio, Pietro. *Tutte le Opere*. Ed. Bruno Brunelli. 5 vols. Milano: Mondadori, 1951–65.

Moir, David Macbeth. *Sketches of the Poetical Literature of the Past Half-Century*. Edinburgh: Blackwood, 1856.

Monti, Vincenzo. *Opere Scelte*. Ed. Cesare Angelini. Milan and Rome: Rizzoli, 1940.

Moore, Thomas. *The Poetical Works of Thomas Moore, with a Memoir*, 6 vols. in 3 vols. Boston: Houghton Mifflin, 1855.

Mountain, Arthur Harcourt. *The Romantic Elements in Mrs. Tighe's "Psyche," with an Account of Her Life and a Review of Her Reliques*. M.A. Thesis, University of Chicago, 1921.

O'Brien, Conor. "The Byrnes of Ballymanus." *Wicklow: History and Society*. Ed. Ken Hannigan and William Nolan. Dublin: Geography Publications, 1994. 305–39.

O'Caisade, Seamus. "Printing at Rosanna." *Irish Book Lover* 8 (1916): 17.

O'Donnell, Ruan. *The Rebellion in Wicklow, 1798*. Dublin and Portland: Irish Academic Press, 1998.

O'Sullivan, Seumas. "Mrs. Tighe and 'Psyche.'" *The Dublin Magazine* 1:5 (1923): 445–46.

Pipkin, John. *The Line Invisible: Intertextuality and the Men and Women Poets of British Romanticism*. Ph.D. Thesis, Rice University, 1997.

———. "The Material Sublime of Women Romantic Poets." *Studies in English Literature* 38:4 (Autumn 1998): 597–619.

Porter, Anna Maria. *Ballad Romances, and Other Poems*. London: Longman, 1811.

Priestman, Martin. *Romantic Atheism: Poetry and Freethought, 1780–1830*. Cambridge and New York: Cambridge University Press, 1999.

Quint, David, trans. *The Stanze of Angelo Poliziano*. Amherst: University of Massachusetts Press, 1979.

Review of *Psyche, with Other Poems*. *The British Critic* 38 (Dec. 1811): 631–32.

Review of *Psyche, with Other Poems*. *The British Review* 1 (June 1811): 277–98.

Review of *Psyche, with Other Poems*. *The Critical Review, or, Annals of Literature* s4, 1 (June 1812): 606–9.

Review of *Psyche, with Other Poems*. *The Eclectic Review* 9 (Mar. 1813): 217–29.

Review of *Psyche, with Other Poems*. *The Gentleman's Magazine* 82:2 (Nov. 1812): 464–67.

Review of *Psyche, with Other Poems*. *The Glasgow Magazine* 2 (Aug. 1811): 304–5.

Review of *Psyche, with Other Poems*. *The Monthly Review* 66 (Oct. 1811): 138–52.

Review of *Psyche, with Other Poems*. *New Annual Register, or, General Repository of History, Politics, and Literature* 32 (1811): 364–72.

Review of *Psyche, with Other Poems*. *The Poetical Register* 8 (1811): 604.

Review of *Psyche, with Other Poems*. *The Quarterly Review* 5:10 (May 1811): 471–85.

Roscoe, William Stanley. *Poems by William Stanley Roscoe*. London: William Pickering, 1834.

Ross, Marlon. *The Contours of Masculine Desire: Romanticism and the Rise of Women's Poetry*. New York: Oxford University Press, 1989.

Saglia, Diego. "The Dangers of Over-Refinement: The Language of Luxury in Romantic Poetry by Women, 1793–1811." *Studies in Romanticism* 38:4 (Winter 1999): 641–72.

———. "Interior Luxury and Poetic Narratives of Identity: From Tighe and Hunt to Keats and Tennyson." *Keats-Shelley Journal* 52 (2003): 130–65.

Sharp, Elizabeth. *Women's Voices: An Anthology of the Most Characteristic Poems by English, Scotch and Irish Women*. London: White and Allen, 1887.

Smith, Mrs. Richard Smith. *The Life of the Rev. Henry Moore; The Biographer and Executor of the Rev. John Wesley; including the Autobiography; and the Continuation, Written from His Own Papers*. London: Simpkin, Marshall, 1844.

Sym, Robert. *Noctes Ambrosianae* 21, *Blackwood's Edinburgh Magazine* (Sept. 1825). *Noctes Ambrosianae*. 5 vols. Ed. R. Shelton Mackenzie. New York: Redfield, 1855. 2:102–3.

Symons, Arthur. *The Romantic Movement in English Poetry*. London: Constable, 1909.

Tighe, Wilfred. "A History of the Tighe Family." *Ashford and District Historical Journal* 5 (July 1998): 49–55.

Voiture, Vincent. *Les OEuvres de Monsieur de Voiture*. Paris: Augustin Courbé, 1650.

Ward, Humphrey, and W. Roberts. *Romney: A Biographical and Critical Essay with a Catalogue Raisonné of His Works*. 2 vols. New York: Charles Scribner's, 1904.

Wesley, John. *The Journals of the Rev. John Wesley*. Ed. Ernest Rhys. 4 vols. London: Dent, 1906.

———. *The Works of the Rev. John Wesley*. 14 vols. London: Wesleyan Methodist Book Room, 1872.

Wilding, John. "The Tighes of Rossanagh." *Ashford and District Historical Journal* 2 (July 1992): 37–38.

Williams, Anne. *Art of Darkness: A Poetics of Gothic*. Chicago: University of Chicago Press, 1995.

Williams, Jane. *The Literary Women of England*. London: Saunders, 1861.

Wilson, John. *Noctes Ambrosianae* 2, *Blackwood's Edinburgh Magazine* (Sept. 1819). *Noctes Ambrosianae*. 5 vols. Ed. R. Shelton Mackenzie. New York: Redfield, 1855. 1:75.

Wolfson, Susan. "'Domestic Affections' and 'the spear of Minerva': Felicia Hemans and the Dilemma of Gender." *Re-Visioning Romanticism: British Women Writers, 1776–1837.* Ed. Carol Shiner Wilson and Joel Haefner. Philadelphia: University of Pennsylvania Press, 1994. 128–66.

Wordsworth, Jonathan. "Ann Yearsley to Caroline Norton: Women Poets of the Romantic Period." *The Wordsworth Circle* 26 (1995): 114–24.

Index of Titles and First Lines